VOLPONE AND OTHER PLAYS

BEN JONSON was born in 1572, the posthumous son of a minister, and thanks to an unknown patron was educated at Westminster School. After this he was for a brief time apprenticed to his stepfather as a bricklayer. He served as a soldier in the Low Countries and married sometime between 1592 and 1595. In 1597 he began to work for Henslowe's company as a player and playwright and during the following two years two groundbreaking comedies, *Every Man in his Humour* and *Every Man out of his Humour*, were produced. These were followed by *Cynthia's Revels* (1600) and *The Poetaster* (1601). Jonson's great run of comedies consists of *Volpone* (1606), *Epicoene, or the Silent Woman* (1609), *The Alchemist* (1610) and *Bartholomew Fair* (1614). In addition to his comic writing Jonson also produced two powerful Roman tragedies, *Sejanus, his Fall* (1603) and *Catiline, his Conspiracy* (1611). After 1616 Jonson abandoned the public theatre for a decade, concentrating his efforts entirely on the court masques, a form of entertainment that reached its highest elaboration in his hands, and his sporadic returns to comic drama in the Caroline period met with less popular success than his Jacobean masterpieces. In 1616 he was granted a royal pension and made, in effect, Poet Laureate. His latter years were unhappy, though. Under Charles I he lost favour and was replaced as masque-writer after quarrelling with Inigo Jones, the masque-designer. He also suffered from paralysis and was unable to publish the second volume of his *Workes*. Ben Jonson died on 6 August 1637.

MICHAEL JAMIESON studied at the University of Aberdeen, Princeton University, and King's College, Cambridge. He was on the staff of the University of Keele for two years before going to the University of Sussex in 1962 as a lecturer in the School of English and American Studies. He has also taught at the University of Rome and the University of California at Santa Cruz. He has published a study of *As You Like It* and articles on Elizabethan acting and on modern theatres for Shakespeare.

BEN JONSON

Volpone and Other Plays

Edited with an Introduction and Notes by
MICHAEL JAMIESON

PENGUIN BOOKS

PENGUIN BOOKS

Published by the Penguin Group
Penguin Books Ltd, 80 Strand, London WC2R ORL, England
Penguin Group (USA), Inc., 375 Hudson Street, New York, New York 10014, USA
Penguin Books Australia Ltd, 250 Camberwell Road, Camberwell, Victoria 3124, Australia
Penguin Books Canada Ltd, 10 Alcorn Avenue, Toronto, Ontario, Canada M4V 3B2
Penguin Books India (P) Ltd, 11 Community Centre, Panchsheel Park, New Delhi – 110 017, India
Penguin Books (NZ) Ltd, Cnr Rosedale and Airborne Roads, Albany, Auckland, New Zealand
Penguin Books (South Africa) (Pty) Ltd, 24 Sturdee Avenue, Rosebank 2196, South Africa

Penguin Books Ltd, Registered Offices: 80 Strand, London WC2R ORL, England

www.penguin.com

This collection published in the Penguin English Library 1966
Reprinted in Penguin Classics 1985 as *Three Comedies*
Reprinted under present title 2004
1

Introduction and Notes copyright © Michael Jamieson, 1966
All rights reserved

Set in Bembo Monotype
Printed in England by Clays Ltd, St Ives plc

CONTENTS

INTRODUCTION

I

> ... Then to the well-trod stage anon,
> If Jonson's learnèd sock be on,
> Or sweetest Shakespeare, Fancy's child,
> Warble his native wood-notes wild.

THIS, I suppose, is the context in which many of us as school-children first came upon the mere name of Ben Jonson. It occurs in John Milton's *L'Allegro*, in that passage where the poet, talking of the nocturnal pleasures of city life, enthuses over the comic theatre. It is ironic that the second line, which contains Milton's tribute to the master of English comedy, should have become a puzzling allusion which young minds are required to explain at O-level. Yet Jonson belongs with those writers whom one is often expected to know about rather than to have read.

I was fortunate in that I next came upon Jonson in the theatre, when Donald Wolfit was playing Volpone and relishing that arch-predator's sardonic villainies. That Jonson could still be a great entertainer came as a revelation. He belongs on the boards, as Milton indeed was suggesting in the expression 'well-trod stage', but the doubly allusive lines from *L'Allegro* seem, from the way in which they demand foot-noting, sadly symbolic of Jonson's re-putation among readers today. The 'learnèd socks' are the slippers Greek and Roman actors wore in comedies; in these lines Jonson, the classically erudite writer of comedy, is epitomized in an allu-sion from the theatre of the Ancients by a poet of even greater classical erudition. But Milton expected his readers to recognize also a graceful compliment to Ben Jonson, for in this author's own poem in Shakespeare's memory prefaced to the First Folio, 'sock' is similarly used:

> And though thou hadst small Latin and less Greek,
> From thence to honour thee I would not seek
> For names; but call forth thund'ring Aeschylus,
> Euripides, and Sophocles to us. ...

Or, when thy socks were on,
Leave thee alone, for the comparison
Of all that insolent Greece or haughty Rome
Sent forth, or since did from their ashes come.

In Milton's four lines we seem to find several aspects of Jonson which are daunting to the general reader of books – his classicism, his great learning, his tendency (like Milton with 'learnèd sock') to need explanatory notes, and, of course, his complete contrast to William Shakespeare. Milton is, in fact, praising Jonson, placing him first, and being, if anything, condescending about Shakespeare. But that is not how the lines strike us at first reading today, for we put a higher value than Milton did on spontaneity, and are quick to sniff pedantry in a 'classical' writer. There *is* something daunting about Jonson's present-day reputation; and anyone introducing a volume of his plays has to begin by stressing what ought to be obvious – that his three best comedies are still very funny, that they make splendid reading, and that they are vivid, lucid, and marvellously actable stage-plays.

Critics have already dwelt, a shade lugubriously, on this daunting aspect of Jonson's work. In 1919 T. S. Eliot wrote:

The reputation of Jonson has been of the most deadly kind that can be compelled upon the memory of a great poet. To be universally accepted; to be damned by the praise that quenches all desire to read the book; to be afflicted by the imputation of the virtues which excite the least pleasure; and to be read only by historians and antiquaries – this is the most perfect conspiracy of approval.[1]

In 1938 Professor Harry Levin continued in a similar vein:

Ben Jonson's position, three hundred years after his death, is more than secure; it might almost be called impregnable. He is still the greatest unread English author. . . . Jonson has always had more attention from antiquarians than from critics, and has too often served as a cadaver over which to read a lecture on the lore of language and custom.[2]

1. 'Ben Jonson', *Selected Essays* (enlarged edition, 1951), p. 147; reprinted in *Ben Jonson: A Collection of Critical Essays*, edited by J. A. Barish (1963), p. 14.
2. Introduction to *Ben Jonson: Selected Works* (n.d. [1938]), p. 1.

And in 1948 Edmund Wilson commented, just as bleakly:

... among a thousand people, say, who have some knowledge and love of Shakespeare, and even some taste for Webster and Marlowe, I doubt whether you could find half a dozen who have any enthusiasm for Jonson or who have seriously read his plays. T. S. Eliot, admitting the long neglect into which Ben Jonson's work had fallen, put up ... a strong plea for Jonson as an artist, and thus made a respect for this poet *de rigueur* in literary circles. But one's impression is that what people have read has been, not Jonson, but Eliot's essay.[1]

Readers are still put off by talk of Jonson's monumental learning and by the constant, artificial twinning, as in Milton's lines, of a Jonson laboriously theoretical and a Shakespeare effortlessly inspired. Many critical discussions of Jonsonian comedy are bedevilled by the fact that writers on Shakespeare use Jonson as the convenient representative writer of 'classical' comedy, in order to contrast that *genre* with the richer Shakespearean comedy exemplified in *Twelfth Night*, *As You Like It*, or *The Tempest*. Jonson's two great comedies, *Volpone* and *The Alchemist*, are not examples of a kind of play which is inherently inferior to Shakespearean comedy. They are comic masterpieces in their own right, but in a different tradition. Jonson's best work for the theatre operates within narrow limits; it does not have the diversity of Shakespeare's comedies, histories, and tragedies. The three plays reprinted here are the best three – though a case could be made for displacing *Bartholomew Fair* with *The Silent Woman* – and they are plays of the same broad, satiric scope. This makes it necessary, in the sections on individual plays, to emphasize their differences as well as their similarities, as a step towards evaluating them critically.

Jonson's biography and the critical theories behind his plays are of secondary importance, despite the facts that Jonson's was a life of compelling interest to the literary historian and that he was hugely respected in his own day as a prescriptive literary theorist. But some knowledge of the details of Jonson's life, of his theories about literary composition and about what constituted literary excellence, and of his artistic assumptions, helps to put the three comedies in perspective for modern readers and playgoers.

1. 'Morose Ben Jonson', *The Triple Thinkers* (new edition, 1952), p. 204; reprinted by Barish, p. 61.

II

Jonson was a great and colourful character. He probably killed a man in a hand-to-hand fight while soldiering in the Low Countries, and he certainly killed the actor Gabriel Spencer in a duel. He was imprisoned several times. He once worked as a bricklayer. He was a bonhomous, opinionated, and highly prized drinking companion in literary London, and the William Hickeys of this world might write him down as an *habitué* of the Mermaid Tavern, the Sun, the Dog, the Triple Tun, and the Apollo Room upstairs above the Old Devil. His output – as printed in his own Folio *Workes* or in the eleven stout, splendid, Oxonian volumes edited and annotated by C. H. Herford and Percy and Evelyn Simpson – demonstrates, however, that the greater part of his crowded life must have been spent in what W. B. Yeats once called 'the sedentary toil of creative art'. It is as a writer that he is of interest to us today, not as a personality.

Ben Jonson was born, the posthumous son of a minister, in 1572, and, thanks to an unknown patron, he was educated at one of the great schools of the day, Westminster, where the headmaster was the scholar and antiquarian, William Camden. At a time when he might have expected to go up to Cambridge or Oxford, he was apprenticed, briefly and humiliatingly, to his stepfather as a bricklayer. He served as a soldier in the Low Countries, married, and was for a time an actor. From around 1597 he wrote plays for Philip Henslowe, working on such get-penny entertainments as *Hot Anger Soon Cold* and *Richard Crookback* as well as on the superb additions to the ever-popular melodrama *The Spanish Tragedy*. His first truly Jonsonian comedies were *Everyman in his Humour*, in which William Shakespeare acted in 1598, and *Everyman out of his Humour*; both are 'comedies of humours', in which each character is a type dominated by a ruling passion or obsession. To the complicated literary feud known as 'The War of the Theatres' Jonson contributed *Poetaster* and he was himself attacked in *Satiromastix, or The Untrussing of the Humorous Poet*. Soon after, however, he collaborated with Chapman and one of his attackers, Marston, on a racy London comedy *Eastward Ho!*, which contained a joke ('I ken the man weel. He's ane of my thirty pound knights') about King James's Scots accent and his mercenary creation of knights. The collaborators were imprisoned. Yet already Jonson had won favour at Court and had created his first royal masque, *The Masque of Blackness*. He became the greatest English writer and contriver of these splendid Renaissance entertainments, producing thirty-three for King James, and inventing the grotesque comic interlude, the anti-masque. In most of these he collaborated with the famous architect and stage-designer, Inigo Jones, whose spectacular scenes and machines were later to eclipse Jonson's poetry and songs.

Jonson's great run of comedies consists of *Volpone* (1606), *The Silent Woman* (1609), *The Alchemist* (1610), written, like Shakespeare's plays, for the King's Men, and *Bartholomew Fair* (1614). His two Roman tragedies, correct by classical standards, *Sejanus, his Fall* (1603) and *Catiline, his Conspiracy* (1611) were failures in the theatre, but Professor G. E. Bentley's researches have shown that *Catiline* was the most respected play of the seventeenth century, the tragedy educated people were expected to admire.[1] Jonson's later plays, which Dryden termed 'dotages', show a sad falling-off.

In 1616 Jonson published in folio *The Workes of Beniamin Jonson*, a daring act which had important reverberations. The *Workes* included not only epistles, satires, and epigrams (respectable literary *genres*) but also masques and nine play-scripts, edited as meticulously as if they had been philosophical treatises or a Spenserian epic. None of the early hack-work for Henslowe was printed, but the use of the title *Workes* for mere stage-plays was greeted with scorn and derision. Had Jonson not put his plays before the public in this collected edition, the actors Heming and Condell might never have undertaken the great posthumous collection of plays, many not previously printed, by William Shakespeare, the First Folio of 1623. The gossip John Aubrey records, 'Ben Jonson was never a good Actor, but an excellent Instructor', which suggests that he insisted on supervising rehearsals of his own plays – something in keeping with his finicky and exacting temperament and his (justifiable) pride in his work.

1. *Shakespeare and Jonson: Their Reputations in the Seventeenth Century Compared* (1945), vol. I, pp. 109–12; *The Jacobean and Caroline Stage* (1941–), vol. IV, p. 608.

In the year his *Workes* were published in Folio, Jonson was granted a royal pension and made, in effect, Poet Laureate. King James wanted to make him a knight. He was uniquely honoured among Jacobean writers: Cambridge and Oxford gave him honorary degrees, and when he walked to Edinburgh in 1618 he was made an honorary burgess and entertained at a civic banquet costing £220 6s. 4d., Scots – the Scots pound being worth 1s. 8d. He made a long stay with William Drummond of Hawthornden, the Scots poet, who jotted down his table-talk, which was pithy, opinionated, and revealing. His last years in London were unhappy. His library was burned. He became paralysed, and was unable to get out the second volume of his *Workes*. Under King Charles, James's Laureate did not find favour: he quarrelled with Inigo Jones and was replaced as masque-writer at Court by Aurelian Townshend. He died on 6 August 1637, and his burial at Westminster Abbey was attended by 'all or the greatest part of the nobility and gentry then in town'. C. H. Herford and Percy Simpson in their Oxford edition end the biography thus:

Neglected as his later years had been, the passing of Ben was, for the entire world of letters, the passing of its king – a king who had perhaps ceased to govern, but who still reigned.[1]

In 1638 appeared a collection of thirty-three poems, *Jonsonus Virbius, or The Memory of Ben Jonson Revived By The Friends of the Muses*. The projected memorial to him in the Abbey never materialized. Instead, a square of marble was inscribed, at a cost (according to Aubrey) of eighteen-pence: 'O Rare Ben Jonson.'

Jonson was, in a way that Shakespeare never was, a celebrity and a man of letters. He was a poet, a writer of court-masques, a literary theorist, a grammarian, a dramatist, and a pundit. His theories about composition and rhetoric are easily accessible in *Timber, or Discoveries*, posthumously pieced together from Jonson's commonplace book, or even from lecture-notes, by Sir Kenelm Digby. There is nothing there specifically about the writing of comedies, but Jonson's ideas on this subject would have matched Sir Philip Sidney's definition:

1. *Ben Jonson* (1925–52), vol. I, p. 115.

Comedy is an imitation of the common errors of our life, which he presenteth in the most ridiculous and scornful sort that may be; so as it is impossible that any beholder can be content to be such a one.

The Prologue to *Every Man in his Humour* tells of the author's ambition to offer models of comedy-writing:

> He rather prays, you will be pleased to see
> One such, today, as other plays should be.

Jonson promises:

> . . . deeds and language, such as men do use,
> And persons, such as Comedy would choose,
> When she would show an image of the times,
> And sport with human follies, not with crimes.

This, like the epistle-dedicatory of *Volpone*, aligns him with the satiric tradition of comedy – where comedy is didactic and offers moral correction. It points also to that classical notion of comedy as concerned, not like tragedy with kings and princes but with people placed low in the social scale, people of the city and the streets. Professor Nevill Coghill has usefully demonstrated that two traditions of comedy existed in Elizabethan times, with different antecedents, both stemming from theoretical reversals of Aristotle's notions of tragedy. Romantic Comedy begins with wretchedness and the threat of danger but ends happily. Satiric Comedy teaches by exposing the errors of city folk. Shakespeare and Jonson, Professor Coghill argues, exemplify the two comic forms:

Compared with the comedies of Shakespeare, those of Ben Jonson are no laughing matter. A harsh ethic in them yokes punishment with derision; foibles are persecuted and vices flayed; the very simpletons are savaged for being what they are. The population . . . [of] his comedies . . . is a congeries of cits, parvenus, mountebanks, cozeners, dupes, braggarts, bullies, and bitches. No one loves anyone . . .
    In Shakespeare things are different. Princes and dukes, lords and ladies, jostle with merchants, weavers, joiners, country sluts, friendly rogues, schoolmasters, and village policemen, hardly one of whom is incapable of a generous impulse.[1]

1. 'The Basis of Shakespearean Comedy', *Shakespeare Criticism, 1935–60*, edited by Anne Ridler (1963), p. 201.

And of the two traditions Professor Coghill remarks:

Faced by a choice in such matters, a writer is wise if he follows his own temperament. Ben Jonson knotted his cat-o'-nine-tails. Shakespeare reached for his Chaucer.[1]

The excellencies and the limitations of Jonson's comedies are closely related to his chosen *genre*. It is a mistake to regard him as *the* exemplar of 'classical' comic dramaturgy. As Professor Levin reminds us 'Jonson is commonly conceived as a man who wrote comedies because he had a theory about why comedies ought to be written.'[2] In our own day the writer with a sound theoretical basis for his art is somehow suspect, and to brand Jonson as a comic theorist gives his plays a forbidding, pedantic image. The neoclassical views on wide reading, knowledge of rhetoric, constant practice of one's own style, and imitation of past masters which Jonson set down and refined upon in *Discoveries* have a pragmatic and very English bent, and remind us of the *obiter dicta* preserved by William Drummond. While the reader should not too readily assume that Jonson's dramatic practice squared rigidly with his critical precepts, it still seems both appropriate and meaningful to say that Jonson's greatest comedies, *Volpone* and *The Alchemist*, display 'classical' virtues of lucidity and meticulous construction.

The quality of a Jonsonian comedy, however, lies not only in its construction and in its presentation of character as obsession, but also in its language, which often has a positively *nourishing* quality; it has the 'feel' of the life of his time. In fact, Jonson's evocation of contemporary London low-life is at times so dense, so detailed that for a modern reader it is at first confusing; *Volpone*, set in Venice, is as a result the most immediately accessible of his comedies.

The master-theme in Jonson's satirical comedies is human folly, particularly that obsessive human greed which betrays fools into the hands of expert and opportunist manipulators. The action always culminates in exposure and often in punishment. The comedy is harsh, single-minded, and inhospitable to sentiment,

1. *Shakespeare Criticism, 1935–60*, p. 206.
2. Introduction to *Ben Jonson: Selected Works*, p. 5.

pathos, and irrelevance. In the end Jonsonian comedy *is* more limited than Shakespeare's great succession of comedies, but the *genre* is purer. Imitation of past masters and the observance of rules helped Jonson to write well; his own acute observation, moral concern, and mastery of words made him a great comic dramatist. Later, imitation of their master guided 'the tribe of Ben' to write less badly, and made Jonson the most celebrated father-figure in English literature.

III

Volpone is Jonson's greatest and most intense comedy. It is a savage and sardonic satire on human greed and rapacity, but the brilliance of the design and the execution, together with the comments of critics primarily concerned with the literary qualities of the play, should not prevent us from recognizing its perennial vitality as a piece of theatre.

Jonson presents both his characters and their backgrounds with deliberate precision. The people of the play are, through their names, invested with animal symbolism (Wolf, Fly, Vulture, Raven, and Crow), and linked with the creatures of medieval *fabliaux*, with Reynard the Fox and his victims. But where animals behaving like human beings, whether in the *Fables* of Robert Henryson or in the cartoons of Walt Disney, have the charm and fantasy of creatures viewed from a novel perspective, men behaving like animals and predatory birds are seen to be debased and degenerate. Nor is it by chance that these people are Venetians. Venice, already familiar on the Elizabethan stage as the city of Shakespeare's usurer, Shylock, was famed as the most affluent, acquisitive, glittering, and corrupt city in Renaissance Europe. In the modern theatre one envisages for this play an opulence of production and *décors* as peculiarly necessary to emphasize the preoccupation with affluence and acquisitiveness which the play exposes.

Several literary critics, approaching the opening scenes of *Volpone*, have pointed to the thorough reversal of traditional religious and moral values in the play, and demonstrated how the language and imagery reinforce this total reversal. The play opens with a literary convention, with a character waking to greet the dawn:

> Good morning to the day; and next, my gold!
> Open the shrine, that I may see my saint!

And, as Mosca draws a curtain to disclose the treasures heaped up behind, Volpone's speech becomes a perverted act of worship:

> Hail the world's soul, and mine! More glad than is
> The teeming earth to see the longed-for sun
> Peep through the horns of the celestial Ram,
> Am I, to view thy splendour darkening his . . .

Volpone here uses an image of the earth's potential richness and fertility as it awaits the life-quickening sun in spring to describe his own expectant state; already within these lines, gold has eclipsed the sun, an idea that is made more explicit a moment later with his apostrophe:

> O, thou son of Sol
> (But brighter than thy father) let me kiss,
> With adoration, thee, and every relic
> Of sacred treasure in this blessèd room.

Here the reversal of values and the perverse misappropriation of traditional language ('adoration', 'relic', 'sacred', 'blessèd') become complete, and the myth that gold is indeed child of Sol, the sun, associates Volpone with alchemists and their pursuit of the Philosopher's Stone. The dehumanizing and debasing aspects of Volpone's worship of gold are apparent in the lines where the normal, happy lives of others are contemptuously dismissed. And at the end of the first act, Mosca clinches his seductive description of Celia by comparing her beauty, finally, not with living things but with gold itself. Throughout *Volpone*, religious and erotic language and imagery are perverted and debased, expressing (as their very names do) the inner corruption and animality of the main characters. Jonson also uses language and imagery in such a way that we of the audience are led to make our own moral judgements. Volpone's speeches are often memorably beautiful, but the poetry is never purely ornamental. Thus although, in his more splendid passages, Volpone's energy, intelligence, and thrust may seem to link him in our minds with Dr Faustus and Tamburlaine the Great, the Marlovian over-reachers, we see that he has none of their heroic aspirations. Volpone's habitual disguise as an old man sick unto death, his assumed diseases and senility, ironically point to his own inner sickness; his energy and intelligence shine out in the early scenes of the play principally in contrast to the drab and joyless self-interest and miserliness of his dupes, Voltore, Corbaccio, and Corvino. He gets more pleasure from manipulating them, and from watching them squirm, than from anything their gold, diamonds, and pearls enable him to do. Volpone's function in these scenes is almost judicial:

> What a rare punishment
> Is avarice to itself!

While analysis of the poetry, the imagery, the larger metaphor of animal names, and the like helps to direct and control our moral and emotional responses to *Volpone*, such a critical approach tends to ignore the vitality of the play as a piece of theatre, and literary commentators have insufficiently stressed the superb *theatricalism* of Jonson's great comedy, which stems in part from Volpone's self-congratulatory acting throughout the play. He is a consummate actor, delighting in impersonation and in the details of make-up and costume; on his virtuosity depend the early scenes of the play. Despite Jonson's paucity of stage-directions, it is clear that Volpone's huge bed should dominate the stage. At the very beginning of the play he is discovered there, awakening. Later he lies in bed, receiving the tributes from his 'clients', shamming sickness and senility, and all the while critically eyeing and evaluating their presents and making sardonic comments *sotto voce* to Mosca. There are wonderful opportunities here for by-play by the actor playing Volpone; in Sir Donald Wolfit's performance he 'leered through the curtains and twiddled his toes under the bed-clothes for sheer enjoyment as the gifts kept coming in'.[1] Similarly, the scene in which Volpone disguises himself as the Mountebank and harangues the crowd provides Volpone (and the actor playing him) with unlimited opportunities. Later, the bed is again the main stage-furniture in the scene in which Corvino eagerly leads his wife to the bedside of the sick Volpone to prostitute her to his

1. *Ben Jonson*, vol. IX, p. 205.

potential benefactor. This is the central scene of the play, and it is a great moment in the theatre when, as Celia droops by the bed, Volpone throws off the furs, the caps, the make-up of the senile invalid, and leaps from the bed to stand before her as a Renaissance gallant, glorying in his potency:

> Nay, fly me not,
> Nor let thy false imagination
> That I was bed-rid, make thee think I am so:
> Thou shalt not find it. I am, now, as fresh,
> As hot, as high, and in as jovial plight
> As when, in that so celebrated scene,
> At recitation of our comedy,
> For entertainment of the great Valois,
> I acted young Antinous, and attracted
> The eyes and ears of all the ladies present,
> T'admire each graceful gesture, note, and footing.

Typically, Volpone here recalls his past triumph as an actor, and the sex-appeal he had for the ladies of the Court. Typically, too, he links himself, in the pun on 'jovial', with Jove, who metamorphosed himself for so many erotic adventures with earthly maidens. And in the song, which originates in Catullus, Volpone presses Celia with the argument, insidious to traditional moralists, that Time is passing, that the only sin is to be found out, and that they are superior beings:

> Cannot *we* delude the eyes
> Of a few poor household spies? . . .
> To be taken, to be seen,
> These have crimes accounted been.

His dazzling speech beginning 'Why droops my Celia?' is a speech of temptation. Running through it there is an unchallenged assumption that everyone has a price ('A diamond would have bought Lollia Paulina'). And when, in the next speech, Volpone depicts their future life together, the sensuality becomes more blatant:

> Our drink shall be preparèd gold and amber,
> Which we will take until my roof whirl round
> With the vertigo; and my dwarf shall dance,
> My eunuch sing, my fool make up the antic.

> Whilst we, in changèd shapes, act Ovid's tales,
> Thou like Europa now, and I like Jove,
> Then I like Mars, and thou like Erycine;
> So of the rest, till we have quite run through,
> And wearied all the fables of the gods.
> Then will I have thee in more modern forms,
> Attirèd like some sprightly dame of France . . .
> Or some quick Negro, or cold Russian. . .

The perversity, the artificial stimulation of passion, reminds us (if Mosca is a truthful witness) of the real children of Volpone: the dwarf, the eunuch, the hermaphrodite – the three freaks – and:

> Bastards,
> Some dozen, or more, that he begot on beggars,
> Gypsies, and Jews, and black-moors, when he was drunk.

It reminds us, too, of Nano's song, sung while he impersonated the Mountebank's zany, which vainly promised eternal youth and beauty, and the preservation of the life of the senses. Volpone, the eloquent seducer, fails to move Celia. He resorts to rape. Bonario rushes in, in the nick of time, to save Celia; but Jonson in this play is not much interested in human goodness, and the wronged wife and stalwart young man are minor, unrealized figures in the comedy. Coleridge was not alone in expressing disappointment at this: 'Bonario and Celia should have been made in some way or other principals in the plot . . . If it were possible to lessen the paramountcy of Volpone himself, a most delightful comedy might have been produced, by making Celia the ward or niece of Corvino, instead of his wife, and Bonario her lover.'[1] But there is a sense in which 'the paramountcy of Volpone' *is* the play; and who would sacrifice the distinctive harsh tone of *Volpone* for yet another 'most delightful comedy'?

Bonario's intervention momentarily casts Volpone and Mosca down: they even talk of suicide. Soon they start manipulating the changed circumstances to their advantage, and their machinations seem, for a time, likely to triumph. In the end, these over-reachers come tumbling down, but it is not the virtuous Bonario and Celia who prove their undoing, nor the feeble processes of Venetian

1. T. M. Raysor, *Coleridge's Miscellaneous Criticism* (1936), p. 55.

law. Volpone's own relish for extemporizing to meet the new complications proves his ruin: for the gleeful experience of watching his clients' discomfiture he feigns his own death, and installs Mosca as his heir. The parasite has learned from the patron; the mutual admiration society is dissolved: they undo each other. The end of the comedy is harsh and punitive: no one 'scapes whipping. And where, in Coleridge's 'delightful comedy', virtue would triumph and Celia be married at the play's end, the pallid heroine is restored, with her dowry, to her parents. *Volpone* does not end with wedding-bells but with Volpone, the unmasked Fox, speaking the epilogue.

Throughout the comedy Sir Politic Would-be and his Fine Madame play a secondary, never an essential, part. They remain English visitors in a world of Italianate machinations which they never understand. Lady Would-be is merely a *poseuse*, a minor Mrs Malaprop, a figure of fun – the role has been played, broadly and effectively, as a dame part. Sir Politic is something more. In the theatre he emerges as the befuddled Englishman abroad, secure only in his suspicion of foreigners and his own better understanding of how things are organized by the natives. His ludicrous speculative ventures parallel Volpone's successful fleecing of his dupes; and are part of the play's satirical attack upon an irrationally acquisitive, capitalistic society. Sir Pol is a contemporary satirical portrait of the English traveller. He is also, in the play's bestiary, the parrot, chattering away at second hand, and memorable for his bland stupidity and his vague 'general notions'. Sir Politic has been excellently played by Michael Hordern and by Jonathan Miller, and it is his essential *Englishness* which makes him funny. The Would-be pair are expendable; but to cut them from a performance of the comedy leaves the Italian dupes and manipulators relatively unfocused. They earn their part in the play.

IV

The Alchemist is a humbler, a more domestic *Volpone*. Once more the characters are men dominated and exploited by others through their own desires to get rich quick. A sucker seems to have been born every minute in Jonson's comic world, and in the Philosopher's Stone, which was supposed to turn base metals into gold,

Jonson found a wonderful correlative for his gulls' selfish and inordinate desire for wealth, influence, and power. It is by holding out to the gulls the prospect of possessing the Stone, that the triumvirate of confidence-tricksters, Face, Subtle, and Dol Common, manipulate them, and win a living. But their world is very different from the rich, remote world of Volpone's Venice. Their environment is Jacobean London, vividly and saltily evoked by Jonson; and where Volpone operated in part for the sheer perverse exhilaration of controlling others, these three uneasy allies are desperate chancers living on their wits. The play opens explosively with Face and Subtle quarrelling, and we are early reminded how near the bread-line Subtle has been used to living. Dol Common and Subtle are the under-dogs of the Elizabethan underworld.

The great *technical* achievement of this comedy is that Jonson was able to compress so much local life, so many special slangs and jargons, within his lively and supple blank verse. The density of the dialogue, the contemporaneity of the comedy to a Jacobean audience, makes *The Alchemist* (like *Bartholomew Fair*) more difficult than *Volpone* for readers and playgoers today. While the theme of human greed and gullibility is universal, the types, the references, the vocabularies are Jacobean. The idiom is often obscure, but the dialogue and the pace of the action are fast, and carry the reader with them. The play moves with classical, almost clockwork precision, each act stepping on the heels of the preceding one, and the action is virtually continuous from (according to the Herford–Simpson edition) 9 a.m., when Dapper calls, until 3 p.m., when Lovewit unexpectedly returns home and the coney-catchers are unmasked and dispersed. *The Alchemist* is, in essence, farcical; but its quality lies in the Jonsonian synthesis of two seemingly irreconcilable elements – farce and intellect.

The structure of *The Alchemist* resembles *Volpone* in that, one by one, the principal dupes are introduced to us as they pay their morning calls. Jonson provides a superb array of types – the upstart clerk, Dapper; the shy little tobacconist, Abel Drugger, whom Garrick delighted to act; the elephantine voluptuary, Sir Epicure Mammon; and the insidious kill-joy Puritans, Ananias and Tribulation Wholesome. Each is governed by self-interest, and each is betrayed into the opportunists' hands by a dream of wealth. Even the card-sharper, Surly, who seems to embody common sense – rather like those reasonable brothers-in-law in Molière who show up the obsessions of the Miser or the Imaginary Invalid – ends by trying to make a wealthy match with Dame Pliant. For each Jonson creates an appropriate diction and speech-rhythm: Drugger is shy and halting, the Puritans are sanctimonious, and Subtle has a splendid line in alchemical blarney. Sir Epicure's speeches *sound* almost as seductive, Marlovian, and sumptuous as Volpone's, but they are transparently silly and self-deluding. He is closer to Sir Politic Would-be than to Tamburlaine.

The end of *The Alchemist* is more indulgent than that of *Volpone*. Lovewit, the rightful owner, returns suddenly, and is not really surprised at the uses to which his town house has been put. Dol Common and Subtle make their get-away, none the richer for their ingenious cozenings. Captain Face dwindles again to being Jeremy, the butler, and blandly triumphs by helping his master to a rich wife. He remains the complete opportunist. That he dodges retribution is psychologically right, and reminds the audience that con-men, like the poor, are always with us. Like Flatterie at the end of Sir David Lyndsay's great morality *The Three Estates*, Face goes scot-free; the audience must be wary.

When Sir Tyrone Guthrie directed *The Alchemist* at London's Old Vic in 1962, the play was performed in modern dress. In part this was because the desire for wealth still makes people gullible today, so that the theme of the comedy remains universal. Guthrie gave a further reason in his programme-note: '. . . modern dress gives more point to the frequent disguises and impersonations used by the trio of rogues. In Jacobean dress, who would know when Face was a Captain or a House Servant? Whether Subtle was a Divine or a Doctor?' The point was well taken, and Guthrie's production was fast and farcical and marvellously entertaining, reminding us, perhaps, that of Jonson's three best comedies this one shone longest and brightest on the English stage. But because Jonson used contemporary idiom and place-reference so vividly, some obscurity is nowadays unavoidable, and a director may well want to make cuts. This is not a recent problem. David Garrick's acting version, shortened and with most of the lime-light on the Little Tobacconist, had – according to the Jonsonian stage-historian Robert Gale Noyes – 'one hundred and fifty four cuts, varying from one line to three pages'[1] – though not all were made because of obscurity. Two hundred and fifty lines were excised from Sir Epicure Mammon's part, including the one about 'the swelling unctuous paps of a fat pregnant sow'. The problem the men of the theatre still need to solve – Guthrie no less than Garrick – is how to do justice to Jonson's fusion of farce and intellectual satire. Guthrie certainly did well by Sir Epicure, who emerged in his production as a Jonsonian 'humour', a monumental caricature, but elsewhere his version, rightly hilarious, missed the moral comment which is implicit in the play's language and structure. Guthrie's *Alchemist* was great fun; Jonson's *Alchemist* is a great comedy. Dryden regarded it as Jonson's highest achievement, although *Volpone* now claims first place. Between them they demonstrate Jonson's variety within the narrow range of satirical comedy.

V

There remains Jonson's later prose-comedy, *Bartholomew Fair*. When in 1950 the Old Vic Company revived this entertainment on the open stage of the Assembly Hall at Edinburgh and later in London, Mr T. C. Worsley, usually a sympathetic critic, found the play 'the most crashing old bore'[2] and Mr Kenneth Tynan announced that 'the play, to stand up, certainly needs crutches'.[3] Part of their dissatisfaction may be attributed to the production by George Devine which, though enjoyable, was insufficiently serious, substituting a riot of false noses and actors laughing at their own stale jokes for Jonson's contemporary realism. The reviewers prompted a critical revaluation of this play. It is, of course, a lesser work than either *Volpone* or *The Alchemist*, although some academic critics rate it more highly.

Bartholomew Fair is a 'panoramic' structure, looser and more comprehensive than Jonson's other great comedies. It is a festive entertainment in the literal sense that it dramatizes a popular holiday, and into it Jonson packed a great deal of London life and

1. *Ben Jonson on the English Stage, 1660–1776* (1935), p. 143.
2. *The Fugitive Art: Dramatic Commentaries, 1947–51* (1952), p. 183.
3. *Curtains* (1961), p. 3.

London idiom. The first act, which is almost a prologue to the four which follow, is essentially expository. It introduces one segment of the large cast of characters, those people who, though already united through kinship, friendship, business, or Puritanical religious zeal, are really linked by one thing: their desire to go to the Fair. They are presented in ones and twos – an idiosyncratic, well-drawn gallery of types – and the opening act culminates in the entrance of the monstrous, black figure of the Puritan-hypocrite, Rabbi Zeal-of-the-Land Busy. In the second act we move to the Fair (or rather, in the Elizabethan theatre, the Fair moves to us), where another monstrous, authoritarian figure, Justice Overdo, is disguising himself in order to move, like a good Governor or Magistrate in the Elizabethan drama, unrecognized among the people. But this Justice, so bent on uncovering 'enormities', learns very little from his experience. The people of the Fair who are introduced in the second act have something in common with the trio in *The Alchemist* – they live by their wits. The prose-pamphlets of Thomas Nashe and others[1] testify to the Elizabethans' intense interest in the sheer mechanics of roguery, but the moral drift of this festive comedy is that the dupes are no better than the confidence-tricksters and villains. As the comedy progresses, the people of Act One meet and mingle with the folk of the Fair, itself a symbol of the world. There seems little to choose between the fools and the knaves, especially as some of the latter have a touch of the agility and roguish skill of Face, Subtle, and Dol. At the centre of the Fair and of the comedy stands Ursula, the Pig Woman, raucous, sweating, Falstaffian. She seems almost an Earth-Mother figure, but, like the other crooks, she should not be over-romanticized by critics: after all, it is she who, as the unofficial, accommodating lavatory-attendant at the Fair, tries to entice Mistress Littlewit and Mistress Overdo into prostitution.

The structure of the comedy appears to be casual – the fresh complications of Quarlous's disguise and of Dame Purecraft's falling in love with a madman are brought in almost off-handedly at the closing moments of Act Four – but the underlying design is always clear. *Bartholomew Fair* ends genially: the sober, hypo-

1. See A. V. Judges (editor), *The Elizabethan Underworld* (1930), *passim*.

critical, and authoritarian figures, the Puritan and the Justice, killjoys both, are discomfited. Zeal-of-the-Land Busy, with his prodigious rhetorical tirade against the theatre, is out-manoeuvred in debate after the puppet-play-within-the-play by Lantern's puppet, and retires crestfallen. Justice Overdo (whose Christian name Adam suggests that he is a universal figure) sheds his disguise for that final moment towards which all satiric comedy inexorably moves – the judgement:

Now to my enormities: look upon me, O London! and see me, O Smithfield! The example of justice, and mirror of magistrates, the true top of formality, and scourge of enormity. Hearken unto my labours . . . !

But Overdo is silenced when one of the 'prostitutes' is unmasked, and turns out to be Mistress Overdo. The end of the play is good-humoured and forgiving, prolonging the spirit of holiday: Justice Overdo invites all the *dramatis personae* back to his house for supper. The motives of the 'upright' have been questioned; the knaves and the opportunists go free.

The appeal of *Bartholomew Fair* is in the rich and vivid execution rather than in any moral content. This execution presents difficulties for today's reader – difficulties that, as in *The Alchemist*, spring from Jonson's rich and detailed evocation of Jacobean life through contemporary and local reference, and through specific jargons and slang. Although the modern reader quickly appreciates the *vitality* of this comedy, its rich comprehensiveness, he is bound to find a good deal of it (Dan Knockem's 'vapours', for example, or Whit's stage-Irish) very tiresome. And while certain characters spring vividly to life – the Justice, Zeal-of-the-Land Busy, Humphrey Wasp, Ursula – others in the large cast of characters nowadays remain obscure. Part of the pleasure for the first audiences must have been that shock of recognition as they saw their own great Fair put vividly and realistically upon the stage of the Hope Theatre at Bankside in October 1614, only a couple of months after the Fair itself had been held as usual at Smithfield.

Kenneth Tynan once called *Bartholomew Fair* 'a documentary'[1]

1. *Curtains*, p. 3.

and another drama critic, Professor Eric Bentley, regards Shakespeare's major history-sequence as forming *with this comedy of Jonson's* 'the great masterpiece of social realism in English'.[1] Jonson, in an almost pedantic way, crammed a great mass of Jacobean life, idiom, and local colour, into *Bartholomew Fair*. The term 'documentary' is a somewhat bleak description of his achievement in this comedy and does scant justice to its exuberance and its richness of caricature. I should prefer to call *Bartholomew Fair* a cartoon, and to regard as distinctive its animation, its vigour, and its 'panoramic' coverage of Jacobean types. Some day, I hope, Miss Joan Littlewood will direct the play in such a way as to bring to life in modern stage terms both its stylization and its realism, and to give us 'the beauty of it hot', for, literary and intellectual though Jonson's desire to cram everything in may have been, the play has analogies with the visual arts. *Bartholomew Fair* may be inferior to *Volpone* and *The Alchemist*, but it links Jonson with that other celebrant of the riotous life of Bartholomew Fair, the great English cartoonist, Thomas Rowlandson.

VI

The aims of the present edition are modest. The text of *Volpone* and *The Alchemist* is that of the First Folio *Workes* (1616) seen through the press by Jonson himself; that of *Bartholomew Fair* is based upon the posthumous Second Folio (1640), sheets of which Jonson may have seen and partly corrected before his death.

Jonson took great pains to see that his play-scripts were accurately presented to the Jacobean reader, and he adopted a standard method for the printing of the plays. Like other Elizabethan dramatists he did not give locations for his scenes save for a general indication that the action was set in London or in Venice. His practice was to start off at Act I Scene I, and usually to begin a new scene (Scene II, Scene III, etc.) at the entrance of another character, a style which never became standard for printing plays in England as it did in France. At the head of each scene he listed the characters appearing in it: *Subtle. Face. Dol. Mammon.*, etc. The first-named character is always the first speaker, and Jonson never gave any further attribution of the opening speech. He did

1. *In Search of Theater* (1953), p. 129.

not indicate the precise point at which a character enters or exits when these entrances or exits do not mark the beginning or end of a scene. He gave few stage-directions (save for *Bartholomew Fair*, where the largeness of the cast and the 'busy' action seems to have made stage-directions more necessary), and these were always printed in the margin. The following conventions have been used in this edition:

SPELLING AND PUNCTUATION

The spelling has been modernized throughout, as has the punctuation, to make the sense clear to the modern reader. Thus I print *murder* where Jonson used *murther*, *venture* for his *venter* (save where rhyme has to be preserved), and so on. Obvious misprints have been silently corrected. The minor emendations and corrections which are standard in modern editions have likewise been silently included, but, where a new reading has been adopted from a recent scholarly edition, the fact has been recorded among the critical notes at the back. Jonson's plays survive in an uncommonly good state, and I have not included a list of textual variants, knowing as I do that scholars and graduate-students who need access to the full bibliographical and textual apparatus will always prefer to use the Folios themselves, or the Oxford edition, or some other old-spelling reprint. In past participles Jonson's *'d* has been extended to *ed*, and his *ed* has been stressed *èd*. Jonson's *th'*, *i'*, *ha'*, *gi'*, etc. (for *the*, *in*, *have*, *give*, etc.) have been retained; they reflect the idiomatic usages and the pronunciation of his own day, and in dialect speeches especially they are necessary – and helpful – to the actor. The colloquial *an* (if), which Jonson spelt *and* or *an'*, has been spelt *an'*. Jonson habitually used italics for outlandish and technical words. These have usually been dispensed with. Capitals have sometimes been introduced for clarity or emphasis, and to guide the reader or the actor.

ACT- AND SCENE-DIVISION

It would be pedantic to adhere rigidly to Jonson's scene-divisions in a modern edition, especially as so much of the action in his comedies is continuous. Editorial scene-divisions have been made only when a change of location has to be indicated (see below), and all these are printed in square brackets: [SCENE TWO]. Jonson's own scene-divisions have been retained in abbreviated form and placed towards the margin: I, i, I, ii, I, iii, etc. The reader can thus appreciate at a glance the scenic structure of the comedies, while not experiencing the sense of a break in the action. Also, there is an advantage in preserving Jonson's scene-divisions for students who wish to use this text while referring to the commentaries in, say, the Oxford edition. The running-titles throughout use the editorial scene-divisions, though square brackets are here dispensed with.

LOCATIONS AND STAGE-DIRECTIONS

At the top of the first page of the original prompt-copy for the King's Men's performances of *Volpone* there may well have been scrawled 'A bed thrust out. Volpone in it'. In this edition locations are added in square brackets: [*Volpone's house.*] or [*The Fair.*]. These locations have been kept brief, and it is emphasized that they are sometimes conjectural. In the front-matter to the individual comedies I have summarized the sort of problems that occasionally arise about the precise location of particular scenes – problems which a director or a stage-designer can solve by adopting a composite-set.

Jonson's marginal stage-directions have usually been retained, though seldom kept in the margin. Square brackets indicate editorial stage-directions (many of them stemming from nineteenth- and twentieth-century editors), but sometimes a cryptically brief authorial stage-direction has been superseded by one in square brackets. Occasionally a stage-direction by Jonson has been placed in round brackets within a speech.

SPEECH-TAGS

The names of speakers are usually printed as contractions in the Jacobean editions of Jonson's comedies. These have here been expanded throughout, so that similar speech-tags like *Volp.* and *Volt.*, *Corb.* and *Corv.*, no longer confuse the reader, but are replaced by *Volpone*, *Voltore*, *Corbaccio*, and *Corvino*. The *Win.* and

Winw. (which muddled the first printers of *Bartholomew Fair*) are here replaced by *Mistress Littlewit* and *Winwife.*

ANNOTATION

The notes in any edition of plays by Jonson present a problem, for the range of his classical, contemporary, topographical, and other references is immense. The appropriateness of a mythological allusion or the sharpness of a Jacobean reference can often be appreciated by a present-day reader only if he refers to the notes. I have tried to divide notes into two broad categories – glosses on Jacobean expressions and on words that have changed their meaning are printed as footnotes, while explanatory notes on classical and literary references, proper- and place-names, and allusions to Jacobean life appear with the longer critical comments at the back. Occasionally, where the reader might miss the point of a speech, the word 'Note' appears at the foot of the page to refer him to the back of this book. Usually no such indication has been considered necessary, and it is hoped that the reader who is puzzled by a particular difficulty *will* find it explained in a note. At times he will look in vain for this help. Comprehensive annotation of all three comedies would lay too heavy a burden upon Jonson, and most readers will prefer, first time through, being carried forward by the pace of the developing action and by the rhythm and buoyancy of the dialogue, to being slavishly dependent on what S. Potter once called 'the dispiriting apparatus of notes'.[1]

As the line-numbering of *The Alchemist* and of the verse-scenes of *Volpone* corresponds with that in the standard Oxford edition by Herford and the Simpsons, a zealous reader can make full use of the thorough annotation in their volumes of commentaries. For the prose-scenes of *Volpone* and for *Bartholomew Fair* my abbreviations of Jonson's own scene-divisions (I, i, I, ii, etc.) should also make for easy reference to massively annotated editions. I have made no attempt to make a comprehensive survey of the numerous parallels with classical and Renaissance authors, nor have I tried to explain every learned allusion. Those who want to know, for example, that in *The Alchemist*, I, i, I, Subtle's 'I fart at

1. *The Muse in Chains: A Study in Education* (1937), p. 42.

thee!' is like the Latin *oppedo* and the Greek καταπέρδω will want to make use of Volume X of the Oxford *Ben Jonson*; others of us will continue to believe that such words were actually heard sometimes on the lips of Jonson's contemporaries.

ACKNOWLEDGEMENTS

In preparing the text and notes I have, of course, benefited greatly from the work of my many predecessors, particularly the labours of C. H. Herford and Percy and Evelyn Simpson. Professor Harry Levin's excellent one-volume *Ben Jonson: Selected Works* was, alas, unannotated, but, throughout, I have been guided, enlightened, and occasionally inhibited, by the scholarship of previous editors and by the insight of critics and commentators. Any editor is greatly indebted to others. For example, a casual glance at the editions of *Bartholomew Fair* by Eugene M. Waith (1963) and Edward B. Partridge (1964) will reveal how deep is their debt to E. A. Horsman's edition for the Revels Plays (1960); I had the good fortune to be able to consult and make use of the work of all three gentlemen. I am grateful to Professor David Daiches and Mr R. P. C. Mutter for advice and encouragement.

FURTHER READING

The bibliography on p. 33 and the prefatory matter to the three separate comedies show that there is no lack of critical and scholarly books on Ben Jonson. There has indeed been something of a Jonson revival in the United States with Professor Levin, dedicatee of at least two striking books on the dramatist, as the *doyen* of American Jonsonians. The general reader must be warned, however, that Jonson's notorious learning has called forth an answering pedantry in some of his more recent American commentators and scholarly exegetes which is manifested either in a fancy line in chapter headings, 'Comoedy of Affliction' and '(Although no Paralel)', or in mandarin prose:

With Zeal-of-the-Land Busy ... we are back on the highroad of linguistic caricature, where every cobblestone, every pebble, shrieks

affectation, and the whole gives off a lurid phosphorescence more like that of a Martian than an earthly landscape . . .
Unlike Busy . . . Overdo is auto-intoxicate.

Scholars who have immolated themselves in some part of 'The Background' (Renaissance philosophy, rhetoric, satire, psychology, alchemy, the Great Chain of Being itself) are sometimes slow to get back to Jonson's marvellous liveliness on the printed page and to the theatrical potentialities of his comedies.

Had I put an epigraph on the title-page, I should have adapted · some words of Jonson's from the epilogue to *Cynthia's Revels, or The Fountain of Self-Love:*

> By God 'tis good, and if you lik't, you may.

Falmer House,   M. S. J.
The University of Sussex,
Brighton
St Bartholomew's Day, 1965

SELECT BIBLIOGRAPHY

1. BIBLIOGRAPHIES

W. W. GREG. *A Bibliography of the English Printed Drama to the Restoration*, 4 vols., 1940–59.

S. A. TANNENBAUM. *Ben Jonson (A Concise Bibliography)*, 1938.

S. A. and DOROTHY R. TANNENBAUM. *Supplement to Ben Jonson, A Concise Bibliography*, 1947

2. SCHOLARLY WORKS OF REFERENCE

G. E. BENTLEY. *The Jacobean and Caroline Stage*, 7 vols., 1941–68.

E. K. CHAMBERS. *The Elizabethan Stage*, 4 vols., 1923.

3. COLLECTED EDITIONS

The Workes of Beniamin Jonson, 1616.

The Workes of Benjamin Jonson, 2 vols., 1640.

C. H. HERFORD and PERCY and EVELYN SIMPSON, editors. *Ben Jonson*, 11 vols., 1925–52.

A. B. KERNAN and R. B. YOUNG, general editors. *The Yale Ben Jonson*, in progress, 1962–.

4. BIOGRAPHICAL, CRITICAL, AND OTHER STUDIES

J. B. BAMBOROUGH. *Ben Jonson*, 1959.

J. A. BARISH. *Ben Jonson and the Language of Prose Comedy*, 1960.

J. A. BARISH, editor. *Ben Jonson: A Collection of Critical Essays*, 1963.

G. E. BENTLEY. *Shakespeare and Jonson, Their Reputations in the Seventeenth Century Compared*, 2 vols., 1945; *The Swan of Avon and the Bricklayer of Westminster*, 1946.

M. C. BRADBROOK. *The Growth and Structure of Elizabethan Comedy*, 1955.

O. J. CAMPBELL. *Comicall Satyre and Shakespeare's 'Troilus and Cressida'*, 1938.

MARCHETTE CHUTE. *Ben Jonson of Westminster*, 1954.

T. S. ELIOT. 'Ben Jonson', *Selected Essays*, 1932; revised edition, 1951; reprinted by J. A. Barish, editor, *Ben Jonson: A Collection of Critical Essays*, 1963.

SELECT BIBLIOGRAPHY

J. J. ENCK. *Jonson and the Comic Truth*, 1957.

D. J. ENRIGHT. 'Poetic Satire and Satire in Verse: A Consideration of Ben Jonson and Philip Massinger', *The Apothecary's Shop*, 1957.

BRIAN GIBBONS. *Jacobean City Comedy: A Study of Satiric Plays by Jonson, Marston and Middleton*, 1968.

A. B. KERNAN. *The Cankered Muse: Satire of the English Renaissance*, 1959.

L. C. KNIGHTS. 'Ben Jonson, Dramatist', *The Pelican Guide to English Literature, 2, The Age of Shakespeare*, Boris Ford, editor, 1955; *Drama and Society in the Age of Jonson*, 1937.

HARRY LEVIN. Introduction to *Ben Jonson: Selected Works*, n.d. [1938]; reprinted by J. A. Barish, editor, *Ben Jonson: A Collection of Critical Essays*, 1963.

ERIC LINKLATER. *Ben Jonson and King James: Biography and Portrait*, 1931.

ROBERT GALE NOYES. *Ben Jonson on the English Stage, 1660–1776*, 1935.

JOHN PALMER. *Ben Jonson*, 1934.

E. B. PARTRIDGE. *The Broken Compass: A Study of the Major Comedies of Ben Jonson*, 1958.

A. H. SACKTON. *Rhetoric as a Dramatic Language in Ben Jonson*, 1948.

FREDA L. TOWNSEND. *Apologie for Bartholmew Fayre: The Art of Jonson's Comedies*, 1947.

WESLEY TRIMPI. *Ben Jonson's Poems: A Study of the Plain Style*, 1962.

EDMUND WILSON. 'Morose Ben Jonson', *The Triple Thinkers*, revised edition, 1952; reprinted by J. A. Barish, editor, *Ben Jonson: A Collection of Critical Essays*, 1963.

VOLPONE,
OR
THE FOX

PRELIMINARY NOTE

I. STAGE-HISTORY AND FIRST PUBLICATION

Volpone was first acted in late 1605 or early 1606 by the leading company of the times, the King's Men, led by Richard Burbage, who probably played Mosca with John Lowin as Volpone. It was successfully performed by them at Oxford and Cambridge. The play was published in quarto in 1607, prefaced by verse-eulogies from John Donne, George Chapman, Francis Beaumont, and John Fletcher, and was dedicated by Jonson 'To the Most Noble and Most Equal Sisters, the Two Famous Universities for their Love and Acceptance Shown to his Poem in the Presentation'. It was printed in the Folio *Workes* in 1616 and in the enlarged posthumous Folio of 1640. The play was regularly staged in London throughout the seventeenth and for most of the eighteenth century. After 1785 it does not seem to have been revived until the nineteen-twenties, when it was given two performances by the Phoenix Society and also played by Cambridge undergraduates. Donald Wolfit first appeared as Volpone at the Westminster Theatre in London in 1938, and included the play in several of his annual far-flung provincial tours in the forties. Sir Donald also appeared in the play on B.B.C. television. In 1952 Sir Ralph Richardson played Volpone at the Shakespeare Memorial Theatre at Stratford-upon-Avon. Peter Woodthorpe was Volpone in the Marlowe Society production at Cambridge in 1955, when Jonathan Miller played Sir Politic Would-be. It was performed in modern dress under the direction of Joan Littlewood (who played Lady Would-be) by Theatre Workshop in 1955, a production more acclaimed in Paris than in London.

In 1926 Stefan Zweig made a German version, which was later translated into French by Jules Romains and played in Paris in 1928 by Charles Dullin in a multiple set by André Barsacq. This script was the basis of the memorable French film with Harry Baur as Volpone and Louis Jouvet as Mosca. Jean-Louis Barrault keeps the Zweig–Romains adaptation in his Parisian repertory.

Ruth Langner *actually translated Zweig's version back into English* for a Broadway production, with Alfred Lunt as Mosca, in 1928. José Ferrer appeared on Broadway in 1948 in Jonson's play; but the much-heralded production announced by Orson Welles in 1955 with himself as Mosca to Jackie Gleason's Volpone did not materialize. In 1964 *Volpone* was seen at the new Tyrone Guthrie Repertory Theatre in Minneapolis, Minnesota, starring Douglas Cambell. An opera with music by Malcolm Williamson based on *Volpone* was seen in London in 1964, and in that year Bert Lahr appeared on Broadway in a musical *Foxy*, set in Alaska during the Gold Rush, and remotely inspired by Jonson's play. In 1965 John Neville played Mosca in a production at the Nottingham Playhouse. Leo McKern appeared as Volpone in Oxford and London in 1966–67 under the direction of Frank Hauser, a production which won more critical acclaim than Guthrie's for the National Theatre in 1968, when fussy business and good and bad ideas (animal costumes and movement; animal noises) blurred the lucid story-line.

2. LOCATION AND TIME-SCHEME

The action in *Volpone* takes place in Volpone's bedroom, inside and outside Corvino's house, in Sir Politic's lodging, in the Scrutineo, and in the street. The action covers one day, from Volpone's awakening (and Voltore's 'early visitation') to the sentences passed on Volpone and Mosca late in the afternoon.

3. EDITIONS AND CRITICAL COMMENT

Volpone has been reprinted in various collected and selected editions of Jonson, and in many anthologies. It has been edited and annotated by J. D. Rea (1919), by Arthur Sale (1951), by David Cook (1962), and, as the first volume of the new Yale Ben Jonson, by A. B. Kernan (1962). J. J. Enck and E. B. Partridge have chapters on the play (the latter is concerned with imagery and what it tells us); J. A. Barish's compendium of Jonsonian criticism includes his own demonstration that Sir Politic and Lady Would-be are relevant to the play as a whole; and Professor Harry Levin has contributed a learned analysis of Mosca's interlude in I, ii to *Philological Quarterly*, XXII (1943).

BEN: IONSON

his

VOLPONE

Or

THE FOXE.

—— *Simul & iucunda, & idonea dicere vitæ.*

Printed for *Thomas Thorppe.*
1 6 0 7.

Facsimile of the title-page of the first edition, the quarto of 1607.

EPISTLE

To the
Most Noble And Most Equal Sisters,
The Two Famous Universities,
For Their
Love and Acceptance Shown to His Poem
In The Presentation;
Ben. Jonson,
The Grateful Acknowledger,
Dedicates Both It And Himself.

There follows an Epistle, if   10
you dare venture on the length.

Never, most equal Sisters, had any man a wit so presently excellent as that it could raise itself; but there must come both matter, occasion, commenders, and favourers to it. If this be true, and that the fortune of all writers doth daily prove it, it behooves the careful to provide well toward these accidents, and, having acquired them, to preserve that part of reputation most tenderly wherein the benefit of a friend is also defended. Hence is it that I now render myself grateful and am studious to justify the bounty of your act, to which, though your mere authority were satisfying, 20 yet, it being an age wherein poetry and the professors of it hear so ill on all sides, there will a reason be looked for in the subject. It is certain, nor can it with any forehead be opposed, that the too much licence of poetasters in this time hath much deformed their mistress, that, every day, their manifold and manifest ignorance doth stick unnatural reproaches upon her; but for their petulancy it were an act of the greatest injustice either to let the learned suffer, or so divine a skill (which indeed should not be attempted

6. *In The Presentation:* in performance.
21. *professors:* practitioners, i.e. poets.
23. *forehead:* good sense.
25. *their mistress:* their muse, the art of poetry itself.

41

with unclean hands) to fall under the least contempt. For, if men
will impartially, and not asquint, look toward the offices and
function of a poet, they will easily conclude to themselves the
impossibility of any man's being the good poet without first being a good man. He that is said to be able to inform young men
to all good disciplines, inflame grown men to all great virtues,
keep old men in their best and supreme state, or, as they decline
to childhood, recover them to their first strength; that comes forth
the interpreter and arbiter of nature, a teacher of things divine no
less than human, a master in manners; and can alone, or with a
few, effect the business of mankind: this, I take him, is no subject
for pride and ignorance to exercise their railing rhetoric upon. But
it will here be hastily answered that the writers of these days are
other things: that not only their manners, but their natures, are
inverted, and nothing remaining with them of the dignity of poet
but the abused name, which every scribe usurps; that now, especially in dramatic, or, as they term it, stage poetry, nothing but
ribaldry, profanation, blasphemy, all licence of offence to God and
man is practised. I dare not deny a great part of this, and am sorry
I dare not, because in some men's abortive features (and would
they had never boasted the light) it is over-true; but that all are
embarked in this bold adventure for hell is a most uncharitable
thought, and, uttered, a more malicious slander. For my particular,
I can, and from a most clear conscience, affirm that I have ever
trembled to think toward the least profaneness, have loathed the
use of such foul and unwashed bawdry as is now made the food
of the scene. And, howsoever I cannot escape, from some, the imputation of sharpness, but that they will say I have taken a pride,
or lust, to be bitter, and not my youngest infant but hath come
into the world with all his teeth; I would ask of these supercilious
politics, what nation, society, or general order, or state I have provoked? what public person? whether I have not in all these preserved their dignity, as mine own person, safe? My works are

33. *inform:* train, mould.
48. *abortive features:* premature, ill-considered dramatic works.
54. *the food of the scene:* the staple of our theatrical diet, or subject-
matter for plays.
57. *youngest infant:* i.e. *Sejanus.* Note.

read, allowed (I speak of those that are entirely mine); look into them. What broad reproofs have I used? where have I been particular? where personal? except to a mimic, cheater, bawd, or buffoon, creatures for their insolencies worthy to be taxed? Yet to which of these so pointingly as he might not either ingenuously have confessed or wisely dissembled his disease? But it is not rumour can make men guilty, much less entitle me to other men's crimes. I know that nothing can be so innocently writ or carried, but may be made obnoxious to construction; marry, whilst I bear *70* mine innocence about me, I fear it not. Application is now grown a trade with many, and there are that profess to have a key for the deciphering of everything; but let wise and noble persons take heed how they be too credulous, or give leave to these invading interpreters to be over-familiar with their fames, who cunningly, and often, utter their own virulent malice under other men's simplest meanings. As for those that will (by faults which charity hath raked up, or common honesty concealed) make themselves a name with the multitude, or (to draw their rude and beastly claps) care not whose living faces they entrench with their petulant *80* styles, may they do it without a rival, for me. I choose rather to lie graved in obscurity than share with them in so preposterous a fame. Nor can I blame the wishes of those severe and wiser patriots, who, providing the hurts these licentious spirits may do in a state, desire rather to see fools and devils, and those antique relics of barbarism retrieved, with all other ridiculous and exploded follies, than behold the wounds of private men, of princes, and nations. For, as Horace makes Trebatius speak, among these:

– *Sibi quisque timet, quamquam est intactus, et odit.*

And men may justly impute such rages, if continued, to the writer, *90* as his sports. The increase of which lust in liberty, together with

62. *allowed:* given critical acceptance.
62. *entirely mine:* all my own work, i.e. uncontaminated by collaboration.
70. *made obnoxious to construction:* exposed to misconstruction.
71. *Application:* the identification of characters in plays with actual persons.
82. *graved:* buried.

the present trade of the stage, in all their misc'line interludes, what
learned or liberal soul doth not already abhor? where nothing but
the filth of the time is uttered, and that with such impropriety of
phrase, such plenty of solecisms, such dearth of sense, so bold pro-
lepses, so racked metaphors, with brothelry able to violate the ear
of a pagan, and blasphemy to turn the blood of a Christian to
water. I cannot but be serious in a cause of this nature, wherein my
fame and the reputations of divers honest and learned are the
100 question; when a name so full of authority, antiquity, and all great
mark, is, through their insolence, become the lowest scorn of the
age; and those men subject to the petulancy of every vernaculous
orator that were wont to be the care of kings and happiest mon-
archs. This it is that hath not only rapt me to present indignation,
but made me studious heretofore, and by all my actions to stand
off from them; which may most appear in this my latest work –
which you, most learned Arbitresses, have seen, judged, and, to
my crown, approved – wherein I have laboured, for their instruction and amendment, to reduce not only the ancient forms,
110 but manners of the scene: the easiness, the propriety, the innocence, and last, the doctrine, which is the principal end of poesie,
to inform men in the best reason of living. And though my
catastrophe may in the strict rigour of comic law meet with
censure, as turning back to my promise, I desire the learned and
charitable critic to have so much faith in me to think it was done
of industry: for with what ease I could have varied it nearer his
scale (but that I fear to boast my own faculty) I could here insert.
But, my special aim being to put the snaffle in their mouths that
cry out: We never punish vice in our interludes, &c., I took the
120 more liberty, though not without some lines of example drawn
even in the ancients themselves, the goings-out of whose comedies

92. *misc'line:* mixed, chaotic.

100. *a name:* i.e. the name, or profession, of poet.

102. *vernaculous:* ill-bred.

107. *most learned Arbitresses:* i.e. the 'Equal Sisters', Oxford and Cambridge.

109. *reduce:* recover, bring back into use.

113. *catastrophe:* i.e. in *Volpone* itself; the climax of the action.

114. *my promise:* Note.   116. *of industry:* deliberately.

121. *goings-out:* endings, resolutions.

are not always joyful, but oft-times the bawds, the servants, the rivals, yea, and the masters are mulcted, and fitly, it being the office of a comic poet to imitate justice, and instruct to life, as well as purity of language, or stir up gentle affections. To which I shall take the occasion elsewhere to speak. For the present, most reverenced Sisters, as I have cared to be thankful for your affections past, and here made the understanding acquainted with some ground of your favours, let me not despair their continuance, to the maturing of some worthier fruits; wherein, if my muses be *130* true to me, I shall raise the despised head of poetry again, and, stripping her out of those rotten and base rags wherewith the times have adulterated her form, restore her to her primitive habit, feature, and majesty, and render her worthy to be embraced and kissed of all the great and master-spirits of our world. As for the vile and slothful, who never affected an act worthy of celebration or are so inwards with their own vicious natures, as they worthily fear her and think it a high point of policy to keep her in contempt with their declamatory and windy invectives; she shall out of just rage incite her servants (who are *genus irritabile*) to spout ink in *140* their faces that shall eat, farther than their marrow, into their fames, and not Cinnamus the barber with his art shall be able to take out the brands, but they shall live, and be read, till the wretches die, as things worst deserving of themselves in chief, and then of all mankind.

From my house in the Blackfriars,
this 11th day of February, 1607.

---

133. *primitive:* ancient, original.

THE PERSONS OF THE PLAY

VOLPONE, *a Magnifico*
MOSCA, *his Parasite*
VOLTORE, *an Advocate*
CORBACCIO, *an old Gentleman*
CORVINO, *a Merchant*
AVOCATORI, *four Magistrates*
NOTARIO, *the Register*
NANO, *a Dwarf*
CASTRONE, *an Eunuch*
[SIR] POLITIC WOULD-BE, *a Knight*
PEREGRINE, *a Gentleman-traveller*
BONARIO, *a young Gentleman, son of Corbaccio*
FINE MADAME WOULD-BE, *the Knight's wife*
CELIA, *the Merchant's wife*
COMMENDATORI, *Officers*
MERCATORI, *three Merchants*
ANDROGYNO, *a Hermaphrodite*
SERVITORE, *a servant*
GREGE, *crowd*
WOMEN

The Scene:
VENICE

VOLPONE,

OR

THE FOX

V olpone, childless, rich, feigns sick, despairs,
O ffers his state to hopes of several heirs,
L ies languishing; his Parasite receives
P resents of all, assures, deludes; then weaves
O ther cross-plots, which ope themselves, are told.
N ew tricks for safety are sought; they thrive; when, bold,
E ach tempts th' other again, and all are sold.

PROLOGUE

Now, luck yet send us, and a little wit
   Will serve to make our play hit;
According to the palates of the season,
   Here is rhyme not empty of reason.
This we were bid to credit from our poet,
   Whose true scope, if you would know it,
In all his poems still hath been this measure:
   To mix profit with your pleasure;
And not as some, whose throats their envy failing,
   Cry hoarsely, 'All he writes is railing,'
And when his plays come forth, think they can flout them,   *10*
   With saying, 'He was a year about them.'
To these there needs no lie but this his creature,
   Which was two months since no feature;
And though he dares give them five lives to mend it,
   'Tis known, five weeks fully penned it,
From his own hand, without a coadjutor,
   Novice, journeyman, or tutor.

17. coadjutor, novice, etc.: Note.

Yet thus much I can give you as a token
20   Of his play's worth: no eggs are broken,
Nor quaking custards with fierce teeth affrighted,
    Wherewith your rout are so delighted;
Nor hales he in a gull old ends reciting,
    To stop gaps in his loose writing,
With such a deal of monstrous and forced action,
    As might make Bedlam a faction;
Nor made he his play for jests stol'n from each table,
    But makes jests to fit his fable.
And so presents quick comedy refined,
30   As best critics have designed;
The laws of time, place, persons he observeth,
    From no needful rule he swerveth.
All gall and copperas from his ink he draineth,
    Only a little salt remaineth,
Wherewith he'll rub your cheeks, till, red with laughter,
    They shall look fresh a week after.

21. *quaking custards:* Note.
29. *quick:* lively.
33. *copperas:* an acid.

ACT ONE

[Volpone's house.]

[Volpone in a large bed. Enter MOSCA. VOLPONE *awakes.]*
[VOLPONE:] Good morning to the day; and next, my gold!
    Open the shrine, that I may see my saint.
    *[*MOSCA *draws a curtain, revealing piles of gold.]*
    Hail the world's soul, and mine! More glad than is
    The teeming earth to see the longed-for sun
    Peep through the horns of the celestial Ram,
    Am I, to view thy splendour darkening his;
    That lying here, amongst my other hoards,
    Show'st like a flame by night, or like the day
    Struck out of chaos, when all darkness fled
    Unto the centre. O, thou son of Sol   10
    (But brighter than thy father) let me kiss,
    With adoration, thee, and every relic
    Of sacred treasure in this blessèd room.
    Well did wise poets by thy glorious name
    Title that age which they would have the best,
    Thou being the best of things, and far transcending
    All style of joy in children, parents, friends,
    Or any other waking dream on earth.
    Thy looks when they to Venus did ascribe,
    They should have giv'n her twenty thousand Cupids,   20
    Such are thy beauties and our loves! Dear saint,
    Riches, the dumb god that giv'st all men tongues,
    That canst do nought, and yet mak'st men do all things;
    The price of souls; even hell, with thee to boot,
    Is made worth heaven! Thou art virtue, fame,
    Honour, and all things else. Who can get thee,
    He shall be noble, valiant, honest, wise –
MOSCA: And what he will, sir. Riches are in fortune

----
8. *the day . . . chaos:* the day of creation.
15. *that age:* the Age of Gold.

A greater good than wisdom is in nature.
30 VOLPONE: True, my belovèd Mosca. Yet, I glory
More in the cunning purchase of my wealth
Than in the glad possession, since I gain
No common way: I use no trade, no venture;
I wound no earth with ploughshares; fat no beasts
To feed the shambles; have no mills for iron,
Oil, corn, or men, to grind 'em into powder;
I blow no subtle glass; expose no ships
To threat'nings of the furrow-facèd sea;
I turn no moneys in the public bank,
40 Nor usure private –
MOSCA: No, sir, nor devour
Soft prodigals. You shall ha' some will swallow
A melting heir as glibly as your Dutch
Will pills of butter, and ne'er purge for 't;
Tear forth the fathers of poor families
Out of their beds, and coffin them, alive,
In some kind, clasping prison, where their bones
May be forthcoming, when the flesh is rotten.
But, your sweet nature doth abhor these courses;
You loathe the widow's or the orphan's tears
50 Should wash your pavements, or their piteous cries
Ring in your roofs, and beat the air for vengeance –
VOLPONE: Right, Mosca, I do loathe it.
MOSCA: And, besides, sir,
You are not like the thresher that doth stand
With a huge flail, watching a heap of corn,
And, hungry, dares not taste the smallest grain,
But feeds on mallows and such bitter herbs;
Nor like the merchant, who hath filled his vaults
With Romagnìa and rich Candian wines,
Yet drinks the lees of Lombard's vinegar.
60 You will not lie in straw, whilst moths and worms

35. *shambles:* slaughter-house.
56. *mallows:* coarse greens.
58. *Romagnìa:* a sweet wine from Greece; *Candian wines:* malmsey from Crete; *Lombard's vinegar:* cheap wine from North Italy.

Feed on your sumptuous hangings and soft beds.
You know the use of riches, and dare give, now,
From that bright heap, to me, your poor observer,
Or to your dwarf, or your hermaphrodite,
Your eunuch, or what other household trifle
Your pleasure allows maint'nance –

VOLPONE: Hold thee, Mosca,
   [*Gives him money.*]
Take, of my hand; thou strik'st on truth in all,
And they are envious term thee parasite.
Call forth my dwarf, my eunuch, and my fool,
And let 'em make me sport.
   [*Exit* MOSCA.]
                                        What should I do   70
But cocker up my genius and live free
To all delights my fortune calls me to?
I have no wife, no parent, child, ally,
To give my substance to; but whom I make
Must be my heir, and this makes men observe me.
This draws new clients, daily, to my house,
Women and men of every sex and age,
That bring me presents, send me plate, coin, jewels,
With hope that when I die (which they expect
Each greedy minute) it shall then return   80
Tenfold upon them; whilst some, covetous
Above the rest, seek to engross me, whole,
And counter-work the one unto the other,
Contend in gifts, as they would seem in love.
All which I suffer, playing with their hopes,
And am content to coin 'em into profit,
And look upon their kindness, and take more,
And look on that; still bearing them in hand,
Letting the cherry knock against their lips,
And draw it by their mouths, and back again. How now!   90

   71. *cocker up my genius:* give free play to my innate talents.

I, ii   [*Enter* MOSCA *with* NANO, ANDROGYNO, *and* CASTRONE.]

[NANO (*reciting*):] Now, room for fresh gamesters, who do will
    you to know,
They do bring you neither play nor university show;
And therefore do entreat you that whatsoever they rehearse,
May not fare a whit the worse, for the false pace of the verse.
If you wonder at this, you will wonder more ere we pass,
For know, here is enclosed the soul of Pythagoras,
    [*Pointing to* ANDROGYNO.]
That juggler divine, as hereafter shall follow;
Which soul, fast and loose, sir, came first from Apollo,
And was breathed into Æthalides, Mercurius's son,
10 Where it had the gift to remember all that ever was done.
From thence it fled forth, and made quick transmigration
To goldy-locked Euphorbus, who was killed in good fashion,
At the siege of old Troy, by the cuckold of Sparta.
Hermotimus was next (I find it in my charta)
To whom it did pass, where no sooner it was missing,
But with one Pyrrhus of Delos it learned to go a-fishing;
And thence did it enter the sophist of Greece.
From Pythagore she went into a beautiful piece,
Hight Aspasia, the meretrix; and the next toss of her
20 Was again of a whore, she became a philosopher,
Crates the Cynic, as itself doth relate it.
Since, kings, knights, and beggars, knaves, lords, and fools gat it,
Besides ox and ass, camel, mule, goat, and brock,
In all which it hath spoke, as in the Cobbler's cock.
But I come not here to discourse of that matter,
Or his one, two, or three, or his great oath, 'By Quater!'
His musics, his trigon, his golden thigh,
Or his telling how elements shift; but I

6. *Pythagoras:* Note.
9. *Æthalides:* the herald of the Argonauts.
12. *Euphorbus:* a Trojan.
13. *cuckold of Sparta:* Menelaus, whose wife Helen was abducted by
Paris.
17. *sophist of Greece:* philosopher – i.e. Pythagoras himself.
26. *'By Quater!':* Note.
27. *musics:* music of the spheres; *trigon:* triangle.

Would ask, how of late thou hast suffered translation,
And shifted thy coat in these days of reformation? 30
ANDROGYNO [*reciting*]: Like one of the reformèd, a fool, as you see,
Counting all old doctrine heresy.
NANO: But not on thine own forbid meats hast thou ventured?
ANDROGYNO: On fish, when first a Carthusian I entered.
NANO: Why, then thy dogmatical silence hath left thee?
ANDROGYNO: Of that an obstreperous lawyer bereft me.
NANO: O wonderful change! When Sir Lawyer forsook thee,
For Pythagore's sake, what body then took thee?
ANDROGYNO: A good, dull moyle.
NANO: And how! by that means
Thou wert brought to allow of the eating of beans? 40
ANDROGYNO: Yes.
NANO: But from the moyle into whom didst thou
    pass?
ANDROGYNO: Into a very strange beast, by some writers called an
    ass;
By others, a precise, pure, illuminate brother,
Of those devour flesh, and sometimes one another,
And will drop you forth a libel, or a sanctified lie,
Betwixt every spoonful of a nativity-pie.
NANO: Now quit thee, for heaven, of that profane nation,
And gently report thy next transmigration.
ANDROGYNO: To the same that I am.
NANO: A creature of delight,
And what is more than a fool, an hermaphrodite? 50
Now, prithee, sweet soul, in all thy variation,
Which body wouldst thou choose to take up thy station?
ANDROGYNO: Troth, this I am in, even here would I tarry.
NANO: 'Cause here the delight of each sex thou canst vary?
ANDROGYNO: Alas, those pleasures be stale and forsaken;
No, 'tis your Fool wherewith I am so taken,
The only one creature that I can call blessèd,
For all other forms I have proved most distressèd.

31. *reformèd*: Protestants.   39. *moyle*: mule.
43. *illuminate*: having experienced religious illumination or vision.
46. *nativity-pie*: Christmas-pie; Note.

NANO: Spoke true, as thou wert in Pythagoras still.
60 This learnèd opinion we celebrate will,
    Fellow eunuch, as behoves us, with all our wit and art,
    To dignify that whereof ourselves are so great and special a part.
VOLPONE: Now, very, very pretty! Mosca, this
    Was thy invention?
MOSCA: If it please my patron,
    Not else.
VOLPONE: It doth, good Mosca.
MOSCA: Then it was, sir.

SONG

        Fools, they are the only nation
        Worth men's envy or admiration;
        Free from care or sorrow-taking,
        Selves and others merry making,
70   All they speak or do is sterling.
        Your Fool, he is your great man's dearling,
        And your ladies' sport and pleasure;
        Tongue and babble are his treasure.
        E'en his face begetteth laughter,
        And he speaks truth free from slaughter;
        He's the grace of every feast,
        And, sometimes, the chiefest guest;
        Hath his trencher and his stool,
        When wit waits upon the Fool.
80   O, who would not be
            He, he, he?

One knocks without.

VOLPONE: Who's that? Away! Look, Mosca.
MOSCA: Fool, begone!
    [*Exeunt* NANO, CASTRONE, *and* ANDROGYNO.]
    'Tis Signior Voltore, the advocate;
    I know him by his knock.
VOLPONE: Fetch me my gown,
    My furs, and night-caps; say my couch is changing,
            85. *changing:* being made.

56

And let him entertain himself awhile
Without i' th' gallery.
   [*Exit* MOSCA.]
                             Now, now, my clients
Begin their visitation! Vulture, kite,
Raven, and gorcrow, all my birds of prey,
That think me turning carcass, now they come.   *90*
I am not for 'em yet.
   [*Enter* MOSCA *with the gown, furs, etc.*]
                       How now? the news?
MOSCA: A piece of plate, sir.
VOLPONE: Of what bigness?
MOSCA: Huge,
Massy, and antique, with your name inscribed,
And arms engraven.
VOLPONE: Good! and not a Fox
Stretched on the earth, with fine delusive sleights
Mocking a gaping Crow – ha, Mosca?
MOSCA: Sharp, sir.
VOLPONE: Give me my furs. Why dost thou laugh so, man?
MOSCA: I cannot choose, sir, when I apprehend
What thoughts he has, without, now, as he walks:
That this might be the last gift he should give;   *100*
That this would fetch you; if you died today,
And gave him all, what he should be tomorrow;
What large return would come of all his ventures;
How he should worshipped be, and reverenced;
Ride with his furs, and foot-cloths; waited on
By herds of fools and clients; have clear way
Made for his moyle, as lettered as himself;
Be called the great and learnèd advocate:
And then concludes, there's nought impossible.
VOLPONE: Yes, to be learnèd, Mosca.
MOSCA: O, no; rich   *110*
Implies it. Hood an ass with reverend purple,
So you can hide his two ambitious ears,
And he shall pass for a cathedral doctor.

        89. *gorcrow:* carrion crow.

VOLPONE: My caps, my caps, good Mosca. Fetch him in.

MOSCA: Stay, sir; your ointment for your eyes.

VOLPONE: That's true;
Dispatch, dispatch. I long to have possession
Of my new present.

MOSCA: That, and thousands more,
I hope to see you lord of.

VOLPONE: Thanks, kind Mosca.

MOSCA: And that, when I am lost in blended dust,
120   And hundreds such as I am, in succession –

VOLPONE: Nay, that were too much, Mosca.

MOSCA: You shall live
Still to delude these harpies.

VOLPONE: Loving Mosca!
'Tis well. My pillow now, and let him enter.
    [*Exit* MOSCA.]
Now, my feigned cough, my phthisic, and my gout,
My apoplexy, palsy, and catarrhs,
Help, with your forcèd functions, this my posture,
Wherein, this three year, I have milked their hopes.
He comes, I hear him – uh! uh! uh! uh! O!
    [VOLPONE *gets into bed.*]

I, iii   [*Enter* MOSCA *with* VOLTORE.]

[MOSCA:] You still are what you were, sir. Only you,
    Of all the rest, are he commands his love,
    And you do wisely to preserve it thus,
    With early visitation, and kind notes
    Of your good meaning to him, which, I know,
    Cannot but come most grateful. Patron, sir.
    Here's Signior Voltore is come –

VOLPONE: What say you?

MOSCA: Sir, Signior Voltore is come this morning
    To visit you.

VOLPONE: I thank him.

MOSCA: And hath brought

124. *phthisic:* consumption.   126. *posture:* imposture, act.

A piece of antique plate, bought of St Mark,   *10*
With which he here presents you.
VOLPONE: He is welcome.
Pray him to come more often.
MOSCA: Yes.
VOLTORE: What says he?
MOSCA: He thanks you and desires you see him often.
VOLPONE: Mosca.
MOSCA: My patron?
VOLPONE: Bring him near, where is he?
I long to feel his hand.
MOSCA: The plate is here, sir.
VOLTORE: How fare you, sir?
VOLPONE: I thank you, Signior Voltore.
Where is the plate? mine eyes are bad.
VOLTORE: I'm sorry
To see you still thus weak.
MOSCA [*aside*]:   That he is not weaker.
VOLPONE. You are too munificent.
VOLTORE: No, sir, would to heaven
I could as well give health to you as that plate!   *20*
VOLPONE: You give, sir, what you can. I thank you. Your love
Hath taste in this, and shall not be unanswered.
I pray you see me often.
VOLTORE: Yes, I shall, sir.
VOLPONE: Be not far from me.
MOSCA: Do you observe that, sir?
VOLPONE: Hearken unto me still; it will concern you.
MOSCA: You are a happy man, sir; know your good.
VOLPONE: I cannot now last long –
MOSCA: You are his heir, sir.
VOLTORE: Am I?
VOLPONE: I feel me going – uh! uh! uh! uh!
I am sailing to my port – uh! uh! uh! uh!
And I am glad I am so near my haven.   *30*
MOSCA: Alas, kind gentleman. Well, we must all go –
VOLTORE: But, Mosca –
MOSCA: Age will conquer.

VOLTORE: Pray thee, hear me.
Am I inscribed his heir for certain?
MOSCA: Are you?
I do beseech you, sir, you will vouchsafe
To write me i' your family. All my hopes
Depend upon your worship. I am lost
Except the rising sun do shine on me.
VOLTORE: It shall both shine and warm thee, Mosca.
MOSCA: Sir,
I am a man that have not done your love
All the worst offices. Here I wear your keys,
See all your coffers and your caskets locked,
Keep the poor inventory of your jewels,
Your plate, and moneys; am your steward, sir,
Husband your goods here.
VOLTORE: But am I sole heir?
MOSCA: Without a partner, sir, confirmed this morning;
The wax is warm yet, and the ink scarce dry
Upon the parchment.
VOLTORE: Happy, happy me!
By what good chance, sweet Mosca?
MOSCA: Your desert, sir;
I know no second cause.
VOLTORE: Thy modesty
Is loath to know it; well, we shall requite it.
MOSCA: He ever liked your course, sir; that first took him.
I oft have heard him say how he admired
Men of your large profession, that could speak
To every cause, and things mere contraries,
Till they were hoarse again, yet all be law;
That, with most quick agility, could turn,
And re-turn; make knots, and undo them;
Give forkèd counsel; take provoking gold
On either hand, and put it up. These men,
He knew, would thrive with their humility.
And, for his part, he thought he should be blessed
To have his heir of such a suffering spirit,

58. *forkèd:* ambiguous.

So wise, so grave, of so perplexed a tongue,
And loud withal, that would not wag, nor scarce
Lie still, without a fee; when every word
Your worship but lets fall, is a chequin!
   Another knocks.
Who's that? One knocks. I would not have you seen, sir.
And yet – pretend you came and went in haste;
I'll fashion an excuse. And, gentle sir,
When you do come to swim in golden lard,   *70*
Up to the arms in honey, that your chin
Is borne up stiff with fatness of the flood,
Think on your vassal; but remember me:
I ha' not been your worst of clients.
VOLTORE: Mosca –
MOSCA: When will you have your inventory brought, sir?
Or see a copy of the will? – Anon. –
I'll bring 'em to you, sir. Away, be gone,
Put business i' your face.
   [*Exit* VOLTORE.]
VOLPONE: Excellent, Mosca!
Come hither, let me kiss thee.
MOSCA: Keep you still, sir.
Here is Corbaccio.
VOLPONE: Set the plate away.   *80*
The vulture's gone, and the old raven's come.

[MOSCA:] Betake you to your silence, and your sleep. –   I, iv
Stand there and multiply. – Now shall we see
A wretch who is indeed more impotent
Than this can feign to be, yet hopes to hop
Over his grave.
   [*Enter* CORBACCIO.]
              Signior Corbaccio!
You're very welcome, sir.
CORBACCIO: How does your patron?
MOSCA: Troth, as he did, sir; no amends.

63. *perplexed:* confusing.   66. *chequin:* a Venetian gold coin.

CORBACCIO [*deaf*]:   What? mends he?

MOSCA [*shouting*]: No, sir. He is rather worse.

CORBACCIO: That's well. Where is he?

MOSCA: Upon his couch, sir, newly fall'n asleep.

10 CORBACCIO: Does he sleep well?

MOSCA: No wink, sir, all this night,
Nor yesterday, but slumbers.

CORBACCIO: Good! He should take
Some counsel of physicians. I have brought him
An opiate here, from mine own doctor –

MOSCA: He will not hear of drugs.

CORBACCIO: Why? I myself
Stood by while 't was made, saw all th' ingredients,
And know it cannot but most gently work.
My life for his, 'tis but to make him sleep.

VOLPONE [*aside*]: Ay, his last sleep, if he would take it.

MOSCA: Sir,
He has no faith in physic.

CORBACCIO: Say you, say you?

20 MOSCA: He has no faith in physic: he does think
Most of your doctors are the greater danger,
And worse disease t' escape. I often have
Heard him protest that your physician
Should never be his heir.

CORBACCIO: Not I his heir?

MOSCA: Not your physician, sir.

CORBACCIO: O, no, no, no,
I do not mean it.

MOSCA: No, sir, nor their fees
He cannot brook; he says they flay a man
Before they kill him.

CORBACCIO: Right, I do conceive you.

MOSCA: And then, they do it by experiment,
30 For which the law not only doth absolve 'em,
But gives them great reward; and he is loath
To hire his death so.

CORBACCIO: It is true, they kill
With as much licence as a judge.

MOSCA: Nay, more;
  For he but kills, sir, where the law condemns,
  And these can kill him too.
CORBACCIO: Ay, or me,
  Or any man. How does his apoplex?
  Is that strong on him still?
MOSCA: Most violent.
  His speech is broken, and his eyes are set,
  His face drawn longer than 't was wont –
CORBACCIO: How? how?
  Stronger than he was wont?
MOSCA: No, sir; his face   40
  Drawn longer than 't was wont.
CORBACCIO: O, good.
MOSCA: His mouth
  Is ever gaping, and his eyelids hang.
CORBACCIO: Good.
MOSCA: A freezing numbness stiffens all his joints,
  And makes the colour of his flesh like lead.
CORBACCIO: 'Tis good.
MOSCA: His pulse beats slow and dull.
CORBACCIO: Good symptoms still.
MOSCA: And from his brain –
CORBACCIO: Ha! how? not from his brain?
MOSCA: Yes, sir, and from his brain –
CORBACCIO: I conceive you; good.
MOSCA: Flows a cold sweat, with a continual rheum,
  Forth the resolvèd corners of his eyes.
CORBACCIO: Is't possible? Yet I am better, ha!   50
  How does he with the swimming of his head?
MOSCA: O, sir, 'tis past the scotomy; he now
  Hath lost his feeling, and hath left to snort;
  You hardly can perceive him that he breathes.
CORBACCIO: Excellent, excellent! sure I shall outlast him!
  This makes me young again, a score of years.
MOSCA: I was a–coming for you, sir.

46. *brain:* Note.   52. *scotomy:* dizziness and loss of sight.
53. *left to snort:* ceased snoring or breathing.

CORBACCIO: Has he made his will?
What has he given me?

MOSCA: No, sir.

CORBACCIO: Nothing? ha!

MOSCA: He has not made his will, sir.

CORBACCIO: Oh, oh, oh.

60   What then did Voltore, the lawyer, here?

MOSCA: He smelled a carcass, sir, when he but heard
My master was about his testament;
As I did urge him to it for your good –

CORBACCIO: He came unto him, did he? I thought so.

MOSCA: Yes, and presented him this piece of plate.

CORBACCIO: To be his heir?

MOSCA: I do not know, sir.

CORBACCIO: True,
I know it too.

MOSCA [*aside*]: By your own scale, sir.

CORBACCIO: Well,
I shall prevent him yet. See, Mosca, look,
Here I have brought a bag of bright chequins,

70   Will quite weigh down his plate.

MOSCA [*taking the bag*]:   Yea, marry, sir,
This is true physic, this your sacred medicine;
No talk of opiates to this great elixir.

CORBACCIO: 'Tis *aurum palpabile*, if not *potabile*.

MOSCA: It shall be ministered to him, in his bowl?

CORBACCIO: Ay, do, do, do.

MOSCA: Most blessèd cordial!
This will recover him.

CORBACCIO: Yes, do, do, do.

MOSCA: I think it were not best, sir.

CORBACCIO: What?

MOSCA: To recover him.

CORBACCIO: O, no, no, no; by no means.

72. *elixir:* a liquor thought to be capable of prolonging life for ever, or in alchemical lore the substance for turning other metals into gold.

73. *aurum palpabile:* Note.

75. *cordial:* a medicine which restores the heart.

MOSCA: Why, sir, this
Will work some strange effect if he but feel it.

CORBACCIO: 'Tis true, therefore forbear; I'll take my venture; 80
Give me 't again.

MOSCA: At no hand. Pardon me.
You shall not do yourself that wrong, sir. I
Will so advise you, you shall have it all.

CORBACCIO: How?

MOSCA: All, sir; 'tis your right, your own; no man
Can claim a part; 'tis yours without a rival,
Decreed by destiny.

CORBACCIO: How, how, good Mosca?

MOSCA: I'll tell you, sir. This fit he shall recover –

CORBACCIO: I do conceive you.

MOSCA: And on first advantage
Of his gained sense, will I re-importune him
Unto the making of his testament, 90
And show him this.

CORBACCIO: Good, good.

MOSCA: 'Tis better yet,
If you will hear, sir.

CORBACCIO: Yes, with all my heart.

MOSCA: Now would I counsel you, make home with speed;
There, frame a will, whereto you shall inscribe
My master your sole heir.

CORBACCIO: And disinherit
My son?

MOSCA: O, sir, the better; for that colour
Shall make it much more taking.

CORBACCIO: O, but colour?

MOSCA: This will, sir, you shall send it unto me.
Now, when I come to enforce, as I will do,
Your cares, your watchings, and your many prayers,
Your more than many gifts, your this day's present, 100
And, last, produce your will; where, without thought
Or least regard unto your proper issue,

96. *colour*: pretence.   97. *taking*: tempting.
103. *proper issue*: legitimate offspring (i.e. Bonario).

A son so brave and highly meriting,
The stream of your diverted love hath thrown you
Upon my master, and made him your heir:
He cannot be so stupid, or stone dead,
But out of conscience and mere gratitude –
CORBACCIO: He must pronounce me his?
MOSCA: 'Tis true.
CORBACCIO: This plot
110   Did I think on before.
MOSCA: I do believe it.
CORBACCIO: Do you not believe it?
MOSCA: Yes, sir.
CORBACCIO: Mine own project.
MOSCA: Which, when he hath done, sir –
CORBACCIO: Published me his heir?
MOSCA: And you so certain to survive him –
CORBACCIO: Ay.
MOSCA: Being so lusty a man –
CORBACCIO: 'Tis true.
MOSCA: Yes, sir –
CORBACCIO: I thought on that too. See, how he should be
The very organ to express my thoughts!
MOSCA: You have not only done yourself a good –
CORBACCIO: But multiplied it on my son?
MOSCA: 'Tis right, sir.
CORBACCIO: Still my invention.
MOSCA: 'Las, sir! Heaven knows
120   It hath been all my study, all my care,
(I e'en grow grey withal) how to work things –
CORBACCIO: I do conceive, sweet Mosca.
MOSCA: You are he
For whom I labour here.
CORBACCIO: Ay, do, do, do.
I'll straight about it.
MOSCA [aside]:   Rook go with you, raven!
CORBACCIO: I know thee honest.
MOSCA [aside]:   You do lie, sir.

124. *Rook go with you*: May you be rooked – fooled.

66

CORBACCIO: And –

MOSCA [*aside*]: Your knowledge is no better than your ears, sir.

CORBACCIO: I do not doubt to be a father to thee.

MOSCA [*aside*]: Nor I to gull my brother of his blessing.

CORBACCIO: I may ha' my youth restored to me, why not?

MOSCA [*aside*]: Your worship is a precious ass – 130

CORBACCIO: What sayst thou?

MOSCA: I do desire your worship to make haste, sir.

CORBACCIO: 'Tis done, 'tis done, I go.

   [*Exit.*]

VOLPONE: O, I shall burst!
  Let out my sides, let out my sides.

MOSCA: Contain
  Your flux of laughter, sir. You know this hope
  Is such a bait it covers any hook.

VOLPONE: O, but thy working, and thy placing it!
  I cannot hold; good rascal, let me kiss thee.
  I never knew thee in so rare a humour.

MOSCA: Alas, sir, I but do as I am taught; 140
  Follow your grave instructions; give 'em words;
  Pour oil into their ears, and send them hence.

VOLPONE: 'Tis true, 'tis true. What a rare punishment
  Is avarice to itself!

MOSCA: Ay, with our help, sir.

VOLPONE: So many cares, so many maladies,
  So many fears attending on old age.
  Yea, death so often called on as no wish
  Can be more frequent with 'em. Their limbs faint,
  Their senses dull, their seeing, hearing, going,
  All dead before them; yea, their very teeth, 150
  Their instruments of eating, failing them;
  Yet this is reckoned life! Nay, here was one,
  Is now gone home, that wishes to live longer!
  Feels not his gout, nor palsy; feigns himself
  Younger by scores of years, flatters his age
  With confident belying it; hopes he may
  With charms, like Æson have his youth restored;

156. *Æson*: Jason's father, who was magically restored to youth by Medea.

And with these thoughts so battens, as if fate
Would be as easily cheated on as he,
And all turns air!

Another knocks

                  Who's that there, now? a third?

160 MOSCA: Close to your couch again; I hear his voice.
It is Corvino, our spruce merchant.

VOLPONE [*lying in bed*]:   Dead.

MOSCA: Another bout, sir, with your eyes. –Who's there?

I, V   [*Enter* CORVINO.]

[MOSCA]: Signior Corvino! come most wished for! O,
How happy were you, if you knew it, now!

CORVINO: Why? what? wherein?

MOSCA: The tardy hour is come, sir.

CORVINO: He is not dead?

MOSCA: Not dead, sir, but as good;
He knows no man.

CORVINO: How shall I do then?

MOSCA: Why, sir?

CORVINO: I have brought him here a pearl.

MOSCA: Perhaps he has
So much remembrance left as to know you, sir.
He still calls on you, nothing but your name
Is in his mouth. Is your pearl orient, sir?

10 CORVINO: Venice was never owner of the like.

VOLPONE: Signior Corvino!

MOSCA: Hark!

VOLPONE: Signior Corvino!

MOSCA: He calls you; step and give it him. He is here, sir.
And he has brought you a rich pearl.

CORVINO: How do you, sir?
Tell him it doubles the twelfth caract.

MOSCA: Sir,
He cannot understand, his hearing's gone,
And yet it comforts him to see you –

CORVINO: Say

9. *orient*: from the East, and therefore especially valuable and lustrous.

I have a diamond for him, too.

MOSCA: Best show 't, sir,
Put it into his hand; 'tis only there
He apprehends, he has his feeling yet.
See how he grasps it!

CORVINO: 'Las, good gentleman!   *20*
How pitiful the sight is!

MOSCA: Tut, forget, sir.
The weeping of an heir should still be laughter
Under a visor.

CORVINO: Why, am I his heir?

MOSCA: Sir, I am sworn, I may not show the will
Till he be dead. But here has been Corbaccio,
Here has been Voltore, here were others too –
I cannot number 'em, they were so many –
All gaping here for legacies; but I,
Taking the vantage of his naming you,
'Signior Corvino, Signior Corvino,' took   *30*
Paper, and pen, and ink, and there I asked him
Whom he would have his heir? 'Corvino.' Who
Should be executor? 'Corvino.' And
To any question he was silent to,
I still interpreted the nods he made,
Through weakness, for consent; and sent home th' others,
Nothing bequeathed them but to cry and curse.
     They embrace.

CORVINO: O, my dear Mosca. Does he not perceive us?

MOSCA: No more than a blind harper. He knows no man,
No face of friend, nor name of any servant,   *40*
Who 't was that fed him last, or gave him drink;
Not those he hath begotten, or brought up,
Can he remember.

CORVINO: Has he children?

MOSCA: Bastards,
Some dozen, or more, that he begot on beggars,
Gypsies, and Jews, and black-moors when he was drunk.
Knew you not that, sir? 'Tis the common fable,

         23. *visor:* mask.

The dwarf, the fool, the eunuch are all his;
He's the true father of his family,
In all save me – but he has given 'em nothing.
50 CORVINO: That's well, that's well. Art sure he does not hear us?
MOSCA: Sure, sir? why, look you, credit your own sense. –
      [*He shouts at* VOLPONE.]
The pox approach and add to your diseases,
If it would send you hence the sooner, sir!
For your incontinence, it hath deserved it
Throughly and throughly, and the plague to boot!
(You may come near, sir.) Would you would once close
Those filthy eyes of yours that flow with slime
Like two frog-pits, and those same hanging cheeks,
Covered with hide instead of skin (Nay, help, sir)
60 That look like frozen dish-clouts set on end.
CORVINO: Or, like an old smoked wall, on which the rain
Ran down in streaks.
MOSCA: Excellent, sir, speak out.
You may be louder yet; a culverin
Discharged in his ear would hardly bore it.
CORVINO: His nose is like a common sewer, still running.
MOSCA: 'Tis good! And what his mouth?
CORVINO: A very draught.
MOSCA: O, stop it up –
CORVINO: By no means.
MOSCA: Pray you, let me.
Faith I could stifle him rarely with a pillow,
As well as any woman that should keep him.
70 CORVINO: Do as you will, but I'll be gone.
MOSCA: Be so.
It is your presence makes him last so long.
CORVINO: I pray you, use no violence.
MOSCA: No, sir? Why?
Why should you be thus scrupulous, pray you, sir?
CORVINO: Nay, at your discretion.
MOSCA: Well, good sir, be gone.
CORVINO: I will not trouble him now to take my pearl?
                63. *culverin:* hand-gun or cannon.

MOSCA: Puh! nor your diamond. What a needless care
Is this afflicts you! Is not all here yours?
Am not I here, whom you have made your creature?
That owe my being to you?

CORVINO: Grateful Mosca!
Thou art my friend, my fellow, my companion,   80
My partner, and shalt share in all my fortunes.

MOSCA: Excepting one.

CORVINO: What's that?

MOSCA: Your gallant wife, sir.
    [Exit CORVINO.]
Now is he gone; we had no other means
To shoot him hence but this.

VOLPONE: My divine Mosca!
Thou hast today outgone thyself.
    Another knocks.

                          Who's there?
I will be troubled with no more. Prepare
Me music, dances, banquets, all delights;
The Turk is not more sensual in his pleasures
Than will Volpone.
    [Exit MOSCA.]
                    Let me see: a pearl!
A diamond! plate! chequins! Good morning's purchase.   90
Why, this is better than rob churches, yet,
Or fat, by eating once a month a man.
    [Enter MOSCA.]
Who is 't?

MOSCA: The beauteous Lady Would-be, sir,
Wife to the English knight, Sir Politic Would-be,
(This is the style, sir, is directed me)
Hath sent to know how you have slept tonight,
And if you would be visited?

VOLPONE: Not now.
Some three hours hence, –

MOSCA: I told the squire so much.

VOLPONE: When I am high with mirth and wine, then, then.
            92. fat: grow fat.

71

100 'Fore heaven, I wonder at the desperate valour
Of the bold English, that they dare let loose
Their wives to all encounters!

MOSCA: Sir, this knight
Had not his name for nothing; he is politic,
And knows, howe'er his wife affect strange airs,
She hath not yet the face to be dishonest.
But had she Signior Corvino's wife's face –

VOLPONE: Has she so rare a face?

MOSCA: O, sir, the wonder,
The blazing star of Italy! a wench
O' the first year! a beauty ripe as harvest!

110 Whose skin is whiter than a swan, all over!
Than silver, snow, or lilies! a soft lip,
Would tempt you to eternity of kissing!
And flesh that melteth in the touch to blood!
Bright as your gold! and lovely as your gold!

VOLPONE: Why had not I known this before?

MOSCA: Alas, sir,
Myself but yesterday discovered it.

VOLPONE: How might I see her?

MOSCA: O, not possible;
She's kept as warily as is your gold,
Never does come abroad, never takes air

120 But at a window. All her looks are sweet
As the first grapes or cherries, and are watched
As near as they are.

VOLPONE: I must see her –

MOSCA: Sir,
There is a guard, of ten spies thick, upon her;
All his whole household; each of which is set
Upon his fellow, and have all their charge,
When he goes out, when he comes in, examined.

VOLPONE: I will go see her, though but at her window.

MOSCA: In some disguise then.

VOLPONE: That is true. I must
Maintain mine own shape still the same: we'll think.
   [*Exeunt.*]

ACT TWO

[The Public Square outside Corvino's house.]

[Enter SIR POLITIC WOULD-BE *and* PEREGRINE.*]*
[SIR POLITIC:] Sir, to a wise man, all the world's his soil.
  It is not Italy, nor France, nor Europe,
  That must bound me, if my fates call me forth.
  Yet, I protest, it is no salt desire
  Of seeing countries, shifting a religion,
  Nor any disaffection to the state
  Where I was bred, and unto which I owe
  My dearest plots, hath brought me out; much less
  That idle, antique, stale, grey-headed project
  Of knowing men's minds, and manners, with Ulysses;   10
  But a peculiar humour of my wife's,
  Laid for this height of Venice, to observe,
  To quote, to learn the language, and so forth –
  I hope you travel, sir, with licence?
PEREGRINE: Yes.
SIR POLITIC: I dare the safelier converse – How long, sir,
  Since you left England?
PEREGRINE: Seven weeks.
SIR POLITIC: So lately!
  You ha' not been with my Lord Ambassador?
PEREGRINE: Not yet, sir.
SIR POLITIC: Pray you, what news, sir, vents our
    climate?
  I heard last night a most strange thing reported
  By some of my lord's followers, and I long   20
  To hear how 'twill be seconded.
PEREGRINE: What was't, sir?

4. *salt:* wanton.   12. *Laid for this height:* aimed for the latitude.
14. *with licence:* with the permission of the Privy Council; legally.
18. *vents our climate:* comes from our country.

SIR POLITIC: Marry, sir, of a raven, that should build
In a ship royal of the King's.

PEREGRINE [*aside*]:   – This fellow,
Does he gull me, trow? or is gulled? – Your name, sir?

SIR POLITIC: My name is Politic Would-be.

PEREGRINE [*aside*]:   – O, that speaks him –
A knight, sir?

SIR POLITIC: A poor knight, sir.

PEREGRINE: Your lady
Lies here, in Venice, for intelligence
Of tires, and fashions, and behaviour
Among the courtesans? The fine Lady Would-be?

30 SIR POLITIC: Yes, sir, the spider and the bee oft-times
Suck from one flower.

PEREGRINE: Good Sir Politic!
I cry you mercy; I have heard much of you.
'Tis true, sir, of your raven.

SIR POLITIC: On your knowledge?

PEREGRINE: Yes, and your lion's whelping in the Tower.

SIR POLITIC: Another whelp!

PEREGRINE: Another, sir.

SIR POLITIC: Now heaven!
What prodigies be these? The fires at Berwick!
And the new star! These things concurring, strange!
And full of omen! Saw you those meteors?

PEREGRINE: I did, sir.

SIR POLITIC: Fearful! Pray you, sir, confirm me,
40 Were there three porpoises seen above the bridge,
As they give out?

PEREGRINE: Six, and a sturgeon, sir.

SIR POLITIC: I am astonished!

PEREGRINE: Nay, sir, be not so;
I'll tell you a greater prodigy than these –

SIR POLITIC: What should these things portend?

PEREGRINE: The very day
(Let me be sure) that I put forth from London,

25. *speaks:* describes.   28. *tires:* attires, clothes.
34. *lion's whelping*, etc.: Note.

74

There was a whale discovered in the river,
As high as Woolwich, that had waited there,
Few know how many months, for the subversion
Of the Stode fleet.
SIR POLITIC: Is't possible? Believe it,
'Twas either sent from Spain, or the Archdukes!   *50*
Spinola's whale, upon my life, my credit!
Will they not leave these projects? Worthy sir,
Some other news.
PEREGRINE: Faith, Stone the fool is dead,
And they do lack a tavern fool extremely.
SIR POLITIC: Is Mas' Stone dead?
PEREGRINE: He's dead, sir; why, I hope
You thought him not immortal? [*Aside.*] – O, this knight,
Were he well known, would be a precious thing
To fit our English stage. He that should write
But such a fellow, should be thought to feign
Extremely, if not maliciously –
SIR POLITIC: Stone dead!.   *60*
PEREGRINE: Dead. Lord, how deeply, sir, you apprehend it!
He was no kinsman to you?
SIR POLITIC: That I know of.
Well, that same fellow was an unknown fool.
PEREGRINE: And yet you know him, it seems?
SIR POLITIC: I did so. Sir,
I knew him one of the most dangerous heads
Living within the state, and so I held him.
PEREGRINE: Indeed, sir?
SIR POLITIC: While he lived, in action.
He has received weekly intelligence,
Upon my knowledge, out of the Low Countries,
For all parts of the world, in cabbages;   *70*
And those dispensed, again, t' ambassadors,
In oranges, musk-melons, apricots,
Lemons, pome-citrons, and suchlike; sometimes
In Colchester oysters, and your Selsey cockles.
PEREGRINE: You make me wonder.
SIR POLITIC: Sir, upon my knowledge.

Nay, I have observed him at your public ordinary
Take his advertisement from a traveller,
A concealed statesman, in a trencher of meat;
And, instantly, before the meal was done,
80   Convey an answer in a toothpick.

PEREGRINE: Strange!
How could this be, sir?

SIR POLITIC: Why, the meat was cut
So like his character, and so laid as he
Must easily read the cipher.

PEREGRINE: I have heard
He could not read, sir.

SIR POLITIC: So 'twas given out,
In policy, by those that did employ him:
But he could read, and had your languages,
And to 't, as sound a noddle –

PEREGRINE: I have heard, sir,
That your baboons were spies, and that they were
A kind of subtle nation near to China.

90 SIR POLITIC: Ay, ay, your Mamuluchi. Faith, they had
Their hand in a French plot, or two; but they
Were so extremely given to women as
They made discovery of all; yet I
Had my advices here, on Wednesday last,
From one of their own coat, they were returned,
Made their relations, as the fashion is,
And now stand fair for fresh employment.

PEREGRINE [aside]:   – Heart!
This Sir Pol will be ignorant of nothing –
It seems, sir, you know all.

76. *ordinary:* eating-house.
77. *advertisement:* information.
78. *concealed statesman:* government agent in disguise.
82. *his character:* his code.
85. *in policy:* for diplomatic reasons.
86. *had your languages:* was a linguist.
87. *And to 't, as sound a noddle:* And, in addition, as good a head.
94. *advices:* bulletins.   95. *coat:* party.
96. *relations:* reports.

SIR POLITIC: Not all, sir. But
I have some general notions; I do love   100
To note and to observe: though I live out,
Free from the active torrent, yet I'd mark
The currents and the passages of things
For mine own private use; and know the ebbs
And flows of state.
PEREGRINE: Believe it, sir, I hold
Myself in no small tie unto my fortunes
For casting me thus luckily upon you,
Whose knowledge, if your bounty equal it,
May do me great assistance in instruction
For my behaviour, and my bearing, which   110
Is yet so rude and raw.
SIR POLITIC: Why? came you forth
Empty of rules for travel?
PEREGRINE: Faith, I had
Some common ones, from out that vulgar grammar,
Which he that cried Italian to me, taught me.
SIR POLITIC: Why, this it is that spoils all our brave bloods,
Trusting our hopeful gentry unto pedants,
Fellows of outside, and mere bark. You seem
To be a gentleman, of ingenuous race –
I not profess it, but my fate hath been
To be where I have been consulted with   120
In this high kind, touching some great men's sons,
Persons of blood and honour –
PEREGRINE: Who be these, sir?

[*Enter* MOSCA *and* NANO, *disguised, with properties for erecting*   II, ii
a scaffold stage.]
[MOSCA:] Under that window, there 't must be. The same.
SIR POLITIC: Fellows to mount a bank! Did your instructor

106. *I hold myself in no small tie unto my fortunes:* I count myself fortunate.
113. *vulgar grammar:* Note.
114. *he that cried Italian to me:* my Italian teacher.
118. *of ingenuous race:* of good family.

In the dear tongues never discourse to you
Of the Italian mountebanks?

PEREGRINE: Yes, sir.

SIR POLITIC: Why,
Here shall you see one.

PEREGRINE: They are quacksalvers,
Fellows that live by venting oils and drugs.

SIR POLITIC: Was that the character he gave you of them?

PEREGRINE: As I remember.

SIR POLITIC: Pity his ignorance.
They are the only knowing men of Europe!

10   Great general scholars, excellent physicians,
Most admired statesmen, professed favourites
And cabinet counsellors to the greatest princes!
The only languaged men of all the world!

PEREGRINE: And I have heard they are most lewd impostors,
Made all of terms and shreds; no less beliers
Of great men's favours than their own vile med'cines;
Which they will utter upon monstrous oaths,
Selling that drug for twopence, ere they part,
Which they have valued at twelve crowns before.

20   SIR POLITIC: Sir, calumnies are answered best with silence.
Yourself shall judge. Who is it mounts, my friends?

MOSCA: Scoto of Mantua, sir.

SIR POLITIC: Is't he? Nay, then
I'll proudly promise, sir, you shall behold
Another man than has been phant'sied to you.
I wonder, yet, that he should mount his bank
Here, in this nook, that has been wont t'appear
In face of the Piazza! Here he comes.

> [*Enter* VOLPONE, *disguised as a Mountebank, and followed by the*
> GREGE, *or crowd.*]

3. *the dear tongues:* the main languages (of Europe).

4. *mountebank:* Note.   5. *quacksalvers:* quacks.

12. *cabinet counsellors:* intimate advisers.

13. *only languaged men:* the best linguists.

15. *terms and shreds:* impressive-sounding jargon, miscellaneous quotations, etc.

24. *phant'sied:* depicted.

VOLPONE [*to* NANO]: Mount, zany.

GREGE: Follow, follow, follow, follow, follow!

SIR POLITIC: See how the people follow him! He's a man
 May write ten thousand crowns in bank here.

 [VOLPONE *mounts the stage*.]

            Note,   30
 Mark but his gesture. I do use to observe
 The state he keeps in getting up!

PEREGRINE: 'Tis worth it, sir.

VOLPONE: Most noble gentlemen, and my worthy patrons, it
 may seem strange that I, your Scoto Mantuano, who was ever
 wont to fix my bank in face of the public Piazza, near the shelter
 of the Portico to the Procuratia, should now, after eight months'
 absence from this illustrious city of Venice, humbly retire myself into an obscure nook of the Piazza.

SIR POLITIC: Did not I now object the same?

PEREGRINE: Peace, sir.

VOLPONE: Let me tell you: I am not, as your Lombard proverb 40
 saith, cold on my feet, or content to part with my commodities
 at a cheaper rate than I accustomed. Look not for it. Nor that
 the calumnious reports of that impudent detractor, and shame
 to our profession (Alessandro Buttone, I mean) who gave out,
 in public, I was condemned a *sforzato* to the galleys, for poison-
 ing the Cardinal Bembo's – cook, hath at all attached, much less
 dejected me. No, no, worthy gentlemen; to tell you true, I
 cannot endure to see the rabble of these ground *ciarlatani* that
 spread their cloaks on the pavement as if they meant to do feats
 of activity, and then come in lamely with their mouldy tales 50
 out of Boccaccio, like stale Tabarine, the fabulist: some of them
 discoursing their travels, and of their tedious captivity in the

39. *the Portico to the Procuratia:* the arcade of the residence of the Pro-
curators – important state officials.

41. *cold on my feet:* forced to sell things cheap.

44. *Buttone:* another mountebank.

48. *ground ciarlatani:* pavement–quacks, without platforms; charlatans.

49. *feats of activity:* acrobatic feats.

51. *Tabarine:* the zany in a troupe of Italian comedians.

Turk's galleys, when, indeed, were the truth known, they were
the Christian's galleys, where very temperately they eat bread,
and drunk water, as a wholesome penance, enjoined them by
their confessors, for base pilferies.

SIR POLITIC: Note but his bearing and contempt of these.

VOLPONE: These turdy-facy-nasty-paty-lousy-fartical rogues,
with one poor groatsworth of unprepared antimony, finely
60 wrapped up in several *scartoccios*, are able, very well, to kill their
twenty a week, and play; yet these meagre, starved spirits, who
have half stopped the organs of their minds with earthly oppilations, want not their favourers among your shrivelled salad-
eating artisans, who are overjoyed that they may have their
half-pe'rth of physic; though it purge 'em into another world,
't makes no matter.

SIR POLITIC: Excellent! ha' you heard better language, sir?

VOLPONE: Well, let 'em go. And, gentlemen, honourable gentlemen, know that for this time our bank, being thus removed
70 from the clamours of the *canaglia*, shall be the scene of pleasure
and delight; for I have nothing to sell, little or nothing to sell.

SIR POLITIC: I told you, sir, his end.

PEREGRINE: You did so, sir.

VOLPONE: I protest, I and my six servants are not able to make of
this precious liquor so fast as it is fetched away from my lodging
by gentlemen of your city, strangers of the Terra Firma, worshipful merchants, ay, and senators too, who, ever since my
arrival, have detained me to their uses by their splendidous
liberalities. And worthily. For what avails your rich man to
have his magazines stuffed with *moscadelli*, or of the purest grape,
80 when his physicians prescribe him, on pain of death, to drink
nothing but water cocted with aniseeds? O health! health! the
blessing of the rich! the riches of the poor! who can buy thee at
too dear a rate, since there is no enjoying this world without

60. *scartoccios*: scraps of paper used to wrap up medicines, etc.
62. *oppilations*: obstructions.
70. *canaglia*: the rabble, or scum (*canaille*).
75. *Terra Firma*: Venetian territory on the mainland.
79. *magazines*: warehouses.
79. *moscadelli*: muscatel wines.   81. *cocted*: boiled.

thee? Be not then so sparing of your purses, honourable gentlemen, as to abridge the natural course of life –

PEREGRINE: You see his end?

SIR POLITIC: Ay, is't not good?

VOLPONE: For, when a humid flux, or catarrh, by the mutability
of air falls from your head into an arm or shoulder, or any other
part, take you a ducat, or your chequin of gold, and apply to the
place affected: see, what good effect it can work. No, no, 'tis   *90*
this blessed *unguento*, this rare extraction, that hath only power
to disperse all malignant humours that proceed either of hot,
cold, moist, or windy causes –

PEREGRINE: I would he had put in dry too.

SIR POLITIC: Pray you, observe.

VOLPONE: To fortify the most indigest and crude stomach, ay,
were it of one that through extreme weakness vomited blood,
applying only a warm napkin to the place, after the unction and
fricace; for the vertigine in the head, putting but a drop into
your nostrils, likewise behind the ears; a most sovereign and
approved remedy: the *mal-caduco*, cramps, convulsions, para-   *100*
lyses, epilepsies, *tremor cordia*, retired nerves, ill vapours of the
spleen, stoppings of the liver, the stone, the strangury, *hernia
ventosa, iliaca passio*; stops a *dysenteria* immediately; easeth the
torsion of the small guts; and cures *melancholia hypocondriaca*,
being taken and applied according to my printed receipt.

Pointing to his bill and his glass.

For, this is the physician, this the medicine; this counsels, this
cures; this gives the direction, this works the effect; and, in sum,
both together may be termed an abstract of the theoric and
practic in the Æsculapian art. 'Twill cost you eight crowns.
And, Zan Fritada, pray thee sing a verse, extempore, in honour   *110*
of it.

92. *malignant humours*: Note.

100 ff. *mal-caduco*: epilepsy; *tremor cordia*: palpitation of the heart;
retired nerves: shrunken sinews; *the stone*: kidney trouble; *strangury*:
urinary complaint; *hernia ventosa*: flatulence caused by hernia; *iliaca
passio*: intestinal pains; *torsion of the small guts*: gripes; *melancholia hypocondriaca*: the 'black bile', chronic depression.

110. *Zan Fritada*: a famous comedian, whose name Volpone borrows to
address his own zany, Nano.

SIR POLITIC: How do you like him, sir?

PEREGRINE: Most strangely, I!

SIR POLITIC: Is not his language rare?

PEREGRINE: But alchemy
I never heard the like, or Broughton's books.

SONG

Had old Hippocrates or Galen,
That to their books put med'cines all in,
But known this secret, they had never,
(Of which they will be guilty ever)
Been murderers of so much paper,
Or wasted many hurtless taper.
120   No Indian drug had e'er been famèd,
Tobacco, sassafras not namèd;
Ne yet of guacum one small stick, sir,
Nor Raymund Lully's great elixir.
Ne had been known the Danish Gonswart,
Or Paracelsus, with his long sword.

PEREGRINE: All this, yet, will not do; eight crowns is high.

VOLPONE: No more. Gentlemen, if I had but time to discourse to
you the miraculous effects of this my oil, surnamed *Oglio del
Scoto*, with the countless catalogue of those I have cured of
130   th'aforesaid, and many more diseases; the patents and privileges
of all the princes and commonwealths of Christendom; or but
the depositions of those that appeared on my part, before the
signiory of the *Sanita* and most learned College of Physicians;
where I was authorized, upon notice taken of the admirable
virtues of my medicaments, and mine own excellency in matter
of rare and unknown secrets, not only to disperse them publicly
in this famous city, but in all the territories that happily joy
under the government of the most pious and magnificent states
of Italy. But may some other gallant fellow say, 'O, there be
140   divers that make profession to have as good and as experimented
receipts as yours.' Indeed, very many have assayed, like apes, in

114. *Hippocrates, Galen*: Greek physicians.
121. *sassafras*: a stimulant.
122. *guacum*: a drug obtained from a resinous wood.

imitation of that which is really and essentially in me, to make of this oil; bestowed great cost in furnaces, stills, alembics, continual fires, and preparation of the ingredients (as indeed there goes to it six hundred several simples, besides some quantity of human fat, for the conglutination, which we buy of the anatomists), but, when these practitioners come to the last decoction, blow, blow, puff, puff, and all flies *in fumo*. Ha, ha, ha! Poor wretches! I rather pity their folly and indiscretion than their loss of time and money; for those may be recovered by industry; but to be a fool born is a disease incurable. For myself, I always from my youth have endeavoured to get the rarest secrets, and book them, either in exchange or for money; I spared nor cost nor labour where anything was worthy to be learned. And, gentlemen, honourable gentlemen, I will undertake, by virtue of chemical art, out of the honourable hat that covers your head to extract the four elements, that is to say, the fire, air, water, and earth, and return you your felt without burn or stain. For, whilst others have been at the balloo, I have been at my book, and am now past the craggy paths of study, and come to the flowery plains of honour and reputation. 150 160

SIR POLITIC: I do assure you, sir, that is his aim.

VOLPONE: But to our price –

PEREGRINE: And that withal, Sir Pol.

VOLPONE: You all know, honourable gentlemen, I never valued this *ampulla*, or vial, at less than eight crowns, but for this time I am content to be deprived of it for six; six crowns is the price, and less in courtesy I know you cannot offer me; take it or leave it, howsoever, both it and I am at your service. I ask you not as the value of the thing, for then I should demand of you a thousand crowns; so the Cardinals Montalto, Farnese, the great Duke of Tuscany, my gossip, with divers other princes have given me; but I despise money. Only to show my affection to you, honourable gentlemen, and your illustrious state here, I have neglected the messages of these princes, mine own offices, 170

145. *simples:* herbal ingredients.   148. *decoction:* boiling to extract.
148. *flies in fumo:* goes up in smoke.
159. *balloo:* a game played in Venice with a large ball.
171. *gossip:* here, god-father, companion.

framed my journey hither, only to present you with the fruits
of my travels. [*To* NANO *and* MOSCA.] Tune your voices once
more to the touch of your instruments, and give the honourable
assembly some delightful recreation.

PEREGRINE: What monstrous and most painful circumstance
180   Is here, to get some three or four *gazets*!
Some threepence i' th' whole! for that 'twill come to.

SONG

You that would last long, list to my song,
Make no more coil, but buy of this oil.
Would you be ever fair? and young?
Stout of teeth? and strong of tongue?
Tart of palate? quick of ear?
Sharp of sight? of nostril clear?
Moist of hand? and light of foot?
Or I will come nearer to't –
190   Would you live free from all diseases?
Do the act your mistress pleases,
Yet fright all aches from your bones?
Here's a med'cine for the nones.

VOLPONE: Well, I am in a humour, at this time, to make a present
of the small quantity my coffer contains to the rich, in courtesy,
and to the poor, for God's sake. Wherefore, now mark: I asked
you six crowns, and six crowns at other times you have paid
me; you shall not give me six crowns, nor five, nor four, nor
three, nor two, nor one; nor half a ducat; no, nor a *moccenigo!*
200   Sixpence it will cost you, or six hundred pound – expect no
lower price, for by the banner of my front, I will not bate a
bagatine; that I will have, only, a pledge of your loves, to carry
something from amongst you to show I am not contemned by

180. *gazet:* a Venetian coin (a penny).
186. *tart of palate:* with a keen sense of taste.
191. *aches:* has two syllables in the song.
199. *moccenigo:* coin of little value.
201. *the banner of my front:* the banner on the mountebank's stage listing
his miraculous cures.
201. *bate a bagatine:* take off a penny.

you. Therefore, now, toss your handkerchiefs, cheerfully, cheerfully; and be advertised that the first heroic spirit that deigns to grace me with a handkerchief, I will give it a little remembrance of something beside, shall please it better than if I had presented it with a double pistolet.

PEREGRINE: Will you be that heroic spark, Sir Pol?

   CELIA *at the window throws down her handkerchief.*

O see! the window has prevented you.   *210*

VOLPONE: Lady, I kiss your bounty, and for this timely grace you have done your poor Scoto of Mantua, I will return you, over and above my oil, a secret of that high and inestimable nature shall make you forever enamoured on that minute wherein your eye first descended on so mean – yet not altogether to be despised – an object. Here is a powder concealed in this paper of which, if I should speak to the worth, nine thousand volumes were but as one page, that page as a line, that line as a word: so short is this pilgrimage of man (which some call life) to the expressing of it. Would I reflect on the price? Why, the *220* whole world were but as an empire, that empire as a province, that province as a bank, that bank as a private purse to the purchase of it. I will, only, tell you: it is the powder that made Venus a goddess (given her by Apollo), that kept her perpetually young, cleared her wrinkles, firmed her gums, filled her skin, coloured her hair. From her derived to Helen, and at the sack of Troy unfortunately lost; till now, in this our age, it was as happily recovered by a studious antiquary out of some ruins of Asia, who sent a moiety of it to the court of France (but much sophisticated), wherewith the ladies there now colour *230* their hair. The rest, at this present, remains with me; extracted to a quintessence, so that wherever it but touches in youth it perpetually preserves, in age restores the complexion; seats your teeth, did they dance like virginal jacks, firm as a wall; makes them white as ivory, that were black as –

[*Enter* CORVINO.]   II, iii

[CORVINO (*to* CELIA):] Spite o' the devil, and my shame!

208. *a double pistolet:* a valuable gold coin.

[*To* VOLPONE]   Come down here;
Come down! No house but mine to make your scene?
He beats away the mountebank, etc.
Signior Flaminio, will you down, sir? down?
What, is my wife your Franciscina, sir?
No windows on the whole Piazza, here,
To make your properties, but mine? but mine?
Heart! ere tomorrow I shall be new christened,
And called the Pantolone di Besogniosi
About the town.
    [*Exit.*]

PEREGRINE: What should this mean, Sir Pol?

10   SIR POLITIC: Some trick of state, believe it. I will home.

PEREGRINE: It may be some design on you.

SIR POLITIC: I know not.
I'll stand upon my guard.

PEREGRINE: It is your best, sir.

SIR POLITIC: This three weeks all my advices, all my letters,
They have been intercepted.

PEREGRINE: Indeed, sir?
Best have a care.

SIR POLITIC: Nay, so I will.

PEREGRINE [*aside*]:   This knight,
I may not lose him, for my mirth, till night.
    [*Exeunt.*]

II, iv   [SCENE TWO]

[VOLPONE'S *house.*]

[*Enter* VOLPONE *and* MOSCA.]
[VOLPONE:] O, I am wounded!

MOSCA: Where, sir?

VOLPONE: Not without;
Those blows were nothing, I could bear them ever.
But angry Cupid, bolting from her eyes,

    6. *to make your properties:* to take over as your stage.

Hath shot himself into me like a flame;
Where, now, he flings about his burning heat,
As in a furnace an ambitious fire
Whose vent is stopped. The fight is all within me.
I cannot live except thou help me, Mosca;
My liver melts, and I, without the hope
Of some soft air from her refreshing breath,   *10*
Am but a heap of cinders.

MOSCA: 'Las, good sir!
Would you had never seen her!

VOLPONE: Nay, would thou
Hadst never told me of her.

MOSCA: Sir, 'tis true;
I do confess I was unfortunate,
And you unhappy; but I'm bound in conscience,
No less than duty, to effect my best
To your release of torment, and I will, sir.

VOLPONE: Dear Mosca, shall I hope?

MOSCA: Sir, more than dear,
I will not bid you to despair of aught
Within a human compass.

VOLPONE: O, there spoke   *20*
My better angel. Mosca, take my keys,
Gold, plate, and jewels, all's at thy devotion;
Employ them how thou wilt; nay, coin me too,
So thou in this but crown my longings, Mosca!

MOSCA: Use but your patience.

VOLPONE: So I have.

MOSCA: I doubt not
To bring success to your desires.

VOLPONE: Nay, then,
I not repent me of my late disguise.

MOSCA: If you can horn him, sir, you need not.

VOLPONE: True.
Besides, I never meant him for my heir.
Is not the colour o' my beard and eyebrows   *30*
To make me known?

7. *vent*: chimney   28. *horn him*: cuckold him.

MOSCA: No jot.
VOLPONE: I did it well.
MOSCA: So well, would I could follow you in mine,
   With half the happiness; and, yet, I would
   Escape your epilogue.
VOLPONE: But were they gulled
   With a belief that I was Scoto?
MOSCA: Sir,
   Scoto himself could hardly have distinguished!
   I have not time to flatter you now; we'll part,
   And as I prosper, so applaud my art.
      [*Exeunt.*]

II, V   [SCENE THREE]

   [CORVINO'S *house.*]

   [*Enter* CORVINO, *dragging in* CELIA.]
[CORVINO:] Death of mine honour, with the city's fool?
   A juggling, tooth-drawing, prating mountebank?
   And at a public window? where, whilst he,
   With his strained action, and his dole of faces,
   To his drug-lecture draws your itching ears,
   A crew of old, unmarried, noted lechers
   Stood leering up like satyrs: and you smile
   Most graciously, and fan your favours forth,
   To give your hot spectators satisfaction!
10 What, was your mountebank their call? their whistle?
   Or were y' enamoured on his copper rings?
   His saffron jewel, with the toad-stone in 't?
   Or his embroiderèd suit, with the cope-stitch,
   Made of a hearse cloth? or his old tilt-feather?
   Or his starched beard? Well, you shall have him, yes!

33. *your epilogue:* Note.
   4. *his strained action:* his excessive theatrical performance.
   4. *his dole of faces:* his range of facial expressions.
   12. *toad-stone:* Note.

He shall come home and minister unto you
The fricace for the mother. Or, let me see,
I think you'd rather mount? would you not mount?
Why, if you'll mount, you may; yes truly, you may,
And so you may be seen, down to th' foot.   20
Get you a cittern, Lady Vanity,
And be a dealer with the virtuous man;
Make one. I'll but protest myself a cuckold,
And save your dowry. I am a Dutchman, I!
For if you thought me an Italian,
You would be damned ere you did this, you whore!
Thou'dst tremble to imagine that the murder
Of father, mother, brother, all thy race,
Should follow as the subject of my justice.

CELIA: Good sir, have patience!

CORVINO [*waving his sword*]:   What couldst thou propose   30
Less to thyself than in this heat of wrath,
And stung with my dishonour, I should strike
This steel into thee, with as many stabs
As thou wert gazed upon with goatish eyes?

CELIA: Alas, sir, be appeased! I could not think
My being at the window should more now
Move your impatience than at other times.

CORVINO: No? not to seek and entertain a parley
With a known knave? before a multitude?
You were an actor with your handkerchief,   40
Which he, most sweetly, kissed in the receipt,
And might, no doubt, return it with a letter,
And 'point the place where you might meet: your sister's,
Your mother's, or your aunt's might serve the turn.

CELIA: Why, dear sir, when do I make these excuses?
Or ever stir abroad but to the church?
And that so seldom –

17. *fricace for the mother*: literally, massage for a fit of hysteria, but here used with suggestive overtones.
18. *mount*: become a mountebank; again with suggestive sexual overtones.
21. *cittern*: zither.   24. *dowry, Dutchman*: Notes.

CORVINO: Well, it shall be less;
And thy restraint before was liberty
To what I now decree; and therefore mark me.
50   First, I will have this bawdy light dammed up;
And till't be done, some two, or three yards off
I'll chalk a line, o'er which if thou but chance
To set thy desp'rate foot, more hell, more horror,
More wild, remorseless rage shall seize on thee
Than on a conjurer that had heedless left
His circle's safety ere his devil was laid.
Then, here's a lock which I will hang upon thee;
And, now I think on 't, I will keep thee backwards:
Thy lodging shall be backwards, thy walks backwards;
60   Thy prospect – all be backwards, and no pleasure,
That thou shalt know but backwards. Nay, since you force
My honest nature, know it is your own
Being too open makes me use you thus.
Since you will not contain your subtle nostrils
In a sweet room, but they must snuff the air
Of rank and sweaty passengers –
     Knock within.

                         One knocks.
Away, and be not seen, pain of thy life;
Not look toward the window; if thou dost –
Nay, stay, hear this – let me not prosper, whore,
70   But I will make thee an anatomy,
Dissect thee mine own self, and read a lecture
Upon thee to the city, and in public.
Away!
     [*Exit* CELIA.]
          Who's there?
     [*Enter* SERVANT.]
SERVANT: 'Tis Signior Mosca, sir.

II, vi [CORVINO:] Let him come in. His master's dead. There's yet
Some good to help the bad.

55. *a conjurer:* Note.   57. *lock:* chastity-belt.
58. *backwards:* at the rear of his house.   70. *anatomy:* Note.

90

[*Enter* MOSCA.]

My Mosca, welcome!
I guess your news.

MOSCA: I fear you cannot, sir.

CORVINO: Is't not his death?

MOSCA: Rather the contrary.

CORVINO: Not his recovery?

MOSCA: Yes, sir.

CORVINO: I am cursed,
I am bewitched, my crosses meet to vex me.
How? how? how? how?

MOSCA: Why, sir, with Scoto's oil!
Corbaccio and Voltore brought of it,
Whilst I was busy in an inner room –

CORVINO: Death! that damned mountebank! but for the law,   10
Now, I could kill the rascal; 't cannot be
His oil should have that virtue. Ha' not I
Known him a common rogue, come fiddling in
To th' *osterìa*, with a tumbling whore,
And, when he has done all his forced tricks, been glad
Of a poor spoonful of dead wine, with flies in 't?
It cannot be. All his ingredients
Are a sheep's gall, a roasted bitch's marrow,
Some few sod earwigs, pounded caterpillars,
A little capon's grease, and fasting spittle;   20
I know 'em to a dram.

MOSCA: I know not, sir;
But some on 't, they poured into his ears,
Some in his nostrils, and recovered him,
Applying but the fricace.

CORVINO: Pox o' that fricace.

MOSCA: And since, to seem the more officious
And flatt'ring of his health, there they have had,

---

14. *th' osterìa*: the inn.

14. *a tumbling whore*: 'tumbling' here suggests both acrobatic dancing and 'tumbling in the hay'.

20. *fasting spittle*: the spittle of someone who is fasting, or starving.

At extreme fees, the College of Physicians
Consulting on him how they might restore him;
Where one would have a cataplasm of spices,
30 Another a flayed ape clapped to his breast,
A third would ha' it a dog, a fourth an oil
With wild cats' skins. At last, they all resolved
That to preserve him was no other means
But some young woman must be straight sought out,
Lusty, and full of juice, to sleep by him;
And to this service, most unhappily
And most unwillingly, am I now employed,
Which here I thought to pre-acquaint you with,
For your advice, since it concerns you most,
40 Because I would not do that thing might cross
Your ends, on whom I have my whole dependence, sir.
Yet, if I do it not they may delate
My slackness to my patron, work me out
Of his opinion; and there all your hopes,
Ventures, or whatsoever, are all frustrate.
I do but tell you, sir. Besides, they are all
Now striving who shall first present him. Therefore,
I could entreat you, briefly, conclude somewhat.
Prevent 'em if you can.

CORVINO: Death to my hopes!
50 This is my villainous fortune! Best to hire
Some common courtesan?

MOSCA: Ay, I thought on that, sir.
But they are all so subtle, full of art,
And age again doting and flexible,
So as – I cannot tell – we may perchance
Light on a quean may cheat us all.

CORVINO: 'Tis true.

MOSCA: No, no; it must be one that has no tricks, sir,
Some simple thing, a creature made unto it;
Some wench you may command. Ha' you no kinswoman?

27. *At extreme fees:* at huge cost.
29. *cataplasm:* poultice, or plaster.
42. *delate:* report.
47. *present him:* give him what he requires.
55. *quean:* whore.

God's so – Think, think, think, think, think, think, sir.
One o' the doctors offered there his daughter.   60
CORVINO: How!
MOSCA: Yes, Signior Lupo, the physician.
CORVINO: His daughter!
MOSCA: And a virgin, sir. Why, alas,
He knows the state of 's body, what it is;
That nought can warm his blood, sir, but a fever;
Nor any incantation raise his spirit;
A long forgetfulness hath seized that part.
Besides, sir, who shall know it? Some one or two –
CORVINO: I pray thee give me leave.
     [*Walks aside, talking to himself.*]
                                    If any man
But I had had this luck – The thing in 't self,
I know, is nothing – Wherefore should not I   70
As well command my blood and my affections
As this dull doctor? In the point of honour
The cases are all one of wife and daughter.
MOSCA [*aside*]: I hear him coming.
CORVINO: She shall do 't. 'Tis done.
'Slight, if this doctor, who is not engaged,
Unless 't be for his counsel, which is nothing,
Offer his daughter, what should I that am
So deeply in? I will prevent him. Wretch!
Covetous wretch! – Mosca, I have determined.
MOSCA: How, sir?
CORVINO: We'll make all sure. The party you wot of   80
Shall be mine own wife, Mosca.
MOSCA: Sir, the thing,
But that I would not seem to counsel you,
I should have motioned to you at the first.
And make your count, you have cut all their throats.
Why, 'tis directly taking a possession!

59. *God's so*: Note.
75. *is not engaged*: has no ulterior purpose (i.e. is not one of Volpone's
'clients').
84. *make your count*: be assured.

93

And in his next fit, we may let him go.
'Tis but to pull the pillow from his head,
And he is throttled; 't had been done before
But for your scrupulous doubts.

CORVINO: Ay, a plague on 't,
90   My conscience fools my wit! Well, I'll be brief,
And so be thou, lest they should be before us.
Go home, prepare him, tell him with what zeal
And willingness I do it; swear it was
On the first hearing, as thou mayst do, truly,
Mine own free motion.

MOSCA: Sir, I warrant you,
I'll so possess him with it that the rest
Of his starved clients shall be banished all;
And only you received. But come not, sir,
Until I send, for I have something else
100   To ripen for your good, you must not know 't.
CORVINO: But do not you forget to send now.
MOSCA: Fear not.
        [*Exit* MOSCA.]

II, vii [CORVINO:] Where are you, wife? My Celia? wife?
        [*Enter* CELIA, *weeping*.]

                                          What, blubbering?
Come, dry those tears. I think thou thought'st me in earnest?
Ha? by this light I talked so but to try thee.
Methinks the lightness of the occasion
Should ha' confirmed thee. Come, I am not jealous.
CELIA: No?
CORVINO: Faith I am not, I, nor never was;
It is a poor unprofitable humour.
Do not I know if women have a will
They'll do 'gainst all the watches o' the world?
10   And that the fiercest spies are tamed with gold?
Tut, I am confident in thee, thou shalt see 't;
And see, I'll give thee cause, too, to believe it.
Come, kiss me. Go, and make thee ready straight

In all thy best attire, thy choicest jewels,
Put 'em all on, and, with 'em, thy best looks.
We are invited to a solemn feast
At old Volpone's, where it shall appear
How far I am free from jealousy or fear.
　　[*Exeunt.*]

ACT THREE

[SCENE ONE]

[A street.]

[Enter MOSCA.*]*
[MOSCA:] I fear I shall begin to grow in love
    With my dear self and my most prosp'rous parts,
    They do so spring and burgeon; I can feel
    A whimsy i' my blood. I know not how,
    Success hath made me wanton. I could skip
    Out of my skin now, like a subtle snake,
    I am so limber. O! your parasite
    Is a most precious thing, dropped from above,
    Not bred 'mongst clods and clodpolls, here on earth.
10   I muse the mystery was not made a science,
    It is so liberally professed! Almost
    All the wise world is little else in nature
    But parasites or sub-parasites. And yet,
    I mean not those that have your bare town-art,
    To know who's fit to feed 'em; have no house,
    No family, no care, and therefore mould
    Tales for men's ears, to bait that sense; or get
    Kitchen-invention, and some stale receipts
    To please the belly, and the groin; nor those,
20   With their court-dog tricks, that can fawn and fleer,
    Make their revènue out of legs and faces,
    Echo my lord, and lick away a moth.

10. *the mystery:* the skilled craft or profession; *a science:* a systematic field of learning recognized by universities, academies, etc.

11. *liberally professed:* widely practised like an academic discipline.

14. *town-art:* art of getting one's living by knowing one's way around the city.

18. *kitchen-invention and some stale receipts:* culinary skill and old recipes.

19. *the groin:* this suggests a cook-pander.

20. *fleer:* smile sycophantically.

21. *legs and faces:* bowing and scraping.

But your fine, elegant rascal, that can rise
And stoop, almost together, like an arrow;
Shoot through the air as nimbly as a star;
Turn short as doth a swallow; and be here,
And there, and here, and yonder, all at once;
Present to any humour, all occasion;
And change a visor swifter than a thought,
This is the creature had the art born with him;   30
Toils not to learn it, but doth practise it
Out of most excellent nature: and such sparks
Are the true parasites, others but their zanies.

[*Enter* BONARIO.]   III, ii
[MOSCA:] Who's this? Bonario? Old Corbaccio's son?
    The person I was bound to seek. Fair sir,
    You are happ'ly met.
BONARIO: That cannot be by thee.
MOSCA: Why, sir?
BONARIO: Nay, pray thee know thy way and leave me:
    I would be loath to interchange discourse
    With such a mate as thou art.
MOSCA: Courteous sir,
    Scorn not my poverty.
BONARIO: Not I, by heaven;
    But thou shalt give me leave to hate thy baseness.
MOSCA: Baseness?
BONARIO: Ay, answer me, is not thy sloth
    Sufficient argument? thy flattery?   10
    Thy means of feeding?
MOSCA: Heaven be good to me!
    These imputations are too common, sir,
    And eas'ly stuck on virtue when she's poor.
    You are unequal to me, and howe'er

28. *present to any humour, all occasion:* prepared to cope with any whim
and any event (i.e. thoroughly opportunist).

29. *change a visor:* literally, change a mask; adopt any attitude or play
any part.

Your sentence may be righteous, yet you are not,
That ere you know me, thus proceed in censure.
St Mark bear witness 'gainst you, 'tis inhuman.
[*He weeps.*]
BONARIO [*aside*]: What? does he weep? the sign is soft and good.
I do repent me that I was so harsh.
20 MOSCA: 'Tis true that, swayed by strong necessity,
I am enforced to eat my careful bread
With too much obsequy; 'tis true, beside,
That I am fain to spin mine own poor raiment
Out of my mere observance, being not born
To a free fortune; but that I have done
Base offices, in rending friends asunder,
Dividing families, betraying counsels,
Whispering false lies, or mining men with praises,
Trained their credulity with perjuries,
30 Corrupted chastity, or am in love
With mine own tender ease, but would not rather
Prove the most ruggèd and laborious course,
That might redeem my present estimation,
Let me here perish, in all hope of goodness.
BONARIO [*aside*]: This cannot be a personated passion! –
I was to blame, so to mistake thy nature;
Pray thee forgive me and speak out thy business.
MOSCA: Sir, it concerns you, and though I may seem
At first to make a main offence in manners,
40 And in my gratitude unto my master,
Yet, for the pure love which I bear all right,
And hatred of the wrong, I must reveal it.
This very hour your father is in purpose
To disinherit you –
BONARIO: How!
MOSCA: And thrust you forth
As a mere stranger to his blood; 'tis true, sir.
The work no way engageth me, but as

23. *spin my own poor raiment*: keep myself in clothes.
28. *mining*: undermining.
35. *personated*: impersonated or acted.

I claim an interest in the general state
Of goodness and true virtue, which I hear
T' abound in you, and for which mere respect,
Without a second aim, sir, I have done it.   50
BONARIO: This tale hath lost thee much of the late trust
Thou hadst with me; it is impossible.
I know not how to lend it any thought
My father should be so unnatural.
MOSCA: It is a confidence that well becomes
Your piety, and formed, no doubt, it is
From your own simple innocence, which makes
Your wrong more monstrous and abhorred. But, sir,
I now will tell you more. This very minute
It is, or will be, doing; and if you   60
Shall be but pleased to go with me, I'll bring you,
I dare not say where you shall see, but where
Your ear shall be a witness of the deed;
Hear yourself written bastard and professed
The common issue of the earth.
BONARIO: I'm 'mazed!
MOSCA: Sir, if I do it not, draw your just sword
And score your vengeance on my front and face;
Mark me your villain. You have too much wrong,
And I do suffer for you, sir. My heart
Weeps blood in anguish –
BONARIO: Lead, I follow thee.   70
    [Exeunt.]

[SCENE TWO]   III, iii

[VOLPONE'S house.]

    [Enter VOLPONE.]
[VOLPONE:] Mosca stays long, methinks. Bring forth your sports
And help to make the wretched time more sweet.
    [Enter NANO, CASTRONE, and ANDROGYNO.]
NANO [reciting]: Dwarf, fool, and eunuch, well met here we be.
A question it were now, whether of us three,

Being, all, the known delicates of a rich man,
In pleasing him, claim the precedency can?
CASTRONE: I claim for myself.
ANDROGYNO: And so doth the Fool.
NANO: 'Tis foolish indeed, let me set you both to school.
First for your dwarf, he's little and witty,
10 And everything, as it is little, is pretty;
Else, why do men say to a creature of my shape,
So soon as they see him, 'It's a pretty little ape'?
And, why a pretty ape? but for pleasing imitation
Of greater men's action, in a ridiculous fashion.
Beside, this feat body of mine doth not crave
Half the meat, drink, and cloth one of your bulks will have.
Admit your fool's face be the mother of laughter,
Yet, for his brain, it must always come after;
And though that do feed him, it's a pitiful case
20 His body is beholding to such a bad face.
    One knocks.
VOLPONE: Who's there? My couch, away, look, Nano, see;
    [*Exit* NANO.]
Give me my caps first – go, inquire.
    [*Exeunt* ANDROGYNO *and* CASTRONE. VOLPONE *gets into his
    bed.*]
                              Now Cupid
Send it be Mosca, and with fair return.
    [*Re-enter* NANO.]
NANO: It is the beauteous Madam –
VOLPONE: Would-be – is it?
NANO: The same.
VOLPONE: Now, torment on me; squire her in,
For she will enter, or dwell here forever.
Nay, quickly, that my fit were past, I fear
    [*Exit* NANO.]
A second hell too: that my loathing this
Will quite expel my appetite to the other.
30 Would she were taking, now, her tedious leave.
Lord, how it threats me, what I am to suffer!
28. *this:* Lady Would-be.   29. *the other:* Celia.

[*Enter* NANO *with* LADY WOULD-BE.]

[LADY WOULD-BE (*to* NANO):] I thank you, good sir. Pray you
    signify
  Unto your patron I am here – This band
  Shows not my neck enough. – I trouble you, sir;
  Let me request you bid one of my women
  Come hither to me. In good faith, I am dressed
  Most favourably today! It is no matter;
  'Tis well enough.
    [*Enter* 1ST WOMAN.]
                Look, see these petulant things!
  How they have done this!
VOLPONE [*aside*]:   I do feel the fever
  Ent'ring in at mine ears. O for a charm
  To fright it hence!
LADY WOULD-BE: Come nearer. Is this curl   *10*
  In his right place? or this? Why is this higher
  Than all the rest? You ha' not washed your eyes yet?
  Or do they not stand even i' your head?
  Where's your fellow? Call her.
    [*Exit* 1ST WOMAN.]
NANO [*aside*]:   Now, St Mark
  Deliver us! Anon she'll beat her women
  Because her nose is red.
    [*Re-enter* 1ST WOMAN *with* 2ND WOMAN.]
LADY WOULD-BE: I pray you, view
  This tire, forsooth: are all things apt, or no?
1ST WOMAN: One hair a little, here, sticks out, forsooth.
LADY WOULD-BE: Does't so, forsooth? And where was your
    dear sight
  When it did so, forsooth? What now! Bird-eyed?   *20*
  And you too? Pray you both approach and mend it.
  Now, by that light, I muse you're not ashamed!
  I, that have preached these things so oft unto you,
  Read you the principles, argued all the grounds,
  Disputed every fitness, every grace,
  Called you to counsel of so frequent dressings –

20. *bird-eyed*: staring.

NANO [*aside*]: More carefully than of your fame or honour.

LADY WOULD-BE: Made you acquainted what an ample dowry
   The knowledge of these things would be unto you,
30 Able, alone, to get you noble husbands
   At your return; and you, thus, to neglect it!
   Besides, you seeing what a curious nation
   Th' Italians are, what will they say of me?
   'The English lady cannot dress herself.'
   Here's a fine imputation to our country!
   Well, go your ways, and stay i' the next room.
   This fucus was too coarse, too; it's no matter.
   Good sir, you'll give 'em entertainment?
   [*Exit* NANO *with* WOMEN.]

VOLPONE: The storm comes toward me.

LADY WOULD-BE: How does my Volp?

40 VOLPONE: Troubled with noise, I cannot sleep; I dreamt
   That a strange fury entered, now, my house,
   And, with the dreadful tempest of her breath,
   Did cleave my roof asunder.

LADY WOULD-BE: Believe me, and I
   Had the most fearful dream, could I remember 't –

VOLPONE [*aside*]: Out on my fate! I ha' giv'n her the occasion
   How to torment me. She will tell me hers.

LADY WOULD-BE: Methought the golden mediocrity,
   Polite, and delicate –

VOLPONE: Oh, if you do love me,
   No more; I sweat, and suffer, at the mention
50 Of any dream; feel how I tremble yet.

LADY WOULD-BE: Alas, good soul! the passion of the heart.
   Seed-pearl were good now, boiled with syrup of apples,
   Tincture of gold, and coral, citron-pills,
   Your elecampane root, myrobalanes –

VOLPONE [*aside*]: Ay me, I have ta'en a grasshopper by the wing!

37. *fucus*: a skin cosmetic.
47. *golden mediocrity*: Note.
52. *seed-pearl*: a stimulant for the heart made of crushed seed-pearls
dissolved in liquid.
54. *elecampane root*: the root of a medicinal plant.

LADY WOULD-BE: Burnt silk and amber. You have muscadel
Good in the house –

VOLPONE:　　　　　You will not drink and part?

LADY WOULD-BE: No, fear not that. I doubt we shall not get
Some English saffron, half a dram would serve,
Your sixteen cloves, a little musk, dried mints,　　　　　*60*
Bugloss, and barley-meal –

VOLPONE [*aside*]:　　　　　She's in again.
Before I feigned diseases, now I have one.

LADY WOULD-BE: And these applied with a right scarlet cloth.

VOLPONE [*aside*]: Another flood of words! a very torrent!

LADY WOULD-BE: Shall I, sir, make you a poultice?

VOLPONE:　　　　　　　　No, no, no.
I'm very well, you need prescribe no more.

LADY WOULD-BE: I have a little studied physic; but now
I'm all for music, save, i' the forenoons,
An hour or two for painting. I would have
A lady, indeed, t'have all letters and arts,　　　　　*70*
Be able to discourse, to write, to paint,
But principal (as Plato holds) your music,
(And so does wise Pythagoras, I take it)
Is your true rapture, when there is concent
In face, in voice, and clothes, and is, indeed,
Our sex's chiefest ornament.

VOLPONE:　　　　　The poet,
As old in time as Plato, and as knowing,
Says that your highest female grace is silence.

LADY WOULD-BE: Which o' your poets? Petrarch? or Tasso? or
Dante?
Guarini? Ariosto? Aretine?　　　　　*80*
Cieco di Hadria? I have read them all.

VOLPONE [*aside*]: Is everything a cause to my destruction?

LADY WOULD-BE: I think I ha' two or three of 'em about
me.

VOLPONE [*aside*]: The sun, the sea, will sooner both stand still
Than her eternal tongue! Nothing can 'scape it.

LADY WOULD-BE: Here's *Pastor Fido* –

61. *Bugloss:* another herb.　　　　74. *concent:* harmony.

VOLPONE [*aside*]:   Profess obstinate silence;
That's now my safest.
LADY WOULD-BE: All our English writers,
I mean such as are happy in th' Italian,
Will deign to steal out of this author, mainly;
90   Almost as much as from Montagnié:
He has so modern and facile a vein,
Fitting the time, and catching the court-ear.
Your Petrarch is more passionate, yet he,
In days of sonneting, trusted 'em with much.
Dante is hard, and few can understand him.
But for a desperate wit, there's Aretine!
Only, his pictures are a little obscene –
You mark me not.
VOLPONE: Alas, my mind's perturbed.
LADY WOULD-BE: Why, in such cases, we must cure ourselves,
100   Make use of our philosophy –
VOLPONE: O'y me!
LADY WOULD-BE: And as we find our passions do rebel,
Encounter 'em with reason, or divert 'em
By giving scope unto some other humour
Of lesser danger: as, in politic bodies
There's nothing more doth overwhelm the judgement,
And clouds the understanding, than too much
Settling and fixing, and, as 'twere, subsiding
Upon one object. For the incorporating
Of these same outward things into that part
110   Which we call mental, leaves some certain fæces
That stop the organs, and, as Plato says,
Assassinates our knowledge.
VOLPONE [*aside*]:   Now, the spirit
Of patience help me!
LADY WOULD-BE: Come, in faith, I must
Visit you more a-days and make you well.
Laugh and be lusty!
VOLPONE [*aside*]:   My good angel save me!
LADY WOULD-BE: There was but one sole man in all the world

104. *politic bodies:* çountries.

With whom I e'er could sympathize; and he
Would lie you often, three, four hours together
To hear me speak; and be sometime so rapt,
As he would answer me quite from the purpose,   *120*
Like you, and you are like him, just. I'll discourse,
(An't be but only, sir, to bring you asleep)
How we did spend our time and loves together,
For some six years.
VOLPONE: Oh, oh, oh, oh, oh, oh!
LADY WOULD-BE: For we were *coætanei*, and brought up -
VOLPONE [*aside*]: Some power, some fate, some fortune rescue me!

     [*Enter* MOSCA.]   III, V
[MOSCA:] God save you, madam!
LADY WOULD-BE: Good sir.
VOLPONE: Mosca, welcome!
  Welcome to my redemption.
MOSCA: Why, sir?
VOLPONE [*aside to* MOSCA]:   Oh,
  Rid me of this my torture quickly, there,
  My madam with the everlasting voice;
  The bells in time of pestilence ne'er made
  Like noise, or were in that perpetual motion!
  The cock-pit comes not near it. All my house,
  But now, steamed like a bath with her thick breath.
  A lawyer could not have been heard; nor scarce
  Another woman, such a hail of words   *10*
  She has let fall. For hell's sake, rid her hence.
MOSCA: Has she presented?
VOLPONE: Oh, I do not care;
  I'll take her absence upon any price,
  With any loss.
MOSCA: Madam -
LADY WOULD-BE: I ha' brought your patron
  A toy, a cap here, of mine own work.

        125. *coætanei*: exact contemporaries.
        12. *presented*: given a present.

MOSCA: 'Tis well.
I had forgot to tell you I saw your knight
Where you'd little think it.

LADY WOULD-BE: Where?

MOSCA: Marry,
Where yet, if you make haste, you may apprehend him,
Rowing upon the water in a gondole,
20   With the most cunning courtesan of Venice.

LADY WOULD-BE: Is't true?

MOSCA: Pursue 'em, and believe your eyes.
Leave me to make your gift.
    [*Exit* LADY WOULD-BE.]
                         I knew 'twould take.
For lightly, they that use themselves most licence,
Are still most jealous.

VOLPONE: Mosca, hearty thanks
For thy quick fiction and delivery of me.
Now to my hopes, what sayst thou?
    [*Re-enter* LADY WOULD-BE.]

LADY WOULD-BE: But do you hear, sir?

VOLPONE: Again! I fear a paroxysm.

LADY WOULD-BE: Which way
Rowed they together?

MOSCA: Toward the Rialto.

LADY WOULD-BE: I pray you lend me your dwarf.

MOSCA: I pray you,
take him.
    [*Exit* LADY WOULD-BE.]
30 Your hopes, sir, are like happy blossoms fair,
And promise timely fruit, if you will stay
But the maturing; keep you at your couch.
Corbaccio will arrive straight with the will;
When he is gone, I'll tell you more.
    [*Exit* MOSCA.]

VOLPONE: My blood,
My spirits are returned; I am alive;
And, like your wanton gamester at primero,

        36. *primero*: a card-game.

Whose thought had whispered to him, not go less,
Methinks I lie, and draw – for an encounter.
[VOLPONE *draws the curtains of his bed.*]

[MOSCA *leads in* BONARIO *and hides him.*]   III, vi
[MOSCA:] Sir, here concealed you may hear all. But pray you
    One knocks.
Have patience, sir; the same's your father knocks.
I am compelled to leave you.
BONARIO: Do so. – Yet
Cannot my thought imagine this a truth.

[MOSCA *admits* CORVINO *with* CELIA.]   III, vi
[MOSCA:] Death on me! you are come too soon, what meant you?
Did not I say I would send?
CORVINO: Yes, but I feared
You might forget it, and then they prevent us.
MOSCA: Prevent! [*Aside*] Did e'er man haste so for his horns?
A courtier would not ply it so for a place. –
Well, now there's no helping it, stay here;
I'll presently return.
    [*He crosses the stage.*]
CORVINO: Where are you, Celia?
You know not wherefore I have brought you hither?
CELIA: Not well, except you told me.
CORVINO: Now I will:
Hark hither.
    [*They talk apart.*]
MOSCA (*To* BONARIO): Sir, your father hath sent word,   10
It will be half an hour ere he come;
And therefore, if you please to walk the while
Into that gallery – at the upper end
There are some books to entertain the time.
And I'll take care no man shall come unto you, sir.

3. *they prevent us:* i.e. the various other 'clients'.
4. *his horns:* the horns of a cuckold.

BONARIO: Yes, I will stay there. [*Aside*] I do doubt this fellow.
[*Exit.*]

MOSCA: There, he is far enough; he can hear nothing.
And for his father, I can keep him off.
[MOSCA *stands by* VOLPONE'S *bed.*]

CORVINO: Nay, now, there is no starting back, and therefore
20   Resolve upon it: I have so decreed.
It must be done. Nor would I move 't afore,
Because I would avoid all shifts and tricks,
That might deny me.

CELIA: Sir, let me beseech you,
Affect not these strange trials; if you doubt
My chastity, why, lock me up forever;
Make me the heir of darkness. Let me live
Where I may please your fears, if not your trust.

CORVINO: Believe it, I have no such humour, I.
All that I speak I mean; yet I am not mad,
30   Not horn-mad, see you? Go to, show yourself
Obedient, and a wife.

CELIA: O heaven!

CORVINO: I say it,
Do so.

CELIA: Was this the train?

CORVINO: I've told you reasons:
What the physicians have set down; how much
It may concern me; what my engagements are;
My means, and the necessity of those means
For my recovery; wherefore, if you be
Loyal and mine, be won, respect my venture.

CELIA: Before your honour?

CORVINO: Honour! tut, a breath.
There's no such thing in nature; a mere term
40   Invented to awe fools. What, is my gold

---

21. *move:* urge.

34. *my engagements:* my business commitments.

35–6. *the necessity of those means:* the necessity of adopting certain methods (i.e. becoming Volpone's sole heir through Celia's prostitution); *my recovery:* my *financial* recovery.

The worse for touching? clothes for being looked on?
Why, this 's no more. An old, decrepit wretch,
That has no sense, no sinew; takes his meat
With others' fingers; only knows to gape
When you do scald his gums; a voice, a shadow;
And what can this man hurt you?

CELIA: Lord! what spirit
Is this hath entered him?

CORVINO: And for your fame,
That's such a jig; as if I would go tell it,
Cry it, on the Piazza! Who shall know it
But he that cannot speak it, and this fellow,   50
Whose lips are i' my pocket, save yourself –
If you'll proclaim 't, you may. I know no other
Should come to know it.

CELIA: Are heaven and saints then nothing?
Will they be blind, or stupid?

CORVINO: How?

CELIA: Good sir,
Be jealous still, emulate them, and think
What hate they burn with toward every sin.

CORVINO: I grant you: if I thought it were a sin
I would not urge you. Should I offer this
To some young Frenchman, or hot Tuscan blood
That had read Aretine, conned all his prints,   60
Knew every quirk within lust's labyrinth,
And were professed critic in lechery;
And I would look upon him, and applaud him,
This were a sin; but here, 'tis contrary,
A pious work, mere charity, for physic
And honest policy to assure mine own.

CELIA: O heaven! canst thou suffer such a change?

VOLPONE: Thou art mine honour, Mosca, and my pride,
My joy, my tickling, my delight! Go, bring 'em.

MOSCA [advancing]: Please you draw near, sir.

CORVINO: Come on, what –   70
You will not be rebellious? By that light –

60. prints: Note.

109

[He forces CELIA *to the bed.]*

MOSCA: Sir, Signior Corvino, here, is come to see you.

VOLPONE: Oh!

MOSCA: And hearing of the consultation had,
So lately, for your health, is come to offer,
Or rather, sir, to prostitute –

CORVINO: Thanks, sweet Mosca.

MOSCA: Freely, unasked, or unentreated –

CORVINO: Well.

MOSCA: As the true, fervent instance of his love,
His own most fair and proper wife, the beauty
Only of price in Venice –

CORVINO: 'Tis well urged.

80 MOSCA: To be your comfortress, and to preserve you.

VOLPONE: Alas, I'm past already! Pray you, thank him
For his good care and promptness; but for that,
'Tis a vain labour e'en to fight 'gainst heaven;
Applying fire to a stone: uh, uh, uh, uh!
Making a dead leaf grow again. I take
His wishes gently, though; and you may tell him
What I've done for him. Marry, my state is hopeless!
Will him to pray for me, and t' use his fortune
With reverence when he comes to't.

MOSCA: Do you hear, sir?

90 Go to him with your wife.

CORVINO *[to* CELIA*]*:   Heart of my father!
Wilt thou persist thus? Come, I pray thee, come.
Thou seest 'tis nothing, Celia. By this hand
I shall grow violent. Come, do 't, I say.

CELIA: Sir, kill me rather. I will take down poison,
Eat burning coals, do anything –

CORVINO: Be damned!
Heart! I will drag thee hence home by the hair,
Cry thee a strumpet through the streets, rip up
Thy mouth unto thine ears, and slit thy nose,
Like a raw rochet! – Do not tempt me, come.

100 Yield, I am loth – Death! I will buy some slave

99. *rochet:* a kind of fish.

Whom I will kill, and bind thee to him, alive;
And at my window hang you forth, devising
Some monstrous crime, which I, in capital letters,
Will eat into thy flesh with aquafortis,
And burning cor'sives, on this stubborn breast.
Now, by the blood thou hast incensed, I'll do 't!

CELIA: Sir, what you please, you may; I am your martyr.

CORVINO: Be not thus obstinate, I ha' not deserved it.
Think who it is entreats you. Pray thee, sweet;
Good faith, thou shalt have jewels, gowns, attires,   110
What thou wilt, think and ask. Do but go kiss him.
Or touch him, but. For my sake. At my suit.
This once. No? Not? I shall remember this.
Will you disgrace me thus? D' you thirst my undoing?

MOSCA: Nay, gentle lady, be advised.

CORVINO: No, no.
She has watched her time. God's precious, this is scurvy,
'Tis very scurvy; and you are –

MOSCA: Nay, good sir.

CORVINO: An errant locust, by heaven, a locust! Whore,
Crocodile, that hast thy tears prepared,
Expecting how thou'lt bid 'em flow.

MOSCA: Nay, pray you, sir!   120
She will consider.

CELIA: Would my life would serve
To satisfy.

CORVINO: 'Sdeath! if she would but speak to him,
And save my reputation, 'twere somewhat;
But spitefully to effect my utter ruin!

MOSCA: Ay, now you've put your fortune in her hands.
Why i' faith, it is her modesty; I must quit her.
If you were absent, she would be more coming;
I know it, and dare undertake for her.
What woman can before her husband? Pray you,
Let us depart and leave her here.

CORVINO: Sweet Celia,   130

104. *aquafortis:* nitric acid.   105. *cor'sives:* other corrosives.
126. *quit:* acquit.   127. *coming:* forthcoming.

Thou may'st redeem all yet; I'll say no more.
If not, esteem yourself as lost. Nay, stay there.
   [*Exeunt* MOSCA *and* CORVINO.]
CELIA: O God, and his good angels! whither, whither,
   Is shame fled human breasts? that with such ease
   Men dare put off your honours, and their own?
   Is that, which ever was a cause of life,
   Now placed beneath the basest circumstance,
   And modesty an exile made, for money?
VOLPONE: Ay, in Corvino, and such earth-fed minds,
   He leaps off from the couch.
140 That never tasted the true heaven of love.
   Assure thee, Celia, he that would sell thee,
   Only for hope of gain, and that uncertain,
   He would have sold his part of Paradise
   For ready money, had he met a cope-man.
   Why art thou 'mazed to see me thus revived?
   Rather applaud thy beauty's miracle;
   'Tis thy great work, that hath, not now alone,
   But sundry times raised me in several shapes,
   And, but this morning, like a mountebank,
150 To see thee at thy window. Ay, before
   I would have left my practice for thy love,
   In varying figures I would have contended
   With the blue Proteus, or the hornèd flood.
   Now, art thou welcome.
CELIA: Sir!
VOLPONE: Nay, fly me not,
   Nor let thy false imagination
   That I was bed-rid, make thee think I am so:
   Thou shalt not find it. I am, now, as fresh,
   As hot, as high, and in as jovial plight
   As when, in that so celebrated scene,
160 At recitation of our comedy,
   For entertainment of the great Valois,

144. *cope-man:* dealer.   153. *hornèd flood:* Note.
158. *jovial plight:* cheerful spirits; but the word-play suggests Jovial also
- Jove, the seducer of maidens.

I acted young Antinous, and attracted
The eyes and ears of all the ladies present,
T' admire each graceful gesture, note, and footing.

SONG

    Come, my Celia, let us prove,
    While we can, the sports of love;
    Time will not be ours forever,
    He, at length, our good will sever;
    Spend not then his gifts in vain.   *170*
    Suns that set may rise again;
    But if once we lose this light,
    'Tis with us perpetual night.
    Why should we defer our joys?
    Fame and rumour are but toys.
    Cannot we delude the eyes
    Of a few poor household spies?
    Or his easier ears beguile,
    Thus removèd by our wile?
    'Tis no sin love's fruits to steal,   *180*
    But the sweet thefts to reveal:
    To be taken, to be seen,
    These have crimes accounted been.

CELIA: Some serene blast me, or dire lightning strike
  This my offending face.
VOLPONE: Why droops my Celia?
Thou hast in place of a base husband found
A worthy lover; use thy fortune well,
With secrecy and pleasure. See, behold,
What thou art queen of; not in expectation,
As I feed others, but possessed and crowned.   *190*
See, here, a rope of pearl, and each more orient
Than that the brave Egyptian queen caroused;

165. SONG: Note.
184. *serene:* 'A light fall of moisture or fine rain after sunset in hot countries, formerly regarded as a noxious dew or mist.' - *O.E.D.*
191. *more orient:* of greater value.

Dissolve and drink 'em. See, a carbuncle
May put out both the eyes of our St Mark;
A diamond would have bought Lollia Paulina
When she came in like star-light, hid with jewels
That were the spoils of provinces; take these,
And wear, and lose 'em; yet remains an ear-ring
To purchase them again, and this whole state.
200   A gem but worth a private patrimony
Is nothing: we will eat such at a meal.
The heads of parrots, tongues of nightingales,
The brains of peacocks, and of estriches
Shall be our food, and, could we get the phœnix,
Though nature lost her kind, she were our dish.
  CELIA: Good sir, these things might move a mind affected
With such delights; but I, whose innocence
Is all I can think wealthy, or worth th' enjoying,
And which, once lost, I have nought to lose beyond it,
210   Cannot be taken with these sensual baits.
If you have conscience –
  VOLPONE: 'Tis the beggar's virtue.
If thou hast wisdom, hear me, Celia.
Thy baths shall be the juice of July-flowers,
Spirit of roses, and of violets,
The milk of unicorns, and panthers' breath
Gathered in bags and mixed with Cretan wines.
Our drink shall be preparèd gold and amber,
Which we will take until my roof whirl round
With the vertigo; and my dwarf shall dance,
220   My eunuch sing, my fool make up the antic.
Whilst we, in changèd shapes, act Ovid's tales,
Thou like Europa now, and I like Jove,
Then I like Mars, and thou like Erycine;
So of the rest, till we have quite run through,
And wearied all the fables of the gods.
Then will I have thee in more modern forms,
Attirèd like some sprightly dame of France,
Brave Tuscan lady, or proud Spanish beauty;

220. *antic*: grotesque dance.

Sometimes unto the Persian Sophy's wife,
Or the Grand Signior's mistress; and, for change, *230*
To one of our most artful courtesans,
Or some quick Negro, or cold Russian;
And I will meet thee in as many shapes;
Where we may so transfuse our wand'ring souls
Out at our lips and score up sums of pleasures,
    That the curious shall not know
     How to tell them as they flow;
    And the envious, when they find
     What their number is, be pined.

CELIA: If you have ears that will be pierced, or eyes *240*
That can be opened, a heart may be touched,
Or any part that yet sounds man about you;
If you have touch of holy saints, or heaven,
Do me the grace to let me 'scape. If not,
Be bountiful and kill me. You do know
I am a creature hither ill betrayed
By one whose shame I would forget it were.
If you will deign me neither of these graces,
Yet feed your wrath, sir, rather than your lust,
(It is a vice comes nearer manliness) *250*
And punish that unhappy crime of nature,
Which you miscall my beauty: flay my face,
Or poison it with ointments for seducing
Your blood to this rebellion. Rub these hands
With what may cause an eating leprosy,
E'en to my bones and marrow; anything
That may disfavour me, save in my honour,
And I will kneel to you, pray for you, pay down
A thousand hourly vows, sir, for your health;
Report, and think you virtuous –

VOLPONE: Think me cold, *260*
Frozen, and impotent, and so report me?
That I had Nestor's hernia thou wouldst think.
I do degenerate and abuse my nation
To play with opportunity thus long;

   230. *the Grand Signior:* the Sultan of Turkey.

I should have done the act, and then have parleyed.
Yield, or I'll force thee.
[*He seizes her.*]
CELIA: O! just God!
VOLPONE: In vain –
BONARIO: Forbear, foul ravisher! libidinous swine!
    He leaps out from where MOSCA *had placed him.*
    Free the forced lady, or thou diest, impostor.
    But that I am loath to snatch thy punishment
270 Out of the hand of justice, thou shouldst yet
    Be made the timely sacrifice of vengeance,
    Before this altar, and this dross, thy idol.
    Lady, let's quit the place, it is the den
    Of villainy; fear nought, you have a guard;
    And he ere long shall meet his just reward.
        [*Exeunt* BONARIO *and* CELIA.]
VOLPONE: Fall on me, roof, and bury me in ruin!
    Become my grave, that wert my shelter! O!
    I am unmasked, unspirited, undone,
    Betrayed to beggary, to infamy –

III, viii   [*Enter* MOSCA, *wounded and bleeding.*]
    [MOSCA:] Where shall I run, most wretched shame of men,
    To beat out my unlucky brains?
VOLPONE: Here, here.
    What! dost thou bleed?
MOSCA: O, that his well-driven sword
    Had been so courteous to have cleft me down
    Unto the navel, ere I lived to see
    My life, my hopes, my spirits, my patron, all
    Thus desperately engagèd by my error.
VOLPONE: Woe on thy fortune!
MOSCA: And my follies, sir.
VOLPONE: Th' hast made me miserable.
MOSCA: And myself, sir.
10 Who would have thought he would have hearkened so?
VOLPONE: What shall we do?

MOSCA: I know not; if my heart
Could expiate the mischance, I'd pluck it out.
Will you be pleased to hang me, or cut my throat?
And I'll requite you, sir. Let's die like Romans,
Since we have lived like Grecians.
    They knock without.
VOLPONE: Hark! who's there?
I hear some footing; officers, the *Saffi*,
Come to apprehend us! I do feel the brand
Hissing already at my forehead; now,
Mine ears are boring.
MOSCA: To your couch, sir; you
Make that place good, however. Guilty men   20
Suspect what they deserve still.
    [MOSCA *admits* CORBACCIO.]
                    Signior Corbaccio!

[CORBACCIO:] Why, how now, Mosca?   III, ix
MOSCA: O, undone, amazed, sir.
Your son, I know not by what accident,
Acquainted with your purpose to my patron,
Touching your will, and making him your heir,
Entered our house with violence, his sword drawn,
Sought for you, called you wretch, unnatural,
Vowed he would kill you.
CORBACCIO: Me?
MOSCA: Yes, and my patron.
CORBACCIO: This act shall disinherit him indeed.
Here is the will.
MOSCA: 'Tis well, sir.
CORBACCIO: Right and well.
Be you as careful now for me.
    [*Enter* VOLTORE, *behind.*]
MOSCA: My life, sir,   10
Is not more tendered; I am only yours.
CORBACCIO: How does he? Will he die shortly, think'st thou?

17. *the brand:* No e.   19. *boring:* Note.

117

MOSCA: I fear
  He'll outlast May.
CORBACCIO: Today?
MOSCA [*shouting*]:   No, last out May, sir.
CORBACCIO: Couldst thou not gi' him a dram?
MOSCA: O, by no means, sir.
CORBACCIO: Nay, I'll not bid you.
VOLTORE: This is a knave, I see.
MOSCA [*aside*]: How! Signior Voltore! Did he hear me?
VOLTORE: Parasite!
MOSCA: Who's that? O, sir, most timely welcome.
VOLTORE: Scarce
  To the discovery of your tricks, I fear.
  You are his, only? And mine, also, are you not?
  [CORBACCIO *stands aside*.]
20 MOSCA: Who? I, sir?
VOLTORE: You, sir. What device is this
  About a will?
MOSCA: A plot for you, sir.
VOLTORE: Come,
  Put not your foists upon me; I shall scent 'em.
MOSCA: Did you not hear it?
VOLTORE: Yes, I hear Corbaccio
  Hath made your patron there his heir.
MOSCA: 'Tis true,
  By my device, drawn to it by my plot,
  With hope –
VOLTORE: Your patron should reciprocate?
  And you have promised?
MOSCA: For your good I did, sir.
  Nay, more, I told his son, brought, hid him here,
  Where he might hear his father pass the deed;
30 Being persuaded to it by this thought, sir:
  That the unnaturalness, first, of the act,
  And then his father's oft disclaiming in him
  (Which I did mean t' help on) would sure enrage him
  To do some violence upon his parent.
  On which the law should take sufficient hold,

And you be stated in a double hope.
Truth be my comfort, and my conscience,
My only aim was to dig you a fortune
Out of these two old, rotten sepulchres –
VOLTORE: I cry thee mercy, Mosca.
MOSCA: Worth your patience,   40
And your great merit, sir. And see the change!
VOLTORE: Why? what success?
MOSCA: Most hapless! you must help, sir,
Whilst we expected th' old raven, in comes
Corvino's wife, sent hither by her husband –
VOLTORE: What, with a present?
MOSCA: No, sir, on visitation;
(I'll tell you how anon) and staying long,
The youth he grows impatient, rushes forth,
Seizeth the lady, wounds me, makes her swear
(Or he would murder her, that was his vow)
T' affirm my patron to have done her rape,   50
Which how unlike it is, you see! and hence,
With that pretext, he's gone t' accuse his father,
Defame my patron, defeat you –
VOLTORE: Where's her husband?
Let him be sent for straight.
MOSCA: Sir, I'll go fetch him.
VOLTORE: Bring him to the *Scrutineo*.
MOSCA: Sir, I will.
VOLTORE: This must be stopped.
MOSCA: O, you do nobly, sir.
Alas, 'twas laboured all, sir, for your good;
Nor was there want of counsel in the plot.
But Fortune can, at any time, o'erthrow
The projects of a hundred learnèd clerks, sir.   60
CORBACCIO: What's that?
VOLTORE [*to* CORBACCIO]: Will 't please you, sir, to go along?
    [*Exeunt* CORBACCIO *and* VOLTORE.]
MOSCA: Patron, go in and pray for our success.
VOLPONE: Need makes devotion; heaven your labour bless!
    [*Exeunt*]

ACT FOUR

[SCENE ONE]

[*A street in Venice.*]

[*Enter* SIR POLITIC *and* PEREGRINE.]

[SIR POLITIC:] I told you, sir, it was a plot; you see
    What observation is! You mentioned me
    For some instructions: I will tell you, sir,
    Since we are met here in this height of Venice,
    Some few particulars I have set down
    Only for this meridian, fit to be known
    Of your crude traveller; and they are these.
    I will not touch, sir, at your phrase, or clothes,
    For they are old.
PEREGRINE: Sir, I have better.
SIR POLITIC: Pardon,
10   I meant as they are themes.
PEREGRINE: O, sir, proceed.
    I'll slander you no more of wit, good sir.
SIR POLITIC: First, for your garb, it must be grave and serious,
    Very reserved and locked; not tell a secret
    On any terms, not to your father; scarce
    A fable but with caution; make sure choice
    Both of your company and discourse; beware
    You never speak a truth –
PEREGRINE: How!
SIR POLITIC: Not to strangers,
    For those be they you must converse with most;
    Others I would not know, sir, but at distance,
20   So as I still might be a saver in 'em.
    You shall have tricks, else, passed upon you hourly.

    8. *phrase:* way of speaking. By '*your* phrase' Sir Politic means 'one's',
but Peregrine takes – or pretends to take – it personally.
    10. *themes:* general topics.   12. *garb:* appearance, bearing.
    20. *So as I still might be a saver in 'em:* obscure.

And then, for your religion, profess none,
But wonder at the diversity of all;
And, for your part, protest were there no other
But simply the laws o' th' land, you could content you.
Nick Machiavel and Monsieur Bodin both
Were of this mind. Then must you learn the use
And handling of your silver fork at meals,
The metal of your glass (these are main matters
With your Italian), and to know the hour   30
When you must eat your melons and your figs.
PEREGRINE: Is that a point of state too?
SIR POLITIC: Here it is.
For your Venetian, if he see a man
Preposterous in the least, he has him straight;
He has, he strips him. I'll acquaint you, sir.
I now have lived here 'tis some fourteen months;
Within the first week of my landing here,
All took me for a citizen of Venice,
I knew the forms so well –
PEREGRINE [aside]:   And nothing else.
SIR POLITIC: I had read Contarini, took me a house,   40
Dealt with my Jews to furnish it with movables –
Well, if I could but find one man, one man
To mine own heart, whom I durst trust, I would –
PEREGRINE: What, what, sir?
SIR POLITIC: Make him rich, make him a fortune:
He should not think again. I would command it.
PEREGRINE: As how?
SIR POLITIC: With certain projects that I have,
Which I may not discover.
PEREGRINE [aside]:   If I had
But one to wager with, I would lay odds, now,
He tells me instantly.
SIR POLITIC: One is (and that
I care not greatly who knows) to serve the state   50
Of Venice with red herrings for three years,

29. metal: material.   34. preposterous: unconventional.
46. projects: speculative enterprises.

And at a certain rate, from Rotterdam,
Where I have correspondence. There's a letter
Sent me from one o' th' States, and to that purpose;
He cannot write his name, but that's his mark.

PEREGRINE: He is a chandler?

SIR POLITIC: No, a cheesemonger.
There are some other too with whom I treat
About the same negotiation;
And I will undertake it: for 'tis thus

60   I'll do 't with ease, I've cast it all. Your hoy
Carries but three men in her, and a boy;
And she shall make me three returns a year.
So, if there come but one of three, I save;
If two, I can defalk. But this is now
If my main project fail.

PEREGRINE: Then you have others?

SIR POLITIC: I should be loath to draw the subtle air
Of such a place without my thousand aims.
I'll not dissemble, sir; where'er I come
I love to be considerative, and 'tis true

70   I have at my free hours thought upon
Some certain goods unto the state of Venice,
Which I do call my cautions; and, sir, which
I mean, in hope of pension, to propound
To the Great Council, then unto the Forty,
So to the Ten. My means are made already –

PEREGRINE: By whom?

SIR POLITIC: Sir, one that though his place be obscure,
Yet he can sway, and they will hear him. He's
A *commendatore*.

PEREGRINE: What, a common sergeant?

SIR POLITIC: Sir, such as they are put it in their mouths

80   What they should say, sometimes, as well as greater.
I think I have my notes to show you –

PEREGRINE: Good sir.

60. *hoy:* a kind of trading-boat.
64. *defalk:* cut or lop off (here, show a profit).
73. *pension:* i.e. for service to the State.

SIR POLITIC: But you shall swear unto me, on your gentry,
  Not to anticipate –
PEREGRINE: I, sir?
SIR POLITIC: Nor reveal
  A circumstance – My paper is not with me.
PEREGRINE: O, but you can remember, sir.
SIR POLITIC: My first is
  Concerning tinder-boxes. You must know
  No family is here without its box.
  Now, sir, it being so portable a thing,
  Put case that you or I were ill affected
  Unto the state; sir, with it in our pockets   *90*
  Might not I go into the Arsenal?
  Or you? Come out again? And none the wiser?
PEREGRINE: Except yourself, sir.
SIR POLITIC: Go to, then. I therefore
  Advertise to the state how fit it were
  That none but such as were known patriots,
  Sound lovers of their country, should be suffered
  T' enjoy them in their houses; and even those
  Sealed at some office, and at such a bigness
  As might not lurk in pockets.
PEREGRINE: Admirable!
SIR POLITIC: My next is, how t' inquire, and be resolved   *100*
  By present demonstration, whether a ship
  Newly arrivèd from Syria, or from
  Any suspected part of all the Levant,
  Be guilty of the plague. And where they use
  To lie out forty, fifty days, sometimes,
  About the *Lazaretto* for their trial,
  I'll save that charge and loss unto the merchant,
  And in an hour clear the doubt.
PEREGRINE: Indeed, sir!
SIR POLITIC: Or – I will lose my labour.
PEREGRINE: My faith, that's much.

89. *put case:* supposing.
97. *t' enjoy them:* to keep them (tinder-boxes).
106. *the Lazaretto:* a quarantine hospital.

110 SIR POLITIC: Nay, sir, conceive me. 'Twill cost me, in onions,
   Some thirty livres –
   PEREGRINE: Which is one pound sterling.
   SIR POLITIC: Beside my waterworks. For this I do, sir:
   First, I bring in your ship 'twixt two brick walls –
   But those the state shall venture. On the one
   I strain me a fair tarpaulin, and in that
   I stick my onions, cut in halves; the other
   Is full of loopholes, out at which I thrust
   The noses of my bellows; and those bellows
   I keep, with waterworks, in perpetual motion,
120 Which is the easiest matter of a hundred.
   Now, sir, your onion, which doth naturally
   Attract th' infection, and your bellows blowing
   The air upon him, will show instantly
   By his changed colour if there be contagion,
   Or else remain as fair as at the first.
   Now 'tis known, 'tis nothing.
   PEREGRINE: You are right, sir.
   SIR POLITIC: I would I had my note.
   PEREGRINE: Faith, so would I.
   But you ha' done well for once, sir.
   SIR POLITIC: Were I false,
   Or would be made so, I could show you reasons
130 How I could sell this state, now, to the Turk –
   Spite of their galleys, or their –
   PEREGRINE: Pray you, Sir Pol.
   SIR POLITIC: I have 'em not about me.
   PEREGRINE: That I feared.
   They're there, sir?
   SIR POLITIC: No, this is my diary,
   Wherein I note my actions of the day.
   PEREGRINE: Pray you let's see, sir. What is here? – 'Notandum,
   A rat had gnawn my spur leathers; notwithstanding,
   I put on new and did go forth; but first
   I threw three beans over the threshold. Item,
   I went and bought two toothpicks, whereof one

114. *venture:* put up the money for.

124

I burst, immediately, in a discourse   *140*
With a Dutch merchant 'bout *ragion del stato*.
From him I went and paid a *moccenigo*
For piecing my silk stockings; by the way
I cheapened sprats, and at St Mark's I urined.'
Faith, these are politic notes!

SIR POLITIC: Sir, I do slip
No action of my life, thus, but I quote it.

PEREGRINE: Believe me it is wise!

SIR POLITIC: Nay, sir, read forth.

[*Enter* LADY WOULD-BE, NANO, *and two* WOMEN.]   IV, ii
[LADY WOULD-BE:] Where should this loose knight be, trow?
    Sure, he's housed.

NANO: Why, then he's fast.

LADY WOULD-BE: Ay, he plays both with me.
    I pray you stay. This heat will do more harm
    To my complexion than his heart is worth.
    I do not care to hinder, but to take him.
    How it comes off! [*Rubbing her rouged cheeks.*]

1ST WOMAN: My master's yonder.

LADY WOULD-BE: Where?

2ND WOMAN: With a young gentleman.

LADY WOULD-BE: The same's the party!
    In man's apparel! Pray you, sir, jog my knight.
    I will be tender to his reputation,
    However he demerit.

SIR POLITIC: My lady!

PEREGRINE: Where?   *10*

SIR POLITIC: 'Tis she indeed; sir, you shall know her. She is,
    Were she not mine, a lady of that merit
    For fashion, and behaviour, and for beauty
    I durst compare –

---

141. *ragion del stato:* affairs of state.
142. *moccenigo:* a coin worth little.   144. *cheapened:* haggled over.
    7. *the party:* i.e. the 'cunning courtesan' Mosca told her of in III, v, 20.

PEREGRINE: It seems you are not jealous,
That dare commend her.

SIR POLITIC: Nay, and for discourse –

PEREGRINE: Being your wife, she cannot miss that.

SIR POLITIC: Madam,
Here is a gentleman; pray you, use him fairly;
He seems a youth, but he is –

LADY WOULD-BE: None?

SIR POLITIC: Yes, one
Has put his face as soon into the world –

20 LADY WOULD-BE: You mean, as early? But today?

SIR POLITIC: How's this?

LADY WOULD-BE: Why, in this habit, sir; you apprehend me!
Well, Master Would-be, this doth not become you.
I had thought the odour, sir, of your good name
Had been more precious to you; that you would not
Have done this dire massàcre on your honour,
One of your gravity, and rank besides!
But knights, I see, care little for the oath
They make to ladies, chiefly their own ladies.

SIR POLITIC: Now, by my spurs, the symbol of my knighthood –

30 PEREGRINE [aside]: Lord, how his brain is humbled for an oath!

SIR POLITIC: I reach you not.

LADY WOULD-BE: Right, sir, your policy
May bear it through thus. [To PEREGRINE] Sir, a word with you,
I would be loath to contest publicly
With any gentlewoman, or to seem
Froward, or violent; as The Courtier says
It comes too near rusticity in a lady,
Which I would shun by all means. And, however
I may deserve from Master Would-be, yet
T' have one fair gentlewoman, thus, be made
40 Th' unkind instrument to wrong another,
And one she knows not, ay, and to persèver,
In my poor judgement, is not warranted
From being a solecism in our sex,
If not in manners.

PEREGRINE: How is this!

SIR POLITIC: Sweet madam,
Come nearer to your aim.

LADY WOULD-BE: Marry, and will, sir.
Since you provoke me with your impudence
And laughter of your light land-siren here,
Your Sporus, your hermaphrodite –

PEREGRINE: What's here?
Poetic fury and historic storms!

SIR POLITIC: The gentleman, believe it, is of worth,   *50*
And of our nation.

LADY WOULD-BE: Ay, your Whitefriars nation!
Come, I blush for you, Master Would-be, ay;
And am ashamed you should ha' no more forehead
Than thus to be the patron, or St George,
To a lewd harlot, a base fricatrice,
A female devil in a male outside.

SIR POLITIC: Nay,
An' you be such a one, I must bid adieu
To your delights. The case appears too liquid.
    [*Exit.*]

LADY WOULD-BE: Ay, you may carry't clear, with your state-
face!
But for your carnival concupiscence,   *60*
Who here is fled for liberty of conscience,
From furious persecution of the marshal,
Her will I disc'ple.

PEREGRINE: This is fine, i' faith!
And do you use this often? Is this part
Of your wit's exercise, 'gainst you have occasion?
Madam –

LADY WOULD-BE: Go to sir.

PEREGRINE: Do you hear me, lady?
Why, if your knight have set you to beg shirts,
Or to invite me home, you might have done it
A nearer way by far.

LADY WOULD-BE: This cannot work you

47. *light land-siren:* irresponsible harlot.
64. *use this:* behave like this.

70 Out of my snare.

PEREGRINE: Why, am I in it, then?
Indeed, your husband told me you were fair,
And so you are; only your nose inclines –
That side that's next the sun – to the queen-apple.

LADY WOULD-BE: This cannot be endured by any patience!

IV, iii   [*Enter* MOSCA.]

[MOSCA:] What's the matter, madam?

LADY WOULD-BE: If the Senate
Right not my quest in this, I will protest 'em
To all the world no aristocracy.

MOSCA: What is the injury, lady?

LADY WOULD-BE: Why, the callet
You told me of, here I have ta'en disguised.

MOSCA: Who? This! What means your ladyship? The creature
I mentioned to you is apprehended, now
Before the Senate. You shall see her –

LADY WOULD-BE: Where?

MOSCA: I'll bring you to her. This young gentleman,
10 I saw him land this morning at the port.

LADY WOULD-BE: Is't possible? How has my judgement wan-
dered!
Sir, I must, blushing, say to you, I have erred;
And plead your pardon.

PEREGRINE: What, more changes yet?

LADY WOULD-BE: I hope y' ha' not the malice to remember
A gentlewoman's passion. If you stay
In Venice, here, please you to use me, sir –

MOSCA: Will you go, madam?

LADY WOULD-BE: Pray you, sir, use me. In faith,
The more you see me, the more I shall conceive
You have forgot our quarrel.

73. *the queen-apple:* Peregrine is saying one side of her nose is red.
  2. *quest:* claim.   4. *callet:* prostitute.
  16. *use me:* let me be of service to you socially; but Lady Would-be is
being too inviting, as 'conceive' suggests.

[*Exeunt* LADY WOULD-BE, MOSCA, NANO, *and* WOMEN.]
PEREGRINE: This is rare!
  Sir Politic Would-be? No, Sir Politic Bawd,   20
  To bring me, thus, acquainted with his wife!
  Well, wise Sir Pol, since you have practised thus
  Upon my freshmanship, I'll try your salt-head,
  What proof it is against a counter-plot.
    [*Exit.*]

[SCENE TWO]   IV, iv

[*The Scrutineo, or Senate House.*]

[*Enter* VOLTORE, CORBACCIO, CORVINO, *and* MOSCA.]
[VOLTORE:] Well, now you know the carriage of the business,
  Your constancy is all that is required,
  Unto the safety of it.
MOSCA: Is the lie
  Safely conveyed amongst us? Is that sure?
  Knows every man his burden?
CORVINO: Yes.
MOSCA: Then shrink not.
CORVINO [*aside to* MOSCA]: But knows the Advocate the truth?
MOSCA: O sir,
  By no means. I devised a formal tale
  That salved your reputation. But be valiant, sir.
CORVINO: I fear no one but him, that this his pleading
  Should make him stand for a co-heir –
MOSCA: Co-halter!   10
  Hang him, we will but use his tongue, his noise,
  As we do Croaker's here. [*Indicating* CORBACCIO.]
CORVINO: Ay, what shall he do?
MOSCA: When we ha' done, you mean?

23. *freshmanship:* inexperience.
  1. *carriage of the business:* way to tackle the business.
  5. *burden:* refrain in a song – i.e. something memorized, in this case 'his lines'.

129

CORVINO: Yes.

MOSCA: Why, we'll think:
Sell him for mummia, he's half dust already.
    (*To* VOLTORE.)
Do not you smile to see this buffalo,
How he doth sport it with his head? – I should,
If all were well and past. (*To* CORBACCIO) Sir, only you
Are he that shall enjoy the crop of all,
And these not know for whom they toil.

CORBACCIO: Ay, peace.

20 MOSCA (*To* CORVINO): But you shall eat it. – Much! –
    (*To* VOLTORE *again*)   Worshipful sir,
Mercury sit upon your thund'ring tongue,
Or the French Hercules, and make your language
As conquering as his club, to beat along,
As with a tempest, flat, our adversaries;
But much more yours, sir.

VOLTORE: Here they come, ha' done.

MOSCA: I have another witness if you need, sir,
I can produce.

VOLTORE: Who is it?

MOSCA: Sir, I have her.

IV, v   [*Enter Four* AVOCATORI, BONARIO, CELIA, NOTARIO,
        COMMENDATORI, *and others*.]

[1ST AVOCATORE:] The like of this the Senate never heard of.

2ND AVOCATORE: 'Twill come most strange to them when we
    report it.

4TH AVOCATORE: The gentlewoman has been ever held
Of unreprovèd name.

3RD AVOCATORE: So the young man.

4TH AVOCATORE: The more unnatural part that of his father.

2ND AVOCATORE: More of the husband.

1ST AVOCATORE: I not know to give

14. *mummia:* substance made from Egyptian mummies, or from corpses,
and used as a drug.
15. *this buffalo:* Corvino, with his cuckold's horns.

His act a name, it is so monstrous!

4TH AVOCATORE: But the impostor, he is a thing created
T' exceed example.

1ST AVOCATORE: And all after-times!

2ND AVOCATORE: I never heard a true voluptuary   10
Described but him.

3RD AVOCATORE: Appear yet those were cited?

NOTARIO: All but the old magnifico, Volpone.

1ST AVOCATORE: Why is not he here?

MOSCA: Please your fatherhoods,
Here is his advocate. Himself's so weak,
So feeble –

4TH AVOCATORE: What are you?

BONARIO: His parasite,
His knave, his pander! I beseech the court
He may be forced to come, that your grave eyes
May bear strong witness of his strange impostures.

VOLTORE: Upon my faith and credit with your virtues,
He is not able to endure the air.   20

2ND AVOCATORE: Bring him, however.

3RD AVOCATORE: We will see him.

4TH AVOCATORE: Fetch him.
    [*Exeunt* OFFICERS.]

VOLTORE: Your fatherhoods' fit pleasures be obeyed,
But sure the sight will rather move your pities
Than indignation. May it please the court,
In the meantime he may be heard in me!
I know this place most void of prejudice,
And therefore crave it, since we have no reason
To fear our truth should hurt our cause.

3RD AVOCATORE: Speak free.

VOLTORE: Then know, most honoured fathers, I must now
Discover to your strangely abusèd ears   30
The most prodigious and most frontless piece
Of solid impudence, and treachery,
That ever vicious nature yet brought forth
To shame the state of Venice. This lewd woman,

9. *example*: precedent.   31. *frontless*: shameless.

131

[*Indicating* CELIA.]
That wants no artificial looks or tears
To help the visor she has now put on,
Hath long been known a close adulteress
To that lascivious youth, there;
    [*Indicating* BONARIO.]
                                not suspected,
I say, but known, and taken, in the act,
40   With him; and by this man, the easy husband,
    [*Indicating* CORVINO.]
Pardoned; whose timeless bounty makes him now
Stand here, the most unhappy, innocent person
That ever man's own goodness made accused.
For these, not knowing how to owe a gift
Of that dear grace but with their shame, being placed
So above all powers of their gratitude,
Began to hate the benefit, and in place
Of thanks, devise t' extirp the memory
Of such an act. Wherein, I pray your fatherhoods
50   To observe the malice, yea, the rage of creatures
Discovered in their evils; and what heart
Such take, even from their crimes. But that anon
Will more appear. This gentleman, the father,
    [*Indicating* CORBACCIO.]
Hearing of this foul fact, with many others,
Which daily struck at his too tender ears,
And grieved in nothing more than that he could not
Preserve himself a parent (his son's ills
Growing to that strange flood) at last decreed
To disinherit him.
  1ST AVOCATORE: These be strange turns!
60 2ND AVOCATORE: The young man's fame was ever fair and honest.
  VOLTORE: So much more full of danger is his vice,
That can beguile so under shade of virtue.
But as I said, my honoured sires, his father
Having this settled purpose (by what means
To him betrayed, we know not) and this day

48. *extirp:* wipe out.

Appointed for the deed, that parricide,
(I cannot style him better) by confederacy
Preparing this his paramour to be there,
Entered Volpone's house – who was the man,
Your fatherhoods must understand, designed   70
For the inheritance – there sought his father.
But with what purpose sought he him, my lords?
I tremble to pronounce it, that a son
Unto a father, and to such a father,
Should have so foul, felonious intent:
It was to murder him! When, being prevented
By his more happy absence, what then did he?
Not check his wicked thoughts? No, now new deeds!
(Mischief doth ever end where it begins)
An act of horror, fathers! He dragged forth   80
The agèd gentleman, that had there lain bed-rid
Three years and more, out off his innocent couch,
Naked upon the floor, there left him; wounded
His servant in the face; and, with this strumpet,
The stale to his forged practice, who was glad
To be so active (I shall here desire
Your fatherhoods to note but my collections
As most remarkable) thought at once to stop
His father's ends, discredit his free choice
In the old gentleman, redeem themselves   90
By laying infamy upon this man,
To whom, with blushing, they should owe their lives.

1ST AVOCATORE: What proofs have you of this?

BONARIO: Most honoured fathers,
I humbly crave there be no credit given
To this man's mercenary tongue.

2ND AVOCATORE: Forbear.

BONARIO: His soul moves in his fee.

3RD AVOCATORE: O, sir!

BONARIO: This fellow,
For six sols more would plead against his Maker.

1ST AVOCATORE: You do forget yourself.

85. *stale:* decoy; *forged practice:* contrived plot.   97. *sols:* coins.

133

VOLTORE: Nay, nay, grave fathers,
Let him have scope. Can any man imagine
100 That he will spare 's accuser, that would not
Have spared his parent?
1ST AVOCATORE: Well, produce your proofs.
CELIA: I would I could forget I were a creature!
VOLTORE: Signor Corbaccio!
4TH AVOCATORE: What is he?
VOLTORE: The father.
2ND AVOCATORE: Has he had an oath?
NOTARIO: Yes.
CORBACCIO: What must I do now?
NOTARIO: Your testimony's craved.
CORBACCIO [not hearing]:   Speak to the knave?
I'll ha' my mouth first stopped with earth. My heart
Abhors his knowledge. I disclaim in him.
1ST AVOCATORE: But for what cause?
CORBACCIO: The mere portent of nature.
He is an utter stranger to my loins.
110 BONARIO: Have they made you to this?
CORBACCIO: I will not hear thee,
Monster of men, swine, goat, wolf, parricide!
Speak not, thou viper.
BONARIO: Sir, I will sit down,
And rather wish my innocence should suffer,
Than I resist the authority of a father.
VOLTORE: Signor Corvino!
2ND AVOCATORE: This is strange.
1ST AVOCATORE: Who's this?
NOTARIO: The husband.
4TH AVOCATORE: Is he sworn?
NOTARIO: He is.
3RD AVOCATORE: Speak, then.
CORVINO: This woman, please your fatherhoods, is a whore
Of most hot exercise, more than a partridge,
Upon recòrd –

108. *mere portent of nature:* utter monster.
118. *partridge:* widely regarded as a lecherous bird.

IST AVOCATORE: No more.

CORVINO: Neighs like a jennet.

NOTARIO: Preserve the honour of the court.

CORVINO: I shall, 120
And modesty of your most reverend ears.
And, yet, I hope that I may say these eyes
Have seen her glued unto that piece of cedar,
That fine, well-timbered gallant; and that here
[Indicating his brow.]
The letters may be read, thorough the horn,
That make the story perfect.

MOSCA: Excellent, sir.

CORVINO [to MOSCA]: There is no shame in this now, is there?

MOSCA: None.

CORVINO: Or if I said I hoped that she were onward
To her damnation, if there be a hell
Greater than whore and woman; a good Catholic 130
May make the doubt.

3RD AVOCATORE: His grief hath made him frantic.

IST AVOCATORE: Remove him hence.

She [CELIA] swoons.

2ND AVOCATORE: Look to the woman!

CORVINO: Rare!
Prettily feigned! Again!

4TH AVOCATORE: Stand from about her.

IST AVOCATORE: Give her the air.

3RD AVOCATORE [to MOSCA]: What can you say?

MOSCA: My wound,
May 't please your wisdoms, speaks for me, received
In aid of my good patron, when he missed
His sought-for father, when that well-taught dame
Had her cue given her to cry out a rape.

BONARIO: O most laid impudence! Fathers –

3RD AVOCATORE: Sir, be silent,
You had your hearing free, so must they theirs. 140

2ND AVOCATORE: I do begin to doubt th' imposture here.

4TH AVOCATORE: This woman has too many moods.

119. *jennet:* high-spirited horse.

VOLTORE: Grave fathers,
She is a creature of a most professed
And prostituted lewdness.

CORVINO: Most impetuous,
Unsatisfied, grave fathers!

VOLTORE: May her feignings
Not take your wisdoms; but this day she baited
A stranger, a grave knight, with her loose eyes
And more lascivious kisses. This man saw 'em
Together on the water in a gondola.

150 **MOSCA:** Here is the lady herself that saw 'em too,
Without; who, then, had in the open streets
Pursued them, but for saving her knight's honour.

1ST AVOCATORE: Produce that lady.

[*Exit* MOSCA.]

2ND AVOCATORE: Let her come.

4TH AVOCATORE: These things,
They strike with wonder!

3RD AVOCATORE: I am turned a stone!

IV, vi [*Re-enter* MOSCA *with* LADY WOULD-BE.]
[MOSCA:] Be resolute, madam.

LADY WOULD-BE [*pointing to* CELIA]: Ay, this same is she.
Out, thou chameleon harlot! Now thine eyes
Vie tears with the hyena. Dar'st thou look
Upon my wrongèd face? – I cry your pardons.
I fear I have forgettingly transgressed
Against the dignity of the court –

2ND AVOCATORE: No, madam.

LADY WOULD-BE: And been exorbitant –

4TH AVOCATORE: You have not, lady.
These proofs are strong.

LADY WOULD-BE: Surely, I had no purpose
To scandalize your honours, or my sex's.

3RD AVOCATORE: We do believe it.

3. *hyena*: regarded as a treacherous, deceitful beast. Hyena's tears would
be like crocodile's tears.

LADY WOULD-BE: Surely, you may believe it.   *10*
2ND AVOCATORE: Madam, we do.
LADY WOULD-BE: Indeed, you may; my breeding
Is not so coarse –
4TH AVOCATORE: We know it.
LADY WOULD-BE: To offend
With pertinacy –
3RD AVOCATORE: Lady –
LADY WOULD-BE: Such a presence.
No, surely.
1ST AVOCATORE: We well think it.
LADY WOULD-BE: You may think it.
1ST AVOCATORE: Let her o'ercome. [*To* BONARIO] What wit-
nesses have you
To make good your report?
BONARIO: Our consciences.
CELIA: And heaven, that never fails the innocent.
4TH AVOCATORE: These are no testimonies.
BONARIO: Not in your courts,
Where multitude and clamour overcomes.
1ST AVOCATORE: Nay, then you do wax insolent.

    VOLPONE *is brought in, as impotent.*

VOLTORE: Here, here,   *20*
The testimony comes that will convince,
And put to utter dumbness their bold tongues.
See here, grave fathers, here's the ravisher,
The rider on men's wives, the great impostor,
The grand voluptuary! Do you not think
These limbs should affect venery? Or these eyes
Covet a concubine? Pray you, mark these hands.
Are they not fit to stroke a lady's breasts?
Perhaps he doth dissemble!
BONARIO: So he does.
VOLTORE: Would you ha' him tortured?
BONARIO: I would have him proved.   *30*
VOLTORE: Best try him, then, with goads, or burning irons;
Put him to the strappado. I have heard

13. *pertinacy:* evidently a malapropism.   32. *strappado:* a form of torture.

137

The rack hath cured the gout. Faith, give it him
And help him of a malady; be courteous.
I'll undertake, before these honoured fathers,
He shall have yet as many left diseases
As she has known adulterers, or thou strumpets.
O my most equal hearers, if these deeds,
Acts of this bold and most exorbitant strain,
40 May pass with sufferance, what one citizen
But owes the forfeit of his life, yea, fame,
To him that dares traduce him? Which of you
Are safe, my honoured fathers? I would ask,
With leave of your grave fatherhoods, if their plot
Have any face or colour like to truth?
Or if, unto the dullest nostril here,
It smell not rank and most abhorrèd slander?
I crave your care of this good gentleman,
Whose life is much endangered by their fable;
50 And as for them, I will conclude with this:
That vicious persons, when they are hot and fleshed
In impious acts, their constancy abounds:
Damned deeds are done with greatest confidence.

1ST AVOCATORE: Take 'em to custody, and sever them.

[CELIA and BONARIO are led away.]

2ND AVOCATORE: 'Tis pity two such prodigies should live.

1ST AVOCATORE: Let the old gentleman be returned with
care.

I'm sorry our credulity wronged him.

[VOLPONE is carried out.]

4TH AVOCATORE: These are two creatures!

3RD AVOCATORE: I have an earthquake in me!

2ND AVOCATORE: Their shame, even in their cradles, fled their
faces.

60 4TH AVOCATORE [to VOLTORE]: You've done a worthy service
to the state, sir,
In their discovery.

1ST AVOCATORE: You shall hear ere night

45. *face or colour like to truth*: appearance of truth.
51. *fleshed*: hardened.   55. *prodigies*: monsters, 'holy terrors'.

138

What punishment the court decrees upon 'em.

VOLTORE: We thank your fatherhoods. –

   [*Exeunt* AVOCATORI, NOTARIO, *and others.*]

                               How like you it?

MOSCA: Rare.

I'd ha' your tongue, sir, tipped with gold for this;

I'd ha' you be the heir to the whole city;

The earth I'd have want men, ere you want living.

They're bound to erect your statue in St Mark's.

Signor Corvino, I would have you go

And show yourself, that you have conquered.

CORVINO: Yes.

MOSCA: It was much better than you should profess   *70*

Yourself a cuckold, thus, than that the other

Should have been proved.

CORVINO: Nay, I considered that.

Now, it is her fault.

MOSCA: Then, it had been yours.

CORVINO: True. I do doubt this advocate still.

MOSCA: I' faith,

You need not; I dare ease you of that care.

CORVINO: I trust thee, Mosca.

MOSCA: As your own soul, sir.

   [*Exit* CORVINO.]

CORBACCIO: Mosca!

MOSCA: Now for your business, sir.

CORBACCIO: How! Ha' you business?

MOSCA: Yes, yours, sir.

CORBACCIO: O, none else?

MOSCA: None else, not I.

CORBACCIO: Be careful then.

MOSCA: Rest you with both your eyes, sir.

CORBACCIO: Dispatch it.

MOSCA: Instantly.

CORBACCIO: And look that all   *80*

     66. *living:* means of livelihood.

     71. *the other:* i.e. your prostitution of Celia to Volpone.

     74. *doubt this advocate:* mistrust Voltore.

Whatever be put in: jewels, plate, moneys,
Household-stuff, bedding, curtains.
MOSCA: Curtain-rings, sir;
Only the advocate's fee must be deducted.
CORBACCIO: I'll pay him now; you'll be too prodigal.
MOSCA: Sir, I must tender it.
CORBACCIO: Two chequins is well?
MOSCA: No, six, sir.
CORBACCIO: 'Tis too much.
MOSCA: He talked a great while,
You must consider that, sir.
CORBACCIO: Well, there's three –
MOSCA: I'll give it him.
CORBACCIO: Do so, and there's for thee.
    [*Exit.*]
MOSCA [*aside*]: Bountiful bones! What horrid, strange offence
90 Did he commit 'gainst nature in his youth,
Worthy this age? [*To* VOLTORE] You see, sir, how I work
Unto your ends; take you no notice.
VOLTORE: No,
I'll leave you.
    [*Exit* VOLTORE.]
MOSCA: All is yours – the devil and all,
Good advocate! – [*To* LADY WOULD-BE] Madam, I'll bring
you home.
LADY WOULD-BE: No, I'll go see your patron.
MOSCA: That you shall not.
I'll tell you why: my purpose is to urge
My patron to reform his will, and for
The zeal you've shown today, whereas before
You were but third or fourth, you shall be now
100 Put in the first; which would appear as begged
If you were present. Therefore –
LADY WOULD-BE: You shall sway me.
    [*Exeunt.*]

81. *put in:* entered in the inventory.   89. *Bountiful bones:* Note.
91. *worthy this age:* so that he deserves to be like this in his old age.
97. *reform:* revise.

ACT FIVE

[VOLPONE's *house.*]

[*Enter* VOLPONE.]

[VOLPONE:] Well, I am here, and all this brunt is past.
I ne'er was in dislike with my disguise
Till this fled moment. Here, 'twas good, in private,
But in your public – *Cavè*, whilst I breathe.
'Fore God, my left leg 'gan to have the cramp,
And I apprehended, straight, some power had struck me
With a dead palsy. Well, I must be merry
And shake it off. A many of these fears
Would put me into some villainous disease
Should they come thick upon me. I'll prevent 'em.　　　　10
Give me a bowl of lusty wine to fright
This humour from my heart. Hum, hum, hum!
　He drinks.
'Tis almost gone already; I shall conquer.
Any device, now, of rare, ingenious knavery
That would possess me with a violent laughter,
Would make me up again. So, so, so, so.
　Drinks again.
This heat is life; 'tis blood by this time! Mosca!

[*Enter* MOSCA.]　　　　　　　　　　　　　V, ii

[MOSCA:] How now, sir? Does the day look clear again?
Are we recovered? and wrought out of error
Into our way, to see our path before us?
Is our trade free once more?

　　　1. *brunt:* confusion.
　　　3. *this fled moment:* the time immediately preceding this.
　　　4. *Cavè:* Beware.
　　16. *make me up again:* put me in my old spirits.
　　　4. *our trade:* i.e. legacy-hunting.

VOLPONE: Exquisite Mosca!

MOSCA: Was it not carried learnedly?

VOLPONE: And stoutly.
Good wits are greatest in extremities.

MOSCA: It were a folly beyond thought to trust
Any grand act unto a cowardly spirit.
You are not taken with it enough, methinks?

10 VOLPONE: O, more than if I had enjoyed the wench.
The pleasure of all womankind's not like it.

MOSCA: Why, now you speak, sir! We must here be fixed;
Here we must rest. This is our masterpiece;
We cannot think to go beyond this.

VOLPONE: True,
Th'ast played thy prize, my precious Mosca.

MOSCA: Nay, sir,
To gull the court –

VOLPONE: And quite divert the torrent
Upon the innocent.

MOSCA: Yes, and to make
So rare a music out of discords –

VOLPONE: Right.
That yet to me 's the strangest; how th'ast borne it!

20 That these, being so divided 'mongst themselves,
Should not scent somewhat, or in me or thee,
Or doubt their own side.

MOSCA: True, they will not see't.
Too much light blinds 'em, I think. Each of 'em
Is so possessed and stuffed with his own hopes
That anything unto the contrary,
Never so true, or never so apparent,
Never so palpable, they will resist it –

VOLPONE: Like a temptation of the devil.

MOSCA: Right, sir.
Merchants may talk of trade, and your great signiors

30 Of land that yields well; but if Italy
Have any glebe more fruitful than these fellows,
I am deceived. Did not your advocate rare?

32. *rare:* rarely, i.e. 'Did not your advocate plead exceptionally well?'

VOLPONE: O – 'My most honoured fathers, my grave
    fathers,
    Under correction of your fatherhoods,
    What face of truth is here? If these strange deeds
    May pass, most honoured fathers' – I had much ado
    To forbear laughing.

MOSCA: 'T seemed to me you sweat, sir.

VOLPONE: In troth, I did a little.

MOSCA: But confess, sir;
    Were you not daunted?

VOLPONE: In good faith, I was
    A little in a mist, but not dejected;
    Never but still myself.   *40*

MOSCA: I think it, sir.
    Now, so truth help me, I must needs say this, sir,
    And out of conscience for your advocate:
    He's taken pains, in faith, sir, and deserved,
    In my poor judgement, I speak it under favour,
    Not to contrary you, sir, very richly –
    Well – to be cozened.

VOLPONE: Troth, and I think so too,
    By that I heard him in the latter end.

MOSCA: O, but before, sir, had you heard him first
    Draw it to certain heads, then aggravate,   *50*
    Then use his vehement figures – I looked still
    When he would shift a shirt; and doing this
    Out of pure love, no hope of gain –

VOLPONE: 'Tis right.
    I cannot answer him, Mosca, as I would,
    Not yet; but for thy sake, at thy entreaty,
    I will begin e'en now to vex 'em all,
    This very instant.

MOSCA: Good, sir.

46. *contrary:* contradict.

50. *Draw it to certain heads:* arrange his subject-matter under headings.

51. *vehement figures:* emphatic figures of speech.

52. *shift a shirt:* change his shirt (i.e. Voltore gesticulated like a man changing his shirt; or possibly, sweated so much as to require a fresh shirt).

VOLPONE: Call the dwarf
And eunuch forth.

MOSCA: Castrone! Nano!

[*Enter* CASTRONE *and* NANO.]

NANO: Here.

VOLPONE: Shall we have a jig now?

MOSCA: What you please, sir.

VOLPONE: Go,
60 Straight give out about the streets, you two,
That I am dead; do it with constancy,
Sadly, do you hear? Impute it to the grief
Of this late slander.

[*Exeunt* CASTRONE *and* NANO.]

MOSCA: What do you mean, sir?

VOLPONE: O,
I shall have instantly my vulture, crow,
Raven, come flying hither on the news
To peck for carrion, my she-wolf and all,
Greedy and full of expectation –

MOSCA: And then to have it ravished from their mouths?

VOLPONE: 'Tis true. I will ha' thee put on a gown,
70 And take upon thee as thou wert mine heir;
Show 'em a will. Open that chest and reach
Forth one of those that has the blanks. I'll straight
Put in thy name.

MOSCA: It will be rare, sir.

VOLPONE: Ay,
When they e'en gape, and find themselves deluded –

MOSCA: Yes.

VOLPONE: And thou use them scurvily! Dispatch,
Get on thy gown.

MOSCA: But what, sir, if they ask
After the body?

VOLPONE: Say it was corrupted.

MOSCA: I'll say it stunk, sir; and was fain t' have it
Coffined up instantly and sent away.

80 VOLPONE: Anything, what thou wilt. Hold, here's my will.

70. *take upon thee*: act in such a way.

144

Get thee a cap, a count-book, pen and ink,
Papers afore thee; sit as thou wert taking
An inventory of parcels. I'll get up
Behind the curtain, on a stool, and hearken;
Sometime peep over, see how they do look,
With what degrees their blood doth leave their faces.
O, 'twill afford me a rare meal of laughter!

MOSCA: Your advocate will turn stark dull upon it.

VOLPONE: It will take off his oratory's edge.

MOSCA But your *clarissimo*, old round-back, he   90
Will crump you like a hog-louse with the touch.

VOLPONE: And what Corvino?

MOSCA: O sir, look for him
Tomorrow morning with a rope and dagger
To visit all the streets; he must run mad.
My lady too, that came into the court
To bear false witness for your worship –

VOLPONE: Yes,
And kissed me 'fore the fathers, when my face
Flowed all with oils –

MOSCA: And sweat, sir. Why, your gold
Is such another med'cine, it dries up
All those offensive savours! It transforms   100
The most deformèd, and restores 'em lovely
As 'twere the strange poetical girdle. Jove   *Cestus.*
Could not invent t' himself a shroud more subtle
To pass Acrisius' guards. It is the thing
Makes all the world her grace, her youth, her beauty.

VOLPONE: I think she loves me.

MOSCA: Who? The lady, sir?
She's jealous of you.

VOLPONE: Dost thou say so?
    [*Knocking without.*]

88. *dull*: foolish, insensible.

90. *clarissimo*: Venetian nobleman (i.e. Corbaccio).

91. *crump you like a hog-louse with the touch*: curl up like a louse when
it is touched.

93. *rope and dagger*: Note.

MOSCA: Hark,
There's some already.
VOLPONE: Look!
MOSCA [*looking out*]: It is the vulture;
He has the quickest scent.
VOLPONE: I'll to my place,
110 Thou to thy posture.
MOSCA: I am set.
VOLPONE: But Mosca,
Play the artificer now, torture 'em rarely.
[VOLPONE *hides*.]

V, iii [*Enter* VOLTORE.]
[VOLTORE:] How now, my Mosca?
MOSCA [*writing*]: Turkey carpets, nine –
VOLTORE: Taking an inventory? That is well.
MOSCA: Two suits of bedding, tissue –
VOLTORE: Where's the will?
Let me read that the while.
[*Enter servants, carrying* CORBACCIO *in a chair*.]
CORBACCIO: So, set me down,
And get you home.
[*Exeunt servants*.]
VOLTORE: Is he come now, to trouble us?
MOSCA: Of cloth of gold, two more –
CORBACCIO: Is it done, Mosca?
MOSCA: Of several velvets, eight –
VOLTORE: I like his care.
CORBACCIO: Dost thou not hear?
[*Enter* CORVINO.]
CORVINO: Ha! Is the hour come, Mosca?
VOLPONE [*aside*]: Ay, now they muster!
Volpone peeps from behind a traverse.
CORVINO: What does the advocate here,

111. *artificer*: skilled craftsman (i.e. at teasing the legacy-hunters).
7. *velvets*: velvet curtains, or bales of velvet.
9. *traverse*: a curtain, or a screen made of fabric.

Or this Corbaccio?

CORBACCIO: What do these here?

[*Enter* LADY WOULD-BE.]

LADY WOULD-BE: Mosca! 10
Is his thread spun?

MOSCA: Eight chests of linen –

VOLPONE [*aside*]: O,
My fine Dame Would-be, too!

CORVINO: Mosca, the will,
That I may show it these and rid 'em hence.

MOSCA: Six chests of diaper, four of damask – There.
[*He gives them the will and continues writing.*]

CORBACCIO: Is that the will?

MOSCA: Down-beds, and bolsters –

VOLPONE [*aside*]: Rare!
Be busy still. Now they begin to flutter;
They never think of me. Look, see, see, see!
How their swift eyes run over the long deed
Unto the name, and to the legacies,
What is bequeathed them there.

MOSCA: Ten suits of hangings – 20

VOLPONE [*aside*]: Ay, i' their garters, Mosca. Now their hopes
Are at the gasp.

VOLTORE: Mosca the heir!

CORBACCIO: What's that?

VOLPONE [*aside*]: My advocate is dumb; look to my merchant.
He has heard of some strange storm, a ship is lost,
He faints; my lady will swoon. Old glazen-eyes
He hath not reached his despair, yet.

CORBACCIO: All these
Are out of hope; I'm sure the man.

CORVINO: But, Mosca –

MOSCA: Two cabinets –

CORVINO: Is this in earnest?

11. *Is his thread spun?*: euphemism for 'Is he dead?', referring to the
three Fates who spun, measured, and then cut the thread of a man's life.
21. *i' their garters*: a pun on 'hanging'.
25. *Old glazen-eyes*: a reference to Corbaccio's spectacles.

MOSCA: One
Of ebony –
CORVINO: Or do you but delude me?
30 MOSCA: The other, mother of pearl – I am very busy.
Good faith, it is a fortune thrown upon me –
Item, one salt of agate – not my seeking.
LADY WOULD-BE: Do you hear, sir?
MOSCA: A perfumed box – pray you forbear,
You see I'm troubled – made of an onyx –
LADY WOULD-BE: How?
MOSCA: Tomorrow, or next day, I shall be at leisure
To talk with you all.
CORVINO: Is this my large hope's issue?
LADY WOULD-BE: Sir, I must have a fairer answer.
MOSCA: Madam!
Marry, and shall: pray you, fairly quit my house.
Nay, raise no tempest with your looks; but hark you,
40 Remember what your ladyship offered me
To put you in an heir; go to, think on 't.
And what you said e'en your best madams did
For maintenance, and why not you? Enough.
Go home and use the poor Sir Pol, your knight, well,
For fear I tell some riddles. Go, be melancholic.
     [Exit LADY WOULD-BE.]
VOLPONE [aside]: O my fine devil!
CORVINO: Mosca, pray you a word.
MOSCA: Lord! Will not you take your dispatch hence yet?
Methinks of all you should have been th' example.
Why should you stay here? With what thought? What promise?
50 Hear you: do not you know I know you an ass,
And that you would most fain have been a wittol
If fortune would have let you? That you are
A declared cuckold, on good terms? This pearl,
You'll say, was yours? Right. This diamond?
I'll not deny't, but thank you. Much here else?
It may be so. Why, think that these good works
May help to hide your bad. I'll not betray you,

32. *salt*: salt-cellar.   51. *wittol*: complaisant cuckold.

148

Although you be but extraordinary,
And have it only in title, it sufficeth.
Go home, be melancholic too, or mad.   60

    [*Exit* CORVINO.]

VOLPONE [*aside*]: Rare, Mosca! How his villainy becomes him!
VOLTORE: Certain he doth delude all these for me.
CORBACCIO: Mosca the heir?
VOLPONE [*aside*]:   O, his four eyes have found it!
CORBACCIO. I'm cozened, cheated, by a parasite slave!
Harlot, th'ast gulled me.
MOSCA: Yes, sir. Stop your mouth,
Or I shall draw the only tooth is left.
Are not you he, that filthy, covetous wretch
With the three legs, that here, in hope of prey,
Have, any time this three year, snuffed about
With your most grov'ling nose, and would have hired   70
Me to the pois'ning of my patron, sir?
Are not you he that have, today, in court,
Professed the disinheriting of your son?
Perjured yourself? Go home, and die, and stink.
If you but croak a syllable, all comes out.
Away, and call your porters! Go, go stink.

    [*Exit* CORBACCIO.]

VOLPONE [*aside*]: Excellent varlet!
VOLTORE: Now, my faithful Mosca,
I find thy constancy –
MOSCA: Sir?
VOLTORE: Sincere.
MOSCA [*writing again*]:   A table
Of porphyry – I mar'l you'll be thus troublesome.
VOLTORE: Nay, leave off now, they are gone.
MOSCA: Why, who are you? 80
What, who did send for you? O, cry you mercy,
Reverend sir! Good faith, I am grieved for you,

58–59. *extraordinary*: i.e. Corvino isn't really a cuckold, because Celia only appears to be adulterous.
  63. *his four eyes*: another reference to Corbaccio's spectacles.
  68. *the three legs*: a reference to Corbaccio's walking-stick.

That any chance of mine should thus defeat
Your (I must needs say) most deserving travails.
But I protest, sir, it was cast upon me,
And I could, almost, wish to be without it,
But that the will o' th' dead must be observed.
Marry, my joy is that you need it not;
You have a gift, sir (thank your education)
90 Will never let you want while there are men
And malice to breed causes. Would I had
But half the like, for all my fortune, sir.
If I have any suits – as I do hope,
Things being so easy and direct, I shall not –
I will make bold with your obstreperous aid;
Conceive me, for your fee, sir. In meantime,
You that have so much law, I know ha' the conscience
Not to be covetous of what is mine.
Good sir, I thank you for my plate; 'twill help
100 To set up a young man. Good faith, you look
As you were costive; best go home and purge, sir.
    [*Exit* VOLTORE.]
VOLPONE: Bid him eat lettuce well! My witty mischief,
    [*Coming from behind the curtains.*]
Let me embrace thee. O that I could now
Transform thee to a Venus – Mosca, go,
Straight take my habit of *clarissimo*,
And walk the streets; be seen, torment 'em more.
We must pursue as well as plot. Who would
Have lost this feast?
MOSCA: I doubt it will lose them.
VOLPONE: O, my recovery shall recover all.
110 That I could now but think on some disguies
To meet 'em in, and ask 'em questions.
How I would vex 'em still at every turn!
MOSCA: Sir, I can fit you.
VOLPONE: Canst thou?
MOSCA: Yes, I know

102. *lettuce*: thought to be a laxative.
105. *habit of clarissimo*: nobleman's robe.

One o' th' *commendatori*, sir, so like you;
Him will I straight make drunk, and bring you his habit.
VOLPONE: A rare disguise, and answering thy brain!
O, I will be a sharp disease unto 'em.
MOSCA: Sir, you must look for curses –
VOLPONE: Till they burst;
The Fox fares ever best when he is cursed.
    [*Exeunt.*]

[SCENE TWO]   V, iv

[SIR POLITIC's *lodging.*]

[*Enter* PEREGRINE, *disguised, and three* MERCHANTS.]
[PEREGRINE:] Am I enough disguised?
1ST MERCHANT: I warrant you.
PEREGRINE: All my ambition is to fright him only.
2ND MERCHANT: If you could ship him away, 'twere excellent.
3RD MERCHANT: To Zant, or to Aleppo?
PEREGRINE: Yes, and ha' his
Adventures put i' th' Book of Voyages,
And his gulled story registered for truth?
Well, gentlemen, when I am in a while,
And that you think us warm in our discourse,
Know your approaches.
1ST MERCHANT: Trust it to our care.
    [*Exeunt* MERCHANTS.]
    [*Enter* WOMAN.]
PEREGRINE: Save you, fair lady. Is Sir Pol within?
WOMAN: I do not know, sir.   10
PEREGRINE: Pray you say unto him,
Here is a merchant, upon earnest business,
Desires to speak with him.
WOMAN: I will see, sir.
PEREGRINE: Pray you.
    [*Exit* WOMAN.]

114. *commendatori:* Court officials.

151

I see the family is all female here.
[*Re-enter* WOMAN.]
WOMAN: He says, sir, he has weighty affairs of state
That now require him whole; some other time
You may possess him.
PEREGRINE: Pray you, say again,
If those require him whole, these will exact him,
Whereof I bring him tidings.
[*Exit* WOMAN.]   What might be
20 His grave affair of state now? How to make
Bolognian sausages here in Venice, sparing
One o' th' ingredients?
[*Re-enter* WOMAN.]
WOMAN: Sir, he says he knows
By your word 'tidings' that you are no statesman,
And therefore wills you stay.
PEREGRINE: Sweet, pray you return him:
I have not read so many proclamations
And studied them for words, as he has done,
But – Here he deigns to come.
[*Enter* SIR POLITIC.]
SIR POLITIC: Sir, I must crave
Your courteous pardon. There hath chanced today
Unkind disaster 'twixt my lady and me,
30 And I was penning my apology
To give her satisfaction, as you came now.
PEREGRINE: Sir, I am grieved I bring you worse disaster:
The gentleman you met at th' port today,
That told you he was newly arrived –
SIR POLITIC: Ay, was
A fugitive punk?
PEREGRINE: No, sir, a spy set on you,
And he has made relation to the Senate
That you professed to him to have a plot
To sell the state of Venice to the Turk.
SIR POLITIC: O me!
PEREGRINE: For which warrants are signed by this time
40 To apprehend you and to search your study

For papers –
SIR POLITIC: Alas, sir, I have none but notes
   Drawn out of play-books –
PEREGRINE: All the better, sir.
SIR POLITIC: And some essays. What shall I do?
PEREGRINE: Sir, best
   Convey yourself into a sugar-chest,
   Or, if you could lie round, a frail were rare,
   And I could send you aboard.
SIR POLITIC: Sir, I but talked so
   For discourse' sake merely.
      They knock without.
PEREGRINE: Hark, they are there.
SIR POLITIC: I am a wretch, a wretch!
PEREGRINE: What will you do, sir?
   Ha' you ne'er a currant-butt to leap into?
   They'll put you to the rack, you must be sudden.   50
SIR POLITIC: Sir, I have an engine –
3RD MERCHANT [*outside*]:   Sir Politic Would-be!
2ND MERCHANT [*outside*]: Where is he?
SIR POLITIC: That I have thought up-
   on beforetime.
PEREGRINE: What is it?
SIR POLITIC: I shall ne'er endure the torture!
   Marry, it is, sir, of a tortoise-shell,
   Fitted for these extremities. Pray you, sir, help me.
   [*He gets into a large tortoise-shell.*]
   Here I've a place, sir, to put back my legs;
   Please you to lay it on, sir. With this cap
   And my black gloves, I'll lie, sir, like a tortoise,
   Till they are gone.
PEREGRINE: And call you this an engine?
SIR POLITIC: My own device – Good sir, bid my wife's women   60
   To burn my papers.
      They [the three MERCHANTS] *rush in.*

42. *play-books:* plays printed in quarto.
45. *frail:* a rush basket in which figs, raisins, etc., were packed.
51. *engine:* invention.   55. *fitted:* designed.

1ST MERCHANT: Where's he hid?

3RD MERCHANT: We must,
And will, sure, find him.

2ND MERCHANT: Which is his study?

1ST MERCHANT: What
Are you, sir?

PEREGRINE: I'm a merchant that came here
To look upon this tortoise.

3RD MERCHANT: How!

1ST MERCHANT: St Mark!
What beast is this?

PEREGRINE: It is a fish.

2ND MERCHANT [*kicking the 'tortoise'*]: Come out here!

PEREGRINE: Nay, you may strike him, sir, and tread upon him.
He'll bear a cart.

1ST MERCHANT: What, to run over him?

PEREGRINE: Yes.

3RD MERCHANT: Let's jump upon him.

2ND MERCHANT: Can he not go?

PEREGRINE: He creeps, sir.

1ST MERCHANT: Let's see him creep. [*Goading him.*]

PEREGRINE: No, good sir, you will hurt
him.

70 2ND MERCHANT: Heart, I'll see him creep, or prick his guts.

3RD MERCHANT: Come out here!

PEREGRINE [*aside to* SIR POLITIC]: Pray you, sir, creep a little.

1ST MERCHANT: Forth!

2ND MERCHANT: Yet further.

PEREGRINE [*aside to* SIR POLITIC]: Good sir, creep!

2ND MERCHANT: We'll see his legs.

3RD MERCHANT: Godso, he has garters!

1ST MERCHANT: Ay, and gloves!
They pull off the shell and discover him.

2ND MERCHANT: Is this
Your fearful tortoise?

PEREGRINE: Now, Sir Pol, we are even;
For your next project I shall be prepared.

73. *Godso:* an expletive. Note.

154

I am sorry for the funeral of your notes, sir.

1ST MERCHANT: 'Twere a rare motion to be seen in Fleet Street.

2ND MERCHANT: Ay, i' the term.

1ST MERCHANT: Or Smithfield, in the fair.

3RD MERCHANT: Methinks 'tis but a melancholic sight.

PEREGRINE: Farewell, most politic tortoise!

    [*Exeunt* PEREGRINE *and the three* MERCHANTS.]

    [*Re-enter* WOMAN.]

SIR POLITIC: Where's my lady?   *80*

Knows she of this?

WOMAN: I know not, sir.

SIR POLITIC: Inquire.

    [*Exit* WOMAN.]

O, I shall be the fable of all feasts,

The freight of the *gazetti*, ship-boys' tale,

And, which is worst, even talk for ordinaries.

    [*Re-enter* WOMAN.]

WOMAN: My lady's come most melancholic home,

And says, sir, she will straight to sea, for physic.

SIR POLITIC: And I, to shun this place and clime forever,

Creeping with house on back, and think it well

To shrink my poor head in my politic shell.

    [*Exeunt.*]

[SCENE THREE]   V, V

[VOLPONE'S *house.*]

[*Enter* VOLPONE *and* MOSCA.] *The first in the habit of a Com-*
    mendatore; the other [*in that*] *of a Clarissimo.*

[VOLPONE:] Am I then like him?

---

76. *funeral:* burning. See above, lines 60–61.

77. *motion:* puppet-show; see also *Bartholomew Fair.*

78. *term:* period when the law-courts were sitting, and roughly equiva-
lent to 'the London season'. *Smithfield* was the site of Bartholomew Fair.

82. *the fable of all feasts:* i.e. people will 'dine out on' the story of Sir
Pol's misadventure.

83. *freight:* topic; *gazetti:* news-sheets.   84. *ordinaries:* taverns.

MOSCA: O sir, you are he;
No man can sever you.

VOLPONE: Good.

MOSCA: But what am I?

VOLPONE: 'Fore heav'n, a brave *clarissimo*, thou becom'st it!
Pity thou wert not born one.

MOSCA [*aside*]: If I hold
My made one, 'twill be well.

VOLPONE: I'll go and see
What news, first, at the court.
[*Exit.*]

MOSCA: Do so. My Fox
Is out on his hole, and ere he shall re-enter,
I'll make him languish in his borrowed case,
Except he come to composition with me.
10 Androgyno, Castrone, Nano!
[*Enter* ANDROGYNO, CASTRONE, *and* NANO.]

ALL: Here!

MOSCA: Go recreate yourselves abroad, go sport.
[*Exeunt.*]
So, now I have the keys and am possessed.
Since he will needs be dead afore his time,
I'll bury him, or gain by him. I'm his heir,
And so will keep me, till he share at least.
To cozen him of all were but a cheat
Well placed; no man would cònstrue it a sin.
Let his sport pay for 't. This is called the fox-trap.
[*Exit.*]

V, vi [SCENE FOUR]

[*A street.*]

[*Enter* CORBACCIO *and* CORVINO.]
[CORBACCIO:] They say the court is set.

---

2. *sever:* tell apart.   4. *My made one:* my assumed role.
6–7. *My Fox . . . :* reference to a children's game, Fox-in-the-hole.
8. *case:* covering, disguise.   9. *composition:* bargain.

CORVINO: We must maintain
Our first tale good, for both our reputations.
CORBACCIO: Why, mine's no tale! My son would, there, have
killed me.
CORVINO: That's true, I had forgot. Mine is, I am sure.
But for your will, sir.
CORBACCIO: Ay, I'll come upon him
For that hereafter, now his patron's dead.
[*Enter* VOLPONE, *disguised.*]
VOLPONE: Signor Corvino! And Corbaccio! Sir,
Much joy unto you.
CORVINO: Of what?
VOLPONE: The sudden good
Dropped down upon you –
CORBACCIO: Where?
VOLPONE: And none knows how,
From old Volpone, sir.
CORBACCIO: Out, arrant knave!   10
VOLPONE: Let not your too much wealth, sir, make you furious.
CORBACCIO: Away, thou varlet.
VOLPONE: Why, sir?
CORBACCIO: Dost thou mock me?
VOLPONE: You mock the world, sir; did you not change wills?
CORBACCIO: Out, harlot!
VOLPONE: O! belike you are the man,
Signor Corvino? Faith, you carry it well;
You grow not mad withal, I love your spirit.
You are not over-leavened with your fortune.
You should ha' some would swell now like a wine-vat
With such an autumn – Did he gi' you all, sir?
CORVINO: Avoid, you rascal.
VOLPONE: Troth, your wife has shown   20
Herself a very woman! But you are well,
You need not care, you have a good estate
To bear it out, sir, better by this chance.
Except Corbaccio have a share?
CORBACCIO: Hence, varlet!

17. *over-leavened*: puffed-up.

VOLPONE: You will not be a'known, sir? Why, 'tis wise.
Thus do all gamesters, at all games, dissemble.
No man will seem to win.
    [*Exeunt* CORVINO *and* CORBACCIO.]
                    Here comes my vulture,
Heaving his beak up i' the air, and snuffing.

V, vii   [*Enter* VOLTORE *to* VOLPONE.]
[VOLTORE:] Outstripped thus, by a parasite! A slave,
Would run on errands, and make legs for crumbs?
Well, what I'll do –
VOLPONE: The court stays for your worship.
I e'en rejoice, sir, at your worship's happiness,
And that it fell into so learnèd hands,
That understand the fingering –
VOLTORE: What do you mean?
VOLPONE: I mean to be a suitor to your worship
For the small tenement, out of reparations,
That at the end of your long row of houses,
10   By the *Pescheria*; it was, in Volpone's time,
Your predecessor, ere he grew diseased,
A handsome, pretty, customed bawdy-house
As any was in Venice – none dispraised –
But fell with him. His body and that house
Decayed together.
VOLTORE: Come, sir, leave your prating.
VOLPONE: Why, if your worship give me but your hand,
That I may ha' the refusal, I have done.
'Tis a mere toy to you, sir, candle-rents.
As your learnèd worship knows –
VOLTORE: What do I know?
20 VOLPONE: Marry, no end of your wealth, sir, God decrease it.

25. *a'known:* publicly recognized (as the heir).
2. *make legs:* bow, humble himself.
10. *Pescheria:* fish-market.
12. *customed:* much frequented.
18. *candle-rents:* rents from decaying property.

VOLTORE: Mistaking knave! What, mock'st thou my misfortune?

VOLPONE: His blessing on your heart, sir; would 'twere more!

    [*Exit* VOLTORE.]

Now, to my first again, at the next corner.

    [VOLPONE *stands apart. Enter* CORBACCIO *and* CORVINO.]   V, viii
    [MOSCA *passes across the stage.*]

[CORBACCIO:] See, in our habit! See the impudent varlet!

CORVINO: That I could shoot mine eyes at him, like gun-stones!

    [*Exit* MOSCA.]

VOLPONE: But is this true, sir, of the parasite?

CORBACCIO: Again t' afflict us? Monster!

VOLPONE: In good faith, sir,
I'm heartily grieved a beard of your grave length
Should be so over-reached. I never brooked
That parasite's hair; methought his nose should cozen.
There still was somewhat in his look did promise
The bane of a *clarissimo*.

CORBACCIO: Knave –

VOLPONE: Methinks

Yet you, that are so traded i' the world,   10
A witty merchant, the fine bird Corvino,
That have such moral emblems on your name,
Should not have sung your shame, and dropped your cheese,
To let the Fox laugh at your emptiness.

CORVINO: Sirrah, you think the privilege of the place,
And your red, saucy cap, that seems to me
Nailed to your jolt-head with those two chequins,
Can warrant your abuses. Come you hither:
You shall perceive, sir, I dare beat you. Approach.

VOLPONE: No haste, sir. I do know your valour well,   20
Since you durst publish what you are, sir.

   1. *in our habit:* dressed like people of our class (i.e. as a *clarissimo*).
   2. *gun-stones:* cannon-balls made of stone.
  12–14. *moral emblems:* Note.
  15. *privilege of the place:* safety of a public street.
  17. *chequins:* gold buttons.

CORVINO: Tarry,
  I'd speak with you.
VOLPONE: Sir, sir, another time –
CORVINO: Nay, now.
VOLPONE: O God, sir! I were a wise man
  Would stand the fury of a distracted cuckold.
    MOSCA *walks by 'em.*
CORBACCIO: What, come again?
VOLPONE [*aside*]:   Upon 'em, Mosca; save me.
CORBACCIO: The air's infected where he breathes.
CORVINO: Let's fly him.
  [*Exeunt* CORVINO *and* CORBACCIO.]
VOLPONE: Excellent basilisk! Turn upon the vulture!

V, ix   [*Enter* VOLTORE.]
  [VOLTORE:] Well, flesh-fly, it is summer with you now;
  Your winter will come on.
MOSCA: Good advocate,
  Pray thee not rail, nor threaten out of place thus;
  Thou'lt make a solecism, as Madam says.
  Get you a biggen more; your brain breaks loose.
    [*Exit.*]
VOLTORE: Well, sir.
VOLPONE: Would you ha' me beat the insolent slave?
  Throw dirt upon his first good clothes?
VOLTORE: This same
  Is doubtless some familiar!
VOLPONE: Sir, the court,
  In troth, stays for you. I am mad, a mule
10 That never read Justinian should get up
  And ride an advocate! Had you no quirk
  To avoid gullage, sir, by such a creature?
  I hope you do but jest; he had not done 't;
  This's but confederacy to blind the rest.

27. *basilisk:* a reptile thought to be able to kill with a look.
  5. *biggen:* a lawyer's skull-cap.
  8. *familiar:* evil spirit.   11. *quirk:* trick, legal quibble.

You are the heir?

VOLTORE: A strange, officious,
Troublesome knave! Thou dost torment me.

VOLPONE [aside]:   I know –
It cannot be, sir, that you should be cozened;
'Tis not within the wit of man to do it.
You are so wise, so prudent, and 'tis fit
That wealth and wisdom still should go together.   20
  [Exeunt.]

[SCENE FIVE]   V, X

[The Scrutineo.]

[Enter Four AVOCATORI, NOTARIO, COMMENDATORI,
   BONARIO, CELIA, CORBACCIO, and CORVINO.]

[1ST AVOCATORE:] Are all the parties here?

NOTARIO: All but the advocate.

2ND AVOCATORE: And here he comes.

  [Enter VOLTORE followed by VOLPONE, disguised.]

AVOCATORI: Then bring 'em forth to sentence.

VOLTORE: O my most honoured fathers, let your mercy
Once win upon your justice, to forgive –
I am distracted –

VOLPONE [aside]: What will he do now?

VOLTORE: O,
I know not which t' address myself to first,
Whether your fatherhoods, or these innocents –

CORVINO [aside]: Will he betray himself?

VOLTORE: Whom equally,
I have abused, out of most covetous ends –

CORVINO: The man is mad!

CORBACCIO: What's that?

CORVINO: He is possessed.   10

VOLTORE: For which, now struck in conscience, here I prostrate
Myself at your offended feet, for pardon.

10. possessed: possessed by a devil.

[*He kneels.*]

IST, 2ND AVOCATORI: Arise.

CELIA: O heav'n, how just thou art!

VOLPONE [*aside*]: I'm caught
I' mine own noose.

CORVINO [*aside to* CORBACCIO]: Be constant, sir, nought now
Can help but impudence.

IST AVOCATORE: Speak forward.

COMMENDATORE: Silence!

VOLTORE: It is not passion in me, reverend fathers,
But only conscience, conscience, my good sires,
That makes me now tell truth. That parasite,
That knave, hath been the instrument of all.

20 AVOCATORI: Where is that knave? Fetch him.

VOLPONE: I go.
[*Exit.*]

CORVINO: Grave fathers,
This man's distracted, he confessed it now,
For, hoping to be old Volpone's heir,
Who now is dead –

3RD AVOCATORE: How!

2ND AVOCATORE: Is Volpone dead?

CORVINO: Dead since, grave fathers –

BONARIO: O sure vengeance!

IST AVOCATORE: Stay.
Then he was no deceiver.

VOLTORE: O, no, none;
The parasite, grave fathers.

CORVINO: He does speak
Out of mere envy, 'cause the servant's made
The thing he gaped for. Please your fatherhoods,
This is the truth; though I'll not justify
30 The other, but he may be some-deal faulty.

VOLTORE: Ay, to your hopes, as well as mine, Corvino.
But I'll use modesty. Pleaseth your wisdoms
To view these certain notes, and but confer them;
As I hope favour, they shall speak clear truth.

27. *gaped*: yearned.

CORVINO: The devil has entered him!

BONARIO: Or bides in you.

4TH AVOCATORE: We have done ill, by a public officer
  To send for him, if he be heir.

2ND AVOCATORE: For whom?

4TH AVOCATORE: Him that they call the parasite.

3RD AVOCATORE: 'Tis true,
  He is a man of great estate now left.

4TH AVOCATORE: Go you, and learn his name, and say the court *40*
  Entreats his presence here, but to the clearing
  Of some few doubts.

    [*Exit* NOTARIO.]

2ND AVOCATORE: This same's a labyrinth!

1ST AVOCATORE: Stand you unto your first report?

CORVINO: My state,
  My life, my fame –

BONARIO: Where is't?

CORVINO: Are at the stake.

1ST AVOCATORE: Is yours so too?

CORBACCIO: The advocate's a knave,
  And has a forkèd tongue –

2ND AVOCATORE: Speak to the point.

CORBACCIO: So is the parasite too.

1ST AVOCATORE: This is confusion.

VOLTORE: I do beseech your fatherhoods, read but those.

CORVINO: And credit nothing the false spirit hath writ.
  It cannot be but he is possessed, grave fathers. *50*

[SCENE SIX]   V, xi

  [*A street.*]

  [*Enter* VOLPONE, *alone.*]

[VOLPONE:] To make a snare for mine own neck! And run
  My head into it wilfully, with laughter!
  When I had newly 'scaped, was free and clear!
  Out of mere wantonness! O, the dull devil

Was in this brain of mine when I devised it,
And Mosca gave it second; he must now
Help to sear up this vein, or we bleed dead.
 [*Enter* NANO, ANDROGYNO, *and* CASTRONE.]
How now! Who let you loose? Whither go you now?
What, to buy gingerbread, or to drown kitlings?
10 NANO: Sir, Master Mosca called us out of doors,
 And bid us all go play, and took the keys.
ANDROGYNO: Yes.
VOLPONE: Did Master Mosca take the keys? Why, so!
 I am farther in. These are my fine conceits!
 I must be merry, with a mischief to me!
 What a vile wretch was I, that could not bear
 My fortune soberly; I must ha' my crotchets
 And my conundrums! Well, go you and seek him.
 His meaning may be truer than my fear.
 Bid him, he straight come to me to the court;
20 Thither will I, and if't be possible,
 Unscrew my advocate, upon new hopes.
 When I provoked him, then I lost myself.
  [*Exeunt.*]

V, xii   [SCENE SEVEN]

 [*The Scrutineo.*]

 [*Enter four* AVOCATORI, NOTARIO, VOLTORE, BONARIO,
  CELIA, CORBACCIO, *and* CORVINO.]
[1ST AVOCATORE:] These things can ne'er be reconciled. He here
 Professeth that the gentleman was wronged,
 And that the gentlewoman was brought thither,
 Forced by her husband, and there left.
VOLTORE: Most true.
CELIA: How ready is heav'n to those that pray!

   6. *gave it second:* seconded it.
   7. *sear up:* stop bleeding by cauterizing with a hot iron.
   9. *kitlings:* kittens.   16. *crotchets:* whims.

1ST AVOCATORE: But that
  Volpone would have ravished her, he holds
  Utterly false, knowing his impotence.
CORVINO: Grave fathers, he is possessed; again, I say,
  Possessed. Nay, if there be possession
  And obsession, he has both.
3RD AVOCATORE: Here comes our officer.   10
  [*Enter* VOLPONE, *disguised.*]
VOLPONE: The parasite will straight be here, grave fathers.
4TH AVOCATORE: You might invent some other name, Sir
  Varlet.
3RD AVOCATORE: Did not the notary meet him?
VOLPONE: Not that I know.
4TH AVOCATORE: His coming will clear all.
2ND AVOCATORE: Yet, it is misty.
VOLTORE: May't please your fatherhoods –
VOLPONE: Sir, the parasite
    VOLPONE *whispers* [*to*] *the* ADVOCATE.
  Willed me to tell you that his master lives;
  That you are still the man; your hopes the same;
  And this was only a jest –
VOLTORE: How?
VOLPONE: Sir, to try
  If you were firm, and how you stood affected.
VOLTORE: Art sure he lives?
VOLPONE: Do I live, sir?   20
VOLTORE: O me!
  I was too violent.
VOLPONE: Sir, you may redeem it:
  They said you were possessed: fall down, and seem so.
  I'll help to make it good.
    VOLTORE *falls.*
               God bless the man!
  – Stop your wind hard, and swell – See, see, see, see!
  He vomits crooked pins! His eyes are set

---

    9. *possession:* being possessed internally by a devil.
    10. *obsession:* being controlled from without by a devil.
    25. *crooked pins,* etc.: Note.

Like a dead hare's hung in a poulter's shop!
His mouth's running away! Do you see, signior?
Now, 'tis in his belly.

CORVINO: Ay, the devil!

VOLPONE: Now, in his throat.

CORVINO: Ay, I perceive it plain.

30 VOLPONE: 'Twill out, 'twill out! Stand clear. See where it flies!
In shape of a blue toad, with a bat's wings!
Do you not see it, sir?

CORBACCIO: What? I think I do.

CORVINO: 'Tis too manifest.

VOLPONE: Look! He comes t' himself.

VOLTORE: Where am I?

VOLPONE: Take good heart, the worst is past, sir.
You are dispossessed.

1ST AVOCATORE: What accident is this?

2ND AVOCATORE: Sudden, and full of wonder!

3RD AVOCATORE: If he were
Possessed, as it appears, all this is nothing.

CORVINO: He has been often subject to these fits.

1ST AVOCATORE: Show him that writing – Do you know it, sir?

40 VOLPONE [aside]: Deny it sir, forswear it, know it not.

VOLTORE: Yes, I do know it well, it is my hand;
But all that it contains is false.

BONARIO: O practice!

2ND AVOCATORE: What maze is this!

1ST AVOCATORE: Is he not guilty then,
Whom you, there, name the parasite?

VOLTORE: Grave fathers,
No more than his good patron, old Volpone.

4TH AVOCATORE: Why, he is dead.

VOLTORE: O, no, my honoured fathers.
He lives –

1ST AVOCATORE: How! lives?

VOLTORE: Lives.

2ND AVOCATORE: This is subtler yet!

3RD AVOCATORE: You said he was dead.

VOLTORE: Never.

3RD AVOCATORE: You said so!

CORVINO: I heard so.

4TH AVOCATORE: Here comes the gentleman, make him way.
   [*Enter* MOSCA.]

3RD AVOCATORE: A stool!

4TH AVOCATORE: A proper man and, were Volpone dead,   50
  A fit match for my daughter.

3RD AVOCATORE: Give him way.

VOLPONE [*aside to* MOSCA]: Mosca, I was almost lost; the advo-
  cate
  Had betrayed all; but now it is recovered.
  All's o' the hinge again. Say I am living.

MOSCA: What busy knave is this? Most reverend fathers,
  I sooner had attended your grave pleasures,
  But that my order for the funeral
  Of my dear patron did require me –

VOLPONE [*aside*]:   Mosca!

MOSCA: Whom I intend to bury like a gentleman.

VOLPONE [*aside*]: Ay, quick, and cozen me of all.

2ND AVOCATORE: Still stranger!   60
  More intricate!

1ST AVOCATORE: And come about again!

4TH AVOCATORE [*aside*]: It is a match, my daughter is bestowed.

MOSCA [*aside to* VOLPONE]: Will you gi' me half?

VOLPONE [*aside*]:   First I'll be hanged.

MOSCA [*aside*]:   I know
  Your voice is good, cry not so loud.

1ST AVOCATORE: Demand
  The advocate. Sir, did not you affirm
  Volpone was alive?

VOLPONE: Yes, and he is;
  This gent'man told me so. [*Aside to* MOSCA] Thou shalt have half.

MOSCA: Whose drunkard is this same? Speak, some that know
  him.
  I never saw his face. [*Aside to* VOLPONE] I cannot now
  Afford it you so cheap.

VOLPONE [*aside*]:   No?

1ST AVOCATORE [*to* VOLTORE]: What say you?   70

VOLTORE: The officer told me.

VOLPONE: I did, grave fathers,
And will maintain he lives with mine own life,
And that this creature told me. [*Aside*] I was born
With all good stars my enemies!

MOSCA: Most grave fathers,
If such an insolence as this must pass
Upon me, I am silent; 'twas not this
For which you sent, I hope.

2ND AVOCATORE: Take him away.

VOLPONE [*aside*]: Mosca!

3RD AVOCATORE: Let him be whipped.

VOLPONE [*aside*]:   Wilt thou betray me?
Cozen me?

3RD AVOCATORE: And taught to bear himself
80   Toward a person of his rank.

[*The* OFFICERS *seize* VOLPONE.]

4TH AVOCATORE: Away!

MOSCA: I humbly thank your fatherhoods.

VOLPONE [*aside*]:   Soft, soft. Whipped?
And lose all that I have? If I confess,
It cannot be much more.

4TH AVOCATORE [*to* MOSCA]: Sir, are you married?

VOLPONE [*aside*]: They'll be allied anon; I must be resolute:
The Fox shall here uncase.

He puts off his disguise.

MOSCA: Patron!

VOLPONE: Nay, now
My ruins shall not come alone; your match
I'll hinder sure. My substance shall not glue you,
Nor screw you, into a family.

MOSCA: Why, patron!

VOLPONE: I am Volpone, and this is my knave;
90   This, his own knave; this, avarice's fool;
This, a chimera of wittol, fool, and knave.

85. *uncase:* cast off disguise.   87. *substance:* wealth.
91. *chimera:* originally, in Greek mythology, a monster, part lion, part
goat, part serpent.

And, reverend fathers, since we all can hope
Nought but a sentence, let's not now despair it.
You hear me brief.

CORVINO: May it please your fatherhoods –

COMMENDATORE: Silence.

1ST AVOCATORE: The knot is now undone by miracle!

2ND AVOCATORE: Nothing can be more clear.

3RD AVOCATORE: Or can more prove
These innocent.

1ST AVOCATORE: Give 'em their liberty.

BONARIO: Heaven could not long let such gross crimes be hid.

2ND AVOCATORE: If this be held the highway to get riches,
May I be poor!

3RD AVOCATORE: This's not the gain, but torment.   *100*

1ST AVOCATORE: These possess wealth as sick men possess fevers,
Which trulier may be said to possess them.

2ND AVOCATORE: Disrobe that parasite.

CORVINO, MOSCA: Most honoured fathers –

1ST AVOCATORE: Can you plead aught to stay the course of
justice?
If you can, speak.

CORVINO, VOLTORE: We beg favour.

CELIA: And mercy.

1ST AVOCATORE: You hurt your innocence, suing for the guilty.
Stand forth; and first the parasite. You appear
T'have been the chiefest minister, if not plotter,
In all these lewd impostures; and now, lastly,
Have with your impudence abused the court,   *110*
And habit of a gentleman of Venice,
Being a fellow of no birth or blood.
For which our sentence is, first thou be whipped;
Then live perpetual prisoner in our galleys.

VOLPONE: I thank you for him.

MOSCA: Bane to thy wolfish nature.

1ST AVOCATORE: Deliver him to the *Saffi*.
[MOSCA *is led out.*]
        Thou, Volpone,

115. *bane:* destruction.   116. *Saffi:* sergeants, bailiffs.

By blood and rank a gentleman, canst not fall
Under like censure; but our judgement on thee
Is that thy substance all be straight confiscate
120 To the hospital of the *Incurabili.*
And since the most was gotten by imposture,
By feigning lame, gout, palsy, and such diseases,
Thou art to lie in prison, cramped with irons,
Till thou be'st sick and lame indeed. Remove him.

VOLPONE: This is called mortifying of a Fox.

1ST AVOCATORE: Thou, Voltore, to take away the scandal
Thou hast giv'n all worthy men of thy profession,
Art banished from their fellowship, and our state.
Corbaccio, bring him near! We here possess
130 Thy son of all thy state, and confine thee
To the monastery of *San Spirito;*
Where, since thou knew'st not how to live well here,
Thou shalt be learned to die well.

CORBACCIO [*not hearing*]: Ha! What said he?

COMMENDATORE: You shall know anon, sir.

1ST AVOCATORE: Thou, Corvino, shalt
Be straight embarked from thine own house, and rowed
Round about Venice, through the Grand Canal,
Wearing a cap with fair long ass's ears
Instead of horns; and so to mount, a paper
Pinned on thy breast, to the *Berlina* –

CORVINO: Yes,
140 And have mine eyes beat out with stinking fish,
Bruised fruit, and rotten eggs – 'Tis well, I'm glad
I shall not see my shame yet.

1ST AVOCATORE: And to expiate
Thy wrongs done to thy wife, thou art to send her
Home to her father, with her dowry trebled.
And these are all your judgements.

ALL: Honoured fathers!

1ST AVOCATORE: Which may not be revoked. Now you begin,
When crimes are done and past, and to be punished,

120. *Incurabili:* incurables.
125. *mortifying:* Note. 139. *the Berlina:* the Venetian stocks.

To think what your crimes are. Away with them!
Let all that see these vices thus rewarded,
Take heart, and love to study 'em. Mischiefs feed
Like beasts, till they be fat, and then they bleed.
   [*Exeunt.*]

   [VOLPONE *comes forward.*]

VOLPONE: The seasoning of a play is the applause.
  Now, though the Fox be punished by the laws,
  He yet doth hope there is no suff'ring due
  For any fact which he hath done 'gainst you.
  If there be, censure him; here he doubtful stands.
  If not, fare jovially, and clap your hands.

THE END

THE ALCHEMIST

PRELIMINARY NOTE

I. STAGE-HISTORY AND FIRST PUBLICATION

The Alchemist was first acted at the Globe Theatre by the King's Men in 1610, probably with Richard Burbage as Face and John Lowin as Sir Epicure Mammon. It was first published in quarto in 1612 and reprinted in the Folio *Workes* four years later. Soon after its London opening, the King's Men took the play to Oxford, and it was also acted in Dublin. At the Restoration, the comedy was quickly revived, and it was popular throughout the eighteenth century. Colley Cibber played Subtle 'with great art', and Theophilus Cibber overplayed Abel Drugger. In 1743 David Garrick first played Drugger, and in the twenty-nine years from 1747 to 1776 in which Drury Lane was, under his management, the greatest theatre in Europe, he appeared each season as the little tobacconist. His acting version cut many of the alchemical terms, lines like Mammon's 'the unctuous paps of a fat pregnant sow' were expurgated, and Abel Drugger became the leading part. In the nineteenth century the play was probably considered too coarse for revival, though Charles Dickens (whose amateur productions of *Every Man in his Humour* in the years 1845–8 were notable) thought of producing the play for charity in 1848. In 1899 William Poel's Elizabethan Stage Society mounted the comedy at Blackfriars, and in 1902 at Cambridge, where in 1914 it was acted by the Marlowe Society with the future Professor Sir Dennis Robertson as Subtle. It was also acted by the Birmingham Repertory Theatre in 1916, by the Phoenix Society for two performances in 1923, and at the Malvern Festival of 1932 (with Cedric Hardwicke as Drugger). In 1947 the Old Vic Company gave the play an eighteenth-century setting; Ralph Richardson was Face and Alec Guinness Drugger. Tyrone Guthrie directed the Liverpool Old Vic Company in a modern-dress revival of the play during the Playhouse repertory season, 1944–5; and at the Edinburgh Festival of 1950 he directed *The Atom Doctor* by Eric Linklater, which turned out to be an adaptation of *The Alchemist* set in modern Edinburgh. During the Old Vic season 1962–3 Guthrie again produced the play in modern dress, with contemporary 'gags'; Leo McKern was Subtle, and Lee Montague Face. In 1961 Peter Dews directed a brilliant television version from the B.B.C.'s Midland Studios, and in 1964 there was a production by Frank Hauser at the Oxford Playhouse.

2. LOCATION AND TIME-SCHEME

The Alchemist is set inside Lovewit's house, and outside his front door. The fluidity of the Elizabethan Theatre or of a modern composite stage-setting is necessary in performance, and the acting-area has to indicate two or three rooms inside the house, the street, and possibly the garden. The pace of the action is fast. Act II follows briskly upon Act I, and perhaps Sir Epicure Mammon and Pertinax Surly should already be coming into the audience's view in the street when Dol, inside the house, describes Sir Epicure's approach in the last lines of Act I, so that the action is really continuous. Act IV seems to require several locations – the principal room in Lovewit's house, two smaller rooms, and the garden, but Jonson did not specify locations, and an ingenious director, following the example of Sir Tyrone Guthrie in 1962, could set the scenes in the main area of traffic, and on the staircase, the balcony, and so on. The *décor* for *The Alchemist*, as for any modern farce, requires many doors and exit-points, including the privy in which Dapper is incarcerated. In the Herford–Simpson edition the time-scheme has been worked out from internal evidence as follows: 9 a.m.: arrival of Dapper; 10 a.m.: Mammon seen approaching; 11 a.m.: Ananias threatened if he does not return quickly with more money; noon: Ananias returns on the stroke of the hour; 1 p.m.: Dapper comes back as requested; 2 p.m.: Surly arrives in disguise; 3 p.m.: Lovewit returns home unexpectedly.

3. EDITIONS AND CRITICAL COMMENTARY

The Alchemist is reprinted in many editions of Jonson and in anthologies, including *Elizabethan and Stuart Plays*, edited by C. R.

Baskervill, V. B. Heltzel, and A. H. Nethercot (1934). It has been edited by Felix E. Schelling (1903), by C. S. Alden (1904), and by G. E. Bentley (1947). F. H. Mares' edition for the Revels Plays (1967) appeared after the present volume. The editor for the Yale Ben Jonson is R. B. Young. J. J. Enck and E. B. Partridge both devote chapters to the play. Brian Gibbons in *Jacobean City Comedy* relates *The Alchemist* to other comedies satirizing life and to the coney-catching pamphlets. J. A. Barish's anthology of criticism reprints a section of Paul Goodman's *The Structure of Literature* (1954), which is an Aristotelian analysis of its comic plot. It was Coleridge who said 'Upon my word, I think the *Oedipus Tyrannus, The Alchemist,* and *Tom Jones* the three most perfect plots ever planned.' (*Table Talk:* 5 July 1834.)

A NOTE ON ALCHEMY

The Alchemist is not primarily about alchemy, nor is Subtle a genuine alchemist. Throughout the comedy Jonson exploits alchemy and alchemical language as supreme instances of roguery and the bewitching verbal arts of the confidence-trickster. Although dramatic logic does not demand it, Jonson's use of alchemical terms, always theatrically telling, is usually accurate also. That Jonson made himself familiar with alchemical scholarship may be a further illustration of that massive erudition and pedantic thoroughness mentioned in the first pages of the introduction. Professor Edgar Hill Duncan has assured us that Jonson's knowledge of alchemy 'was greater than that of any other major English literary figure, with the possible exceptions of Chaucer and Donne'. The preoccupation with accuracy may be pedantry on Jonson's part, but it is surely significant that the various characters within the comedy who use alchemical terms use them more or less correctly – the credulous Sir Epicure, who is willingly dazzled by the lights of perverted science; the quick-talking Subtle, who is not a 'cunning-man', but a con-man; and the sceptical Surly, who pours sardonic comments over Subtle's ill-founded but convincingly expressed pretensions. The main point of Jonson's satire, in this play as in *Volpone*, is that human greed and gullibility put men in the power of unscrupulous manipulators, but the accuracy of alchemical reference possibly indicates incidental Jonsonian satire on alchemy itself. Through the speeches of Sir Epicure, Jonson was able to make fun of the claims of the alchemists without having to resort to fantastic inventions of his own; their own claims, reproduced from alchemical treatises, seemed exaggerated enough. And in presenting his audience with Subtle, a bogus alchemist who sounds authentic, Jonson may have been hinting that all authentic-sounding alchemists were bogus also. It was the practice of alchemists to conceal their discoveries in symbolic language and in elaborate pictorial allegories and diagrams which remained mysterious and impenetrable to the uninitiated layman. This complex symbolism has subsequently fascinated historians of ideas and others – for an account by a great modern European mind of the archetypal patterns in the alchemists' world-picture, see C. G. Jung's *Psychology and Alchemy* (British edition, 1953). The studiously cultivated mystery and obscurantism of the Renaissance alchemists probably amused and enraged the exact Jonson, who made of it comic poetry in *The Alchemist*.

Alchemy has a long history which itself forms the pre-history of chemistry. For some fifteen hundred years the alchemists, many of them sincere and dedicated men of science, pursued the hopeless task of transforming such base metals as lead or copper into silver or gold. The first European alchemical treatises date from the third and fourth centuries A.D. Alchemy existed earlier in China and in India, but the main Western tradition originated in Alexandria around A.D. 100. Medieval and Renaissance alchemists believed, as Sir Epicure does in Jonson's play, that men of former times had possessed the secret of transmuting base metals into gold; their own task was to recover that secret either by experiment or by poring over the mystical writings of their predecessors. The experimental and the scholarly approaches became, increasingly, separate activities, but until the middle of the seventeenth century it was in the laboratories of the alchemists that the apparatus and the experimental techniques of chemistry were developed.

Behind early alchemical thinking lay Greek assumptions about the relation between form and matter, derived from Aristotle, and about spirit. Aristotle believed that there was ultimately only one matter and that it could take any number of forms. F. Sherwood Taylor, the historian of alchemy, thus describes the task of the earliest alchemists: '. . . their endeavour to change, let us say, copper into gold, was planned as the removal of the form of copper (or, more picturesquely, as the death of copper and its corruption), to be followed by the introduction of a new form, that of gold (which process was pictured as a resurrection)'. The notion of spirit or breath is a difficult one; it indicates the subtle, almost immaterial influence which had to be present to make possible, say, the germination of a plant, or the transformation of matter from one form to another. The sentence quoted from

Taylor's book suggests how readily alchemical thinking lent itself
to metaphorical expression. In Medieval and Renaissance times
the language and iconography of alchemy became increasingly
complex, drawing upon many sources. The early metaphor of the
reduction of the metal as the slaying of the dragon was elaborated.
Alchemists talked of the marriage of Sol and Luna, gold and silver,
which, if it could be effected, would produce the Philosopher's
Stone. The symbolic language frequently drew upon religion.
Taylor writes: 'The death of our Lord Jesus Christ and His resurrection in a glorified body was to the alchemists to be compared
to the death of the metals and their rebirth as the glorious Stone.'
These three isolated examples are sufficient to show the range of
mythological, analogical, and religious reference in alchemical
symbolism.

Alchemy, which had disappeared along with Greek philosophy
and science after the fall of Rome, was rediscovered in the Western
world in the eleventh and twelfth centuries, when scholars busied
themselves translating into Latin the scientific and philosophic
works of Islam, including Arabic treatises on alchemy. In the
twelfth and thirteenth centuries such great minds as Albertus
Magnus, Roger Bacon, and St Thomas Aquinas, taking all human
knowledge as their province, pondered very seriously the alchemists' explorations of the nature of matter. The attention they
gave in their encyclopedic works to the alchemists' claims contributed to a revival of alchemical activities both through experimental work (notably by Geber or Jabir, a Spanish alchemist) and
through the writing of mystical and, indeed, occult treatises on
alchemy. In the fourteenth century there appeared more systematic
and clearly written alchemical works, usually attributed to Arnold
de Vallanova and to Ramón Lull, though on uncertain grounds.
In England alchemists, both genuine and bogus, flourished;
Chaucer's *Canon's Yeoman's Tale* is a satire on charlatans. A statute
of 1403 forbade the multiplying of metals; and there are cases
recorded throughout the fifteenth century of people obtaining
royal licences to practise alchemy. English alchemists of the
fifteenth century included Sir George Ripley who studied in Italy
(and who is mentioned in this comedy), Thomas Norton, and
Thomas Daulton.

Readers who wish to find out more about the alchemical background to *The Alchemist* will find a brief, old-fashioned article on Alchemy in *Shakespeare's England* (1917). A helpful book-length survey for the general reader, of which I have made use in this short summary, is F. Sherwood Taylor's *The Alchemists: Founders of Modern Chemistry* (reprinted 1958). More detailed is John Read's *Prelude to Chemistry: An Outline of Alchemy, Its Literature, and Relationships* (1936). Like Jung's *Psychology and Alchemy* both these books contain many illustrations from alchemical treatises, many of Read's plates being in colour. Edgar Hill Duncan's closely written article 'Jonson's *Alchemist* and the Literature of Alchemy' in *Publications of the Modern Language Association of America*, LXI (1946) shows how some speeches in the play become more significant in the light of detailed alchemical knowledge. I have drawn freely on his work in annotating certain passages in *The Alchemist*.

No edition for the general reader or playgoer can hope to cover the alchemical background thoroughly, and I have not tried to explain all the terms either in the glosses or in the longer explanatory notes. Jonson's alchemical terms fall into three main classes: (*a*) materials and substances, (*b*) alchemical equipment and apparatus, (*c*) alchemical processes. The following selective glossary may assist the reader and playgoer.

(a) *Materials, substances etc.*

adrop: the matter out of which mercury is extracted for the Philosopher's Stone; the Stone itself.
aqua fortis: impure vitriol.
aqua regis: a mixture of acids which can dissolve gold.
aqua vitae: alcohol.
argaile: unrefined tartar.
aurum potabile: liquid, drinkable gold.
azoch: mercury.
azot: nitrogen.
calce: powdered substance produced by combustion or 'calcination'.
chibrit: mercury.

chrysosperm: elixir.
cinoper: sulphide of mercury.
kibrit: sulphur.
lac virginis: mercurial water.
lato: a mixed metal which looks like brass.
maistrie: the magisterium or Philosopher's Stone.
realga: a mixture of arsenic and sulphur.
sericon: black tincture.
zernich: auripigment or gold paint.

(b) *Alchemical equipment and apparatus*

alembic: the vessel at the top of the distilling apparatus which holds
 the distilled material.
aludel: subliming pot.
athanor: a furnace.
balneum: bath; or process of heating a vessel.
bolt's head: a long-necked vessel.
cross-let: crucible.
cucurbite: a distilling vessel.
gripes egg: a vessel shaped like a vulture's egg.
lembek: a still.
pelican: an alembic.

(c) *Processes*

ceration: softening hard substances.
chrysopœia: the making of gold.
chymia: alchemy.
cibation: seventh stage in alchemy.
citronize: to become yellow.
cohabation: redistillation.
digestion: preparation of substances by gentle heat.
dulcify: to purify.
inhibition: a bathing process associated with the tenth stage.
inceration: softening to the consistency of wax.
macerate: to steep.
potate: liquified.
projection: the twelfth and last stage in alchemy.

putrefaction: the fifth stage in alchemy whereby impurities were removed by the use of moist heat.

solution: the second stage in alchemy.

spagyrica: the spagiric art; Paracelsian chemistry.

sublimation: conversion into vapour through the agency of heat, and reconversion into solid through the agency of cold.

THE
ALCHEMIST.

VVritten
by
BEN. IONSON.

———Neque, me vt miretur turba, labore:
Contentus paucis lectoribus.

LONDON,
Printed by *Thomas Snodham,* for *Walter Burre,*
and are to be fold by *Iohn Stepneth,* at the
Weſt-end of Paules.
1612.

Facsimile of the title-page of the first edition, the quarto of 1612.

TO THE READER

If thou beest more, thou art an understander, and then I trust thee. If thou art one that tak'st up, and but a pretender, beware at what hands thou receiv'st thy commodity; for thou wert never more fair in the way to be coz'ned than in this age in poetry, especially in plays: wherein now the concupiscence of jigs and dances so reigneth, as to run away from nature and be afraid of her is the only point of art that tickles the spectators. But how out of purpose and place do I name art, when the professors are grown so obstinate contemners of it, and presumers on their own naturals, as they are deriders of all diligence that way, and, by simple mock- 10 ing at the terms when they understand not the things, think to get off wittily with their ignorance! Nay, they are esteemed the more learned and sufficient for this by the multitude, through their excellent vice of judgement. For they commend writers as they do fencers or wrestlers; who, if they come in robustiously and put for it with a great deal of violence, are received for the braver fellows; when many times their own rudeness is the cause of their disgrace, and a little touch of their adversary gives all that boister- ous force the foil. I deny not but that these men who always seek to do more than enough may some time happen on some thing 20 that is good and great – but very seldom, and when it comes, it doth not recompense the rest of their ill. It sticks out, perhaps, and is more eminent, because all is sordid and vile about it; as lights are more discerned in a thick darkness than a faint shadow. I speak not this out of a hope to do good on any man against his will; for I know, if it were put to the question of theirs and mine, the worse would find more suffrages, because the most favour common errors. But I give thee this warning, that there is a great difference between those that (to gain the opinion of copy) utter all they can, however unfitly, and those that use election and a mean. For it is 30 only the disease of the unskillful to think rude things greater than polished, or scattered more numerous than composed.

8. *professors:* practitioners.   29. *copy:* copiousness.

THE PERSONS OF THE PLAY

SUBTLE, *the Alchemist*
FACE, *the House-keeper*
DOL COMMON, *their Colleague*
DAPPER, *a Clerk*
DRUGGER, *a Tobacco-man*
LOVEWIT, *Master of the House*
[SIR] EPICURE MAMMON, *a Knight*
[PERTINAX] SURLY, *a Gamester*
TRIBULATION [WHOLESOME], *a Pastor of Amsterdam*
ANANIAS, *a Deacon there*
KASTRIL, *the Angry Boy*
DAME PLIANT, *his sister, a Widow*
[PARSON]
NEIGHBOURS
OFFICERS
MUTES

The Scene:

LONDON

T he sickness hot, a master quit, for fear,
H is house in town, and left one servant there.
E ase him corrupted, and gave means to know
A Cheater and his punk, who now brought low,
L eaving their narrow practice, were become
C oz'ners at large; and only wanting some
H ouse to set up, with him they here contract,
E ach for a share, and all begin to act.
M uch company they draw, and much abuse,
I n casting figures, telling fortunes, news,   10
S elling of flies, flat bawdry, with the Stone;
T ill it, and they, and all in fume are gone.

PROLOGUE

Fortune, that favours fools, these two short hours
   We wish away, both for your sakes and ours,
Judging spectators; and desire in place,
   To th' author justice, to ourselves but grace.
Our scene is London, 'cause we would make known,
   No country's mirth is better than our own.
No clime breeds better matter for your whore,
   Bawd, squire, impostor, many persons more,
Whose manners, now call'd humours, feed the stage;
   And which have still been subject for the rage   10
Or spleen of comic writers. Though this pen
   Did never aim to grieve, but better men,

  1. *the sickness hot:* the plague (being) virulent; refers to the year 1609.
  4. *punk:* prostitute.
  6. *Coz'ners:* tricksters, confidence-men.
  10. *figures:* horoscope.
  11. *flies:* familiar spirits.
  12. *Stone:* the much sought after Philosopher's Stone, which could turn everything into gold.
   9. *humours:* for Jonson's physiological–psychological theories, see note to *Volpone*, II, ii, 92 (page 467), and the general introduction, p. 10.

Howe'er the age he lives in doth endure
  The vices that she breeds, above their cure.
But when the wholesome remedies are sweet,
  And, in their working, gain and profit meet,
He hopes to find no spirit so much diseased,
  But will with such fair correctives be pleased.
For here he doth not fear who can apply.
20 If there be any that will sit so nigh
Unto the stream, to look what it doth run,
  They shall find things, they'd think, or wish, were done;
They are so natural follies, but so shown,
  As even the doers may see, and yet not own.

ACT ONE

[LOVEWIT'S *house.*]

[*Enter* FACE, *in a Captain's uniform, with his sword drawn, and* SUBTLE, *with a vial, quarrelling, and followed by* DOL COMMON.]

FACE: Believe 't, I will.

SUBTLE: Thy worst. I fart at thee.

DOL COMMON: Ha' you your wits? Why, gentlemen! for love –

FACE: Sirrah, I'll strip you –

SUBTLE: What to do? Lick figs
Out at my –

FACE: Rogue, rogue! – out of all your sleights.

DOL COMMON: Nay, look ye, sovereign, general, are you madmen?

SUBTLE: O, let the wild sheep loose. I'll gum your silks
With good strong water, an' you come.

DOL COMMON: Will you have
The neighbours hear you? Will you betray all?
Hark! I hear somebody.

FACE: Sirrah –

SUBTLE: I shall mar
All that the tailor has made, if you approach.   *10*

FACE: You most notorious whelp, you insolent slave,
Dare you do this?

SUBTLE: Yes, faith; yes, faith.

FACE: Why! who
Am I, my mongrel, who am I?

SUBTLE: I'll tell you,
Since you know not yourself.

FACE: Speak lower, rogue.

SUBTLE: Yes. You were once (time's not long past) the good,
Honest, plain, livery-three-pound-thrum, that kept
Your master's worship's house here in the Friars,

3–4. *Lick figs:* Note.   17. *Friars:* Blackfriars, a fashionable part of
London, scene of the comedy's action.

    For the vacations –

FACE: Will you be so loud?

SUBTLE: Since, by my means, translated suburb-captain.

20 FACE: By your means, Doctor Dog!

SUBTLE: Within man's memory,
  All this I speak of.

FACE: Why, I pray you, have I
  Been countenanced by you, or you by me?
  Do but 'collect, sir, where I met you first.

SUBTLE: I do not hear well.

FACE: Not of this, I think it.
  But I shall put you in mind, sir; – at Pie-corner,
  Taking your meal of steam in, from cooks' stalls,
  Where, like the father of hunger, you did walk
  Piteously costive, with your pinched-horn-nose,
  And your complexion of the Roman wash,
30   Stuck full of black and melancholic worms,
  Like powder-corns shot at th' artillery-yard.

SUBTLE: I wish you could advance your voice a little.

FACE: When you went pinned up in the several rags
  Y' had raked and picked from dunghills, before day;
  Your feet in mouldy slippers, for your kibes;
  A felt of rug, and a thin threaden cloak,
  That scarce would cover your no-buttocks –

SUBTLE: So, sir!

FACE: When all your alchemy, and your algebra,
  Your minerals, vegetals, and animals,
40   Your conjuring, coz'ning, and your dozen of trades,
  Could not relieve your corpse with so much linen
  Would make you tinder, but to see a fire;
  I ga' you count'nance, credit for your coals,
  Your stills, your glasses, your materials;

18. *vacations:* Note.

19. *suburb-captain:* bawd or pander, brothels being located in *suburbs* or low quarters, outwith the City's jurisdiction.

29. *Roman wash:* an ointment for venereal disease?

35. *kibes:* chilblains.   36. *felt of rug:* hat made of coarse felt.

44–5. *stills,* etc.: see note on alchemical terms.

Built you a furnace, drew you customers,
Advanced all your black arts; lent you, beside,
A house to practise in –

SUBTLE: Your master's house!

FACE: Where you have studied the more thriving skill
Of bawdry since.

SUBTLE: Yes, in your master's house.
You and the rats here kept possession.   *50*
Make it not strange. I know you were one could keep
The buttery-hatch still locked, and save the chippings,
Sell the dole-beer to aqua vitae men,
The which, together with your Christmas vails
At post-and-pair, your letting out of counters,
Made you a pretty stock, some twenty marks,
And gave you credit to converse with cobwebs
Here, since your mistress' death hath broke up house.

FACE: You might talk softlier, rascal.

SUBTLE: No, you scarab,
I'll thunder you in pieces. I will teach you   *60*
How to beware to tempt a Fury again
That carries tempest in his hand and voice.

FACE: The place has made you valiant.

SUBTLE: No, your clothes.
Thou vermin, have I ta'en thee out of dung,
So poor, so wretched, when no living thing
Would keep thee company, but a spider or worse?
Raised thee from brooms and dust and wat'ring-pots?
Sublimed thee, and exalted thee, and fixed thee
I' the third region, called our state of grace?
Wrought thee to spirit, to quintessence, with pains   *70*
Would twice have won me the Philosopher's Work?
Put thee in words and fashion? made thee fit
For more than ordinary fellowships?
Giv'n thee thy oaths, thy quarrelling dimensions?
Thy rules to cheat at horse-race, cock-pit, cards,

52–3. *chippings, dole-beer*: Note.   54. *vails*: tips.
55. *post-and-pair*: a game of cards.   64–80. *Thou vermin*, etc.: Note.
74. *quarrelling dimensions*: Note.

Dice, or whatever gallant tincture else?
Made thee a second in mine own great art?
And have I this for thanks! Do you rebel?
Do you fly out i' the projection?

80 Would you be gone now?

DOL COMMON: Gentlemen, what mean you?
Will you mar all?

SUBTLE: Slave, thou hadst had no name –

DOL COMMON: Will you undo yourselves with civil war?

SUBTLE: Never been known, past *equi clibanum* –
The heat of horse-dung – under ground, in cellars,
Or an ale-house darker than deaf John's; been lost
To all mankind, but laundresses and tapsters,
Had not I been.

DOL COMMON: Do you know who hears you, sovereign?

FACE: Sirrah –

DOL COMMON: Nay, general, I thought you were civil.

FACE: I shall turn desperate, if you grow thus loud.

90 SUBTLE: And hang thyself, I care not.

FACE: Hang thee, collier,
And all thy pots and pans, in picture I will,
Since thou hast moved me –

DOL COMMON [*aside*]:   O, this 'll o'erthrow all.

FACE: Write thee up bawd in Paul's; have all thy tricks
Of coz'ning with a hollow coal, dust, scrapings,
Searching for things lost, with a sieve and shears,
Erecting figures in your rows of houses,
And taking in of shadows with a glass,
Told in red letters; and a face cut for thee,
Worse than Gamaliel Ratsey's.

DOL COMMON: Are you sound?

100 Ha' you your senses, masters?

FACE: I will have
A book, but barely reckoning thy impostures,
Shall prove a true Philosopher's Stone to printers.

79. *projection:* Note.
96. *erecting figures:* casting horoscopes.
97. *taking . . . glass:* divining by means of a crystal globe.

SUBTLE: Away, you trencher-rascal!

FACE: Out, you dog-leech!
  The vomit of all prisons –

DOL COMMON: Will you be
  Your own destructions, gentlemen?

FACE: Still spewed out
  For lying too heavy o' the basket.

SUBTLE: Cheater!

FACE: Bawd!

SUBTLE: Cow-herd!

FACE: Conjurer!

SUBTLE: Cut-purse!

FACE: Witch!

DOL COMMON: O me!
  We are ruined! lost! Ha' you no more regard
  To your reputations? Where's your judgement? 'Slight,
  Have yet some care of me, o' your republic –   110

FACE: Away this brach! I'll bring thee, rogue, within
  The statute of sorcery, *tricesimo tertio*
  Of Harry the Eight: ay, and perhaps thy neck
  Within a noose, for laund'ring gold and barbing it.

DOL COMMON: You'll bring your head within a coxcomb, will
    you?
      She catcheth out FACE'S *sword, and breaks* SUBTLE'S *glass.*
  And you, sir, with your menstrue! – Gather it up.
  'Sdeath, you abominable pair of stinkards,
  Leave off your barking, and grow one again,
  Or, by the light that shines, I'll cut your throats.
  I'll not be made a prey unto the marshal   120
  For ne'er a snarling dog-bolt o' you both.
  Ha' you together cozened all this while,
  And all the world, and shall it now be said,
  You've made most courteous shift to cozen yourselves?
  [*To* FACE] You will accuse him! You will bring him in
  Within the statute! Who shall take your word?

110. *republic:* common-weal – i.e. our fraternity.
111. *brach:* bitch.   116. *menstrue:* menses used as a solvent.
121. *dog-bolt:* worthless person.

A whoreson, upstart, apocryphal Captain,
Whom not a Puritan in Blackfriars will trust
So much as for a feather! [*To* SUBTLE] And you, too,
130   Will give the cause, forsooth? You will insult,
And claim a primacy in the divisions?
You must be chief? As if you only had
The powder to project with? and the work
Were not begun out of equality?
The venture tripartite? All things in common?
Without priority? 'Sdeath! you perpetual curs,
Fall to your couples again, and cozen kindly,
And heartily, and lovingly, as you should,
And lose not the beginning of a term,
140   Or, by this hand, I shall grow factious too,
And take my part, and quit you.

FACE: 'T is his fault;
He ever murmurs, and objects his pains,
And says the weight of all lies upon him.

SUBTLE: Why, so it does.

DOL COMMON: How does it? Do not we
Sustain our parts?

SUBTLE: Yes, but they are not equal.

DOL COMMON: Why, if your part exceed today, I hope
Ours may tomorrow match it.

SUBTLE: Ay, they may.

DOL COMMON: May, murmuring mastiff? Ay, and do. Death
on me!
Help me to throttle him.
[*Seizes* SUBTLE *by the throat.*]

SUBTLE: Dorothy! Mistress Dorothy!
150   'Ods precious, I'll do anything. What do you mean?

DOL COMMON: Because o' your fermentation and cibation!

SUBTLE: Not I, by Heaven –

DOL COMMON: Your Sol and Luna – [*To* FACE] Help me.

---

139. *term:* one of the periods when the law-courts were sitting; the
London social 'season'.

151. *fermentation*, etc.: further alchemical processes.

152. *Sol and Luna:* sun and moon, i.e. gold and silver.

SUBTLE: Would I were hanged then! I'll conform myself.

DOL COMMON: Will you, sir? Do so then, and quickly! Swear.

SUBTLE: What should I swear?

DOL COMMON: To leave your faction, sir,
And labour kindly in the common work.

SUBTLE: Let me not breathe if I meant aught beside.
I only used those speeches as a spur
To him.

DOL COMMON: I hope we need no spurs, sir. Do we?

FACE: 'Slid, prove today who shall shark best.

SUBTLE: Agreed.   160

DOL COMMON: Yes, and work close and friendly.

SUBTLE: 'Slight, the knot
Shall grow the stronger for this breach, with me.

DOL COMMON: Why, so, my good baboons! Shall we go make
A sort of sober, scurvy, precise neighbours,
That scarce have smiled twice sin' the king came in,
A feast of laughter at our follies? – rascals,
Would run themselves from breath, to see me ride,
Or you t' have but a hole to thrust your heads in,
For which you should pay ear-rent? No, agree.
And may Don Provost ride a-feasting long,   170
In his old velvet jerkin and stained scarfs,
My noble sovereign, and worthy general,
Ere we contribute a new crewel garter
To his most worsted worship.

SUBTLE: Royal Dol!
Spoken like Claridiana, and thyself.

FACE: For which at supper, thou shalt sit in triumph,
And not be styled Dol Common, but Dol Proper,
Dol Singular; the longest cut at night
Shall draw thee for his Dol Particular.

160. *shark:* swindle, cheat.
164. *sort:* crowd; *precise:* Puritanical.
167. *ride:* i.e. on a public cart (punishment for a prostitute).
168-9. *hole:* in the pillory; *pay ear-rent:* have your ears cut off, as punishment.
173. *crewel:* pun on 'cruel' and 'crewel' (worsted).

[*Bell rings without.*]

180 SUBTLE: Who's that? One rings. To the window, Dol! – Pray
    heav'n
    The master do not trouble us this quarter.

FACE: O, fear not him. While there dies one a week
    O' the plague, he's safe from thinking toward London.
    Beside, he's busy at his hop-yards now –
    I had a letter from him. If he do,
    He'll send such word, for airing o' the house,
    As you shall have sufficient time to quit it.
    Though we break up a fortnight, 't is no matter.

SUBTLE: Who is it, Dol?

DOL COMMON: A fine young quodling.

FACE: O,

190   My lawyer's clerk, I lighted on last night,
    In Holborn, at the Dagger. He would have
    (I told you of him) a familiar,
    To rifle with at horses, and win cups.

DOL COMMON: O, let him in.

SUBTLE: Stay. Who shall do 't?

FACE: Get you
    Your robes on; I will meet him, as going out.

DOL COMMON: And what shall I do?

FACE: Not be seen; away!
    [*Exit* DOL COMMON.]
    Seem you very reserved.

SUBTLE: Enough.
    [*Exit.*]

FACE [*shouting as he goes to the door*]: God b' w' you, sir!
    I pray you, let him know that I was here:
    His name is Dapper. I would gladly have stayed, but –

I, ii [DAPPER (*off-stage*):] Captain, I am here.

FACE: Who's that? – He's come, I think, Doctor.

189. *quodling*: literally a green apple; unsophisticated youth.
191. *the Dagger*: a tavern of low repute.
192. *familiar*: familiar spirit.   193. *rifle*: gamble.

[FACE *admits* DAPPER.]
Good faith, sir, I was going away.
DAPPER: In truth,
I'm very sorry, Captain.
FACE: But I thought
Sure I should meet you.
DAPPER: Ay, I'm very glad.
I had a scurvy writ or two to make,
And I had lent my watch last night to one
That dines today at the shrieve's, and so was robbed
Of my pass-time.
[*Re-enter* SUBTLE *in his Doctor's cap and gown.*]
                       Is this the cunning-man?
FACE: This is his worship.
DAPPER: Is he a Doctor?
FACE: Yes.
DAPPER: And ha' you broke with him, Captain?
FACE: Ay.
DAPPER: And how?   10
FACE: Faith, he does make the matter, sir, so dainty,
I know not what to say.
DAPPER: Not so, good Captain.
FACE: Would I were fairly rid on 't, believe me.
DAPPER: Nay, now you grieve me, sir. Why should you wish so?
I dare assure you, I'll not be ungrateful.
FACE: I cannot think you will, sir. But the law
Is such a thing – and then he says, Read's matter
Falling so lately –
DAPPER: Read? he was an ass,
And dealt, sir, with a fool.
FACE: It was a clerk, sir.
DAPPER: A clerk!
FACE: Nay, hear me, sir. You know the law   20
Better, I think –
DAPPER: I should, sir, and the danger:
You know, I showed the statute to you.

8. *pass-time:* watch; *cunning-man:* magician, fortune-teller.
10. *broke:* broached the subject.

FACE: You did so.

DAPPER: And will I tell then! By this hand of flesh,
Would it might never write good court-hand more,
If I discover. What do you think of me,
That I am a chiaus?

FACE: What's that?

DAPPER: The Turk was here.
As one would say, do you think I am a Turk?

FACE: I'll tell the Doctor so.

DAPPER: Do, good sweet Captain.

FACE: Come, noble Doctor, pray thee, let's prevail;
30 This is the gentleman, and he is no chiaus.

SUBTLE: Captain, I have returned you all my answer.
I would do much, sir, for your love – But this
I neither may, nor can.

FACE: Tut, do not say so.
You deal now with a noble fellow, Doctor,
One that will thank you richly; and he's no chiaus.
Let that, sir, move you.

SUBTLE: Pray you, forbear –

FACE: He has
Four angels here.

SUBTLE: You do me wrong, good sir.

FACE: Doctor, wherein? To tempt you with these spirits?

SUBTLE: To tempt my art and love, sir, to my peril.
40 'Fore heav'n, I scarce can think you are my friend,
That so would draw me to apparent danger.

FACE: I draw you! A horse draw you, and a halter,
You, and your flies together –

DAPPER: Nay, good Captain.

FACE: That know no difference of men.

SUBTLE: Good words, sir.

FACE: Good deeds, sir, Doctor Dogs'-meat. 'Slight, I bring you
No cheating Clim-o'-the-Cloughs or Claribels,
That look as big as five-and-fifty, and flush;
And spit out secrets like hot custard –

26. *chiaus:* Turkish messenger.   37. *angel:* gold coin.
47. *flush:* winning hand in primero, a card game.

DAPPER: Captain!

FACE: Nor any melancholic under-scribe,
Shall tell the vicar; but a special gentle,   50
That is the heir to forty marks a year,
Consorts with the small poets of the time,
Is the sole hope of his old grandmother;
That knows the law, and writes you six fair hands,
Is a fine clerk, and has his ciph'ring perfect;
Will take his oath o' the Greek Xenophon,
If need be, in his pocket; and can court
His mistress out of Ovid.

DAPPER: Nay, dear Captain –

FACE: Did you not tell me so?

DAPPER: Yes, but I'd ha' you
Use Master Doctor with some more respect.   60

FACE: Hang him, proud stag, with his broad velvet head! –
But for your sake, I'd choke ere I would change
An article of breath with such a puck-fist! –
Come, let's be gone. [Going.]

SUBTLE: Pray you, le' me speak with you.

DAPPER: His worship calls you, Captain.

FACE: I am sorry
I e'er embarked myself in such a business.

DAPPER: Nay, good sir; he did call you.

FACE: Will he take then?

SUBTLE: First, hear me –

FACE: Not a syllable, 'less you take.

SUBTLE: Pray ye, sir –

FACE: Upon no terms but an *assumpsit*.

SUBTLE: Your humour must be law.
     He takes the money.

FACE: Why now, sir, talk.   70
Now I dare hear you with mine honour. Speak.
So may this gentleman too.

SUBTLE: Why, sir –

DAPPER: 'Fore Heav'n, you do not apprehend the loss
You do yourself in this.

         63. *puck-fist:* puff-ball – i.e. boaster.

FACE: Wherein? for what?

SUBTLE: Marry, to be so importunate for one
That, when he has it, will undo you all:
He'll win up all the money i' the town.

FACE: How!

SUBTLE: Yes, and blow up gamester after gamester,
As they do crackers in a puppet-play.
80 If I do give him a familiar,
Give you him all you play for; never set him,
For he will have it.

FACE: You're mistaken, Doctor.
Why, he does ask one but for cups and horses,
A rifling fly; none o' your great familiars.

DAPPER: Yes, Captain, I would have it for all games.

SUBTLE: I told you so.

FACE [to DAPPER]: 'Slight, that's a new business!
I understood you, a tame bird, to fly
Twice in a term, or so, on Friday nights,
When you had left the office, for a nag
90 Of forty or fifty shillings.

DAPPER: Ay, 'tis true, sir;
But I do think now I shall leave the law,
And therefore –

FACE: Why, this changes quite the case!
D' you think that I dare move him?

DAPPER: If you please, sir;
All's one to him, I see.

FACE: What! for that money?
I cannot with my conscience; nor should you
Make the request, methinks.

DAPPER: No, sir, I mean
To add consideration.

FACE: Why, then, sir,
I'll try. [Goes to SUBTLE] Say that it were for all games,
Doctor?

SUBTLE: I say then, not a mouth shall eat for him

79. *crackers*: fireworks. See *Bartholomew Fair*: V, iv, 23.
81. *set*: bet against.

At any ordinary, but o' the score,
That is a gaming mouth, conceive me.
FACE: Indeed!
SUBTLE: He'll draw you all the treasure of the realm,
  If it be set him.
FACE: Speak you this from art?
SUBTLE: Ay, sir, and reason too, the ground of art.
  He's o' the only best complexion,
  The Queen of Faery loves.
FACE: What! Is he?
SUBTLE: Peace.
  He'll overhear you. Sir, should she but see him –
FACE: What?
SUBTLE: Do not you tell him.
FACE: Will he win at cards too?
SUBTLE: The spirits of dead Holland, living Isaac,
  You'd swear, were in him; such a vigorous luck   *110*
  As cannot be resisted. 'Slight, he'll put
  Six o' your gallants to a cloak, indeed.
FACE: A strange success, that some man shall be born to!
SUBTLE: He hears you, man –
DAPPER: Sir, I'll not be ingrateful.
FACE: Faith, I have a confidence in his good nature:
  You hear, he says he will not be ingrateful.
SUBTLE: Why, as you please; my venture follows yours.
FACE: Troth, do it, Doctor; think him trusty, and make him.
  He may make us both happy in an hour;
  Win some five thousand pound, and send us two on't.   *120*
DAPPER: Believe it, and I will, sir.
FACE: And you shall, sir.
        FACE *takes him aside.*
  You have heard all?
DAPPER: No, what was't? Nothing, I, sir.
FACE: Nothing?
DAPPER: A little, sir.

100. *ordinary:* tavern; *o'the score:* on credit.
111-12. *put six o' your gallants to a cloak,* 'force five out of six gamblers to
pawn their cloaks' (G. E. Bentley).

FACE: Well, a rare star
Reigned at your birth.
DAPPER: At mine, sir! No.
FACE: The Doctor
Swears that you are –
SUBTLE: Nay, Captain, you'll tell all now.
FACE: Allied to the Queen of Faery.
DAPPER: Who! That I am?
Believe it, no such matter –
FACE: Yes, and that
You were born with a caul o' your head.
DAPPER: Who says so?
FACE: Come,
You know it well enough, though you dissemble it.
130 DAPPER: I' fac, I do not; you are mistaken.
FACE: How!
Swear by your fac? And in a thing so known
Unto the Doctor? How shall we, sir, trust you
I' the other matter? Can we ever think,
When you have won five or six thousand pound,
You'll send us shares in 't, by this rate?
DAPPER: By Jove, sir,
I'll win ten thousand pound, and send you half.
I' fac's no oath.
SUBTLE: No, no, he did but jest.
FACE: Go to. Go thank the Doctor. He's your friend,
To take it so.
DAPPER: I thank his worship.
FACE: So! –
140 Another angel!
DAPPER: Must I?
FACE: Must you! 'Slight,
What else is thanks? Will you be trivial? –
  [DAPPER *gives him the money*.]
                              Doctor,
When must he come for his familiar?

128. *born with a caul:* a sign of good luck. Note.
130. *I' fac:* in faith.

DAPPER: Shall I not ha' it with me?

SUBTLE: O, good sir!
There must a world of ceremonies pass;
You must be bathed and fumigated first;
Besides, the Queen of Faery does not rise
Till it be noon.

FACE: Not if she danced tonight.

SUBTLE: And she must bless it.

FACE: Did you never see
Her Royal Grace yet?

DAPPER: Whom?

FACE: Your aunt of Faery?

SUBTLE: Not since she kissed him in the cradle, Captain;   *150*
I can resolve you that.

FACE: Well, see her Grace,
Whate'er it cost you, for a thing that I know!
It will be somewhat hard to compass; but
However, see her. You are made, believe it,
If you can see her. Her Grace is a lone woman,
And very rich, and if she take a fancy,
She will do strange things. See her, at any hand.
'Slid, she may hap to leave you all she has!
It is the Doctor's fear.

DAPPER: How will't be done, then?

FACE: Let me alone, take you no thought. Do you   *160*
But say to me, 'Captain, I'll see her Grace'.

DAPPER: Captain, I'll see her Grace.

FACE: Enough.

One knocks without.

SUBTLE: Who's there?
Anon! – [*Aside to* FACE] Conduct him forth by the back way –
Sir, against one o'clock prepare yourself;
Till when, you must be fasting; only, take
Three drops of vinegar in at your nose,
Two at your mouth, and one at either ear;
Then bathe your fingers' ends and wash your eyes,
To sharpen your five senses, and cry 'hum'

147. *tonight:* last night.

170   Thrice, and then 'buzz' as often; and then come.
        [Exit.]
FACE: Can you remember this?
DAPPER: I warrant you.
FACE: Well then, away. 'Tis but your bestowing
    Some twenty nobles 'mong her Grace's servants,
    And put on a clean shirt. You do not know
    What grace her Grace may do you in clean linen.
        [Exeunt FACE *and* DAPPER.]

I, iii [SUBTLE *(within, to other clients)*:] Come in! Good wives, I pray
        you, forbear me now;
    Troth, I can do you no good till afternoon. –
        [Enter SUBTLE, *followed by* DRUGGER.]
    What is your name, say you? Abel Drugger?
DRUGGER: Yes, sir.
SUBTLE: A seller of tobacco?
DRUGGER: Yes, sir.
SUBTLE: Umph!
    Free of the Grocers?
DRUGGER: Ay, an't please you.
SUBTLE: Well –
    Your business, Abel?
DRUGGER: This, an't please your worship:
    I am a young beginner, and am building
    Of a new shop, an't like your worship, just
    At corner of a street. (Here's the plot on 't.)
10   And I would know by art, sir, of your worship,
    Which way I should make my door, by necromancy;
    And where my shelves; and which should be for boxes,
    And which for pots. I would be glad to thrive, sir;
    And I was wished to your worship by a gentleman,
    One Captain Face, that says you know men's planets,
    And their good angels, and their bad.
SUBTLE: I do,

173. *nobles:* coins.
    9. *plot:* plan, diagram.   14. *wished:* recommended.

If I do see 'em –
   [*Enter* FACE.]

FACE: What! my honest Abel?
Thou art well met here.

DRUGGER: Troth, sir, I was speaking,
Just as your worship came here, of your worship.
I pray you, speak for me to Master Doctor.   20

FACE: He shall do anything. Doctor, do you hear?
This is my friend, Abel, an honest fellow;
He lets me have good tobacco, and he does not
Sophisticate it with sack-lees or oil,
Nor washes it in muscadel and grains,
Nor buries it in gravel, under ground,
Wrapped up in greasy leather, or pissed clouts,
But keeps it in fine lily-pots that, opened,
Smell like conserve of roses, or French beans.
He has his maple block, his silver tongs,   30
Winchester pipes, and fire of juniper:
A neat, spruce, honest fellow, and no goldsmith.

SUBTLE: He's a fortunate fellow, that I am sure on.

FACE: Already, sir, ha' you found it? Lo thee, Abel!

SUBTLE: And in right way toward riches –

FACE: Sir!

SUBTLE: This summer
He will be of the clothing of his company,
And next spring called to the scarlet, spend what he can.

FACE: What, and so little beard?

SUBTLE: Sir, you must think,
He may have a receipt to make hair come.
But he'll be wise – preserve his youth – and fine for 't;   40
His fortune looks for him another way.

FACE: 'Slid, Doctor, how canst thou know this so soon?
I am amused at that.

24. *sophisticate:* adulterate.
25. *grains:* grains of paradise – a kind of spice.
28–31. *lily-pots,* etc.: Note.   32. *goldsmith:* usurer.
40. *fine:* pay a forfeit rather than take office as Sheriff.
43. *amused:* amazed.

SUBTLE: By a rule, Captain,
In metoposcopy, which I do work by;
A certain star i' the forehead, which you see not.
Your chestnut or your olive-coloured face
Does never fail, and your long ear doth promise.
I knew 't by certain spots, too, in his teeth,
And on the nail of his Mercurial finger.
50 FACE: Which finger's that?
SUBTLE: His little finger. Look.
You were born upon a Wednesday?
DRUGGER: Yes, indeed, sir.
SUBTLE: The thumb, in chiromancy, we give Venus;
The forefinger to Jove; the midst to Saturn;
The ring to Sol; the least to Mercury,
Who was the lord, sir, of his horoscope,
His house of life being Libra; which foreshowed
He should be a merchant, and should trade with balance.
FACE: Why, this is strange! Is't not, honest Nab?
SUBTLE: There is a ship now coming from Ormus,
60 That shall yield him such a commodity
Of drugs – This is the west, and this the south?
  [*Looking at the plan.*]
DRUGGER: Yes, sir.
SUBTLE: And those are your two sides?
DRUGGER: Ay, sir.
SUBTLE: Make me your door then, south; your broad side, west;
And on the east side of your shop, aloft,
Write Mathlai, Tarmiel, and Baraborat;
Upon the north part, Rael, Velel, Thiel.
They are the names of those Mercurial spirits
That do fright flies from boxes.
DRUGGER: Yes, sir.
SUBTLE: And
Beneath your threshold, bury me a loadstone
70 To draw in gallants that wear spurs. The rest,

44. *metoposcopy:* the art of telling a man's fortune from his forehead or face.
69. *loadstone:* magnet.

They'll seem to follow.

FACE: That's a secret, Nab!

SUBTLE: And, on your stall, a puppet, with a vice,
And a court-fucus, to call City-dames.
You shall deal much with minerals.

DRUGGER: Sir, I have,
At home, already –

SUBTLE: Ay, I know, you've arsenic,
Vitriol, sal-tartar, argaile, alkali,
Cinoper: I know all. – This fellow, Captain,
Will come, in time, to be a great distiller,
And give a say – I will not say directly,
But very fair – at the Philosopher's Stone.   80

FACE: Why, how now, Abel! is this true?

DRUGGER [aside to FACE]:   Good Captain,
What must I give?

FACE: Nay, I'll not counsel thee.
Thou hear'st what wealth he says (spend what thou canst)
Th' art like to come to.

DRUGGER: I would gi' him a crown.

FACE: A crown! and toward such a fortune? Heart,
Thou shalt rather gi' him thy shop. No gold about thee?

DRUGGER: Yes, I have a portague, I ha' kept this half-year.

FACE: Out on thee, Nab! 'Slight, there was such an offer –
Shalt keep 't no longer, I'll gi' it him for thee. Doctor,
Nab prays your worship to drink this, and swears   90
He will appear more grateful, as your skill
Does raise him in the world.

DRUGGER: I would entreat
Another favour of his worship.

FACE: What is't, Nab?

DRUGGER: But to look over, sir, my almanac,
And cross out my ill-days, that I may neither
Bargain, nor trust upon them.

FACE: That he shall, Nab.

---

73. *court-fucus:* cosmetic used by Court ladies.
79. *give a say:* make an assay, an attempt.
87. *portague:* gold coin.

Leave it, it shall be done, 'gainst afternoon.

SUBTLE: And a direction for his shelves.

FACE: Now, Nab,
Art thou well pleased, Nab?

DRUGGER: 'Thank, sir, both your worships.

FACE: Away.

[*Exit* DRUGGER.]

100   Why, now, you smoky persecutor of nature!
Now do you see, that something's to be done,
Beside your beech-coal, and your cor'sive waters,
Your crosslets, crucibles, and cucurbites?
You must have stuff brought home to you, to work on!
And yet you think I am at no expense
In searching out these veins, then following 'em,
Then trying 'em out. 'Fore God, my intelligence
Costs me more money than my share oft comes to,
In these rare works.

SUBTLE: You're pleasant, sir.

[*Enter* DOL.]

                                        – How now!

I, iv   What says my dainty Dolkin?

DOL COMMON: Yonder fish-wife
Will not away. And there's your giantess,
The bawd of Lambeth.

SUBTLE: 'Heart, I cannot speak with 'em.

DOL COMMON: Not afore night, I have told 'em in a voice,
Thorough the trunk, like one of your familiars.
But I have spied Sir Epicure Mammon –

SUBTLE: Where?

DOL COMMON: Coming along, at far end of the lane,
Slow of his feet, but earnest of his tongue
To one that's with him.

SUBTLE: Face, go you and shift.

102. *cor'sive:* corrosive.
103. *crosslets*, etc.: apparatus used by alchemists.
5. *trunk:* speaking tube.   9. *shift:* change your clothes.

Dol, you must presently make ready, too.   *10*
   [*Exit* FACE.]
DOL COMMON: Why, what's the matter?
SUBTLE: O, I did look for him
With the sun's rising; marvel he could sleep!
This is the day I am to perfect for him
The magisterium, our great work, the Stone;
And yield it, made, into his hands; of which
He has, this month, talked as he were possessed.
And now he's dealing pieces on 't away.
Methinks I see him ent'ring ordinaries,
Dispensing for the pox, and plaguy houses,
Reaching his dose, walking Moorfields for lepers,   *20*
And off'ring citizens' wives pomander-bracelets
As his preservative, made of the elixir;
Searching the 'spital, to make old bawds young;
And the highways, for beggars to make rich.
I see no end of his labours. He will make
Nature ashamed of her long sleep; when art,
Who's but a step-dame, shall do more than she,
In her best love to mankind, ever could.
If his dream last, he'll turn the age to gold.
   [*Exeunt.*]

19. *plaguy houses:* houses stricken with the plague.
   21. *pomander:* a ball containing perfume as a protection (*preservative*)
against infection.
   23. *'spital:* hospital.

ACT TWO

[SCENE ONE]

[*Outside* LOVEWIT'S *house.*]

[*Enter* SIR EPICURE MAMMON *and* PERTINAX SURLY.]
[MAMMON:] Come on, sir. Now you set your foot on shore
In *Novo Orbe*; here's the rich Peru,
And there within, sir, are the golden mines,
Great Solomon's Ophir! He was sailing to 't
Three years, but we have reached it in ten months.
This is the day wherein, to all my friends,
I will pronounce the happy word, 'Be rich!'
This day you shall be *spectatissimi*.
You shall no more deal with the hollow die,
10   Or the frail card. No more be at charge of keeping
The livery-punk for the young heir, that must
Seal, at all hours, in his shirt; no more,
If he deny, ha' him beaten to 't, as he is
That brings him the commodity; no more
Shall thirst of satin, or the covetous hunger
Of velvet entrails for a rude-spun cloak,
To be displayed at Madam Augusta's, make
The sons of sword and hazard fall before
The golden calf, and on their knees, whole nights,
20   Commit idolatry with wine and trumpets,
Or go a-feasting after drum and ensign.
No more of this. You shall start up young viceroys,
And have your punks and punketees, my Surly.
And unto thee I speak it first, 'Be rich!'
Where is my Subtle there? Within, ho!

8. *spectatissimi:* literally, most gazed at; highly esteemed.
9. *hollow die:* loaded dice.
11. *livery-punk:* prostitute acting as accomplice to a confidence-trickster
(ironically, unknown to Mammon, Dol Common is precisely this).
16. *entrails:* lining.   23. *punketees:* young prostitutes.

[FACE (*within*):]   Sir,
  He'll come to you by and by.
MAMMON: That's his fire-drake,
  His Lungs, his Zephyrus, he that puffs his coals,
  Till he firk nature up, in her own centre.
  You are not faithful, sir. This night I'll change
  All that is metal in my house to gold,   30
  And, early in the morning, will I send
  To all the plumbers and the pewterers
  And buy their tin and lead up; and to Lothbury
  For all the copper.
SURLY: What, and turn that, too?
MAMMON: Yes, and I'll purchase Devonshire and Cornwall,
  And make them perfect Indies! You admire now?
SURLY: No, faith.
MAMMON: But when you see th' effects of the Great Med'cine,
  Of which one part projected on a hundred
  Of Mercury, or Venus, or the Moon,
  Shall turn it to as many of the Sun –   40
  Nay, to a thousand – so *ad infinitum*;
  You will believe me.
SURLY: Yes, when I see 't, I will.
  But if my eyes do cozen me so, and I
  Giving 'em no occasion, sure I'll have
  A whore, shall piss 'em out next day.
MAMMON: Ha! Why?
  Do you think I fable with you? I assure you,
  He that has once the flower of the sun,
  The perfect ruby, which we call elixir,
  Not only can do that, but by its virtue,
  Can confer honour, love, respect, long life;   50
  Give safety, valour, yea, and victory,
  To whom he will. In eight-and-twenty days,
  I'll make an old man of fourscore a child.

---

26. *fire-drake*: dragon.
  27. *Lungs*: Mammon's nickname for Face – Subtle's 'bellows' and
laboratory-assistant.   28. *firk*: stir.
  29. *faithful*: believing (i.e. in alchemy).   36. *admire*: wonder

SURLY: No doubt he's that already.

MAMMON: Nay, I mean,
Restore his years, renew him, like an eagle,
To the fifth age; make him get sons and daughters,
Young giants, as our philosophers have done –
The ancient patriarchs, afore the flood –
But taking, once a week, on a knife's point,

60   The quantity of a grain of mustard of it;
Become stout Marses, and beget young Cupids.

SURLY: The decayed vestals of Pickt-hatch would thank you,
That keep the fire alive there.

MAMMON: 'Tis the secret
Of nature naturized 'gainst all infections,
Cures all diseases coming of all causes;
A month's grief in a day, a year's in twelve;
And, of what age soever, in a month,
Past all the doses of your drugging doctors.
I'll undertake, withal, to fright the plague

70   Out o' the kingdom in three months.

SURLY: And I'll
Be bound, the players shall sing your praises then,
Without their poets.

MAMMON: Sir, I'll do 't. Meantime,
I'll give away so much unto my man,
Shall serve th' whole City with preservative
Weekly; each house his dose, and at the rate –

SURLY: As he that built the water-work does with water?

MAMMON: You are incredulous.

SURLY: Faith, I have a humour,
I would not willingly be gulled. Your Stone
Cannot transmute me.

MAMMON: Pertinax, my Surly,

80   Will you believe antiquity? records?
I'll show you a book where Moses, and his sister,
And Solomon have written of the art;
Ay, and a treatise penned by Adam –

63–9. *the secret*, etc.: Note.
71. *the players*: Note.   81–3. *Moses, Solomon*, etc.: Note.

SURLY: How!
MAMMON: O' the Philosopher's Stone, and in High Dutch.
SURLY: Did Adam write, sir, in High Dutch?
MAMMON: He did;
    Which proves it was the primitive tongue.
SURLY: What paper?
MAMMON: On cedar board.
SURLY: O that, indeed, they say,
    Will last 'gainst worms.
MAMMON: 'Tis like your Irish wood
    'Gainst cobwebs. I have a piece of Jason's fleece, too,
    Which was no other than a book of alchemy,   90
    Writ in large sheepskin, a good fat ram-vellum.
    Such was Pythagoras' thigh, Pandora's tub,
    And all that fable of Medea's charms,
    The manner of our work: the bulls, our furnace,
    Still breathing fire; our *argent-vive*, the dragon;
    The dragon's teeth, mercury sublimate,
    That keeps the whiteness, hardness, and the biting;
    And they are gathered into Jason's helm,
    Th' alembic, and then sowed in Mars's field,
    And thence sublimed so often, till they're fixed.   100
    Both this, th' Hesperian garden, Cadmus' story,
    Jove's shower, the boon of Midas, Argus' eyes,
    Boccace's Demogorgon, thousands more,
    All abstract riddles of our Stone.

[SCENE TWO]   II, ii

    [FACE, *disguised as* SUBTLE'S *servant*, LUNGS *or* ULEN
    SPIEGEL, *admits them into the house.*]
[MAMMON:]   – How now!
    Do we succeed? Is our day come? And holds it?
FACE: The evening will set red upon you, sir;
    You have colour for it, crimson; the red ferment

89–104. *Jason's fleece*, etc.: Note.   95. *argent-vive*: quicksilver.
102. *Demogorgon*: Note.

Has done his office; three hours hence prepare you
To see projection.

MAMMON: Pertinax, my Surly,
Again I say to thee, aloud, 'Be rich!'
This day thou shalt have ingots, and tomorrow
Give lords th' affront. – Is it, my Zephyrus, right?
Blushes the bolt's head?

FACE: Like a wench with child, sir,
10 That were but now discovered to her master.

MAMMON: Excellent, witty Lungs! – My only care is
Where to get stuff enough now, to project on;
This town will not half serve me.

FACE: No, sir? Buy
The covering off o' churches.

MAMMON: That's true.

FACE: Yes.
Let 'em stand bare, as do their auditory,
Or cap 'em new with shingles.

MAMMON: No, good thatch –
Thatch will lie light upo' the rafters, Lungs.
Lungs, I will manumit thee from the furnace;
I will restore thee thy complexion, Puff,
20 Lost in the embers; and repair this brain,
Hurt wi' the fume o' the metals.

FACE: I have blown, sir,
Hard, for your worship; thrown by many a coal,
When 't was not beech; weighed those I put in, just,
To keep your heat still even. These bleared eyes
Have waked to read your several colours, sir,
Of the pale citron, the green lion, the crow,
The peacock's tail, the plumèd swan.

MAMMON: And lastly,
Thou hast descried the flower, the *sanguis agni*?

FACE: Yes, sir.

MAMMON: Where's Master?

FACE: At's prayers, sir, he;

9. *bolt's head:* flask.   14. *auditory:* congregation.
23. *just:* exactly.   28. *sanguis agni:* blood of the Lamb.

Good man, he's doing his devotions 30
For the success.

MAMMON: Lungs, I will set a period
To all thy labours; thou shalt be the master
Of my seraglio.

FACE: Good, sir.

MAMMON: But do you hear?
I'll geld you, Lungs.

FACE: Yes, sir.

MAMMON: For I do mean
To have a list of wives and concubines
Equal with Solomon, who had the Stone
Alike with me; and I will make me a back
With the elixir, that shall be as tough
As Hercules, to encounter fifty a night. –
Th'art sure thou saw'st it blood?

FACE: Both blood and spirit, sir. 40

MAMMON: I will have all my beds blown up, not stuffed:
Down is too hard; and then, mine oval room
Filled with such pictures as Tiberius took
From Elephantis, and dull Aretine
But coldly imitated. Then, my glasses
Cut in more subtle angles, to disperse
And multiply the figures, as I walk
Naked between my *succubae*. My mists
I'll have of perfume, vapoured 'bout the room,
To lose our selves in; and my baths, like pits 50
To fall into, from whence we will come forth,
And roll us dry in gossamer and roses. –
Is it arrived at ruby? – Where I spy
A wealthy citizen, or rich lawyer,
Have a sublimed, pure wife, unto that fellow
I'll send a thousand pound to be my cuckold.

FACE: And I shall carry it?

MAMMON: No, I'll ha' no bawds
But fathers and mothers – they will do it best,
Best of all others. And my flatterers

48. *succubae*: here, concubines.

219

60   Shall be the pure and gravest of divines
       That I can get for money. My mere fools
       Eloquent burgesses, and then my poets
       The same that writ so subtly of the fart,
       Whom I will entertain still for that subject.
       The few that would give out themselves to be
       Court- and town-stallions and each-where bely
       Ladies who are known most innocent, for them,
       These will I beg, to make me eunuchs of,
       And they shall fan me with ten estrich tails
70   Apiece, made in a plume to gather wind.
       We will be brave, Puff, now we ha' the med'cine.
       My meat shall all come in, in Indian shells,
       Dishes of agate set in gold, and studded
       With emeralds, sapphires, hyacinths, and rubies.
       The tongues of carps, dormice, and camels' heels,
       Boiled i' the spirit of Sol, and dissolved pearl
       (Apicius' diet, 'gainst the epilepsy);
       And I will eat these broths with spoons of amber,
       Headed with diamond and carbuncle.
80   My foot-boy shall eat pheasants, calvered salmons,
       Knots, godwits, lampreys. I myself will have
       The beards of barbels served instead of salads;
       Oiled mushrooms; and the swelling unctuous paps
       Of a fat pregnant sow, newly cut off,
       Dressed with an exquisite and poignant sauce;
       For which, I'll say unto my cook, 'There's gold;
       Go forth, and be a knight!'

FACE: Sir, I'll go look
       A little, how it heightens.
         [*Exit.*]

74. *hyacinth*: a precious stone.

76. *spirit of Sol*: gold.

80. *calvered*: unknown – evidently an elaborate way of preparing fish while alive.

81. *knots*: a kind of sandpiper, *godwits*: a kind of snipe.

82. *barbel*: a kind of fresh-water fish.

87. *be a knight*: Note.

MAMMON: Do. – My shirts
  I'll have of taffeta-sarsnet, soft and light
  As cobwebs; and for all my other raiment,   *90*
  It shall be such as might provoke the Persian,
  Were he to teach the world riot anew.
  My gloves of fishes' and birds' skins, perfumed
  With gums of paradise, and Eastern air –
SURLY: And do you think to have the Stone with this?
MAMMON: No, I do think t' have all this with the Stone.
SURLY: Why, I have heard he must be *homo frugi*,
  A pious, holy, and religious man,
  One free from mortal sin, a very virgin.
MAMMON: That makes it, sir; he is so. But I buy it;   *100*
  My venture brings it me. He, honest wretch,
  A notable, superstitious, good soul,
  Has worn his knees bare and his slippers bald
  With prayer and fasting for it. And, sir, let him
  Do it alone, for me, still. Here he comes.
  Not a profane word afore him; 'tis poison –

  [*Enter* SUBTLE.]   II, iii

MAMMON: Good morrow, father.
SUBTLE: Gentle son, good morrow,
  And to your friend there. What is he is with you?
MAMMON: An heretic, that I did bring along,
  In hope, sir, to convert him.
SUBTLE: Son, I doubt
  You're covetous, that thus you meet your time
  I' the just point; prevent your day at morning.
  This argues something worthy of a fear
  Of importune and carnal appetite.
  Take heed you do not cause the blessing leave you,
  With your ungoverned haste. I should be sorry   *10*
  To see my labours, now e'en at perfection,
  Got by long watching and large patience,

    89. *taffeta-sarsnet:* very fine silk.
    97. *homo frugi:* a temperate man.   6. *just:* exact.

Not prosper where my love and zeal hath placed 'em:
Which (Heaven I call to witness, with your self,
To whom I have poured my thoughts) in all my ends,
Have looked no way, but unto public good,
To pious uses, and dear charity,
Now grown a prodigy with men. Wherein
If you, my son, should now prevaricate,
And to your own particular lusts employ
So great and catholic a bliss, be sure
A curse will follow, yea, and overtake
Your subtle and most secret ways.

MAMMON: I know, sir,
You shall not need to fear me. I but come
To ha' you confute this gentleman.

SURLY: Who is,
Indeed, sir, somewhat costive of belief
Toward your Stone; would not be gulled.

SUBTLE: Well, son,
All that I can convince him in, is this,
The work is done, bright Sol is in his robe.
We have a med'cine of the triple soul,
The glorified spirit. Thanks be to Heaven,
And make us worthy of it! –
    [*Calling to* FACE.]
                                    Ulen Spiegel!

FACE [*within*]: Anon, sir.

SUBTLE: Look well to the register,
And let your heat still lessen by degrees,
To the aludels.

FACE [*within*]:   Yes, sir.

SUBTLE: Did you look
O' the bolt's-head yet?

FACE [*within*]:   Which? On D., sir?

SUBTLE: Ay.
What's the complexion?

FACE [*within*]:   Whitish.

SUBTLE: Infuse vinegar,
To draw his volatile substance and his tincture,

And let the water in glass E. be filtered,
And put into the gripe's egg. Lute him well;   40
And leave him closed *in balneo*.
FACE [*within*]:   I will, sir.
SURLY [*aside*]: What a brave language here is! next to canting!
SUBTLE: I have another work you never saw, son,
 That three days since passed the Philosopher's Wheel,
 In the lent heat of Athanor, and 's become
 Sulphur o' Nature.
MAMMON: But 'tis for me?
SUBTLE: What need you?
 You have enough in that is perfect.
MAMMON: O, but –
SUBTLE: Why, this is covetise!
MAMMON: No, I assure you,
 I shall employ it all in pious uses,
 Founding of colleges and grammar schools,   50
 Marrying young virgins, building hospitals,
 And, now and then, a church.
  [*Enter* FACE.]
SUBTLE: How now!
FACE: Sir, please you,
 Shall I not change the filter?
SUBTLE: Marry, yes;
 And bring me the complexion of glass B.
  [*Exit* FACE.]
MAMMON: Ha' you another?
SUBTLE: Yes, son; were I assured
 Your piety were firm, we would not want
 The means to glorify it. But I hope the best.
 I mean to tinct C. in sand-heat tomorrow,
 And give him imbibition.
MAMMON: Of white oil?
SUBTLE: No, sir, of red. F. is come over the helm too,   60
 I thank my maker, in St Mary's bath,
 And shows *lac virginis*. Blessèd be heaven!

   42. *canting*: rogues' slang or jargon.
   48. *covetise*: covetousness.

I sent you of his fæces there calcined;
Out of that calx, I ha' won the salt of mercury.

MAMMON: By pouring on your rectifièd water?

SUBTLE: Yes, and reverberating in Athanor.

   [*Re-enter* FACE.]

How now! what colour says it?

FACE: The ground black, sir.

MAMMON: That's your crow's head?

SURLY [*aside*]:   Your cox-comb's, is it not?

SUBTLE: No, 'tis not perfect. Would it were the crow!
70   That work wants something.

SURLY [*aside*]:   O, I looked for this,
The hay is a-pitching.

SUBTLE: Are you sure you loosed 'em
I' their own menstrue?

FACE: Yes, sir, and then married 'em,
And put 'em in a bolt's-head nipped to digestion,
According as you bade me, when I set
The liquor of Mars to circulation
In the same heat.

SUBTLE: The process then was right.

FACE: Yes, by the token, sir, the retort brake,
And what was saved was put into the pelican,
And signed with Hermes' seal.

SUBTLE: I think 't was so
80   We should have a new amalgama.

SURLY [*aside*]:   O, this ferret
Is rank as any polecat.

SUBTLE: But I care not;
Let him e'en die; we have enough beside
In embrion. H. has his white shirt on?

FACE: Yes, sir,
He's ripe for inceration, he stands warm,
In his ash-fire. I would not you should let
Any die now, if I might counsel, sir,

71. *hay:* a net for catching rabbits; 'coney-catching' in Jacobean times meant confidence-tricking.

75. *liquor of Mars:* molten iron.

For luck's sake to the rest. It is not good.

MAMMON: He says right.

SURLY [aside]:   Ay, are you bolted?

FACE: Nay, I know 't, sir,

I've seen th' ill fortune. What is some three ounces

Of fresh materials?

MAMMON: Is 't no more?

FACE: No more, sir,   90

Of gold, t' amalgam with some six of mercury.

MAMMON: Away, here's money. What will serve?

FACE: Ask him, sir.

MAMMON: How much?

SUBTLE: Give him nine pound; you may gi' him ten.

SURLY [aside]: Yes, twenty, and be cozened; do.

MAMMON: There 'tis.

    [*Gives* FACE *the money.*]

SUBTLE: This needs not; but that you will have it so,

To see conclusions of all. For two

Of our inferior works are at fixation,

A third is in ascension. Go your ways.

Ha' you set the oil of Luna in kemia?

FACE: Yes, sir.

SUBTLE: And the Philosopher's Vinegar?

FACE: Ay.   100

    [*Exit.*]

SURLY [aside]: We shall have a salad!

MAMMON: When do you make projection?

SUBTLE: Son, be not hasty. I exalt our med'cine,

By hanging him *in balneo vaporoso*,

And giving him solution; then congeal him;

And then dissolve him; then again congeal him.

For look, how oft I iterate the work,

So many times I add unto his virtue.

As, if at first one ounce convert a hundred,

After his second loose, he'll turn a thousand;

88. *bolted:* driven by the ferret into the net (develops metaphor in line 71).

99. *kemia:* vessel for distilling in.

110 His third solution, ten; his fourth, a hundred;
After his fifth, a thousand thousand ounces
Of any imperfect metal, into pure
Silver or gold, in all examinations
As good as any of the natural mine.
Get you your stuff here against afternoon,
Your brass, your pewter, and your andirons.
MAMMON: Not those of iron?
SUBTLE: Yes, you may bring them too;
We'll change all metals
SURLY [aside]: I believe you in that.
MAMMON: Then I may send my spits?
SUBTLE: Yes, and your racks.
120 SURLY: And dripping-pans, and pot-hangers, and hooks?
Shall he not?
SUBTLE: If he please.
SURLY: – To be an ass.
SUBTLE: How, sir!
MAMMON: This gent'man you must bear withal.
I told you he had no faith.
SURLY: And little hope, sir;
But much less charity, should I gull myself.
SUBTLE: Why, what have you observed, sir, in our art,
Seems so impossible?
SURLY: But your whole work, no more:
That you should hatch gold in a furnace, sir,
As they do eggs in Egypt!
SUBTLE: Sir, do you
Believe that eggs are hatched so?
SURLY: If I should?
130 SUBTLE: Why, I think that the greater miracle.
No egg but differs from a chicken more
Than metals in themselves.
SURLY: That cannot be.
The egg's ordained by nature to that end,
And is a chicken *in potentia*.
SUBTLE: The same we say of lead and other metals,
Which would be gold if they had time.

226

MAMMON: And that
  Our art doth further.
SUBTLE: Ay, for 't were absurd
  To think that nature in the earth bred gold
  Perfect, i' the instant. Something went before.
  There must be remote matter.
SURLY: Ay, what is that?   *140*
SUBTLE: Marry, we say –
MAMMON: Ay, now it heats! Stand, father,
  Pound him to dust.
SUBTLE: It is, of the one part,
  A humid exhalation, which we call
  Materia liquida, or the unctuous water;
  On th' other part, a certain crass and viscous
  Portion of earth; both which, concorporate,
  Do make the elementary matter of gold;
  Which is not yet *propria materia*,
  But common to all metals and all stones.
  For, where it is forsaken of that moisture,   *150*
  And hath more dryness, it becomes a stone;
  Where it retains more of the humid fatness,
  It turns to sulphur or to quicksilver,
  Who are the parents of all other metals.
  Nor can this remote matter suddenly
  Progress so from extreme unto extreme,
  As to grow gold, and leap o'er all the means.
  Nature doth first beget th' imperfect, then
  Proceeds she to the perfect. Of that airy
  And oily water, mercury is engend'red;   *160*
  Sulphur o' the fat and earthy part; the one
  Which is the last supplying the place of male,
  The other of the female, in all metals.
  Some do believe hermaphrodeity,
  That both do act and suffer. But these two
  Make the rest ductile, malleable, extensive.
  And even in gold they are; for we do find
  Seeds of them by our fire, and gold in them;

157. *means:* intermediate stages.

And can produce the species of each metal
170   More perfect thence, than nature doth in earth.
Beside, who doth not see in daily practice
Art can beget bees, hornets, beetles, wasps,
Out of the carcasses and dung of creatures;
Yea, scorpions of an herb, being rightly placed?
And these are living creatures, far more perfect
And excellent than metals.

MAMMON: Well said, father!
Nay, if he take you in hand, sir, with an argument,
He'll bray you in a mortar.

SURLY: Pray you, sir, stay.
Rather than I'll be brayed, sir, I'll believe
180   That Alchemy is a pretty kind of game,
Somewhat like tricks o' the cards, to cheat a man
With charming.

SUBTLE: Sir?

SURLY: What else are all your terms,
Whereon no one o' your writers 'grees with other?
Of your elixir, your *lac virginis*,
Your Stone, your med'cine, and your chrysosperm,
Your sal, your sulphur, and your mercury,
Your oil of height, your Tree of Life, your blood,
Your marchesite, your tutie, your magnesia,
Your Toad, your Crow, your Dragon, and your Panther,
190   Your sun, your moon, your firmament, your adrop,
Your *lato, azoch, zernich, chibrit, heautarit,*
And then your red man, and your white woman,
With all your broths, your menstrues, and materials
Of piss and egg-shells, women's terms, man's blood,
Hair o' the head, burnt clouts, chalk, merds, and clay,
Powder of bones, scalings of iron, glass,
And worlds of other strange ingredients,
Would burst a man to name?

SUBTLE: And all these, named,

178. *bray:* pulverize.
192. *red man:* sulphur; *white woman:* mercury.
193. *terms:* menses.   195. *merds:* fæces.

Intending but one thing; which art our writers
Used to obscure their art.

MAMMON: Sir, so I told him –   200
Because the simple idiot should not learn it,
And make it vulgar.

SUBTLE: Was not all the knowledge
Of the Egyptians writ in mystic symbols?
Speak not the Scriptures oft in parables?
Are not the choicest fables of the poets,
That were the fountains and first springs of wisdom,
Wrapped in perplexèd allegories?

MAMMON: I urged that,
And cleared to him, that Sisyphus was damned
To roll the ceaseless stone, only because
He would have made ours common.

        DOL *is seen [at the door.]*

                              Who is this?   210

SUBTLE: God's precious! – What do you mean? Go in, good lady,
Let me entreat you.
        [DOL *retires.*]
        [*Calling.*]   Where's this varlet?
        [*Re-enter* FACE.]

FACE: Sir.

SUBTLE: You very knave! do you use me thus?

FACE: Wherein, sir?

SUBTLE: Go in and see, you traitor. Go!
        [*Exit* FACE.]

MAMMON: Who is it, sir?

SUBTLE: Nothing, sir; nothing.

MAMMON: What's the matter, good sir?
I have not seen you thus distemp'red: who is 't?

SUBTLE: All arts have still had, sir, their adversaries;
But ours the most ignorant. –
        FACE *returns.*

                              What now?

FACE: 'Twas not my fault, sir; she would speak with you.   220

SUBTLE: Would she, sir! Follow me.
        [*Exit.*]

MAMMON: Stay, Lungs!

FACE: I dare not, sir.

MAMMON: Stay, man; what is she?

FACE: A lord's sister, sir.

MAMMON: How! Pray thee, stay.

FACE: She's mad, sir, and sent hither –
     He'll be mad too –

MAMMON: I warrant thee. Why sent hither?

FACE: Sir, to be cured.

SUBTLE [*within*]:   Why, rascal!

FACE: Lo, you! – here, sir!
     He goes out.

MAMMON: 'Fore God, a Bradamante, a brave piece!

SURLY: 'Heart, this is a bawdy-house! I'll be burnt else.

MAMMON: O, by this light, no! Do not wrong him. He's
     Too scrupulous that way. It is his vice.
     No, he's a rare physician, do him right.
230 An excellent Paracelsian! And has done
     Strange cures with mineral physic. He deals all
     With spirits, he. He will not hear a word
     Of Galen, or his tedious recipes. –
         FACE *again.*

                         How now, Lungs!

FACE: Softly, sir; speak softly. I meant
     To ha' told your worship all. This must not hear.

MAMMON: No, he will not be gulled; let him alone.

FACE: Y'are very right, sir; she is a most rare scholar,
     And is gone mad with studying Broughton's works.
     If you but name a word touching the Hebrew,
240 She falls into her fit, and will discourse
     So learnedly of genealogies,
     As you would run mad, too, to hear her, sir.

MAMMON: How might one do t' have conference with her,
     Lungs?

FACE: O, divers have run mad upon the conference.
     I do not know, sir. I am sent in haste
     To fetch a vial.

224. *I warrant thee:* 'I promise to protect you (against Subtle's anger).'

230

SURLY: Be not gulled, Sir Mammon.

MAMMON: Wherein? Pray ye, be patient.

SURLY: Yes, as you are,
  And trust confederate knaves and bawds and whores.

MAMMON: You are too foul, believe it. – Come here, Ulen,
  One word.

FACE: I dare not, in good faith.

MAMMON: Stay, knave!   250

FACE: He's extreme angry that you saw her, sir.

MAMMON: Drink that. [*Gives him money.*] What is she when she's
  out of her fit?

FACE: O, the most affablest creature, sir! so merry!
  So pleasant! She'll mount you up, like quicksilver
  Over the helm, and circulate like oil,
  A very vegetal; discourse of state,
  Of mathematics, bawdry, anything –

MAMMON: Is she no way accessible? no means,
  No trick to give a man a taste of her – wit –
  Or so?

SUBTLE [*within*]: Ulen!

FACE: I'll come to you again, sir.   260
  [*Exit.*]

MAMMON: Surly, I did not think one o' your breeding
  Would traduce personages of worth.

SURLY: Sir Epicure,
  Your friend to use; yet still loath to be gulled:
  I do not like your philosophical bawds.
  Their Stone is lechery enough to pay for,
  Without this bait.

MAMMON: 'Heart, you abuse yourself.
  I know the lady, and her friends, and means,
  The original of this disaster. Her brother
  Has told me all.

SURLY: And yet you ne'er saw her
  Till now!

MAMMON: O yes, but I forgot. I have, believe it,   270
  One o' the treacherous'st memories, I do think,
  Of all mankind.

SURLY: What call you her brother?

MAMMON: My Lord –
He wi' not have his name known, now I think on 't.

SURLY: A very treacherous memory!

MAMMON: O' my faith –

SURLY: Tut, if you ha' it not about you, pass it
Till we meet next.

MAMMON: Nay, by this hand, 'tis true.
He's one I honour, and my noble friend;
And I respect his house.

SURLY: 'Heart! can it be
That a grave sir, a rich, that has no need,
280 A wise sir, too, at other times, should thus,
With his own oaths and arguments make hard means
To gull himself? An' this be your elixir,
Your *lapis mineralis*, and your lunary,
Give me your honest trick yet at primero,
Or gleek; and take your *lutum sapientis*,
Your *menstruum simplex*! I'll have gold before you,
And with less danger of the quicksilver,
Or the hot sulphur.

[*Re-enter* FACE.]

FACE (*To* SURLY): Here's one from Captain Face, sir,
Desires you meet him i' the Temple–church,
290 Some half-hour hence, and upon earnest business.

He whispers MAMMON.

Sir, if you please to quit us now, and come
Again within two hours, you shall have
My master busy examining o' the works;
And I will steal you in unto the party,
That you may see her converse. [*To* SURLY] Sir, shall I say
You'll meet the Captain's worship?

SURLY: Sir, I will. –
[*Aside*] But, by attorney, and to a second purpose.

283. *lapis mineralis*: Philosopher's Stone.
284–5. *primero, gleek*: games of cards.
287. *danger of the quicksilver*: refers to the standard treatment of venereal disease, as does *sulphur*: line 288.

Now I am sure it is a bawdy-house;
I'll swear it, were the Marshal here to thank me!
The naming this commander doth confirm it.
Don Face! Why he's the most authentic dealer   *300*
I' these commodities, the superintendent
To all the quainter traffickers in town!
He is their visitor, and does appoint
Who lies with whom, and at what hour, what price,
Which gown, and in what smock, what fall, what tire.
Him will I prove, by a third person, to find
The subtleties of this dark labyrinth:
Which if I do discover, dear Sir Mammon,
You'll give your poor friend leave, though no philosopher,
To laugh; for you that are, 'tis thought, shall weep.   *310*
FACE: Sir, he does pray you'll not forget.
SURLY: I will not, sir.
Sir Epicure, I shall leave you?
    [*Exit.*]
MAMMON: I follow you straight.
FACE: But do so, good sir, to avoid suspicion.
This gent'man has a parlous head.
MAMMON: But wilt thou, Ulen,
Be constant to thy promise?
FACE: As my life, sir.
MAMMON: And wilt thou insinuate what I am, and praise me,
And say I am a noble fellow?
FACE: O, what else, sir?
And that you'll make her royal with the Stone,
An empress; you yourself King of Bantam.
MAMMON: Wilt thou do this?   *320*
FACE: Will I, sir!
MAMMON: Lungs, my Lungs!
I love thee.
FACE: Send your stuff, sir, that my master
May busy himself about projection.
MAMMON: Thou'st witched me, rogue. Take, go.
    [*Gives him money.*]

          307. *fall:* veil or ruff; *tire:* head-dress.

233

FACE: Your jack, and all, sir.

MAMMON: Thou art a villain – I will send my jack,
And the weights too. Slave, I could bite thine ear.
Away, thou dost not care for me.

FACE: Not I, sir?

MAMMON: Come, I was born to make thee, my good weasel;
Set thee on a bench, and ha' thee twirl a chain
With the best lord's vermin of 'em all.

330 FACE: Away, sir.

MAMMON: A Count, nay, a Count Palatine –

FACE: Good sir, go.

MAMMON: – shall not advance thee better; no, nor faster.
[*Exit.*]

II, iv   [*Enter* SUBTLE *and* DOL.]
[SUBTLE:] Has he bit? has he bit?

FACE: And swallowed, too, my Subtle.
I ha' given him line, and now he plays, i' faith.

SUBTLE: And shall we twitch him?

FACE: Thorough both the gills.
A wench is a rare bait, with which a man
No sooner's taken, but he straight firks mad.

SUBTLE: Dol, my Lord What's-hum's sister, you must now
Bear yourself *statelich*.

DOL COMMON: O, let me alone.
I'll not forget my race, I warrant you.
I'll keep my distance, laugh and talk aloud;
10   Have all the tricks of a proud scurvy lady,
And be as rude's her woman.

FACE: Well said, Sanguine!

SUBTLE: But will he send his andirons?

FACE: His jack too,
And 's iron shoeing-horn. I ha' spoke to him. Well,
I must not lose my wary gamester yonder.

SUBTLE: O, Monsieur Caution, that will not be gulled?

FACE: Ay, if I can strike a fine hook into him, now,

323. *jack:* a turnspit.   5. *firks:* runs.
11. *Sanguine:* literally ruddy (flattering term of endearment).

The Temple-church, there I have cast mine angle.
Well, pray for me. I'll about it.
  One knocks.
SUBTLE: What, more gudgeons!
  Dol, scout, scout!
  [DOL *looks out of the window.*]
               Stay, Face, you must go to the door.
  Pray God it be my Anabaptist – Who is 't, Dol?   *20*
DOL COMMON: I know him not. He looks like a gold-end-man.
SUBTLE: Godso! 'tis he; he said he would send – what call you
  him?
  The sanctifièd elder, that should deal
  For Mammon's jack and andirons. Let him in.
  Stay, help me off, first, with my gown.
  [*Exit* FACE.]
                    Away,
  Madam, to your withdrawing chamber. Now,
  [*Exit* DOL.]
  In a new tune, new gesture, but old language.
  This fellow is sent from one negotiates with me
  About the Stone, too, for the holy Brethren
  Of Amsterdam, the exiled Saints, that hope   *30*
  To raise their discipline by it. I must use him
  In some strange fashion now, to make him admire me.

  [*Enter* ANANIAS.]   II, V
[SUBTLE:] Where is my drudge?
  [*Re-enter* FACE.]
FACE: Sir?
SUBTLE: Take away the recipient,
  And rectify your menstrue from the *phlegma.*
  Then pour it o' the Sol, in the *cucurbite,*
  And let 'em macerate together.

21. *gold-end man:* dealer in odds and ends of gold.
30. *exiled Saints:* group of fanatical Puritans who moved from England
to Holland.
31. *discipline:* form of church government.

FACE: Yes, sir.
And save the ground?
SUBTLE: No. *Terra damnata*
Must not have entrance in the work. – Who are you?
ANANIAS: A faithful Brother, if it please you.
SUBTLE: What's that?
A Lullianist? a Ripley? *Filius artis*?
Can you sublime and dulcify? calcine?
Know you the *sapor pontic*? *sapor stiptic*?
Or what is homogene, or heterogene?
ANANIAS: I understand no heathen language, truly.
SUBTLE: Heathen! You Knipperdoling! Is *Ars sacra*,
Or *chrysopœia*, or *spagyrica*,
Or the *pamphysic*, or panarchic knowledge,
A heathen language?
ANANIAS: Heathen Greek, I take it.
SUBTLE: How! heathen Greek?
ANANIAS: All's heathen but the Hebrew.
SUBTLE: Sirrah my varlet, stand you forth and speak to him
Like a philosopher. Answer i' the language.
Name the vexations, and the martyrizations
Of metals in the work.
FACE: Sir, putrefaction,
Solution, ablution, sublimation,
Cohobation, calcination, ceration, and
Fixation.
SUBTLE: This is heathen Greek, to you, now? –
And when comes vivification?
FACE: After mortification.
SUBTLE: What's cohobation?
FACE: 'Tis the pouring on
Your *aqua regis*, and then drawing him off,
To the trine circle of the Seven Spheres.
SUBTLE: What's the proper passion of metals?
FACE: Malleation.
SUBTLE: What's your *ultimum supplicium auri*?
FACE: *Antimonium*.
SUBTLE: This's heathen Greek to you? – And what's your mercury?

FACE: A very fugitive, he will be gone, sir.

SUBTLE: How know you him?

FACE: By his viscosity,
His oleosity, and his suscitability.

SUBTLE: How do you sublime him?

FACE: With the calce of egg-shells,
White marble, talc.

SUBTLE: Your magisterium now,
What's that?

FACE: Shifting, sir, your elements,
Dry into cold, cold into moist, moist into hot,
Hot into dry.

SUBTLE: This's heathen Greek to you still? –
Your *Lapis Philosophicus*?

FACE: 'Tis a stone,   40
And not a stone; a spirit, a soul, and a body,
Which if you do dissolve, it is dissolved;
If you coagulate, it is coagulated;
If you make it to fly, it flieth.

SUBTLE: Enough.
    [*Exit* FACE.]
This's heathen Greek to you? What are you, sir?

ANANIAS: Please you, a servant of the exiled Brethren,
That deal with widows' and with orphans' goods,
And make a just account unto the Saints –
A deacon.

SUBTLE: O, you are sent from Master Wholesome,   50
Your teacher?

ANANIAS: From Tribulation Wholesome,
Our very zealous pastor.

SUBTLE: Good! I have
Some orphans' goods to come here.

ANANIAS: Of what kind, sir?

SUBTLE: Pewter and brass, andirons and kitchen-ware,
Metals, that we must use our med'cine on:
Wherein the Brethren may have a penn'orth
For ready money.

ANANIAS: Were the orphans' parents

Sincere professors?

SUBTLE: Why do you ask?

ANANIAS: Because
We then are to deal justly, and give, in truth,
Their utmost value.

SUBTLE: 'Slid, you'd cozen else,
60   And if their parents were not of the faithful? –
I will not trust you, now I think on't,
Till I ha' talked with your pastor. Ha' you brought money
To buy more coals?

ANANIAS: No, surely.

SUBTLE: No? How so?

ANANIAS: The Brethren bid me say unto you, sir,
Surely, they will not venture any more
Till they may see projection.

SUBTLE: How!

ANANIAS: You've had,
For the instruments, as bricks, and loam, and glasses,
Already thirty pound; and, for materials,
They say, some ninety more. And they have heard since,
70   That one at Heidelberg made it of an egg,
And a small paper of pin-dust.

SUBTLE: What's your name?

ANANIAS: My name is Ananias.

SUBTLE: Out, the varlet
That cozened the Apostles! Hence, away!
Flee, mischief! Had your holy consistory
No name to send me, of another sound
Than wicked Ananias? Send your elders
Hither to make atonement for you, quickly,
And gi' me satisfaction; or out goes
The fire, and down th' alembics, and the furnace,
80   *Piger Henricus*, or what not. Thou wretch!
Both *sericon* and *bufo* shall be lost,
Tell 'em. All hope of rooting out the bishops,
Or th' Anti-Christian hierarchy shall perish,
If they stay threescore minutes; the aqueity,

57. *professors*: believers, Puritans.

Terreity, and sulphureity
Shall run together again, and all be annulled,
Thou wicked Ananias!
    [*Exit* ANANIAS.]
                      This will fetch 'em,
And make 'em haste towards their gulling more.
A man must deal like a rough nurse, and fright
Those that are froward to an appetite.   *90*

    [*Enter* FACE, *in his Captain's uniform, with* DRUGGER.]   II, vi
[FACE:] He's busy with his spirits, but we'll upon him.
SUBTLE: How now! What mates, what Bayards ha' we here?
FACE: I told you he would be furious. – Sir, here's Nab
  Has brought you another piece of gold to look on;
  (We must appease him. Give it me.) and prays you,
  You would devise – what is it, Nab?
DRUGGER: A sign, sir.
FACE: Ay, a good lucky one, a thriving sign, Doctor.
SUBTLE: I was devising now.
FACE [*aside to* SUBTLE]:   'Slight, do not say so,
  He will repent he ga' you any more. –
  What say you to his constellation, Doctor,   *10*
  The Balance?
SUBTLE: No, that way is stale and common.
  A townsman, born in Taurus, gives the bull,
  Or the bull's head; in Aries, the ram, –
  A poor device! No, I will have his name
  Formed in some mystic character, whose radii,
  Striking the senses of the passers-by,
  Shall, by a virtual influence, breed affections,
  That may result upon the party owns it;
  As thus –
FACE: Nab!
SUBTLE: He first shall have *a bell*, that's *Abel*:
  And by it standing one whose name is *Dee*,   *20*
  In a *rug* gown, there's *D.*, and *Rug*, that's *Drug*;
               21. *rug:* coarse cloth.

And right anenst him a dog snarling *er*;
There's *Drugger, Abel Drugger*. That's his sign.
And here's now mystery and hieroglyphic!

FACE: Abel, thou art made.

DRUGGER: Sir, I do thank his worship.

FACE: Six o' thy legs more will not do it, Nab.
He has brought you a pipe of tobacco, Doctor.

DRUGGER: Yes, sir.
I have another thing I would impart –

FACE: Out with it, Nab.

DRUGGER: Sir, there is lodged, hard by me,

30   A rich young widow –

FACE: Good! a bona roba?

DRUGGER: But nineteen at the most.

FACE: Very good, Abel.

DRUGGER: Marry, she's not in fashion yet; she wears
A hood, but 't stands a-cop.

FACE: No matter, Abel.

DRUGGER: And I do now and then give her a fucus –

FACE: What! dost thou deal, Nab?

SUBTLE: I did tell you, Captain.

DRUGGER: And physic too, sometime, sir; for which she trusts me
With all her mind. She's come up here of purpose
To learn the fashion.

FACE: Good (his match too!) – On, Nab.

DRUGGER: And she does strangely long to know her fortune.

40 FACE: God's lid, Nab, send her to the Doctor, hither.

DRUGGER: Yes, I have spoke to her of his worship already;
But she's afraid it will be blown abroad,
And hurt her marriage.

FACE: Hurt it! 'tis the way
To heal it, if 'twere hurt; to make it more
Followed and sought. Nab, thou shalt tell her this.
She'll be more known, more talked of; and your widows
Are ne'er of any price till they be famous.
Their honour is their multitude of suitors.

26. *legs*: bows.   30. *a bona roba?*: a fine gown (hence, a courtesan).
33. *a-cop*: on the top of her head.   34. *fucus*: a cosmetic.

Send her, it may be thy good fortune. What?
Thou dost not know?

DRUGGER: No, sir, she'll never marry   50
Under a knight. Her brother has made a vow.

FACE: What! and dost thou despair, my little Nab,
Knowing what the Doctor has set down for thee,
And seeing so many o' the City dubbed?
One glass o' thy water, with a madam I know,
Will have it done, Nab. What's her brother? a knight?

DRUGGER: No, sir, a gentleman newly warm in's land, sir,
Scarce cold in his one-and-twenty, that does govern
His sister here; and is a man himself
Of some three thousand a year, and is come up   60
To learn to quarrel, and to live by his wits,
And will go down again, and die i' the country.

FACE: How! to quarrel?

DRUGGER: Yes, sir, to carry quarrels,
As gallants do; to manage 'em by line.

FACE: 'Slid, Nab! The Doctor is the only man
In Christendom for him! He has made a table,
With mathematical demonstrations,
Touching the art of quarrels. He will give him
An instrument to quarrel. Go, bring 'em both,
Him and his sister. And, for thee, with her   70
The Doctor happ'ly may persuade. Go to!
Shalt give his worship a new damask suit
Upon the premises.

SUBTLE: O, good Captain!

FACE: He shall,
He is the honestest fellow, Doctor. Stay not,
No offers; bring the damask, and the parties.

DRUGGER: I'll try my power, sir.

FACE: And thy will too, Nab.

SUBTLE: 'Tis good tobacco, this! What is't an ounce?

FACE: He'll send you a pound, Doctor.

SUBTLE: O no.

54. *dubbed:* made knights.
64. *by line:* according to the rules.

FACE: He will do't.
It is the goodest soul! – Abel, about it.
80   Thou shalt know more anon. Away, be gone.
    [*Exit* DRUGGER.]
A miserable rogue, and lives with cheese,
And has the worms. That was the cause, indeed,
Why he came now. He dealt with me in private,
To get a med'cine for 'em.
SUBTLE: And shall, sir. This works.
FACE: A wife, a wife for one on's, my dear Subtle!
    We'll e'en draw lots, and he that fails shall have
    The more in goods, the other has in tail.
SUBTLE: Rather the less. For she may be so light
    She may want grains.
FACE: Ay, or be such a burden,
90   A man would scarce endure her for the whole.
SUBTLE: Faith, best let's see her first, and then determine.
FACE: Content. But Dol must ha' no breath on't.
SUBTLE: Mum.
    Away you, to your Surly yonder, catch him.
FACE: Pray God I ha' not stayed too long.
SUBTLE: I fear it.
    [*Exeunt.*]

87. *in goods:* in property; *in tail:* pun on legal and colloquial meanings
(a) limited, conditional inheritance to certain heirs – as opposed to getting
something in goods, and (b) *tail* suggesting a woman sexually available.
    89. *grains:* weight.

ACT THREE

[Outside Lovewit's house.]

[Enter TRIBULATION WHOLESOME *and* ANANIAS.*]*

[TRIBULATION:] These chastisements are common to the Saints,
    And such rebukes we of the Separation
    Must bear with willing shoulders, as the trials
    Sent forth to tempt our frailties.

ANANIAS: In pure zeal,
    I do not like the man. He is a heathen,
    And speaks the language of Canaan, truly.

TRIBULATION: I think him a profane person indeed.

ANANIAS: He bears
    The visible mark of the Beast in his forehead.
    And for his Stone, it is a work of darkness,
    And with philosophy blinds the eyes of man.   10

TRIBULATION: Good Brother, we must bend unto all means
    That may give furtherance to the Holy Cause.

ANANIAS: Which his cannot. The Sanctifièd Cause
    Should have a sanctified course.

TRIBULATION: Not always necessary.
    The children of perdition are oft-times
    Made instruments even of the greatest works.
    Beside, we should give somewhat to man's nature,
    The place he lives in, still about the fire,
    And fume of metals, that intoxicate
    The brain of man, and make him prone to passion.   20
    Where have you greater atheists than your cooks?
    Or more profane, or choleric, than your glass-men?
    More Anti-Christian than your bell-founders?
    What makes the devil so devilish, I would ask you,
    Satan, our common enemy, but his being

2. *Separation:* the dissenting sect in Amsterdam.
17. *give somewhat to:* make allowance for.

Perpetually about the fire, and boiling
Brimstone and arsenic? We must give, I say,
Unto the motives, and the stirrers up
Of humours in the blood. It may be so,
30 Whenas the work is done, the Stone is made,
This heat of his may turn into a zeal,
And stand up for the beauteous discipline
Against the menstruous cloth and rag of Rome.
We must await his calling, and the coming
Of the good spirit. You did fault, t' upbraid him
With the Brethren's blessing of Heidelberg, weighing
What need we have to hasten on the work,
For the restoring of the silenced Saints,
Which ne'er will be but by the Philosopher's Stone.
40 And so a learnèd elder, one of Scotland,
Assured me; *aurum potabile* being
The only med'cine for the civil magistrate,
T' incline him to a feeling of the Cause;
And must be daily used in the disease.

ANANIAS: I have not edified more, truly, by man,
Not since the beautiful light first shone on me,
And I am sad my zeal hath so offended.

TRIBULATION: Let us call on him then.

ANANIAS: The motion's good,
And of the spirit; I will knock first.
    [*Knocks.*]   Peace be within!

III, ii   [SCENE TWO]

[SUBTLE *admits* TRIBULATION WHOLESOME *and* ANANIAS
into the house.]

[SUBTLE:] O, are you come? 'Twas time. Your three-score
    minutes
Were at the last thread, you see; and down had gone

---

38. *silenced Saints:* the dissenters were not permitted to preach in
England.

41. *aurum potabile:* drinkable gold (thought to be an elixir); here it means
bribery.

Furnus acediæ, turris circulatorius:
Lembec, bolt-head, retort, and pelican
Had all been cinders. Wicked Ananias!
Art thou returned? Nay, then, it goes down yet.

TRIBULATION: Sir, be appeasèd; he is come to humble
Himself in spirit, and to ask your patience,
If too much zeal hath carried him aside
From the due path.

SUBTLE: Why, this doth qualify!   10

TRIBULATION: The Brethren had no purpose, verily,
To give you the least grievance; but are ready
To lend their willing hands to any project
The spirit and you direct.

SUBTLE: This qualifies more!

TRIBULATION: And for the orphans' goods, let them be valued,
Or what is needful else to the holy work,
It shall be numb'red. Here, by me, the Saints
Throw down their purse before you.

SUBTLE: This qualifies most!
Why, thus it should be, now you understand.
Have I discoursed so unto you of our Stone,   20
And of the good that it shall bring your cause?
Showed you (beside the main of hiring forces
Abroad, drawing the Hollanders, your friends,
From th' Indies, to serve you, with all their fleet)
That even the med'cinal use shall make you a faction
And party in the realm? As, put the case,
That some great man in state, he have the gout,
Why, you but send three drops of your elixir,
You help him straight. There you have made a friend.
Another has the palsy or the dropsy,   30
He takes of your incombustible stuff,
He's young again: there you have made a friend.
A lady that is past the feat of body,
Though not of mind, and hath her face decayed
Beyond all cure of paintings, you restore
With the oil of talc. There you have made a friend;

10. *qualify:* change the situation.

245

And all her friends. A lord that is a leper,
A knight that has the bone-ache, or a squire
That hath both these, you make 'em smooth and sound

40 With a bare fricace of your med'cine. Still
You increase your friends.

TRIBULATION: Ay, 'tis very pregnant.

SUBTLE: And then the turning of this lawyer's pewter
To plate at Christmas –

ANANIAS: Christ-tide, I pray you.

SUBTLE: Yet, Ananias!

ANANIAS: I have done.

SUBTLE: Or changing
His parcel gilt to massy gold. You cannot
But raise you friends withal, to be of power
To pay an army in the field, to buy
The King of France out of his realms, or Spain
Out of his Indies. What can you not do

50 Against lords spiritual or temporal,
That shall oppone you?

TRIBULATION: Verily, 'tis true.
We may be temporal lords ourselves, I take it.

SUBTLE: You may be anything, and leave off to make
Long-winded exercises, or suck up
Your 'ha!' and 'hum!' in a tune. I not deny,
But such as are not gracèd in a state,
May, for their ends, be adverse in religion,
And get a tune to call the flock together.
For, to say sooth, a tune does much with women

60 And other phlegmatic people; it is your bell.

ANANIAS: Bells are profane; a tune may be religious.

SUBTLE: No warning with you? Then farewell my patience.
'Slight, it shall down! I will not be thus tortured.

TRIBULATION: I pray you, sir.

SUBTLE: All shall perish. I have spoke it.

TRIBULATION: Let me find grace, sir, in your eyes. The man,
He stands corrected. Neither did his zeal,

---

38. *bone-ache:* pox.   40. *fricace:* rubbing or massage.
45. *parcel gilt:* partly gilded articles of silver.

But as yourself, allow a tune somewhere,
Which now, being toward the Stone, we shall not need.
SUBTLE: No, nor your holy vizard, to win widows
To give you legacies, or make zealous wives 70
To rob their husbands for the common cause;
Nor take the start of bonds broke but one day,
And say they were forfeited by providence.
Nor shall you need o'er-night to eat huge meals,
To celebrate your next day's fast the better;
The whilst the Brethren and the Sisters, humbled,
Abate the stiffness of the flesh. Nor cast
Before your hungry hearers scrupulous bones:
As whether a Christian may hawk or hunt,
Or whether matrons of the holy assembly 80
May lay their hair out, or wear doublets,
Or have that idol, starch, about their linen.
ANANIAS: It is indeed an idol.
TRIBULATION: Mind him not, sir.
I do command thee, spirit of zeal, but trouble,
To peace within him! Pray you, sir, go on.
SUBTLE: Nor shall you need to libel 'gainst the prelates,
And shorten so your ears against the hearing
Of the next wire-drawn grace. Nor of necessity
Rail against plays, to please the alderman
Whose daily custard you devour; nor lie 90
With zealous rage till you are hoarse; not one
Of these so singular arts. Nor call yourselves
By names of Tribulation, Persecution,
Restraint, Long-patience, and such-like, affected
By the whole family or wood of you,
Only for glory, and to catch the ear
Of the disciple.
TRIBULATION: Truly, sir, they are
Ways that the godly Brethren have invented,

68. *being toward:* being almost in possession of.
78. *scrupulous bones:* doctrinal points of minor importance and interest.
87. *shorten . . . ears:* have your ears cut off as a punishment in the pillory.
95. *wood:* company.

For propagation of the glorious Cause,
100 As very notable means, and whereby also
Themselves grow soon and profitably famous.
SUBTLE: O, but the Stone, all's idle to't! Nothing!
The art of angels, nature's miracle,
The divine secret that doth fly in clouds
From east to west, and whose tradition
Is not from men, but spirits.
ANANIAS: I hate traditions!
I do not trust them –
TRIBULATION: Peace!
ANANIAS: They are Popish all.
I will not peace! I will not –
TRIBULATION: Ananias!
ANANIAS: Please the profane to grieve the godly,
I may not.
110 SUBTLE: Well, Ananias, thou shalt overcome.
TRIBULATION: It is an ignorant zeal that haunts him, sir,
But truly else a very faithful Brother,
A botcher, and a man by revelation
That hath a competent knowledge of the truth.
SUBTLE: Has he a competent sum there i' the bag
To buy the goods within? I am made guardian,
And must, for charity and conscience' sake,
Now see the most be made for my poor orphan,
Though I desire the Brethren, too, good gainers;
120 There they are within. When you have viewed and bought 'em,
And ta'en the inventory of what they are,
They are ready for projection; there's no more
To do. Cast on the med'cine, so much silver
As there is tin there, so much gold as brass,
I'll gi' it you in by weight.
TRIBULATION: But how long time,
Sir, must the Saints expect yet?
SUBTLE: Let me see,
How's the moon now? Eight, nine, ten days hence,
He will be silver potate; then three days

113. *botcher:* tailor.

Before he citronize. Some fifteen days,
The magisterium will be perfected.   *130*

ANANIAS: About the second day of the third week,
  In the ninth month?

SUBTLE: Yes, my good Ananias.

TRIBULATION: What will the orphans' goods arise to, think you?

SUBTLE: Some hundred marks, as much as filled three cars,
  Unladed now. You'll make six millions of 'em –
  But I must ha' more coals laid in.

TRIBULATION: How?

SUBTLE: Another load,
  And then we ha' finished. We must now increase
  Our fire to *ignis ardens*; we are past
  Fimus equinus, balnei, cineris,
  And all those lenter heats. If the holy purse   *140*
  Should with this draught fall low, and that the Saints
  Do need a present sum, I have a trick
  To melt the pewter, you shall buy now instantly,
  And with a tincture make you as good Dutch dollars
  As any are in Holland.

TRIBULATION: Can you so?

SUBTLE: Ay, and shall bide the third examination.

ANANIAS: It will be joyful tidings to the Brethren.

SUBTLE: But you must carry it secret.

TRIBULATION: Ay; but stay,
  This act of coining, is it lawful?

ANANIAS: Lawful!
  We know no magistrate; or, if we did,   *150*
  This's foreign coin.

SUBTLE: It is no coining, sir.
  It is but casting.

TRIBULATION: Ha! you distinguish well.
  Casting of money may be lawful.

ANANIAS: 'Tis, sir.

TRIBULATION: Truly, I take it so.

SUBTLE: There is no scruple,

---

129. *citronize:* becomes yellow.
150. *know:* recognize the authority of.

Sir, to be made of it, believe Ananias.
This case of conscience he is studied in.

TRIBULATION: I'll make a question of it to the Brethren.

ANANIAS: The Brethren shall approve it lawful, doubt not.
Where shall't be done?

SUBTLE: For that we'll talk anon.
   Knock without.

160 There's some to speak with me. Go in, I pray you,
And view the parcels. That's the inventory.
I'll come to you straight.
   [*Exeunt* TRIBULATION WHOLESOME *and* ANANIAS.]
                    Who is it? – Face! appear.

III, iii   [*Enter* FACE *in his Captain's uniform.*]

[SUBTLE:] How now! Good prize?

FACE: Good pox! Yon costive cheater
Never came on.

SUBTLE: How then?

FACE: I ha' walked the round
Till now, and no such thing.

SUBTLE: And ha' you quit him?

FACE: Quit him! An' Hell would quit him too, he were happy.
'Slight! would you have me stalk like a mill-jade,
All day, for one that will not yield us grains?
I know him of old.

SUBTLE: O, but to ha' gulled him,
Had been a mastery.

FACE: Let him go, black boy,
And turn thee, that some fresh news may possess thee.

10   A noble count, a Don of Spain (my dear
Delicious compeer, and my party-bawd),
Who is come hither private for his conscience
And brought munition with him, six great slops,
Bigger than three Dutch hoys, beside round trunks,

---

11. *party-bawd:* partner-bawd or partner in bawdry.
13. *slops:* loose-padded breeches.
14. *hoys:* ships; *trunks:* hose.

Furnished with pistolets, and pieces of eight,
Will straight be here, my rogue, to have thy bath,
(That is the colour) and to make his batt'ry
Upon our Dol, our castle, our Cinque Port,
Our Dover Pier, our what thou wilt. Where is she?
She must prepare perfumes, delicate linen,   *20*
The bath in chief, a banquet, and her wit,
For she must milk his epididymis.
Where is the doxy?
SUBTLE: I'll send her to thee;
And but despatch my brace of little John Leydens
And come again myself.
FACE: Are they within then?
SUBTLE: Numb'ring the sum.
FACE: How much?
SUBTLE: A hundred marks, boy.
    [Exit.]
FACE: Why, this's a lucky day. Ten pounds of Mammon!
Three o' my clerk! a portague o' my grocer!
This o' the Brethren! beside reversions
And states to come, i' the widow, and my Count!   *30*
My share today will not be bought for forty –
    [Enter DOL.]
DOL COMMON: What?
FACE: Pounds, dainty Dorothy! art thou so near?
DOL COMMON: Yes. Say, Lord General, how fares our camp?
FACE: As with the few that had entrenched themselves
Safe, by their discipline, against a world, Dol,
And laughed within those trenches, and grew fat
With thinking on the booties, Dol, brought in
Daily by their small parties. This dear hour,
A doughty Don is taken with my Dol;
And thou mayst make his ransom what thou wilt,   *40*
My Dowsabel; he shall be brought here, fettered
With thy fair looks, before he sees thee; and thrown
In a down-bed, as dark as any dungeon;
Where thou shalt keep him waking with thy drum –

15. *pistolets:* Spanish gold coins.   23. *doxy:* whore.

Thy drum, my Dol, thy drum – till he be tame
As the poor blackbirds were i' the great frost,
Or bees are with a basin; and so hive him
I' the swan-skin coverlid and cambric sheets,
Till he work honey and wax, my little God's-gift.

50 DOL COMMON: What is he, General?

FACE: An *adalantado*,
A grandee, girl. Was not my Dapper here yet?

DOL COMMON: No.

FACE: Nor my Drugger?

DOL COMMON: Neither.

FACE: A pox on 'em,
They are so long a-furnishing! such stinkards
Would not be seen upon these festival days.
  [*Re-enter* SUBTLE.]
How now! ha' you done?

SUBTLE: Done. They are gone; the sum
Is here in bank, my Face. I would we knew
Another chapman now would buy 'em outright.

FACE: 'Slid, Nab shall do't against he ha' the widow,
To furnish household.

SUBTLE: Excellent, well thought on.

60 Pray God he come.

FACE: I pray he keep away
Till our new business be o'erpast.

SUBTLE: But, Face,
How cam'st thou by this secret Don?

FACE: A spirit
Brought me th' intelligence in a paper here,
As I was conjuring yonder in my circle
For Surly. I ha' my flies abroad. Your bath
Is famous, Subtle, by my means. Sweet Dol,
You must go tune your virginal, no losing
O' the least time. And (do you hear?) good action!
Firk like a flounder; kiss like a scallop, close;

46. *great frost*: i.e. of 1608.
48. *God's gift*: 'Dorothea' in Greek means God's gift.
50. *adalantado*: a Spanish governor.

And tickle him with thy mother-tongue. His great   *70*
Verdugoship has not a jot of language –
So much the easier to be cozened, my Dolly.
He will come here in a hired coach, obscure,
And our own coachman, whom I have sent as guide,
No creature else. –
> *One knocks.*
                  Who's that?

SUBTLE: It is not he?

FACE: O no, not yet this hour.

SUBTLE: Who is't?

DOL COMMON [*looking out*]:   Dapper,
Your clerk.

FACE: God's will then, Queen of Faery,
On with your tire.
> [*Exit* DOL.]
            And, Doctor, with your robes.
Let's despatch him for God's sake.

SUBTLE: 'Twill be long.

FACE: I warrant you, take but the cues I give you,   *80*
It shall be brief enough. 'Slight, here are more!
Abel, and, I think, the angry boy, the heir,
That fain would quarrel.

SUBTLE: And the widow?

FACE: No,
Not that I see. Away!
> [*Exit* SUBTLE.]

> [FACE *admits* DAPPER.]   III, iv

[FACE:]   O, sir, you are welcome.
The Doctor is within a-moving for you.
I have had the most ado to win him to it!
He swears you'll be the darling o' the dice;
He never heard her Highness dote till now, he says.

71. *Verdugoship: verdugo* is Spanish for hangman. 'His great hangmanship can't speak a word of English'.

79. *tire:* costume.

Your aunt has giv'n you the most gracious words
That can be thought on.

DAPPER: Shall I see her Grace?

FACE: See her, and kiss her too.

[*Enter* DRUGGER, *followed by* KASTRIL.]

What, honest Nab!
Hast brought the damask?

DRUGGER: No, sir, here's tobacco.

FACE: 'Tis well done, Nab. Thou'lt bring the damask too?

10 DRUGGER: Yes. Here's the gentleman, Captain, Master Kastril,
I have brought to see the Doctor.

FACE: Where's the widow?

DRUGGER: Sir, as he likes, his sister, he says, shall come.

FACE: O, is it so? Good time. Is your name Kastril, sir?

KASTRIL: Ay, and the best o' the Kastrils, I'd be sorry else,
By fifteen hundred a year. Where is this Doctor?
My mad tobacco-boy here tells me of one
That can do things. Has he any skill?

FACE: Wherein, sir?

KASTRIL: To carry a business, manage a quarrel fairly,
Upon fit terms.

FACE: It seems, sir, y' are but young
20 About the town, that can make that a question.

KASTRIL: Sir, not so young but I have heard some speech
Of the angry boys, and seen 'em take tobacco,
And in his shop; and I can take it too.
And I would fain be one of 'em, and go down
And practise i' the country.

FACE: Sir, for the duello,
The Doctor, I assure you, shall inform you,
To the least shadow of a hair; and show you
An instrument he has, of his own making,
Wherewith no sooner shall you make report
30 Of any quarrel, but he will take the height on't
Most instantly, and tell in what degree
Of safety it lies in, or mortality;
And how it may be borne, whether in a right line,

22. *angry boys:* roisterers.

Or a half-circle; or may else be cast
Into an angle blunt, if not acute;
All this he will demonstrate. And then, rules
To give and take the lie by.
KASTRIL: How! to take it?
FACE: Yes, in oblique he'll show you, or in circle;
But never in diameter. The whole town
Study his theorems, and dispute them ordinarily   *40*
At the eating academies.
KASTRIL: But does he teach
Living by the wits, too?
FACE: Anything whatever.
You cannot think that subtlety but he reads it.
He made me a Captain. I was a stark pimp,
Just o' your standing, 'fore I met with him;
It's not two months since. I'll tell you his method:
First, he will enter you at some ordinary.
KASTRIL: No, I'll not come there; you shall pardon me.
FACE: For why, sir?
KASTRIL: There's gaming there, and tricks.
FACE: Why, would you be
A gallant, and not game?
KASTRIL: Ay, 'twill spend a man.   *50*
FACE: Spend you! It will repair you when you are spent.
How do they live by their wits there, that have vented
Six times your fortunes?
KASTRIL: What, three thousand a year!
FACE: Ay, forty thousand.
KASTRIL: Are there such?
FACE: Ay, sir,
And gallants yet. Here's a young gentleman
Is born to nothing – forty marks a year,
Which I count nothing – he's to be initiated,
And have a fly o' the Doctor. He will win you
By unresistible luck, within this fortnight,

38. *in oblique, in circle:* the lie circumstantial.
39. *in diameter:* the lie direct.
47. *ordinary:* eating-house, tavern.   58. *fly:* familiar spirit.

60 Enough to buy a barony. They will set him
  Upmost, at the groom-porter's, all the Christmas!
  And for the whole year through at every place
  Where there is play, present him with the chair,
  The best attendance, the best drink, sometimes
  Two glasses of Canary, and pay nothing;
  The purest linen and the sharpest knife,
  The partridge next his trencher, and somewhere
  The dainty bed, in private, with the dainty.
  You shall ha' your ordinaries bid for him,
70 As playhouses for a poet; and the master
  Pray him aloud to name what dish he affects,
  Which must be buttered shrimps; and those that drink
  To no mouth else, will drink to his, as being
  The goodly president-mouth of all the board.
KASTRIL: Do you not gull one?
FACE: 'Ods my life! Do you think it?
  You shall have a cast commander, (can but get
  In credit with a glover, or a spurrier,
  For some two pair of either's ware aforehand)
  Will, by most swift posts, dealing with him,
80 Arrive at competent means to keep himself,
  His punk, and naked boy, in excellent fashion,
  And be admired for 't.
KASTRIL: Will the Doctor teach this?
FACE: He will do more, sir. When your land is gone,
  (As men of spirit hate to keep earth long),
  In a vacation, when small money is stirring,
  And ordinaries suspended till the term,
  He'll show a perspective, where on one side
  You shall behold the faces and the persons
  Of all sufficient young heirs in town,

61. *groom-porter:* a royal official in charge of gaming at Court, who kept
a free table at Christmas.
  76. *cast:* cashiered, dismissed.
  85. *vacation:* between terms at the law-courts.
  87. *a perspective:* a picture which seems to change as the spectator shifts
his angle of vision.

Whose bonds are current for commodity;   *90*
On th' other side, the merchants' forms, and others,
That without help of any second broker,
Who would expect a share, will trust such parcels;
In the third square, the very street and sign
Where the commodity dwells, and does but wait
To be delivered, be it pepper, soap,
Hops, or tobacco, oatmeal, woad, or cheeses.
All which you may so handle, to enjoy
To your own use, and never stand obliged.

KASTRIL: I' faith! is he such a fellow?

FACE: Why, Nab here knows him.   *100*
And then for making matches for rich widows,
Young gentlewomen, heirs, the fortunat'st man!
He's sent to, far and near, all over England,
To have his counsel, and to know their fortunes.

KASTRIL: God's will, my suster shall see him.

FACE: I'll tell you, sir,
What he did tell me of Nab. It's a strange thing
(By the way, you must eat no cheese, Nab, it breeds melancholy,
And that same melancholy breeds worms) but pass it –
He told me honest Nab here was ne'er at tavern
But once in's life.

DRUGGER: Truth, and no more I was not.   *110*

FACE: And then he was so sick –

DRUGGER: Could he tell you that too?

FACE: How should I know it?

DRUGGER: In troth, we had been a-shooting,
And had a piece of fat ram-mutton to supper,
That lay so heavy o' my stomach –

FACE: And he has no head
To bear any wine; for, what with the noise o' the fiddlers,
And care of his shop, for he dares keep no servants –

DRUGGER: My head did so ache –

FACE: As he was fain to be brought home.
The Doctor told me. And then a good old woman –

DRUGGER: Yes, faith, she dwells in Seacoal Lane, – did cure me,

97. *woad*: a blue dye.

120 With sodden ale, and pellitory o' the wall –
Cost me but twopence. I had another sickness
Was worse than that.

FACE: Ay, that was with the grief
Thou took'st for being 'cessed at eighteenpence
For the waterwork.

DRUGGER: In truth, and it was like
T' have cost me almost my life.

FACE: Thy hair went off?

DRUGGER: Yes, sir; 'twas done for spite.

FACE: Nay, so says the Doctor.

KASTRIL: Pray thee, tobacco-boy, go fetch my suster.
I'll see this learnèd boy before I go;
And so shall she.

FACE: Sir, he is busy now,
130 But if you have a sister to fetch hither,
Perhaps your own pains may command her sooner;
And he by that time will be free.

KASTRIL: I go.
    [*Exit.*]

FACE: Drugger, she's thine! The damask!
    [*Exit* ABEL.]
    [*Aside*]   Subtle and I
Must wrestle for her. – Come on, Master Dapper,
You see how I turn clients here away,
To give your cause dispatch. Ha' you performed
The ceremonies were enjoined you?

DAPPER: Yes, o' the vinegar,
And the clean shirt.

FACE: 'Tis well; that shirt may do you
More worship than you think. Your aunt's afire,
140 But that she will not show it, t' have a sight on you.
Ha' you provided for her Grace's servants?

DAPPER: Yes, here are six score Edward shillings.

FACE: Good!

DAPPER: And an old Harry's sovereign.

---

120. *pellitory o' the wall:* a herb.
123. *'cessed:* assessed, for taxes.

FACE: Very good!
DAPPER: And three James shillings, and an Elizabeth groat,
 Just twenty nobles.
FACE: O, you are too just.
 I would you had had the other noble in Maries.
DAPPER: I have some Philip and Maries.
FACE: Ay, those same
 Are best of all. Where are they? Hark, the Doctor.

 [*Enter*] SUBTLE, *disguised like a Priest of Faery.*   III, V
 [SUBTLE, *in an assumed voice:*] Is yet her Grace's cousin come?
FACE: He is come.
SUBTLE: And is he fasting?
FACE: Yes.
SUBTLE: And hath cried 'hum'?
FACE: Thrice, you must answer.
DAPPER: Thrice.
SUBTLE: And as oft 'buzz'?
FACE: If you have, say.
DAPPER: I have.
SUBTLE: Then, to her coz,
 Hoping that he hath vinegared his senses,
 As he was bid, the Faery Queen dispenses,
 By me, this robe, the petticoat of Fortune;
 Which that he straight put on, she doth importune.
 And though to Fortune near be her petticoat,
 Yet nearer is her smock, the Queen doth note,   10
 And therefore, even of that a piece she hath sent,
 Which, being a child, to wrap him in was rent;
 And prays him for a scarf he now will wear it,
 With as much love as then her Grace did tear it,
 About his eyes, to show he is fortunate;
  They blind[-*fold*] *him with a rag.*
 And, trusting unto her to make his state,
 He'll throw away all worldly pelf about him;
 Which that he will perform, she doth not doubt him.
FACE: She need not doubt him, sir. Alas, he has nothing

20   But what he will part withal as willingly,
     Upon her Grace's word – Throw away your purse –
     As she would ask it – Handkerchiefs and all –
      He throws away, as they bid him.
     She cannot bid that thing but he'll obey. –
     If you have a ring about you, cast it off,
     Or a silver seal at your wrist. Her Grace will send
     Her fairies here to search you, therefore deal
     Directly with her Highness. If they find
     That you conceal a mite, you are undone.

DAPPER: Truly, there's all.

FACE: All what?

DAPPER: My money, truly.

30 FACE: Keep nothing that is transitory about you.
     [*Aside to* SUBTLE] Bid Dol play music. – Look, the elves are come
      DOL *enters with a cittern.*
     To pinch you, if you tell not truth. Advise you.
      They pinch him.

DAPPER: O! I have a paper with a spur-royal in't.

FACE: *Ti, ti.*
     They knew't, they say.

SUBTLE: *Ti, ti, ti, ti.* He has more yet.

FACE: *Ti, ti-ti-ti.* I' the t'other pocket?

SUBTLE: *Titi, titi, titi, titi.*
     They must pinch him or he will never confess, they say.
      [*They pinch him again.*]

DAPPER: O, O!

FACE: Nay, pray you, hold. He is her Grace's nephew!
     Ti, ti, ti? What care you? Good faith, you shall care. –
     Deal plainly, sir, and shame the fairies. Show
40   You are an innocent.

DAPPER: By this good light, I ha' nothing.

SUBTLE: *Ti ti, ti ti to ta.* He does equivocate, she says:
     Ti, ti do ti, ti ti do, ti da; and swears by the light when he is blinded.

27. *directly:* honestly.

31. *Stage-direction, cittern:* a guitar-like instrument, with wire strings; a
zither.

33. *spur-royal:* a gold coin.

DAPPER: By this good dark, I ha' nothing but a half-crown
  Of gold about my wrist, that my love gave me;
  And a leaden heart I wore sin' she forsook me.
FACE: I thought 'twas something. And would you incur
  Your aunt's displeasure for these trifles? Come,
  I had rather you had thrown away twenty half-crowns.
  [*Takes it off.*]
  You may wear your leaden heart still. – How now!
SUBTLE [*aside*]: What news, Dol?
DOL COMMON [*aside*]: Yonder's your knight, Sir Mammon.   50
FACE [*aside*]: God's lid, we never thought of him till now!
  Where is he?
DOL COMMON [*aside*]: Here, hard by. He's at the door.
SUBTLE [*aside*]: And you are not ready now! Dol, get his suit.
  [*Exit* DOL.]
  He must not be sent back.
FACE [*aside*]:   O, by no means.
  What shall we do with this same puffin here,
  Now he's o' the spit?
SUBTLE [*aside*]:   Why, lay him back awhile,
  With some device.
  [*Re-enter* DOL *with* FACE'S *clothes.*]
          – *Ti, ti ti, ti ti ti.* Would her Grace speak with
  me?
  I come. – [*Aside*] Help, Dol!
FACE: – Who's there? Sir Epicure,
  He speaks through the keyhole, the other knocking.
  My master's i' the way. Please you to walk
  Three or four turns, but till his back be turned,   60
  And I am for you. – [*Aside*] Quickly, Dol!
SUBTLE: Her Grace
  Commends her kindly to you, Master Dapper.
DAPPER: I long to see her Grace.
SUBTLE: She now is set
  At dinner in her bed, and she has sent you
  From her own private trencher, a dead mouse
  And a piece of gingerbread, to be merry withal

    53. *his suit:* Face's clothes in his disguise as Lungs.

And stay your stomach, lest you faint with fasting.
Yet if you could hold out till she saw you, she says,
It would be better for you.

FACE: Sir, he shall
70 Hold out, an't were this two hours, for her Highness;
I can assure you that. We will not lose
All we ha' done. –

SUBTLE: He must nor see, nor speak
To anybody, till then.

FACE: For that we'll put, sir,
A stay in's mouth.

SUBTLE: Of what?

FACE: Of gingerbread.
Make you it fit. He that hath pleased her Grace
Thus far, shall not now crinkle for a little. –
Gape, sir, and let him fit you.

   [*They thrust a gag of gingerbread in his mouth.*]

SUBTLE [*aside*]:   Where shall we now
Bestow him?

DOL COMMON [*aside*]: I' the privy.

SUBTLE: Come along, sir,
I now must show you Fortune's privy lodgings.

80 FACE: Are they perfumed, and his bath ready?

SUBTLE: All;
Only the fumigation's somewhat strong.

FACE [*speaking through the keyhole*]: Sir Epicure, I am yours, sir, by
   and by.

   [*Exeunt with* DAPPER.]

ACT FOUR

[SCENE ONE]

[*Lovewit's house.*

[FACE, *disguised as the servant, admits* MAMMON.]
[FACE:] O sir, y' are come i' the only finest time. –
MAMMON: Where's Master?
FACE: Now preparing for projection, sir.
   Your stuff will be all changed shortly.
MAMMON: Into gold?
FACE: To gold and silver, sir.
MAMMON: Silver I care not for.
FACE: Yes, sir, a little to give beggars.
MAMMON: Where's the lady?
FACE: At hand here. I ha' told her such brave things o' you,
   Touching your bounty and your noble spirit –
MAMMON: Hast thou?
FACE: As she is almost in her fit to see you.
   But, good sir, no divinity i' your conference,
   For fear of putting her in rage.
MAMMON: I warrant thee.   10
FACE: Six men will not hold her down. And then,
   If the old man should hear or see you –
MAMMON: Fear not.
FACE: The very house, sir, would run mad. You know it,
   How scrupulous he is, and violent,
   'Gainst the least act of sin. Physic or mathematics,
   Poetry, state, or bawdry, as I told you,
   She will endure, and never startle; but
   No word of controversy.
MAMMON: I am schooled, good Ulen.
FACE: And you must praise her house, remember that,
   And her nobility.   20

10. *in rage:* mad.   16. *state:* affairs of state, politics.
19. *house:* family.

263

20 MAMMON: Let me alone.
No herald, no, nor antiquary, Lungs,
Shall do it better. Go.
FACE [*aside*]: Why, this is yet
A kind of modern happiness, to have
Dol Common for a great lady.
  [*Exit.*]
MAMMON [*alone*]: Now, Epicure,
Heighten thyself, talk to her all in gold;
Rain her as many showers as Jove did drops
Unto his Danaë; show the god a miser,
Compared with Mammon. What! the Stone will do't.
She shall feel gold, taste gold, hear gold, sleep gold;
30 Nay, we will *concumbere* gold. I will be puissant
And mighty in my talk to her.
  [*Re-enter* FACE *with* DOL, *richly dressed.*]
  Here she comes.
FACE [*aside*]: To him, Dol, suckle him. – This is the noble knight
I told your ladyship –
MAMMON: Madam, with your pardon,
I kiss your vesture.
DOL COMMON: Sir, I were uncivil
If I would suffer that; my lip to you, sir.
MAMMON: I hope my Lord your brother be in health, lady.
DOL COMMON: My Lord my brother is, though I no lady, sir.
FACE [*aside*]: Well said, my Guinea-bird.
MAMMON: Right noble madam –
FACE [*aside*]: O, we shall have most fierce idolatry.
40 MAMMON: 'Tis your prerogative.
DOL COMMON: Rather your courtesy.
MAMMON: Were there nought else t' enlarge your virtues to me,
These answers speak your breeding and your blood.
DOL COMMON: Blood we boast none, sir; a poor baron's daughter.
MAMMON: Poor! and gat you? Profane not. Had your father
Slept all the happy remnant of his life
After the act, lien but there still, and panted,

23. *happiness*: appropriateness.   30. *concumbere*: fornicate.
38. *Guinea-bird*: whore.

He'd done enough to make himself, his issue,
And his posterity noble.

DOL COMMON: Sir, although
We may be said to want the gilt and trappings,
The dress of honour, yet we strive to keep   50
The seeds and the materials.

MAMMON: I do see
The old ingredient, virtue, was not lost,
Nor the drug, money, used to make your compound.
There is a strange nobility i' your eye,
This lip, that chin! Methinks you do resemble
One o' the Austriac princes.

FACE [aside]:   Very like!
Her father was an Irish costermonger.

MAMMON: The house of Valois just had such a nose,
And such a forehead yet the Medici
Of Florence boast.

DOL COMMON: Troth, and I have been lik'ned   60
To all these princes.

FACE [aside]:   I'll be sworn, I heard it.

MAMMON: I know not how! it is not any one,
But e'en the very choice of all their features.

FACE [aside]: I'll in, and laugh.
    [Exit.]

MAMMON: A certain touch, or air,
That sparkles a divinity beyond
An earthly beauty!

DOL COMMON: O, you play the courtier.

MAMMON: Good lady, gi' me leave –

DOL COMMON: In faith, I may not,
To mock me, sir.

MAMMON: To burn i' this sweet flame;
The phœnix never knew a nobler death.

DOL COMMON: Nay, now you court the courtier, and destroy   70
What you would build. This art, sir, i' your words,
Calls your whole faith in question.

MAMMON: By my soul –

57. *costermonger:* seller of fruit.

DOL COMMON: Nay, oaths are made o' the same air, sir.

MAMMON: Nature
  Never bestowed upon mortality
  A more unblamed, a more harmonious feature;
  She played the step-dame in all faces else.
  Sweet madam, le' me be particular –

DOL COMMON: Particular, sir! I pray you, know your distance.

MAMMON: In no ill sense, sweet lady, but to ask
80   How your fair graces pass the hours? I see
  Y' are lodged here, i' the house of a rare man,
  An excellent artist; but what's that to you?

DOL COMMON: Yes, sir. I study here the mathematics,
  And distillation.

MAMMON: O, I cry your pardon.
  He's a divine instructor! can extract
  The souls of all things by his art; call all
  The virtues and the miracles of the sun
  Into a temperate furnace; teach dull nature
  What her own forces are. A man, the Emp'ror
90   Has courted above Kelly; sent his medals
  And chains t' invite him.

DOL COMMON: Ay, and for his physic, sir –

MAMMON: Above the art of Æsculapius,
  That drew the envy of the Thunderer!
  I know all this, and more.

DOL COMMON: Troth, I am taken, sir,
  Whole with these studies that contemplate nature.

MAMMON: It is a noble humour. But this form
  Was not intended to so dark a use.
  Had you been crookèd, foul, of some coarse mould,
  A cloister had done well; but such a feature,
100   That might stand up the glory of a kingdom,
  To live recluse is a mere solecism,
  Though in a nunnery. It must not be.
  I muse, my Lord your brother will permit it!

75. *unblamed:* unblemished.   78. *particular:* familiar, personal.
84. *distillation:* chemistry.   103. *muse:* am surprised.

You should spend half my land first, were I he.
Does not this diamond better on my finger
Than i' the quarry?

DOL COMMON: Yes.

MAMMON: Why, you are like it
You were created, lady, for the light.
Here, you shall wear it; take it, the first pledge
Of what I speak, to bind you to believe me.

DOL COMMON: In chains of adamant?

MAMMON: Yes, the strongest bands.   *110*
And take a secret, too: here, by your side,
Doth stand this hour the happiest man in Europe.

DOL COMMON: You are contented, sir?

MAMMON: Nay, in true being,
The envy of princes and the fear of states.

DOL COMMON: Say you so, Sir Epicure?

MAMMON: Yes, and thou shalt
   prove it,
Daughter of honour. I have cast mine eye
Upon thy form, and I will rear this beauty
Above all styles.

DOL COMMON: You mean no treason, sir?

MAMMON: No, I will take away that jealousy.
I am the lord of the Philosopher's Stone,   *120*
And thou the lady.

DOL COMMON: How, sir! ha' you that?

MAMMON: I am the master of the mastery.
This day the good old wretch here o' the house
Has made it for us. Now he's at projection.
Think therefore thy first wish now, let me hear it;
And it shall rain into thy lap, no shower,
But floods of gold, whole cataracts, a deluge,
To get a nation on thee.

DOL COMMON: You are pleased, sir,
To work on the ambition of our sex.

MAMMON: I'm pleased the glory of her sex should know,   *130*

122. *mastery*: i.e. the *magisterium*, process of making anything into
gold.

This nook here of the Friars is no climate
For her to live obscurely in, to learn
Physic and surgery, for the constable's wife
Of some odd hundred in Essex; but come forth,
And taste the air of palaces; eat, drink
The toils of emp'rics, and their boasted practice;
Tincture of pearl, and coral, gold, and amber;
Be seen at feasts and triumphs; have it asked,
What miracle she is; set all the eyes
140   Of court a-fire, like a burning-glass,
And work 'em into cinders, when the jewels
Of twenty states adorn thee, and the light
Strikes out the stars; that, when thy name is mentioned,
Queens may look pale; and, we but showing our love,
Nero's Poppæa may be lost in story!
Thus will we have it.
DOL COMMON: I could well consent, sir.
But in a monarchy, how will this be?
The Prince will soon take notice, and both seize
You and your Stone, it being a wealth unfit
150   For any private subject.
MAMMON: If he knew it.
DOL COMMON: Yourself do boast it, sir.
MAMMON: To thee, my life.
DOL COMMON: O, but beware, sir! You may come to end
The remnant of your days in a loathed prison,
By speaking of it.
MAMMON: 'Tis no idle fear!
We'll therefore go with all, my girl, and live
In a free state, where we will eat our mullets,
Soused in high-country wines, sup pheasants' eggs,
And have our cockles boiled in silver shells;
Our shrimps to swim again, as when they lived,
160   In a rare butter made of dolphins' milk,
Whose cream does look like opals; and with these

131. *Friars:* i.e. Blackfriars, the part of London in which the comedy is
located.   134. *hundred:* the sub-division of a county.
136. *emp'rics:* experimenters, scientists.

Delicate meats set ourselves high for pleasure,
And take us down again, and then renew
Our youth and strength with drinking the elixir,
And so enjoy a perpetuity
Of life and lust! And thou shalt ha' thy wardrobe
Richer than Nature's, still to change thyself,
And vary oft'ner for thy pride than she,
Or Art, her wise and almost-equal servant.
  [*Enter* FACE.]
FACE: Sir, you are too loud. I hear you, every word,   *170*
  Into the laboratory. Some fitter place –
  The garden, or great chamber above. [*Aside*] How like you her?
MAMMON: Excellent, Lungs! There's for thee.
  [*Gives him money.*]
FACE: But do you hear?
  Good sir, beware, no mention of the rabbins.
MAMMON: We think not on 'em.
FACE: O, it is well, sir.
  [*Exeunt* MAMMON *and* DOL.]
                                          – Subtle!

  [*Enter* SUBTLE.]   IV, ii
  Dost thou not laugh?
SUBTLE: Yes. Are they gone?
FACE: All's clear.
SUBTLE: The widow is come.
FACE: And your quarrelling disciple?
SUBTLE: Ay.
FACE: I must to my Captainship again then.
SUBTLE: Stay, bring 'em in first.
FACE: So I meant. What is she?
  A bonnibel?
SUBTLE: I know not.
FACE: We'll draw lots;
  You'll stand to that?
SUBTLE: What else?
FACE: O, for a suit,

4. *Captainship:* captain's disguise.   5. *a bonnibel:* a beauty.

269

To fall now like a curtain, flap!

SUBTLE: To th' door, man.

FACE: You'll ha' the first kiss, 'cause I am not ready.

    [*Exit.*]

SUBTLE: Yes, and perhaps hit you through both the nostrils.

10 FACE [*within*]: Who would you speak with?

KASTRIL [*within*]:   Where's the Captain?

FACE [*within*]:   Gone, sir,

About some business.

KASTRIL [*within*]:   Gone!

FACE [*within*]:   He'll return straight.

But Master Doctor, his lieutenant, is here.

    [*Enter* KASTRIL, *followed by* DAME PLIANT.]

SUBTLE: Come near, my worshipful boy, my *terræ fili*,

That is, my boy of land; make thy approaches.

Welcome; I know thy lusts and thy desires,

And I will serve and satisfy 'em. Begin,

Charge me from thence, or thence, or in this line;

Here is my centre: ground thy quarrel.

KASTRIL: You lie.

SUBTLE: How, child of wrath and anger! the loud lie?

20 For what, my sudden boy?

KASTRIL: Nay, that look you to,

I am aforehand.

SUBTLE: O, this's no true grammar,

And as ill logic! You must render causes, child,

Your first and second intentions, know your canons

And your divisions, moods, degrees, and differences,

Your predicaments, substance, and accident,

Series extern and intern, with their causes

Efficient, material, formal, final,

And ha' your elements perfect –

KASTRIL: What is this?

The angry tongue he talks in?

SUBTLE: That false precept,

30 Of being aforehand, has deceived a number,

> 9. *hit you through both the nostrils:* put your nose out of joint.
> 29. *angry:* quarrel-provoking – as in 'the angry boy'.

And made 'em enter quarrels oftentimes
Before they were aware; and afterward,
Against their wills.

KASTRIL: How must I do then, sir?

SUBTLE: I cry this lady mercy; she should first
Have been saluted. I do call you lady,
Because you are to be one ere't be long,
My soft and buxom widow.

    He kisses her.

KASTRIL: Is she, i' faith?

SUBTLE: Yes, or my art is an egregious liar.

KASTRIL: How know you?

SUBTLE: By inspection on her forehead,
And subtlety of her lip, which must be tasted   *40*
Often to make a judgement.

    He kisses her again.

                            'Slight, she melts
Like a myrobolane. Here is yet a line,
In rivo frontis, tells me he is no knight.

DAME PLIANT: What is he then, sir?

SUBTLE: Let me see your hand.
O, your *linea fortunæ* makes it plain;
And *stella* here *in monte Veneris*.
But, most of all, *junctura annularis*.
He is a soldier, or a man of art, lady,
But shall have some great honour shortly,

DAME PLIANT: Brother,
He's a rare man, believe me!

    [*Re-enter* FACE, *in his Captain's uniform.*]

KASTRIL: Hold your peace.   *50*
Here comes the t'other rare man. – 'Save you, Captain.

FACE: Good master Kastril! Is this your sister?

KASTRIL: Ay, sir.
Please you to kuss her, and be proud to know her.

42. *myrobolane:* sugar-plum.
43. *rivo frontis:* vein of the forehead.
45. *linea fortunæ:* line of fortune (from palmistry like the terms which
follow).

FACE: I shall be proud to know you, lady.
   [*Kisses her.*]
DAME PLIANT: Brother,
   He calls me lady, too.
KASTRIL: Ay, peace; I heard it.
FACE [*aside to* SUBTLE]: The Count is come.
SUBTLE [*aside to* FACE]:   Where is he?
FACE [*aside*]:   At the door.
SUBTLE [*aside*]: Why, you must entertain him.
FACE [*aside*]:   What'll you do
   With these the while?
SUBTLE [*aside*]:   Why, have 'em up, and show 'em
   Some fustian book, or the dark glass.
FACE [*aside*]:   'Fore God,
60   She is a delicate dabchick! I must have her.
   [*Exit.*]
SUBTLE [*aside*]: Must you! Ay, if your fortune will, you must. –
   Come, sir, the Captain will come to us presently.
   I'll ha' you to my chamber of demonstrations,
   Where I'll show you both the grammar and logic
   And rhetoric of quarrelling, my whole method
   Drawn out in tables; and my instrument,
   That hath the several scale upon't shall make you
   Able to quarrel at a straw's-breadth by moonlight.
   And, lady, I'll have you look in a glass,
70   Some half an hour, but to clear your eyesight,
   Against you see your fortune; which is greater
   Than I may judge upon the sudden, trust me.
   [*Exit, followed by* KASTRIL *and* DAME PLIANT.]

IV, iii   [*Enter* FACE.]
   [FACE:] Where are you, Doctor?
SUBTLE [*within*]: I'll come to you presently.
FACE: I will ha' this same widow, now I ha' seen her,
   On any composition.

59. *glass:* crystal ball into which astrologers gazed.
60. *dabchick:* water-hen.   3. *composition:* terms.

[*Enter* SUBTLE.]

SUBTLE: What do you say?

FACE: Ha' you disposed of them?

SUBTLE: I ha' sent 'em up.

FACE: Subtle, in troth, I needs must have this widow.

SUBTLE: Is that the matter?

FACE: Nay, but hear me.

SUBTLE: Go to.
If you rebel once, Dol shall know it all.
Therefore be quiet, and obey your chance.

FACE: Nay, thou art so violent now. Do but conceive,
Thou art old, and canst not serve –

SUBTLE: Who cannot? I?   10
'Slight, I will serve her with thee, for a –

FACE: Nay,
But understand; I'll gi' you composition.

SUBTLE: I will not treat with thee. What! sell my fortune?
'Tis better than my birthright. Do not murmur.
Win her, and carry her. If you grumble, Dol
Knows it directly.

FACE: Well, sir, I am silent.
Will you go help to fetch in Don, in state?
[*Exit.*]

SUBTLE: I follow you, sir. We must keep Face in awe,
Or he will overlook us like a tyrant.
[*Re-enter* FACE, *with* SURLY, *disguised as a Spanish nobleman.*]
Brain of a tailor! who comes here? Don John!   20

SURLY: *Señores, beso las manos à vuestras mercedes.*

SUBTLE: Would you had stooped a little, and kissed our
anos.

FACE: Peace, Subtle!

SUBTLE: Stab me; I shall never hold, man.
He looks in that deep ruff like a head in a platter,
Served in by a short cloak upon two trestles.

---

19. *overlook:* look down upon.

19. (*Stage-direction*): Surly's disguise is evidently a particularly elaborate Spanish costume, hence the jokes about its ruff, etc.

21. *Señores . . . :* 'Gentleman, I kiss your worships' hands.'

FACE: Or what do you say to a collar of brawn, cut down
Beneath the souse, and wriggled with a knife?

SUBTLE: 'Slud, he does look too fat to be a Spaniard.

FACE: Perhaps some Fleming or some Hollander got him
30   In d'Alva's time; Count Egmont's bastard.

SUBTLE: Don,
Your scurvy, yellow, Madrid face is welcome.

SURLY: *Gratia.*

SUBTLE: He speaks out of a fortification.
Pray God he ha' no squibs in those deeps sets.

SURLY: *Por dios, señores, muy linda casa!*

SUBTLE: What says he?

FACE: Praises the house, I think;
I know no more but's action.

SUBTLE: Yes, the *casa*,
My precious Diego, will prove fair enough
To cozen you in. Do you mark? You shall
Be cozened, Diego.

FACE: Cozened, do you see,
40   My worthy Donzel, cozened.

SURLY: *Entiendo.*

SUBTLE: Do you intend it? So do we, dear Don.
Have you brought pistolets or portagues,
My solemn Don? [*To* FACE] Dost thou feel any?
   He feels his pockets.

FACE: Full.

SUBTLE: You shall be emptied, Don, pumpèd and drawn
Dry, as they say.

FACE: Milkèd, in troth, sweet Don.

SUBTLE: See all the monsters; the great lion of all, Don.

SURLY: *Con licencia, se puede ver à esta señora?*

---

26. *brawn*: boar's flesh.
27. *souse*: ear.
32. *Gratia*: 'Thanks'.   33. *sets*: plaits of the ruff.
34. *Por dios* . . . : 'By God, gentlemen, a very fine house.'
40. *Donzel*: little Don; *Entiendo*: I understand.
42. *portagues*: gold coins.
47. *Con licencia* . . .: 'By your leave, may I see the lady?'

SUBTLE: What talks he now?

FACE: O' the señora.

SUBTLE: O, Don,
That is the lioness, which you shall see
Also, my Don.

FACE: 'Slid, Subtle, how shall we do?   50

SUBTLE: For what?

FACE: Why, Dol's employed, you know.

SUBTLE: That's true.
'Fore heav'n I know not: he must stay, that's all.

FACE: Stay! that he must not by no means.

SUBTLE: No! why?

FACE: Unless you'll mar all. 'Slight, he'll suspect it;
And then he will not pay, not half so well.
This is a travelled punk-master, and does know
All the delays; a notable hot rascal,
And looks already rampant.

SUBTLE: 'Sdeath, and Mammon
Must not be troubled.

FACE: Mammon! in no case.

SUBTLE: What shall we do then?

FACE: Think: you must be sudden.   60

SURLY: *Entiendo que la señora es tan hermosa, que cod'icio tan
à verla como la bien aventuránça de mi vida.*

FACE: *Mi vida!* 'Slid, Subtle, he puts me in mind o' the widow.
What dost thou say to draw her to 't, ha!
And tell her it is her fortune? All our venture
Now lies upon't. It is but one man more,
Which on's chance to have her; and beside,
There is no maidenhead to be feared or lost.
What dost thou think on't, Subtle?

SUBTLE: Who, I? why –

FACE: The credit of our house, too, is engaged.   70

SUBTLE: You made me an offer for my share erewhile.
What wilt thou gi' me, i'faith?

FACE: O, by that light,

61-2. *Entiendo . . . :* 'I understand that the lady is so beautiful that I desire
the sight of her as much as good fortune in my life.'

I'll not buy now. You know your doom to me.
E'en take your lot, obey your chance, sir; win her,
And wear her out for me.

SUBTLE: 'Slight, I'll not work her then.

FACE: It is the common cause; therefore bethink you.
Dol else must know it, as you said.

SUBTLE: I care not.

SURLY: *Señores, porque se tarda tanto?*

SUBTLE: Faith, I am not fit, I am old.

FACE: That's now no reason, sir.

80   SURLY: *Puede ser de hazer burla de mi amor?*

FACE: You hear the Don, too? By this air, I call,
And loose the hinges Dol!

SUBTLE: A plague of Hell –

FACE: Will you then do?

SUBTLE: Y'are a terrible rogue!
I'll think of this. Will you, sir, call the widow?

FACE: Yes, and I'll take her, too, with all her faults,
Now I do think on't better.

SUBTLE: With all my heart, sir;
Am I discharged o' the lot?

FACE: As you please.

SUBTLE: Hands.

     [*They shake hands.*]

FACE: Remember now, that upon any change
You never claim her.

SUBTLE: Much good joy and health to you, sir.

90   Marry a whore! Fate, let me wed a witch first.

SURLY: *Por estas honradas barbas –*

SUBTLE: He swears by his beard.
Dispatch, and call the brother, too.

     [*Exit* FACE.]

SURLY: *Tengo duda, señores,*
Que no me hágan alguna traycion.

73. *doom* : decision.   78. *Señores* . . . : 'Gentlemen, why so much delay?'
80. *Puede* . . . : 'Can it be that you are making fun of my love?'
91. *Por estas* . . . : 'By this honoured beard –'
93. *Tengo* . . . : 'I fear, gentlemen, you are playing some trick on me.'

SUBTLE: How, issue on? Yes, *præsto, señor*. Please you
   Enthratha the *chambratha*, worthy Don,
   Where if it please the Fates, in your *bathada*,
   You shall be soaked, and stroked, and tubbed, and rubbed,
   And scrubbed, and fubbed, dear Don, before you go.
   You shall in faith, my scurvy baboon Don,
   Be curried, clawed, and flawed, and tawed, indeed.   *100*
   I will the heartilier go about it now,
   And make the widow a punk so much the sooner,
   To be revenged on this impetuous Face:
   The quickly doing of it is the grace.
     [*Exeunt* SUBTLE *and* SURLY.]

[SCENE TWO]   IV, iv

[*Another room in Lovewit's house.*]

[*Re-enter* FACE, *accompanied by* KASTRIL *and his sister,* DAME
PLIANT.]

[FACE:] Come, lady. [*To* KASTRIL] I knew the Doctor would not
   leave
   Till he had found the very nick of her fortune.
KASTRIL: To be a countess, say you?
FACE: A Spanish countess, sir.
DAME PLIANT: Why, is that better than an English countess?
FACE: Better! 'Slight, make you that a question, lady?
KASTRIL: Nay, she is a fool, Captain, you must pardon her.
FACE: Ask him from your courtier to your inns-of-court-man,
   To your mere milliner. They will tell you all,
   Your Spanish jennet is the best horse; your Spanish
   Stoop is the best garb; your Spanish beard   *10*
   Is the best cut; your Spanish ruffs are the best
   Wear; your Spanish pavan the best dance;
   Your Spanish titillation in a glove

     98. *fubbed* : cheated.
     100. *tawed* : soaked in preparation for tanning.
     10. *garb:* carriage, deportment.

The best perfume; and for your Spanish pike
And Spanish blade, let your poor Captain speak. –
Here comes the Doctor.

[*Enter* SUBTLE *with a paper.*]

SUBTLE: My most honoured lady,
For so I am now to style you, having found
By this my scheme, you are to undergo
An honourable fortune very shortly,
20   What will you say now, if some –
FACE: I ha' told her all, sir,
And her right worshipful brother here, that she shall be
A countess – do not delay 'em, sir – a Spanish countess.
SUBTLE: Still, my scarce-worshipful Captain, you can keep
No secret! Well, since he has told you, madam,
Do you forgive him, and I do.
KASTRIL: She shall do that, sir;
I'll look to't; 'tis my charge.
SUBTLE: Well, then, nought rests
But that she fit her love now to her fortune.
DAME PLIANT: Truly I shall never brook a Spaniard.
SUBTLE: No?
DAME PLIANT: Never sin' eighty-eight could I abide 'em,
30   And that was some three year afore I was born, in truth.
SUBTLE: Come, you must love him, or be miserable;
Choose which you will.
FACE: By this good rush, persuade her.
She will cry strawberries else within this twelvemonth.
SUBTLE: Nay, shads and mackerel, which is worse.
FACE: Indeed, sir!
KASTRIL: God's lid, you shall love him, or I'll kick you.
DAME PLIANT: Why,
I'll do as you will ha' me, brother.
KASTRIL: Do,
Or by this hand I'll maul you.

18. *scheme:* horoscope.
29. *eighty-eight:* i.e. 1588, the year of the destruction of the Spanish
Armada.   33. *cry:* refers to the street-cries of hawkers.

FACE: Nay, good sir,
Be not so fierce.

SUBTLE: No, my enragèd child;
She will be ruled. What, when she comes to taste
The pleasures of a countess! to be courted – 40

FACE: And kissed and ruffled!

SUBTLE: Ay, behind the hangings.

FACE: And then come forth in pomp!

SUBTLE: And know her state!

FACE: Of keeping all th' idolators o' the chamber
Barer to her, than at their prayers!

SUBTLE: Is served
Upon the knee!

FACE: And has her pages, ushers,
Footmen, and coaches –

SUBTLE: Her six mares –

FACE: Nay, eight!

SUBTLE: To hurry her through London, to th' Exchange,
Bedlam, the China-houses –

FACE: Yes, and have
The citizens gape at her, and praise her tires,
And my Lord's goose-turd bands, that rides with her! 50

KASTRIL: Most brave! By this hand, you are not my suster
If you refuse.

DAME PLIANT: I will not refuse, brother.

[*Enter* SURLY.]

SURLY: *Que es esto, señores, que non se venga?*
Esta tardanza me mata!

FACE: It is the Count come!
The Doctor knew he would be here, by his art.

SUBTLE: *En gallanta madama, Don! gallantissima!*

SURLY: *Por todos los dioses, la mas acabada*

47. *Exchange:* shopping area in the City.
50. *goose-turd:* yellowish-green (colour of goose's droppings).
53–4. *Que es . . . :* 'What's the matter, gentlemen, that she does not come? This delay is killing me!'
56–7. *Por todos . . . :* 'By all the gods, the most perfect beauty that I have seen in my life!'

Hermosura, que he visto en mi vida!

FACE: Is't not a gallant language that they speak?

60 KASTRIL: An admirable language! Is't not French?

FACE: No, Spanish, sir.

KASTRIL: It goes like law French,
And that, they say, is the courtliest language.

FACE: List, sir.

SURLY: *El sol ha perdido su lumbre, con el*
Resplandor que tràe esta dama! Valga me dios!

FACE: H'admires your sister.

KASTRIL: Must not she make curt'sy?

SUBTLE: 'Ods will, she must go to him, man, and kiss him!
It is the Spanish fashion, for the women
To make first court.

FACE: 'Tis true he tells you, sir;
His art knows all.

SURLY: *Porque no se acùde?*

70 KASTRIL: He speaks to her, I think.

FACE: That he does, sir.

SURLY: *Por el amor de dios, que es esto que se tàrda?*

KASTRIL: Nay, see : she will not understand him! Gull,
Noddy!

DAME PLIANT: What say you, brother?

KASTRIL: Ass, my suster,
Go kuss him, as the cunning-man would ha' you;
I'll thrust a pin i' your buttocks else.

FACE: O no, sir.

SURLY: *Señora mia, mi persona muy indigna està*
Allegar à tanta hermosura.

FACE: Does he not use her bravely?

KASTRIL: Bravely, i' faith!

FACE: Nay, he will use her better.

KASTRIL: Do you think so?

63–4 *El sol . . .*: 'The sun has lost its light compared to the splendour this
lady brings! God help me!'

69. *Porque . . .*: 'Why don't you come closer?'

71. *Por . . .*: 'For the love of God, why this delay?'

76. *Señora . . .*: 'Madam, my person is entirely unworthy to come near
such beauty.'

SURLY: *Señora, si sera servida, entremos.*　　　　　　　*80*
　　[*Exit with* DAME PLIANT.]
KASTRIL: Where does he carry her?
FACE:　　　　　　　　　　　Into the garden, sir;
　　Take you no thought. I must interpret for her.
SUBTLE [*aside to* FACE]: Give Dol the word.
　　[*Exit* FACE.]
　　　　　　　　　　　– Come, my fierce child, advance,
　　We'll to our quarrelling lesson again.
KASTRIL:　　　　　　　　　　Agreed.
　　I love a Spanish boy with all my heart.
SUBTLE: Nay, and by this means, sir, you shall be brother
　　To a great count.
KASTRIL:　　　　　Ay, I knew that at first.
　　This match will advance the house of the Kastrils.
SUBTLE: 'Pray God your sister prove but pliant!
KASTRIL:　　　　　　　　　　　　　　Why,
　　Her name is so, by her other husband.
SUBTLE:　　　　　　　　How!　　　　　　　*90*
KASTRIL: The Widow Pliant. Knew you not that?
SUBTLE:　　　　　　　　　　No, faith, sir;
　　Yet, by the erection of her figure, I guessed it.
　　Come, let's go practise.
KASTRIL:　　　　　Yes, but do you think, Doctor,
　　I e'er shall quarrel well?
SUBTLE:　　　　　I warrant you.
　　[*Exeunt.*]

　　　　　　　　　　　　　　　　　　　　　　IV, V

　　　　　　　　　[SCENE THREE]

　　[*A room upstairs in Lovewit's house.*]

　　[*Enter* DOL] *in her fit of talking* [*followed by* MAMMON.]
[DOL COMMON:] For, after Alexander's death –
MAMMON:　　　　　　　　　　Good lady –

80. *Señora . . .:* 'Madam, if you will, let's go in.'
92. *figure:* Subtle's pun is based on 'figure' meaning horoscope.

DOL COMMON: That Perdiccas and Antigonus were slain,
  The two that stood, Seleuc' and Ptolemy –
MAMMON: Madam –
DOL COMMON: Made up the two legs, and the fourth beast,
  That was Gog-north and Egypt-south; which after
  Was called Gog-iron-leg and South-iron-leg –
MAMMON: Lady –
DOL COMMON: And then Gog-hornèd. So was Egypt, too:
  Then Egypt-clay-leg, and Gog-clay-leg –
MAMMON: Sweet madam –
DOL COMMON: And last Gog-dust, and Egypt-dust, which fall
10 In the last link of the fourth chain. And these
  Be stars in story, which none see, or look at –
MAMMON: What shall I do?
DOL COMMON: For, as he says, except
  We call the rabbins, and the heathen Greeks –
MAMMON: Dear lady –
DOL COMMON: To come from Salem, and from Athens,
  And teach the people of Great Britain –
  [*Enter* FACE, *in his servant's costume.*]
FACE: What's the matter, sir?
DOL COMMON: To speak the tongue of Eber and Javan –
MAMMON: O,
  She's in her fit.
DOL COMMON: We shall know nothing –
FACE: Death, sir,
  We are undone!
DOL COMMON: Where then a learnèd linguist
  Shall see the ancient used communion
20 Of vowels and consonants –
FACE: My master will hear!
DOL COMMON: A wisdom, which Pythagoras held most high –
MAMMON: Sweet honourable lady!
DOL COMMON: To comprise
  All sounds of voices, in few marks of letters.
FACE: Nay, you must never hope to lay her now.
  They speak together.

16. *tongue of Eber*: Hebrew; *of Javan*: Greek.

DOL: And so we may arrive, by
Talmud skill

And profane Greek, to raise
the building up

Of Helen's house against the
Ishmaelite,

King of Togarmah, and his
habergeons

Brimstony, blue, and fiery;
and the force

Of king Abaddon, and the
beast of Cittim,

Which Rabbi David Kimchi,
Onkelos,

And Aben Ezra do interpret
Rome.

[*Enter* SUBTLE.]

MAMMON: Where shall I hide me!

SUBTLE: How! What sight
is here?

Close deeds of darkness, and that shun the light!
Bring him again. Who is he? What, my son!
O, I have lived too long.

MAMMON: Nay, good, dear father,
There was no unchaste purpose.

SUBTLE: Not? and flee me
When I come in?

MAMMON: That was my error.

SUBTLE: Error?
Guilt, guilt, my son; give it the right name. No marvel
If I found check in our great work within,
When such affairs as these were managing!

FACE: How did you put her
into't?

MAMMON: Alas, I talked
Of a Fifth Monarchy I would
erect

With the Philosopher's
Stone, by chance, and she
Falls on the other four
straight.

FACE: Out of Broughton!
I told you so. 'Slid, stop her
mouth.

MAMMON: Is't best?

FACE: She'll never leave else.
If the old man hear her,   *30*
We are but fæces, ashes.

SUBTLE: What's to do there?

FACE: O, we are lost! Now she
hears him, she is quiet.

Upon
SUBTLE'S
entry they
[FACE *and*
DOL]
disperse.

40

34. *close*: secret.

MAMMON: Why, have you so?

SUBTLE: It has stood still this half-hour,
And all the rest of our less works gone back.
Where is the instrument of wickedness
My lewd false drudge?

MAMMON: Nay, good sir, blame not him;
Believe me, 'twas against his will or knowledge.
I saw her by chance.

SUBTLE: Will you commit more sin,
T'excuse a varlet?

MAMMON: By my hope, 'tis true, sir.

SUBTLE: Nay, then I wonder less, if you, for whom
50   The blessing was prepared, would so tempt Heaven,
And lose your fortunes.

MAMMON: Why, sir?

SUBTLE: This'll retard
The work a month at least.

MAMMON: Why, if it do,
What remedy? But think it not, good father;
Our purposes were honest.

SUBTLE: As they were,
So the reward will prove.
    A great crack and noise within.
                              How now! ay me!
God and all saints be good to us. –
    [*Re-enter* FACE.]
                              What's that?

FACE: O, sir, we are defeated! All the works
Are flown *in fumo*, every glass is burst!
Furnace and all rent down, as if a bolt
60   Of thunder had been driven through the house.
Retorts, receivers, pelicans, bolt-heads,
All struck in shivers!
    SUBTLE *falls down, as in a swoon.*
                              Help, good sir! alas,
Coldness and death invades him. Nay, Sir Mammon,
Do the fair offices of a man! You stand,

54. *honest:* pure, chaste.

As you were readier to depart than he.
 One knocks.
Who's there? My Lord her brother is come.
MAMMON: Ha, Lungs!
FACE: His coach is at the door. Avoid his sight,
 For he's as furious as his sister is mad.
MAMMON: Alas!
FACE: My brain is quite undone with the fume, sir,
 I ne'er must hope to be mine own man again.   *70*
MAMMON: Is all lost, Lungs? Will nothing be preserved
 Of all our cost?
FACE: Faith, very little, sir;
 A peck of coals or so, which is cold comfort, sir.
MAMMON: O, my voluptuous mind! I am justly punished.
FACE: And so am I, sir.
MAMMON: Cast from all my hopes –
FACE: Nay, certainties, sir.
MAMMON: By mine own base affections.
 SUBTLE *seems [to] come to himself.*
SUBTLE: O, the curst fruits of vice and lust!
MAMMON: Good father,
 It was my sin. Forgive it.
SUBTLE: Hangs my roof
 Over us still, and will not fall, O Justice,
 Upon us, for this wicked man!
FACE: Nay, look, sir,   *80*
 You grieve him now with staying in his sight.
 Good sir, the nobleman will come too, and take you,
 And that may breed a tragedy.
MAMMON: I'll go.
FACE: Ay, and repent at home, sir. It may be,
 For some good penance you may ha' it yet;
 A hundred pound to the box at Bedlam –
MAMMON: Yes.
FACE: For the restoring such as ha' their wits.
MAMMON: I'll do't.
FACE: I'll send one to you to receive it.
MAMMON: Do.

Is no projection left?

FACE: All flown, or stinks, sir.

90 MAMMON: Will nought be saved that's good for med'cine, think'st
thou?

FACE: I cannot tell, sir. There will be perhaps
Something about the scraping of the shards,
Will cure the itch, – though not your itch of mind, sir.
It shall be saved for you, and sent home. Good sir,
This way, for fear the lord should meet you.

[*Exit* MAMMON.]

SUBTLE: Face!

FACE: Ay.

SUBTLE: Is he gone?

FACE: Yes, and as heavily
As all the gold he hoped for were in his blood.
Let us be light though.

SUBTLE [*leaping up*]: Ay, as balls, and bound
100 And hit our heads against the roof for joy:
There's so much of our care now cast away.

FACE: Now to our Don.

SUBTLE: Yes, your young widow by this time
Is made a countess, Face; she's been in travail
Of a young heir for you.

FACE: Good, sir.

SUBTLE: Off with your case,
And greet her kindly, as a bridegroom should,
After these common hazards.

FACE: Very well, sir.
Will you go fetch Don Diego off the while?

SUBTLE: And fetch him over too, if you'll be pleased, sir.
Would Dol were in her place, to pick his pockets now!

FACE: Why, you can do it as well, if you would set to't.
110 I pray you prove your virtue.

SUBTLE: For your sake, sir.

[*Exeunt.*]

103. *case*: costume, disguise (i.e. servant's livery).
110. *virtue*: ability.

286

[SCENE FOUR] IV, vi

[The garden of Lovewit's house.]

[Enter SURLY, *in his Spanish costume, and* DAME PLIANT.]
[SURLY:] Lady, you see into what hands you are fall'n;
　'Mongst what a nest of villains! and how near
　Your honour was t'have catched a certain clap,
　Through your credulity, had I but been
　So punctually forward, as place, time,
　And other circumstance would ha' made a man;
　For y'are a handsome woman: would you were wise, too!
　I am a gentleman come here disguised,
　Only to find the knaveries of this citadel;
　And where I might have wronged your honour, and have not, 10
　I claim some interest in your love. You are,
　They say, a widow, rich; and I'm a bachelor
　Worth nought. Your fortunes may make me a man,
　As mine ha' preserved you a woman. Think upon it,
　And whether I have deserved you or no.
DAME PLIANT: I will, sir.
SURLY: And for these household-rogues, let me alone
　To treat with them.

　　[Enter SUBTLE.]

SUBTLE: How doth my noble Diego,
　And my dear madam Countess? Hath the Count
　Been courteous, lady, liberal and open?
　Donzel, methinks you look melancholic, 20
　After your *coitum*, and scurvy! Truly,
　I do not like the dullness of your eye;
　It hath a heavy cast, 'tis upsee Dutch,
　And says you are a lumpish whore-master.
　Be lighter, I will make your pockets so.
　　He falls to picking of them.
SURLY: Will you, Don Bawd and Pick-purse?

　　3. *clap:* calamity or fall, with overtones of venereal disease.
　21. *coitum:* intercourse.

287

[*Knocking him down.*]

How now! Reel you?
Stand up, sir, you shall find, sinse I am so heavy,
I'll gi' you equal weight.

SUBTLE: Help! murder!

SURLY: No, sir,
There's no such thing intended. A good cart
30   And a clean whip shall ease you of that fear.
I am the Spanish Don that should be cozened,
Do you see? Cozened? Where's your Captain Face,
That parcel-broker, and whole-bawd, all rascal?

[*Enter* FACE *in his Captain's uniform.*]

FACE: How, Surly!

SURLY: O, make your approach, good Captain.
I've found from whence your copper rings and spoons
Come now, wherewith you cheat abroad in taverns.
'Twas here you learned t'anoint your boot with brimstone,
Then rub men's gold on't for a kind of touch,
And say 'twas naught, when you had changed the colour,
40   That you might ha't for nothing. And this Doctor,
Your sooty, smoky-bearded compeer, he
Will close you so much gold, in a bolt's-head,
And, on a turn, convey i' the stead another
With sublimed mercury, that shall burst i' the heat,
And fly out all *in fumo!* Then weeps Mammon;
Then swoons his worship. Or, he is the Faustus,

[*Exit* FACE, *quietly.*]

That casteth figures and can conjure, cures
Plagues, piles, and pox, by the ephemerides,
And holds intelligence with all the bawds
50   And midwives of three shires; while you send in –
Captain! – What! is he gone? – damsels with child,
Wives that are barren, or the waiting-maid
With the green sickness.

29. *cart:* the punishment for bawds was to drive them publicly through
the streets.
33. *parcel:* partial, part.
48. *ephemerides:* almanacs of astrology.

[Seizes SUBTLE *as he is escaping.]*
                 – Nay, sir, you must tarry,
Though he be 'scaped; and answer by the ears, sir.

[Re-enter FACE *with* KASTRIL.]   IV, vii

[FACE:] Why, now's the time, if ever you will quarrel
  Well, as they say, and be a true-born child.
  The Doctor and your sister both are abused.
KASTRIL: Where is he? Which is he? He is a slave.
  Whate'er he is, and the son of a whore. – Are you
  The man, sir, I would know?
SURLY: I should be loath, sir,
  To confess so much.
KASTRIL: Then you lie i' your throat.
SURLY: How!
FACE [*to* KASTRIL]: A very arrant rogue, sir, and a cheater,
  Employed here by another conjurer
  That does not love the Doctor, and would cross him,   10
  If he knew how.
SURLY: Sir, you are abused.
KASTRIL: You lie:
  And 'tis no matter.
FACE: Well said, sir! He is
  The impudent'st rascal –
SURLY: You are indeed. Will you hear me, sir?
FACE: By no means. Bid him be gone.
KASTRIL: Begone, sir, quickly.
SURLY: This's strange! – Lady, do you inform your brother.
FACE: There is not such a foist in all the town.
  The Doctor had him presently; and finds yet
  The Spanish Count will come here. – [*Aside*] Bear up, Subtle.
SUBTLE: Yes, sir, he must appear within this hour.
FACE: And yet this rogue would come in a disguise,   20
  By the temptation of another spirit,
  To trouble our art, though he could not hurt it.
KASTRIL: Ay,

16. *foist:* rogue, trickster.

I know – [*To his sister*] Away, you talk like a foolish mauther.

SURLY: Sir, all is truth she says.

FACE: Do not believe him, sir.
He is the lying'st swabber! Come your ways, sir.

SURLY: You are valiant out of company!

KASTRIL: Yes, how then, sir?

[*Enter* DRUGGER *with a piece of damask.*]

FACE: Nay, here's an honest fellow, too, that knows him,
And all his tricks. – [*Aside to* DRUGGER] Make good what I say,
Abel;
This cheater would ha' cozened thee o' the widow. –
30 He owes this honest Drugger here seven pound,
He has had on him in twopenny'orths of tobacco.

DRUGGER: Yes, sir. And's damned himself three terms to pay me.

FACE: And what does he owe for lotion?

DRUGGER: Thirty shillings, sir;
And for six syringes.

SURLY: Hydra of villainy!

FACE: Nay, sir, you must quarrel him out o' the house.

KASTRIL: I will.
– Sir, if you get not out o' doors, you lie;
And you are a pimp.

SURLY: Why, this is madness, sir,
Not valour in you. I must laugh at this.

KASTRIL: It is my humour; you are a pimp and a trig,
40 And an Amadis de Gaul, or a Don Quixote

DRUGGER: Or a knight o' the curious coxcomb, do you see?

[*Enter* ANANIAS.]

ANANIAS: Peace to the household!

KASTRIL: I'll keep peace tor no man.

ANANIAS: Casting of dollars is concluded lawful.

KASTRIL: Is he the Constable?

SUBTLE: Peace, Ananias.

FACE: No, sir.

23. *mauther:* young woman.   32. *damned himself:* sworn.
39. *trig:* coxcomb.
40. *Amadis de Gaul:* a chivalric hero.

KASTRIL: Then you are an otter, and a shad, a whit,
 A very tim.
SURLY: You'll hear me, sir?
KASTRIL: I will not.
ANANIAS: What is the motive?
SUBTLE: Zeal in the young gentleman,
 Against his Spanish slops.
ANANIAS: They are profane,
 Lewd, superstitious, and idolatrous breeches.
SURLY: New rascals!
KASTRIL: Will you be gone, sir?
ANANIAS: Avoid, Satan!   50
 Thou art not of the light! That ruff of pride
 About thy neck betrays thee, and is the same
 With that which the unclean birds, in seventy-seven,
 Were seen to prank it with on divers coasts:
 Thou look'st like Antichrist, in that lewd hat.
SURLY: I must give way.
KASTRIL: Be gone, sir.
SURLY: But I'll take
 A course with you –
ANANIAS: Depart, proud Spanish fiend!
SURLY: Captain and Doctor –
ANANIAS: Child of perdition!
KASTRIL: Hence, sir! –
 [*Exit* SURLY.]
 Did I not quarrel bravely?
FACE: Yes, indeed, sir.
KASTRIL: Nay, an' I give my mind to't, I shall do't.   60
FACE: O, you must follow, sir, and threaten him tame.
 He'll turn again else.
KASTRIL: I'll re-turn him then.
 [*Exit.*]
FACE: Drugger, this rogue prevented us, for thee.
 We had determined that thou should'st ha' come
 In a Spanish suit, and ha' carried her so; and he,

---

45. *tim*: abusive term; exact meaning uncertain.
53. *seventy-seven*: Note.

A brokerly slave, goes, puts it on himself.
Hast brought the damask?

DRUGGER: Yes, sir.

FACE: Thou must borrow
A Spanish suit. Hast thou no credit with the players?

DRUGGER: Yes, sir; did you never see me play the Fool?

70 FACE: I know not, Nab. – [*Aside*] Thou shalt, if I can help it. –
Hieronimo's old cloak, ruff, and hat will serve;
I'll tell thee more when thou bring'st 'em.

   [*Exit* DRUGGER.]

ANANIAS: Sir, I know   SUBTLE
The Spaniard hates the Brethren, and hath spies   *hath*
Upon their actions; and that this was one   *whispered*
I make no scruple. – But the Holy Synod   *with him*
Have been in prayer and meditation for it;   *this while.*
And 'tis revealed no less to them than me,
That casting of money is most lawful.

SUBTLE: True.
But here I cannot do it; if the house
80 Should chance to be suspected, all would out,
And we be locked up in the Tower for ever,
To make gold there for th' state, never come out.
And then you are defeated.

ANANIAS: I will tell
This to the elders and the weaker Brethren,
That the whole company of the Separation
May join in humble prayer again.

SUBTLE: And fasting.

ANANIAS: Yea, for some fitter place. The peace of mind
Rest with these walls!

SUBTLE: Thanks, courteous Ananias.

   [*Exit* ANANIAS.]

FACE: What did he come for?

SUBTLE: About casting dollars,
90 Presently, out of hand. And so I told him,
A Spanish minister came here to spy

68. *suit*: costume; *players*: actors.
71. *Hieronimo*: avenger-hero of Thomas Kyd's *The Spanish Tragedy*.

Against the faithful –

FACE: I conceive. Come, Subtle,
Thou art so down upon the least disaster!
How wouldst thou ha' done, if I had not helped thee out?

SUBTLE: I thank thee, Face, for the angry boy, i' faith.

FACE: Who would ha' looked it should ha' been that rascal
Surly? He had dyed his beard and all. Well, sir,
Here's damask come to make you a suit.

SUBTLE: Where's Drugger?

FACE: He is gone to borrow me a Spanish habit;
I'll be the Count now.

SUBTLE: But where's the widow?   *100*

FACE: Within, with my Lord's sister; Madam Dol
Is entertaining her.

SUBTLE: By your favour, Face,
Now she is honest, I will stand again.

FACE: You will not offer it!

SUBTLE: Why?

FACE: Stand to your word,
Or – here comes Dol! – she knows –

SUBTLE: Y'are tyrannous still.

[*Enter* DOL *hurriedly.*]

FACE: – Strict for my right. – How now, Dol! Hast told her
The Spanish Count will come?

DOL COMMON: Yes, but another is come,
You little looked for!

FACE: Who's that?

DOL COMMON: Your master,
The master of the house.

SUBTLE: How, Dol!

FACE: She lies,
This is some trick. Come, leave your quiblins, Dorothy.   *110*

DOL COMMON: Look out and see.

[FACE *goes to the window.*]

SUBTLE: Art thou in earnest?

96. *looked:* thought, expected.
110. *quiblins:* jokes, verbal quibbles.

DOL COMMON: 'Slight,
Forty o' the neighbours are about him, talking.

FACE: 'Tis he, by this good day.

DOL COMMON: 'Twill prove ill day
For some on us.

FACE: We are undone, and taken.

DOL COMMON: Lost, I'm afraid.

SUBTLE: You said he would not come,
While there died one a week within the liberties.

FACE: No: 'twas within the walls.

SUBTLE: Was't so? Cry you mercy.
I thought the liberties. What shall we do now, Face?

FACE: Be silent: not a word, if he call or knock.
120   I'll into mine old shape again and meet him,
Of Jeremy, the butler. I' the meantime,
Do you two pack up all the goods and purchase
That we can carry i' the two trunks. I'll keep him
Off for today, if I cannot longer, and then
At night, I'll ship you both away to Ratcliff,
Where we will meet tomorrow, and there we'll share.
Let Mammon's brass and pewter keep the cellar;
We'll have another time for that. But, Dol,
'Pray thee go heat a little water quickly;
130   Subtle must shave me. All my Captain's beard
Must off, to make me appear smooth Jeremy.
You'll do't?

SUBTLE: Yes, I'll shave you as well as I can.

FACE: And not cut my throat, but trim me?

SUBTLE: You shall see, sir.
[*Exeunt.*]

116. *liberties:* suburban areas outwith the City's jurisdiction; slums.
122. *purchase:* loot, booty.

ACT FIVE

[Outside Lovewit's house.]

[Enter LOVEWIT *with a Crowd of* NEIGHBOURS.]
[LOVEWIT:] Has there been such resort, say you?
1ST NEIGHBOUR: Daily, sir.
2ND NEIGHBOUR: And nightly, too.
3RD NEIGHBOUR: Ay, some as brave as lords.
4TH NEIGHBOUR: Ladies and gentlewomen.
5TH NEIGHBOUR: Citizens' wives.
1ST NEIGHBOUR: And knights.
6TH NEIGHBOUR: In coaches.
2ND NEIGHBOUR: Yes, and oyster-
    women.
1ST NEIGHBOUR: Beside other gallants.
3RD NEIGHBOUR: Sailors' wives.
4TH NEIGHBOUR: Tobacco-
    men.
5TH NEIGHBOUR: Another Pimlico!
LOVEWIT: What should my knave ad-
    vance,
  To draw this company? He hung out no banners
  Of a strange calf with five legs to be seen,
  Or a huge lobster with six claws?
6TH NEIGHBOUR: No, sir.
3RD NEIGHBOUR: We had gone in then, sir.
LOVEWIT: He has no gift   10
  Of teaching i' the nose that e'er I knew of.
  You saw no bills set up that promised cure
  Of agues or the tooth-ache?

   1. *resort:* visiting, coming and going.
   6. *knave:* servant (i.e. Jeremy *alias* Face).
  11. *teaching i' the nose:* preaching with a nasal intonation, like a Puritan.
  12. *bills:* advertisements, posters.

2ND NEIGHBOUR: No such thing, sir!

LOVEWIT: Nor heard a drum struck for baboons or puppets?

5TH NEIGHBOUR: Neither, sir.

LOVEWIT: What device should he bring
forth now?
I love a teeming wit as I love my nourishment.
'Pray God he ha' not kept such open house,
That he hath sold my hangings, and my bedding!
I left him nothing else. If he have eat 'em,
20 A plague o' the moth, say I! Sure he has got
Some bawdy pictures to call all this ging:
The Friar and the Nun, or the new motion
Of the knight's courser covering the parson's mare;
The boy of six year old, with the great thing;
Or 't may be, he has the fleas that run at tilt
Upon a table, or some dog to dance.
When saw you him?

1ST NEIGHBOUR: Who, sir, Jeremy?

2ND NEIGHBOUR: Jeremy butler?
We saw him not this month.

LOVEWIT: How!

4TH NEIGHBOUR: Not these five weeks, sir.

1ST NEIGHBOUR: These six weeks, at the least.

LOVEWIT: You amaze me
neighbours!
30 5TH NEIGHBOUR: Sure, if your worship know not where he is,
He's slipped away.

6TH NEIGHBOUR: Pray God he be not made away.

LOVEWIT: Ha! It's no time to question, then.
He knocks.

6TH NEIGHBOUR: About
Some three weeks since I heard a doleful cry,
As I sat up a-mending my wife's stockings.

LOVEWIT: This's strange that none will answer! Did'st thou hear
A cry, sayst thou?

21. *ging:* assembly, gang.
22. *motion:* puppet-show. As in *Bartholomew Fair*, throughout.
25. *fleas:* i.e. a flea-circus.

6TH NEIGHBOUR: Yes, sir, like unto a man
That had been strangled an hour, and could not speak.
2ND NEIGHBOUR: I heard it, too, just this day three weeks, at two o'clock
Next morning.
LOVEWIT: These be miracles, or you make 'em so!
A man an hour strangled, and could not speak,⁣   *40*
And both you heard him cry?
3RD NEIGHBOUR: Yes, downward, sir.
LOVEWIT: Thou art a wise fellow. Give me thy hand, I pray thee.
What trade art thou on?
3RD NEIGHBOUR: A smith, an't please your worship.
LOVEWIT: A smith! Then lend me thy help to get this door open.
3RD NEIGHBOUR: That I will presently, sir, but fetch my tools –
    [*Exit.*]
1ST NEIGHBOUR: Sir, best to knock again afore you break it.

[LOVEWIT (*knocks again*):] I will.   V, ii
    [*Enter* FACE *in his butler's livery.*]
FACE: What mean you, sir?
1ST, 2ND, 4TH NEIGHBOURS: O, here's
Jeremy!
FACE: Good sir, come from the door.
LOVEWIT: Why, what's the matter?
FACE: Yet farther, you are too near yet.
LOVEWIT: I' the name of wonder,
What means the fellow!
FACE: The house, sir, has been visited.
LOVEWIT: What, with the plague? Stand thou then farther.
FACE: No, sir,
I had it not.
LOVEWIT: Who had it then? I left
None else but thee i' the house.
FACE: Yes, sir, my fellow,
The cat that kept the buttery, had it on her
A week before I spied it; but I got her
Conveyed away i' the night; and so I shut   *10*

The house up for a month –

LOVEWIT: How!

FACE: Purposing then, sir,
T'have burnt rose-vinegar, treacle, and tar,
And ha' made it sweet, that you should ne'er ha' known it;
Because I knew the news would but afflict you, sir.

LOVEWIT: Breathe less, and farther off! Why this is stranger:
The neighbours tell me all here that the doors
Have still been open –

FACE: How, sir!

LOVEWIT: Gallants, men and women,
And of all sorts, tag-rag, been seen to flock here
In threaves, these ten weeks, as to a second Hogsden,
20 In days of Pimlico and Eye-bright.

FACE: Sir,
Their wisdoms will not say so.

LOVEWIT: Today they speak
Of coaches and gallants. One in a French hood
Went in, they tell me; and another was seen
In a velvet gown at the window. Divers more
Pass in and out.

FACE: They did pass through the doors then,
Or walls, I assure their eyesights, and their spectacles;
For here, sir, are the keys, and here have been,
In this my pocket, now above twenty days!
And for before, I kept the fort alone there.
30 But that 'tis yet not deep i' the afternoon,
I should believe my neighbours had seen double
Through the black pot, and made these apparitions!
For, on my faith to your worship, for these three weeks
And upwards, the door has not been opened.

LOVEWIT: Strange!

1ST NEIGHBOUR: Good faith, I think I saw a coach.

2ND NEIGHBOUR: And I too,
I'd ha' been sworn.

19. *threaves:* droves, crowds.
20. *Eye-bright:* probably the name of a tavern in the area.
32. *through the black pot:* through too much drinking.

LOVEWIT: Do you but think it now?
And but one coach?

4TH NEIGHBOUR: We cannot tell, sir; Jeremy
Is a very honest fellow.

FACE: Did you see me at all?

1ST NEIGHBOUR: No; that we are sure on.

2ND NEIGHBOUR: I'll be sworn o' that.

LOVEWIT: Fine rogues to have your testimonies built on! 40

[*Re-enter* 3RD NEIGHBOUR, *with his tools.*]

3RD NEIGHBOUR: Is Jeremy come?

1ST NEIGHBOUR: O yes; you may leave your
tools;
We were deceived, he says.

2ND NEIGHBOUR: He's had the keys,
And the door has been shut these three weeks.

3RD NEIGHBOUR: Like enough.

LOVEWIT: Peace, and get hence, you changelings.

[*Enter* SURLY *and* MAMMON.]

FACE [*aside*]: Surly come!
And Mammon made acquainted! They'll tell all.
How shall I beat them off? What shall I do?
Nothing's more wretched than a guilty conscience.

[SURLY:] No, sir, he was a great physician. This,   v, iii
It was no bawdy-house, but a mere chancel!
You knew the Lord and his sister.

MAMMON: Nay, good Surly.

SURLY: The happy word, 'Be rich' –

MAMMON: Play not the tyrant.

SURLY: Should be today pronounced to all your friends.
And where be your andirons now? And your brass pots,
That should ha' been golden flagons, and great wedges?

MAMMON: Let me but breathe. What, they ha' shut their doors,
Methinks!

MAMMON *and* SURLY *knock.*

SURLY: Ay, now 'tis holiday with them.

2. *chancel*: temple.

MAMMON: Rogues,
10   Cozeners, impostors, bawds!
FACE: What mean you, sir?
MAMMON: To enter if we can.
FACE: Another man's house!
   Here is the owner, sir; turn you to him,
   And speak your business.
MAMMON: Are you, sir, the owner?
LOVEWIT: Yes, sir.
MAMMON: And are those knaves, within, your cheaters?
LOVEWIT: What knaves, what cheaters?
MAMMON: Subtle and his Lungs.
FACE: The gentleman is distracted, sir! No lungs
   Nor lights ha' been seen here these three weeks, sir,
   Within these doors, upon my word.
SURLY: Your word,
   Groom arrogant!
FACE: Yes, sir. I am the housekeeper,
20   And know the keys ha' not been out o' my hands.
SURLY: This's a new Face.
FACE: You do mistake the house, sir.
   What sign was't at?
SURLY: You rascal! This is one
   O' the confederacy. Come, let's get officers,
   And force the door.
LOVEWIT: Pray you stay, gentlemen.
SURLY: No, sir, we'll come with warrant.
MAMMON: Ay, and then
   We shall ha' your doors open.
      [*Exeunt* MAMMON *and* SURLY.]
LOVEWIT: What means this?
FACE: I cannot tell, sir.
1ST NEIGHBOUR: These are two o' the gallants
   That we do think we saw.
FACE: Two o' the fools!
   You talk as idly as they. Good faith, sir,
   I think the moon has crazed 'em all.
      [*Enter* KASTRIL.]

[*Aside*]   O me,   30
The angry boy come too! He'll make a noise,
And ne'er away till he have betrayed us all.
    KASTRIL *knocks.*
KASTRIL: What, rogues, bawds, slaves, you'll open the door anon!
    Punk, cockatrice, my suster! By this light,
    I'll fetch the marshal to you. You are a whore
    To keep your castle –
FACE: Who would you speak with, sir?
KASTRIL: The bawdy Doctor, and the cozening Captain,
    And Puss, my suster.
LOVEWIT: This is something, sure.
FACE: Upon my trust, the doors were never open, sir.
KASTRIL: I have heard all their tricks told me twice over,   40
    By the fat knight and the lean gentleman.
LOVEWIT: Here comes another.

[*Enter* ANANIAS *and* TRIBULATION WHOLESOME.]

FACE: Ananias, too!
    And his pastor!
TRIBULATION: The doors are shut against us.
    They beat, too, at the door.
ANANIAS: Come forth, you seed of sulphur, sons of fire!
    Your stench it is broke forth; abomination
    Is in the house.
KASTRIL: Ay, my suster's there.
ANANIAS: The place,
    It is become a cage of unclean birds.
KASTRIL: Yes, I will fetch the scavenger, and the constable.
TRIBULATION: You shall do well.
ANANIAS: We'll join to weed them out.
KASTRIL: You will not come then, punk devise, my suster!   50
ANANIAS: Call her not sister; she is a harlot verily.
KASTRIL: I'll raise the street.
LOVEWIT: Good gentlemen, a word.
ANANIAS: Satan, avoid, and hinder not our zeal!

34. *cockatrice:* whore.
50. *punk devise:* perfect harlot, pun on *point-device.*

[*Exeunt* ANANIAS, TRIBULATION WHOLESOME, *and*
KASTRIL.]

LOVEWIT: The world's turned Bedlam.

FACE: These are all broke loose,
Out of St Katherine's, where they use to keep
The better sort of mad-folks.

1ST NEIGHBOUR: All these persons
We saw go in and out here.

2ND NEIGHBOUR: Yes, indeed, sir.

3RD NEIGHBOUR: These were the parties.

FACE: Peace, you drunkards!
Sir,
I wonder at it. Please you to give me leave
60   To touch the door; I'll try an' the lock be changed.

LOVEWIT: It 'mazes me!

FACE [*goes to the door*]: Good faith, sir, I believe
There's no such thing; 'tis all *deceptio visus* –
[*Aside*] Would I could get him away.

        DAPPER *cries out within.*

DAPPER: Master Captain! Master Doctor!

LOVEWIT: Who's that?

FACE [*aside*]:   Our clerk within, that I forgot! –
I know not, sir.

DAPPER [*within*]: For God's sake, when will her Grace be at
    leisure?

FACE: Ha!
Illusions, some spirit o' the air! – [*Aside*] His gag is melted,
And now he sets out the throat.

DAPPER [*within*]:   I am almost stifled –

FACE [*aside*]: Would you were altogether.

LOVEWIT: 'Tis i' the house.
Ha! list.

FACE: Believe it, sir, i' the air.

LOVEWIT: Peace, you.

70   DAPPER [*within*]: Mine aunt's Grace does not use me well.

SUBTLE [*within*]:   You fool
Peace, you'll mar all.

        62. *deceptio visus*: an optical illusion.

FACE [*speaking through the keyhole*]: Or you will else, you rogue.

LOVEWIT [*overhearing* FACE]: O, is it so? Then you converse with
    spirits! –

    Come, sir. No more o' your tricks, good Jeremy.

    The truth, the shortest way.

FACE: Dismiss this rabble, sir. –

    [*Aside*] What shall I do? I am catched.

LOVEWIT: Good neighbours,

    I thank you all. You may depart. –

    [*Exeunt* NEIGHBOURS.]

                        Come, sir,

    You know that I am an indulgent master;

    And therefore conceal nothing. What's your med'cine,

    To draw so many several sorts of wild-fowl?

FACE: Sir, you were wont to affect mirth and wit –   80

    But here's no place to talk on't i' the street.

    Give me but leave to make the best of my fortune,

    And only pardon me th' abuse of your house:

    It's all I beg. I'll help you to a widow,

    In recompense, that you shall gi' me thanks for,

    Will make you seven years younger, and a rich one.

    'Tis but your putting on a Spanish cloak;

    I have her within. You need not fear the house;

    It was not visited.

LOVEWIT: But by me, who came

    Sooner than you expected.

FACE: It is true, sir.   90

    'Pray you forgive me.

LOVEWIT: Well, let's see your widow.

    [*Exeunt.*]

               [SCENE TWO]   V, iv

    [*Inside Lovewit's house.*]

    [*Enter* SUBTLE, *leading in* DAPPER, *with his eyes bound as before.*]

[SUBTLE:] How! ha' you eaten your gag?

DAPPER: Yes, faith, it crumbled
Away i' my mouth.
SUBTLE: You ha' spoiled all then.
DAPPER: No!
I hope my aunt of Faery will forgive me.
SUBTLE: Your aunt's a gracious lady; but in troth
You were to blame.
DAPPER: The fume did overcome me,
And I did do't to stay my stomach. 'Pray you
So satisfy her Grace.
     [*Enter* FACE *in his uniform.*]
                      Here comes the Captain.
FACE: How now! Is his mouth down?
SUBTLE: Ay, he has spoken!
FACE [*aside*]: A pox, I heard him, and you too. [*Aloud*] He's un-
     done then. –
10   [*Aside to* SUBTLE] I have been fain to say, the house is haunted
With spirits, to keep churl back.
SUBTLE [*aside*]:   And hast thou done it?
FACE [*aside*]: Sure, for this night.
SUBTLE [*aside*]:   Why, then triumph and sing
Of Face so famous, the precious king
Of present wits.
FACE [*aside*]:   Did you not hear the coil
About the door?
SUBTLE [*aside*]:   Yes, and I dwindled with it.
FACE [*aside*]: Show him his aunt, and let him be dispatched:
I'll send her to you.
     [*Exit* FACE.]
SUBTLE: Well, sir, your aunt her Grace
Will give you audience presently, on my suit,
And the Captain's word that you did not eat your gag
20   In any contempt of her Highness.
     [*Unbinds his eyes.*]
DAPPER: Not I, in troth, sir.
     [*Enter*] DOL *like the Queen of Faery.*
SUBTLE: Here she is come. Down o' your knees and wriggle:

                  14. *coil:* row.

She has a stately presence.
[DAPPER *kneels and moves towards* DOL.]
                              Good! Yet nearer,
And bid, God save you!
DAPPER: Madam!
SUBTLE: And your aunt.
DAPPER: And my most gracious aunt, God save your Grace.
DOL COMMON: Nephew, we thought to have been angry with
    you;
But that sweet face of yours hath turned the tide,
And made it flow with joy, that ebbed of love.
Arise, and touch our velvet gown.
SUBTLE: The skirts,
And kiss 'em. So!
DOL COMMON: Let me now stroke that head.
Much, nephew, shalt thou win, much shalt thou spend;   30
Much shalt thou give away; much shalt thou lend.
SUBTLE [*aside*]: Ay, much indeed! – Why do you not thank her
    Grace?
DAPPER: I cannot speak for joy.
SUBTLE: See, the kind wretch!
Your Grace's kinsman right.
DOL COMMON: Give me the bird. –
Here is your fly in a purse, about your neck, cousin;
Wear it, and feed it about this day sev'n-night,
On your right wrist –
SUBTLE: Open a vein with a pin
And let it suck but once a week. Till then,
You must not look on't.
DOL COMMON: No. And, kinsman,
Bear yourself worthy of the blood you come on.   40
SUBTLE: Her Grace would ha' you eat no more Woolsack pies,
Nor Dagger frume'ty.
DOL COMMON: Nor break his fast
In Heaven and Hell.

41. *Woolsack:* a tavern.
42. *Dagger:* another tavern; *frume'ty:* a sort of porridge made of wheat
boiled in milk.   43. *Heaven, Hell:* also names of taverns.

SUBTLE: She's with you everywhere!
Nor play with costermongers, at mumchance, tray-trip,
God-make-you-rich (whenas your aunt has done it); but keep
The gallant'st company, and the best games –

DAPPER: Yes, sir.

SUBTLE: Gleek and primero; and what you get, be true to us.

DAPPER: By this hand, I will.

SUBTLE: You may bring's a thousand pound
Before tomorrow night, if but three thousand
50 Be stirring, an' you will.

DAPPER: I swear I will then.

SUBTLE: Your fly will learn you all games.

FACE [*within*]: Ha' you done there?

SUBTLE: Your Grace will command him no more duties?

DOL COMMON: No;
But come and see me often. I may chance
To leave him three or four hundred chests of treasure,
And some twelve thousand acres of fairy land,
If he game well and comely with good gamesters.

SUBTLE: There's a kind aunt; kiss her departing part. –
But you must sell your forty mark a year now.

DAPPER: Ay, sir, I mean.

SUBTLE: Or, gi't away; pox on't!

60 DAPPER: I'll gi't mine aunt. I'll go and fetch the writings.

SUBTLE: 'Tis well; away.

[*Exit* DAPPER. *Re-enter* FACE.]

FACE: Where's Subtle?

SUBTLE: Here. What news?

FACE: Drugger is at the door; go take his suit,
And bid him fetch a parson presently.
Say he shall marry the widow. Thou shalt spend
A hundred pound by the service!

[*Exit* SUBTLE.]

Now, Queen Dol,
Have you packed up all?

DOL COMMON: Yes.

44–5. *mumchance*, etc.: games of chance.
47. *gleek, primero*: card games.

FACE: And how do you like
    The Lady Pliant?
DOL COMMON: A good dull innocent.
    [*Re-enter* SUBTLE.]
SUBTLE: Here's your Hieronimo's cloak and hat.
FACE: Give me 'em.
SUBTLE: And the ruff too?
FACE: Yes; I'll come to you presently.
    [*Exit* FACE.]
SUBTLE: Now he is gone about his project, Dol,   70
    I told you of, for the widow.
DOL COMMON: 'Tis direct
    Against our articles.
SUBTLE: Well, we'll fit him, wench.
    Hast thou gulled her of her jewels or her bracelets?
DOL COMMON: No; but I will do't.
SUBTLE: Soon at night, my Dolly,
    When we are shipped and all our goods aboard,
    Eastward for Ratcliff, we will turn our course
    To Brainford, westward, if thou sayst the word,
    And take our leaves of this o'erweening rascal,
    This peremptory Face.
DOL COMMON: Content; I'm weary of him.
SUBTLE: Thou'st cause, when the slave will run a-wiving, Dol, 80
    Against the instrument that was drawn between us.
DOL COMMON: I'll pluck his bird as bare as I can.
SUBTLE: Yes, tell her
    She must by any means address some present
    To th' cunning-man, make him amends for wronging
    His art with her suspicion; send a ring
    Or chain or pearl; she will be tortured else
    Extremely in her sleep, say, and ha' strange things
    Come to her. Wilt thou?
DOL COMMON: Yes.
SUBTLE: My fine flitter-mouse,

68. *Hieronimo's cloak:* theatrical costume in the Spanish style as promised earlier.

84. *cunning-man:* magician.   88. *flitter-mouse:* bat.

My bird o' the night! We'll tickle it at the Pigeons,
90 When we have all, and may unlock the trunks,
And say, this's mine, and thine; and thine, and mine.
    They kiss.
    [*Re-enter* FACE.]
FACE: What now! a-billing?
SUBTLE: Yes, a little exalted
In the good passage of our stock-affairs.
FACE: Drugger has brought his parson; take him in, Subtle,
And send Nab back again to wash his face.
SUBTLE: I will. And shave himself?
FACE: If you can get him.
    [*Exit* SUBTLE.]
DOL COMMON: You are hot upon it, Face, whate'er it is!
FACE: A trick that Dol shall spend ten pound a month by.
    [*Re-enter* SUBTLE.]
    Is he gone?
SUBTLE: The chaplain waits you i' the hall, sir.
100 FACE: I'll go bestow him.
    [*Exit.*]
DOL COMMON: He'll now marry her instantly.
SUBTLE: He cannot yet, he is not ready. Dear Dol,
Cozen her of all thou canst. To deceive him
Is no deceit, but justice, that would break
Such an inextricable tie as ours was.
DOL COMMON: Let me alone to fit him.
    [*Re-enter* FACE.]
FACE: Come, my venturers,
You ha' packed up all? Where be the trunks? Bring forth.
SUBTLE: Here.
FACE: Let's see 'em. Where's the money?
SUBTLE: Here,
In this.
FACE: Mammon's ten pound; eight score before.
The Brethren's money this. Drugger's and Dapper's?
110 What paper's that?
DOL COMMON: The jewel of the waiting-maid's,

89. *Pigeons:* The Three Pigeons, a tavern at Brainford.

That stole it from her lady, to know certain –
FACE: If she should have precedence of her mistress?
DOL COMMON: Yes.
FACE: What box is that?
SUBTLE: The fish-wives' rings, I think,
And th'ale-wives' single money. Is't not, Dol?
DOL COMMON: Yes, and the whistle that the sailor's wife
Brought you to know an' her husband were with Ward.
FACE: We'll wet it tomorrow; and our silver beakers
And tavern cups. Where be the French petticoats
And girdles and hangers?
SUBTLE: Here, i' the trunk,
And the bolts of lawn.
FACE: Is Drugger's damask there,   120
And the tobacco?
SUBTLE: Yes.
FACE: Give me the keys.
DOL COMMON: Why you the keys?
SUBTLE: No matter, Dol; because
We shall not open 'em before he comes.
FACE: 'Tis true, you shall not open them, indeed;
Nor have 'em forth, do you see? Not forth, Dol.
DOL COMMON: No!
FACE: No, my smock-rampant. The right is, my master
Knows all, has pardoned me, and he will keep 'em.
Doctor, 'tis true – you look – for all your figures!
I sent for him, indeed. Wherefore, good partners,
Both he and she, be satisfied; for here   130
Determines the indenture tripartite
'Twixt Subtle, Dol, and Face. All I can do
Is to help you over the wall, o' the back-side,
Or lend you a sheet to save your velvet gown, Dol.
Here will be officers presently; bethink you
Of some course suddenly to 'scape the dock;
For thither you'll come else.

114. *single-money*: small change.
119. *girdles*: sashes; *hangers*: for swords.
126. *right*: truth.   131. *determines*: terminates.

[*Loud knocking at the door.*]

Hark you, thunder!

SUBTLE: You are a precious fiend!

OFFICERS [*without*]: Open the door!

FACE: Dol, I am sorry for thee, i' faith; but hear'st thou?
140   It shall go hard, but I will place thee somewhere.
Thou shalt ha' my letter to Mistress Amo –

DOL COMMON: Hang you!

FACE: Or Madam Caesarean.

DOL COMMON: Pox upon you, rogue,
Would I had but time to beat thee!

FACE: Subtle,
Let's know where you set up next; I'll send you
A customer now and then, for old acquaintance.
What new course ha' you?

SUBTLE: Rogue, I'll hang myself,
That I may walk a greater devil than thou,
And haunt thee i' the flock-bed and the buttery.
[*Exeunt.*]

V, V   [*Enter* LOVEWIT *in Spanish dress, with the Parson. Loud knocking at the door.*]

[LOVEWIT:] What do you mean, my masters?

MAMMON [*without*]: Open your door,
Cheaters, bawds, conjurers!

OFFICER [*without*]: Or we'll break it open.

LOVEWIT: What warrant have you?

OFFICER [*without*]: Warrant enough, sir, doubt not,
If you'll not open it.

LOVEWIT: Is there an officer there?

OFFICER [*without*]: Yes, two or three for failing.

LOVEWIT: Have but patience,
And I will open it straight.

[*Enter* FACE *in his butler's livery.*]

148. *flock-bed*: mattress stuffed with wool rather than feathers; *i' the flock-bed and buttery*: 'when asleep and when eating'.

FACE: Sir, ha' you done?
Is it a marriage? Perfect?

LOVEWIT: Yes, my brain.

FACE: Off with your ruff and cloak then; be yourself, sir.

SURLY [*without*]: Down with the door.

KASTRIL [*without*]:   'Slight, ding it open.

LOVEWIT [*throwing off his disguise and opening the door*]:   Hold,
Hold, gentlemen, what means this violence?   10

   [*Enter* MAMMON, SURLY, KASTRIL, ANANIAS, TRIBULA-
   TION WHOLESOME, *and* OFFICERS.]

MAMMON: Where is this collier?

SURLY: And my Captain Face?

MAMMON: These day-owls.

SURLY: That are birding in men's purses.

MAMMON: Madam Suppository.

KASTRIL: Doxy, my suster.

ANANIAS: Locusts
Of the foul pit.

TRIBULATION: Profane as Bel and the Dragon.

ANANIAS: Worse than the grasshoppers, or the lice of Egypt.

LOVEWIT: Good gentlemen, hear me. Are you officers,
And cannot stay this violence?

OFFICER: Keep the peace.

LOVEWIT: Gentlemen, what is the matter? Whom do you seek?

MAMMON: The chemical cozener.

SURLY: And the captain pandar.

KASTRIL: The nun, my suster.

MAMMON: Madam Rabbi.

ANANIAS: Scorpions,   20
And caterpillars.

LOVEWIT: Fewer at once, I pray you.

OFFICER: One after another, gentlemen, I charge you,
By virtue of my staff.

ANANIAS: They are the vessels
Of pride, lust, and the cart.

LOVEWIT: Good zeal, lie still
A little while.

12. *birding:* thieving.

311

TRIBULATION: Peace, Deacon Ananias.

LOVEWIT: The house is mine here, and the doors are open;
    If there be any such persons as you seek for,
    Use your authority, search on o' God's name.
    I am but newly come to town, and finding
30   This tumult 'bout my door, to tell you true,
    It somewhat 'mazed me; till my man here, fearing
    My more displeasure, told me he had done
    Somewhat an insolent part, let out my house
    (Belike presuming on my known aversion
    From any air o' the town while there was sickness),
    To a Doctor and a Captain; who, what they are
    Or where they be, he knows not.

MAMMON: Are they gone?

LOVEWIT: You may go in and search, sir.
    They enter.

                                 Here, I find
    The empty walls worse than I left 'em, smoked,
40   A few cracked pots, and glasses, and a furnace;
    The ceiling filled with poesies of the candle,
    And 'Madam with a dildo' writ o' the walls.
    Only one gentlewoman I met here,
    That is within, that said she was a widow –

KASTRIL: Ay, that's my suster; I'll go thump her. Where is she?
    [*Goes in.*]

LOVEWIT: And should ha' married a Spanish count, but he,
    When he came to't, neglected her so grossly,
    That I, a widower, am gone through with her.

SURLY: How! have I lost her, then?

LOVEWIT: Were you the Don, sir?
50   Good faith, now, she does blame you extremely, and says
    You swore, and told her you had ta'en the pains
    To dye your beard, and umber o'er your face,
    Borrowed a suit and ruff, all for her love:
    And then did nothing. What an oversight
    And want of putting forward, sir, was this!

38. *They enter (Stage-direction)*: i.e. the inner rooms.
42. '*Madam with a dildo*': part of a popular ballad.

Well fare an old harquebusier yet,
Could prime his powder, and give fire, and hit,
All in a twinkling!
    MAMMON *comes forth.*
MAMMON: The whole nest are fled!
LOVEWIT: What sort of birds were they?
MAMMON: A kind of choughs,   60
Or thievish daws, sir, that have picked my purse
Of eight-score and ten pounds within these five weeks,
Beside my first materials; and my goods,
That lie i' the cellar, which I am glad they ha' left,
I may have home yet.
LOVEWIT: Think you so, sir?
MAMMON: Ay.
LOVEWIT: By order of law, sir, but not otherwise.
MAMMON: Not mine own stuff?
LOVEWIT: Sir, I can take no knowledge
That they are yours, but by public means.
If you can bring certificate that you were gulled of 'em,
Or any formal writ out of a court,
That you did cozen yourself, I will not hold them.   70
MAMMON: I'll rather lose 'em.
LOVEWIT: That you shall not, sir,
By me, in troth. Upon these terms, they're yours.
What, should they ha' been, sir, turned into gold, all?
MAMMON: No.
I cannot tell. – It may be they should. – What then?
LOVEWIT: What a great loss in hope have you sustained!
MAMMON: Not I; the commonwealth has.
FACE: Ay, he would ha' built
The City new; and made a ditch about it
Of silver, should have run with cream from Hogsden;
That every Sunday in Moorfields the younkers
And tits and tom-boys should have fed on, gratis.   80
MAMMON: I will go mount a turnip-cart, and preach
The end o' the world within these two months. – Surly,

56. *harquebusier:* musketeer.
79. *younkers:* youths.   80. *tits:* girls.

What! in a dream?

SURLY: Must I needs cheat myself
With that same foolish vice of honesty?
Come, let us go and hearken out the rogues.
That Face I'll mark for mine, if e'er I meet him.

FACE: If I can hear of him, sir, I'll bring you word
Unto your lodging; for in troth, they were strangers
To me; I thought 'em honest as myself, sir.
    [*Exeunt* SURLY *and* MAMMON.]
    [ANANIAS *and* TRIBULATION WHOLESOME] *come forth.*

90 TRIBULATION: 'Tis well, the Saints shall not lose all yet. Go
And get some carts –

LOVEWIT: For what, my zealous friends?

ANANIAS: To bear away the portion of the righteous
Out of this den of thieves.

LOVEWIT: What is that portion?

ANANIAS: The goods, sometimes the orphans', that the Brethren
Bought with their silver pence.

LOVEWIT: What, those i' the cellar,
The knight Sir Mammon claims?

ANANIAS: I do defy
The wicked Mammon, so do all the Brethren.
Thou profane man! I ask thee with what conscience
Thou canst advance that idol against us
100 That have the seal? Were not the shillings numb'red
That made the pounds; were not the pounds told out
Upon the second day of the fourth week,
In the eighth month, upon the table dormant,
The year of the last patience of the Saints,
Six hundred and ten?

LOVEWIT: Mine earnest vehement botcher,
And deacon also, I cannot dispute with you;
But if you get you not away the sooner,
I shall confute you with a cudgel.

ANANIAS: Sir!

TRIBULATION: Be patient, Ananias.

85. *hearken:* search.
94. *sometimes:* formerly.   100. *have the seal:* i.e. of God's approval.

ANANIAS: I am strong,
  And will stand up, well girt, against an host   *110*
  That threaten Gad in exile.
LOVEWIT: I shall send you
  To Amsterdam, to your cellar.
ANANIAS: I will pray there,
  Against thy house. May dogs defile thy walls,
  And wasps and hornets breed beneath thy roof,
  This seat of falsehood, and this cave of coz'nage!
    [*Exeunt* ANANIAS *and* TRIBULATION WHOLESOME.]
    DRUGGER *enters.*
LOVEWIT: Another, too?
DRUGGER: Not I, sir, I am no Brother.
LOVEWIT: Away, you Harry Nicholas! do you talk?
  He beats him away.
FACE: No, this was Abel Drugger. (*To the* PARSON) Good sir, go,
  And satisfy him; tell him all is done.
  He stayed too long a-washing of his face.   *120*
  The Doctor, he shall hear of him at Westchester;
  And of the Captain, tell him, at Yarmouth, or
  Some good port-town else, lying for a wind.
    [*Exit* PARSON.]
  If you get off the angry child now, sir –
    [*Enter* KASTRIL, *with his sister,* DAME PLIANT.]
KASTRIL (*To his sister.*): Come on, you ewe, you have matched
    most sweetly, ha' you not?
  Did not I say, I would never ha' you tupped
  But by a dubbed boy, to make you a lady-tom?
  'Slight, you are a mammet! O, I could touse you now.
  Death, mun you marry with a pox!
LOVEWIT: You lie, boy;
  As sound as you; and I'm aforehand with you.
KASTRIL: Anon?   *130*
LOVEWIT: Come, will you quarrel? I will feize you, sirrah;
  Why do you not buckle to your tools?
KASTRIL: God's light,

127. *dubbed boy:* young knight.
128. *mammet:* puppet: *touse:* beat.   131. *feize:* flog.

This is a fine old boy as e'er I saw!

LOVEWIT: What, do you change your copy now? Proceed;
Here stands my dove; stoop at her if you dare.

KASTRIL: 'Slight, I must love him! I cannot choose, i' faith,
An' I should be hanged for 't! Suster, I protest,
I honour thee for this match.

LOVEWIT: O, do you so, sir?

KASTRIL: Yes, an' thou canst take tobacco and drink, old boy,
140 I'll give her five hundred pound more to her marriage,
Than her own state.

LOVEWIT: Fill a pipe full, Jeremy.

FACE: Yes; but go in and take it, sir.

LOVEWIT: We will.
I will be ruled by thee in anything, Jeremy.

KASTRIL: 'Slight, thou art not hide-bound, thou art a jovy boy!
Come, let's in, I pray thee, and take our whiffs.

LOVEWIT: Whiff in with your sister, brother boy.

[*Exeunt* KASTRIL *and* DAME PLIANT.]

                                   That master
That had received such happiness by a servant,
In such a widow, and with so much wealth,
Were very ungrateful, if he would not be
150 A little indulgent to that servant's wit,
And help his fortune, though with some small strain
Of his own candour.

[*Advancing to address the audience.*]

                    Therefore, gentlemen,
And kind spectators, if I have outstripped
An old man's gravity, or strict canon, think
What a young wife and a good brain may do:
Stretch age's truth sometimes, and crack it too.
Speak for thyself, knave.

FACE: So I will, sir.

[*Advancing also.*]   Gentlemen,
My part a little fell in this last scene,

135. *stoop*: a term in falconry. Kastril=Kestrel, a hawk.
144. *jovy*: jovial.
152. *candour*: honesty, integrity.

Yet 'twas decorum. And though I am clean
Got off from Subtle, Surly, Mammon, Dol,   *160*
Hot Ananias, Dapper, Drugger, all
With whom I traded; yet I put myself
On you, that are my country; and this pelf
Which I have got, if you do quit me, rests,
To feast you often, and invite new guests.
    [*Exeunt.*]

159. *decorum:* according to the rules of artistic and dramatic propriety.
164. *country:* jury.

THE END

BARTHOLOMEW FAIR

PRELIMINARY NOTE

I. STAGE-HISTORY

Bartholomew Fair was first acted by the Lady Elizabeth's Men at the Hope Theatre, Bankside, on 31 October 1614, and was played at Court the following day. It was acted after the Restoration, and much liked by that indefatigable playgoer, Samuel Pepys. An anti-Puritan farce based in part on Jonson's play was staged before King Charles II, greatly to the annoyance of Puritan divines. The play was only intermittently performed in the eighteenth century until 1731, and after that time it seems to have completely disappeared from the theatrical repertory, save for one adaptation acted in 1735. Bartholomew Fair itself was last held in 1855. The Phoenix Society gave a single performance of the play in Oxford in 1921. The Marlowe Society of Cambridge produced the play in 1947, and undergraduates at Oxford performed it in 1962. The very large cast makes frequent professional performances unlikely, but in 1950 the Old Vic Company, under the direction of George Devine, acted the comedy on the great open stage of the Assembly Hall of the Church of Scotland in Edinburgh during the Festival, and later brought the production to the Waterloo Road. Mark Dignam played Busy and Roger Livesey Justice Overdo; Alec Clunes and Robert Eddison were especially good as the testy Humphrey Wasp and the ninny Bartholomew Cokes.

2. LOCATION AND TIME-SCHEME

The action of the play takes place in one day: the Feast of St Bartholomew (i.e. 24 August), presumably 1614. The comedy opens early in the morning and ends with Justice Overdo magnanimously inviting the entire *dramatis personae* home to supper. The first act is set in Littlewit's house, and requires no scenic elaboration; the rest of the entertainment takes place at the Fair. The stalls, booths, and stocks may have been on view throughout Act I in the Jacobean performances; it is more likely that at the end of Act I they were erected in full view of the audience by the characters of the Fair themselves, before, after, or even during Justice Overdo's soliloquy. (The official accounts for the second performance – at the Court of King James – include sums of money for 'Canvas for the Boothes and other necessaries for a play called Bartholomew Fair'.) The transformation-scene at Edinburgh whereby the Assembly Hall became the bustling Fair was one of the most striking effects in Devine's production. In any performance characters can retreat into their own stalls when not required, and Ursula's booth, centrally located for most of the play, serves as a curtained 'discovery-place' in which Mistress Littlewit and Mistress Overdo are eventually revealed in the party scene. It is up to individual directors to decide such things as whether the stocks remain on-stage throughout Act IV. Leatherhead's puppet-theatre seems to be re-erected in the central position during Act V, while the real audience and the audience-within-the-play look on.

3. EARLY PUBLICATION

Bartholomew Fair was not included in the 1616 Folio *Workes*; it was printed (very badly for a Jonsonian text) in folio sheets in 1631, but not published until it was included in the Second Folio, the two-volume *Workes* issued posthumously in 1640. Ben Jonson was paralysed from 1628, and his eyesight was failing. Only three plays were set up for the new Folio in his lifetime, and his exemplary standards of proof-reading were not maintained.

Throughout the Folio text Bartholomew Fair is spelt Bartholmew Fair, and this form is used on the title-page printed in 1631 – *Bartholmew Fayre*. This probably shows Jonson's intention to retain contemporary pronunciation. The Jacobean Londoners appear to have stressed the first syllable (hence St Bartle in Nightingale's song – and Bart's as the present-day abbreviation of the famous London teaching hospital), and their pronunciation was probably Bartle-mew or Bartle-my in casual, everyday speech. I have followed Eugene Waith in printing the title *Bartholomew Fair* and using Barthol'mew in the speeches.

4. LATER EDITIONS AND CRITICAL COMMENTARY

Bartholomew Fair has been reprinted in many collected and selected editions of Jonson's works, and in anthologies of drama. It has been edited and annotated in recent years for the Revels Plays by Professor E. A. Horsman (1960), for the Yale Ben Jonson by Eugene M. Waith (1963), for Nebraska's Regents Renaissance Drama series by Edward B. Partridge (1964), and by Maurice Hussey (1964). I have been able to consult their texts and notes. J. J. Enck and J. A. Barish each devote a chapter to the comedy. Dr Enck regards it as a master-work. Dr Barish concentrates on the technicalities of Jonson's prose. Freda Townsend in *Apologie for Bartholmew Fayre* sees the play as the culmination of Jonson's playwriting career, and argues that his brilliant dramatic practice did not always accord with his neo-classical precepts. Brian Gibbons discusses the play in the light of other satirical comedies of London life in *Jacobean City Comedy*.

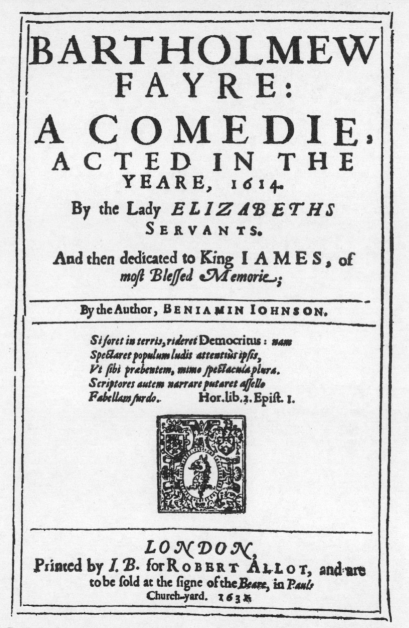

BARTHOLMEW FAYRE:

A COMEDIE,

ACTED IN THE
YEARE, 1614.

By the Lady *ELIZABETHS*
SERVANTS.

And then dedicated to King IAMES, of
moſt Bleſſed Memorie;

By the Author, BENIAMIN IOHNSON.

Si foret in terris, rideret Democritus : *nam*
Spectaret populum ludis attentius ipſis,
Vt ſibi præbentem, mimo spectacula plura.
Scriptores autem narrare putaret aſello
Fabellam ſurdo. Hor.lib.2.Epiſt.1.

LONDON,
Printed by *I.B.* for ROBERT ALLOT, and are
to be ſold at the ſigne of the *Beare*, in *Pauls*
Church-yard. 1631.

Facsimile of the title-page of the first edition, printed in 1631 for the Second Folio (1640)

THE
PROLOGUE
TO
THE KING'S
MAJESTY

Your Majesty is welcome to a Fair;
Such place, such men, such language and such ware,
You must expect; with these the zealous noise
Of your land's faction, scandalized at toys,
As babies, hobby-horses, puppet-plays,
And such like rage, whereof the petulant ways
Yourself have known, and have been vexed with long.
These for your sport, without particular wrong,
Or just complaint of any private man
Who of himself or shall think well or can,
The maker doth present, and hopes tonight
To give you for a fairing true delight.

4. *faction:* the Puritans; *toys:* rubbish, trifles.
5. *babies:* dolls.
8. *particular wrong:* satire directed at individuals rather than types.
12. *fairing:* a present bought at a fair.

THE PERSONS OF THE PLAY

JOHN LITTLEWIT, a *Proctor*
SOLOMON, *his Man*
[MISTRESS] WIN LITTLEWIT, *his Wife*
DAME PURECRAFT, *her Mother and a Widow*
ZEAL-OF-THE-LAND BUSY, *her Suitor, a Banbury man*
[NED] WINWIFE, *his Rival, a Gentleman*
[TOM] QUARLOUS, *his Companion, a Gamester*
BARTHOLOMEW COKES, *an Esquire of Harrow*
HUMPHREY WASP, *his Man*
ADAM OVERDO, *a Justice of Peace*
DAME OVERDO, *his Wife*
GRACE WELLBORN, *his Ward*
LANTERN LEATHERHEAD, *a Hobby-horse-seller*
JOAN TRASH, *a Gingerbread-woman*
EZEKIEL EDGWORTH, *a Cutpurse*
NIGHTINGALE, *a Ballad-singer*
URSULA, *a Pig-woman*
MOONCALF, *her Tapster*
JORDAN KNOCKEM, *a Horse-courser and Ranger o' Turnbull*
VAL CUTTING, *a Roarer*
CAPTAIN WHIT, *a Bawd*
PUNK ALICE, *Mistress o' the Game*
TROUBLE-ALL, *a Madman*
TOBY HAGGIS and DAVY BRISTLE } *Watchmen, three*
POACHER, *a Beadle*
COSTER-MONGER
PASSENGERS

proctor: a law agent or attorney.
gamester: gambler, play-boy or rake (see also Surly in *The Alchemist*).
Cokes: proverbial name for a booby.
horse-courser: a dealer in horses already ridden.
ranger: keeper of a park; synonym for 'gamester'.
roarer: bully, roisterer.
the game: prostitution.
coster-monger: apple-seller.

CORN-CUTTER
TINDERBOX-MAN
NORTHERN, *a Clothier*
PUPPY, *a Wrestler*
FILCHER and SHARKWELL, *Door-keepers*
PUPPETS

[*The Persons in the Induction:*

STAGE-KEEPER
BOOK-HOLDER
SCRIVENER]

[*Enter* STAGE-KEEPER.]

[STAGE-KEEPER:] Gentlemen, have a little patience, they are e'en upon coming, instantly. He that should begin the play, Master Littlewit, the Proctor, has a stitch new fall'n in his black silk stocking; 'twill be drawn up ere you can tell twenty. He plays one o' the Arches, that dwells about the Hospital, and he has a very pretty part. But for the whole play, will you ha' the truth on't? (I am looking, lest the poet hear me, or his man, Master Brome, behind the arras) it is like to be a very conceited scurvy one, in plain English. When't comes to the Fair once, you were e'en as good go to Virginia, for anything there is of Smithfield. 10 He has not hit the humours, he does not know 'em; he has not conversed with the Barthol'mew-birds, as they say; he has ne'er a sword-and-buckler man in his Fair, nor a little Davy to take toll o' the bawds there, as in my time, nor a Kindheart, if anybody's teeth should chance to ache in his play. Nor a juggler with a well-educated ape to come over the chain for the King of England and back again for the Prince, and sit still on his arse for the Pope and the King of Spain! None o' these fine sights! Nor has he the canvas-cut i' the night for a hobby-horse-man to creep in to his she-neighbour and take his leap there! Nothing! 20 No, an' some writer (that I know) had had but the penning o' this matter, he would ha' made you such a jig-a-jog i' the booths, you should ha' thought an earthquake had been i' the Fair! But these master-poets, they will ha' their own absurd courses; they will be informed of nothing! He has, sir reverence, kicked me three or four times about the tiring-house, I thank him, for but

1. *stage-keeper:* the principal stage-hand; for his duties see lines 46-8, below.

8. *arras:* tapestry hanging or curtain.

11. *humours:* here, idiosyncracies, distinctive oddities of types and classes of people.

13. *sword-and-buckler man:* ruffian.

25. *sir reverence:* with apologies, with respect (contraction of 'save your reverence').

26. *tiring-house:* dressing-room; the backstage area, behind the tiered façade of the play-house, where the actors dressed.

offering to put in, with my experience. I'll be judged by you,
gentlemen, now, but for one conceit of mine! Would not a fine
pump upon the stage ha' done well for a property now? And a
30 punk set under upon her head, with her stern upward, and ha'
been soused by my witty young masters o' the Inns o' Court?
What think you o' this for a show, now? He will not hear o'
this! I am an ass, I? And yet I kept the stage in Master Tarlton's
time, I thank my stars. Ho! an' that man had lived to have played
in *Barthol'mew Fair*, you should ha' seen him ha' come in, and
ha' been cozened i' the cloth-quarter, so finely! And Adams, the
rogue, ha' leaped and capered upon him, and ha' dealt his vermin
about as though they had cost him nothing. And then a sub-
stantial watch to ha' stol'n in upon 'em, and taken 'em away
40 with mistaking words, as the fashion is in the stage-practice.

    [*Enter*] BOOK-HOLDER [*and*] SCRIVENER *to him*.

BOOK-HOLDER: How now? What rare discourse you are fall'n
upon, ha! Ha' you found any familiars here, that you are so
free? What's the business?

STAGE-KEEPER: Nothing, but the understanding gentlemen o'
the ground here asked my judgement.

BOOK-HOLDER: Your judgement, rascal? For what? Sweeping
the stage? Or gathering up the broken apples for the bears within? Away rogue, it's come to a fine degree in these spectacles
when such a youth as you pretend to a judgement.

    [*Exit* STAGE-KEEPER.]

50 And yet he may, i' the most o' this matter i' faith; for the author
hath writ it just to his meridian, and the scale of the grounded
judgements here, his play-fellows in wit. – Gentlemen, not for
want of a prologue, but by way of a new one, I am sent out to
you here with a scrivener, and certain articles drawn out in
haste between our author and you; which if you please to hear,

31. *Inns o' Court:* Note.
36. *cloth-quarter:* Note.
37. *vermin:* fleas.   41. *book-holder:* prompter.
44. *understanding:* a pun referring to the 'groundlings' – those spectators standing in the pit immediately below the stage.
47. *bears:* the Hope theatre also featured bear-baiting.
51. *meridian:* fullest stretch of the stage-keeper's understanding.

and as they appear reasonable, to approve of, the play will follow presently. Read, scribe, gi' me the counterpane.

SCRIVENER [*reading*]: 'Articles of Agreement indented between the spectators or hearers at the Hope on the Bankside, in the county of Surrey, on the one party, and the author of *Barthol'-* 60 *mew Fair* in the said place and county, on the other party, the one and thirtieth day of October 1614, and in the twelfth year of the reign of our Sovereign Lord, James, by the grace of God King of England, France, and Ireland, Defender of the Faith; and of Scotland the seven and fortieth.

'INPRIMIS, It is covenanted and agreed, by and between the parties above-said, and the said spectators and hearers, as well the curious and envious as the favouring and judicious, as also the grounded judgements and under-standings do for themselves severally covenant and agree, to remain in the places their 70 money or friends have put them in, with patience, for the space of two hours and an half and somewhat more. In which time the author promiseth to present them, by us, with a new sufficient play called *Barthol'mew Fair*, merry, and as full of noise as sport, made to delight all, and to offend none; provided they have either the wit or the honesty to think well of themselves.

'It is further agreed that every person here have his or their free-will of censure, to like or dislike at their own charge, the author having now departed with his right: it shall be lawful for any man to judge his six pen'orth, his twelve pen'orth, so to 80 his eighteen pence, two shillings, half a crown, to the value of his place; provided always his place get not above his wit. And if he pay for half a dozen, he may censure for all them too, so that he will undertake that they shall be silent. He shall put in for censures here as they do for lots at the lottery; marry, if he drop but sixpence at the door, and will censure a crown's worth, it is thought there is no conscience or justice in that.

'It is also agreed that every man here exercise his own

57. *counterpane:* opposite of an indenture.
78. *censure:* judgement.
80. *six pen'orth*, etc.: refers to the price of admission.
85. *the lottery:* Note.

judgement, and not censure by contagion, or upon trust, from another's voice or face that sits by him, be he never so first in the commission ot wit, as also, that he be fixed and settled in his censure, that what he approves or not approves today, he will do the same tomorrow, and if tomorrow, the next day, and so the next week (if need be), and not to be brought about by any that sits on the bench with him, though they indict and arraign plays daily. He that will swear *Jeronimo* ot *Andronicus* are the best plays yet, shall pass unexcepted at here as a man whose judgement shows it is constant, and hath stood still these five and twenty, or thirty years. Though it be an ignorance, it is a virtuous and staid ignorance; and next to truth, a confirmed error does well; such a one the author knows where to find him.

'It is further covenanted, concluded, and agreed that how great soever the expectation be, no person here is to expect more than he knows, or better ware than a Fair will afford; neither to look back to the sword-and-buckler age of Smithfield, but content himself with the present. Instead of a little Davy to take toll o' the bawds, the author doth promise a strutting horse-courser with a leer drunkard, two or three to attend him in as good equipage as you would wish. And then for Kindheart, the tooth-drawer, a fine oily pig-woman with her tapster to bid you welcome, and a consort of roarers for music. A wise Justice of Peace *meditant*, instead of a juggler with an ape. A civil cut-purse *searchant*. A sweet singer of new ballads *allurant*; and as fresh an hypocrite as ever was broached *rampant*. If there be never a servant-monster i' the Fair, who can help it? he says; nor a nest of antics? He is loth to make nature afraid in his plays, like those that beget *Tales*, *Tempests*, and such like drolleries, to mix his head with other men's heels, let the concupiscence of jigs and dances reign as strong as it will amongst you; yet if the puppets will please anybody, they shall be entreated to come in.

'In consideration of which, it is finally agreed by the foresaid

89. *contagion:* infection, i.e. repeating one's neighbour's opinion.
91. *commission of wit:* authorized body of critics.
109. *equipage:* array, dress.
112. *meditant:* etc.: burlesque of heraldic terms.
115. *servant-monster:* Note.

hearers and spectators that they neither in themselves conceal, nor suffer by them to be concealed, any state-decipherer, or politic picklock of the scene, so solemnly ridiculous as to search out who was meant by the Gingerbread-woman, who by the Hobby-horse-man, who by the Costermonger, nay, who by their wares. Or that will pretend to affirm, on his own inspired ignorance, what Mirror of Magistrates is meant by the Justice, what great lady by the Pig-woman, what concealed statesman by the Seller of Mousetraps, and so of the rest. But that such *130* person or persons, so found, be left discovered to the mercy of the author, as a forfeiture to the stage and your laughter aforesaid. As also, such as shall so desperately or ambitiously play the fool by his place aforesaid, to challenge the author of scurrility because the language somewhere savours of Smithfield, the booth, and the pig-broth; or of profaneness because a madman cries, "God quit you", or "bless you". In witness whereof, as you have preposterously put to your seals already (which is your money), you will now add the other part of suffrage, your hands. The play shall presently begin. And though the *140* Fair be not kept in the same region that some here, perhaps, would have it, yet think that therein the author hath observed a special decorum, the place being as dirty as Smithfield, and as stinking every whit.

'Howsoever, he prays you to believe his ware is still the same; else you will make him justly suspect that he that is so loath to look on a baby or an hobby - horse here, would be glad to take up a commodity of them, at any laughter, or loss, in another place.'

[*Exeunt.*]

128. *Mirror:* paragon. Note.   134. *challenge:* accuse.
138. *preposterously:* in the wrong order.
139. *suffrage:* approval.
143. *decorum:* literary term for fitness or appropriateness as between the form and the content of a work of art.
148. *commodity:* quantity.

ACT ONE

[Littlewit's house.]

[Enter JOHN LITTLEWIT, *holding a licence.]*

[LITTLEWIT:] A pretty conceit, and worth the finding! I ha' such
luck to spin out these fine things still, and like a silk-worm, out
of myself. Here's Master Barthol'mew Cokes, of Harrow o' th'
Hill, i' th' County of Middlesex, Esquire, takes forth his licence
to marry Mistress Grace Wellborn of the said place and county –
and when does he take it forth? Today! The four and twentieth
of August! Barthol'mew Day! Barthol'mew upon Barthol'-
mew! There's the device! Who would have marked such a leap-
frog chance now? A very less than ames-ace on two dice! Well,
go thy ways, John Littlewit, Proctor John Littlewit – one o' the *10*
pretty wits o' Paul's, the Little-wit of London (so thou art called)
and something beside. When a quirk or a quiblin does 'scape
thee, and thou dost not watch, and apprehend it, and bring it
afore the constable of conceit (there now, I speak quib too), let
'em carry thee out o' the archdeacon's court into his kitchen, and
make a Jack of thee, instead of a John. (There I am again, la!)

[Enter MISTRESS LITTLEWIT.]

Win, good morrow, Win. Ay marry, Win! Now you look
finely indeed, Win! This cap does convince! You'd not ha' worn *20*
it, Win, nor ha' had it velvet, but a rough country beaver with
a copper band, like the coney-skin woman of Budge Row!
Sweet Win, let me kiss it! And her fine high shoes, like the
Spanish lady! Good Win, go a little; I would fain see thee pace,
pretty Win! By this fine cap, I could never leave kissing on't.

MISTRESS LITTLEWIT: Come, indeed la, you are such a fool,
still!

---

8. *device:* verbal ingenuity.
9. *ames-ace:* double ace, the lowest throw on two dice.

12. *quirk:* quip.	12. *quiblin:* quibble, pun.
16. *Jack:* servant or labourer.	19. *convince:* overcome, impress.
20. *beaver:* hat of beaver fur.	

337

LITTLEWIT: No, but half a one, Win; you are the tother half:
man and wife make one fool, Win. (Good!) Is there the proctor,
30   or doctor indeed, i' the diocese, that ever had the fortune to win
him such a Win! (There I am again!) I do feel conceits coming
upon me, more than I am able to turn tongue to. A pox o' these
pretenders to wit, your Three Cranes, Mitre, and Mermaid
men! Not a corn of true salt nor a grain of right mustard
amongst them all. They may stand for places or so, again' the
next witfall, and pay twopence in a quart more for their canary
than other men. But gi' me the man can start up a justice of wit
out of six-shillings beer, and give the law to all the poets and
poet-suckers i' town, because they are the players' gossips! 'Slid,
40   other men have wives as fine as the players, and as well dressed.
Come hither, Win.

[*He kisses her.*]

I, ii   [*Enter* NED WINWIFE.]

[WINWIFE:] Why, how now, Master Littlewit? Measuring of lips
or moulding of kisses? Which is it?

LITTLEWIT: Troth, I am a little taken with my Win's dressing
here! Does't not fine, Master Winwife? How do you apprehend, sir? She would not ha' worn this habit. I challenge all
Cheapside to show such another – Moorfields, Pimlico path, or
the Exchange, in a summer evening – with a lace to boot, as this
has. Dear Win, let Master Winwife kiss you. He comes a-woo-
ing to our mother, Win, and may be our father perhaps, Win.
10   There's no harm in him, Win.

WINWIFE: None i' the earth, Master Littlewit.

[*He kisses her.*]

LITTLEWIT: I envy no man my delicates, sir.

WINWIFE: Alas, you ha' the garden where they grow still! A wife

34. *again'*: in anticipation of.   35. *canary*: a sweet wine.
38. *poet-suckers*: young poets.   38. *gossips*: friends.
4. *apprehend*: think.   7. *lace*: stripe.

338

here with a strawberry-breath, cherry-lips, apricot-cheeks, and
a soft velvet head, like a melicotton.

LITTLEWIT: Good i' faith! Now dullness upon me, that I had not
that before him, that I should not light on't as well as he! Velvet
head!

WINWIFE: But my taste, Master Littlewit, tends to fruit of a later
kind: the sober matron, your wife's mother.   20

LITTLEWIT: Ay! we know you are a suitor, sir. Win and I both
wish you well; by this licence here, would you had her, that
your two names were as fast in it, as here are a couple. Win
would fain have a fine young father i' law with a feather, that
her mother might hood it and chain it with Mistress Overdo.
But you do not take the right course, Master Winwife.

WINWIFE: No, Master Littlewit, why?

LITTLEWIT: You are not mad enough.

WINWIFE: How? Is madness a right course?

LITTLEWIT: I say nothing, but I wink upon Win. You have a   30
friend, one Master Quarlous, comes here sometimes?

WINWIFE: Why? he makes no love to her, does he?

LITTLEWIT: Not a tokenworth that ever I saw, I assure you, but –

WINWIFE: What?

LITTLEWIT: He is the more madcap o' the two. You do not apprehend me.

MISTRESS LITTLEWIT: You have a hot coal i' your mouth now,
you cannot hold.

LITTLEWIT: Let me out with it, dear Win.

MISTRESS LITTLEWIT: I'll tell him myself.   40

LITTLEWIT: Do, and take all the thanks, and much good do thy
pretty heart, Win.

MISTRESS LITTLEWIT: Sir, my mother has had her nativity-
water cast lately by the cunning-men in Cow Lane, and they
ha' told her her fortune, and do ensure her she shall never have

15. *melicotton:* a peach grafted on a quince.

25. *hood, chain:* signs of rank (i.e. Mistress Overdo takes pride in her
husband's office).

33. *tokenworth:* a farthing's worth.

43. *nativity-water cast:* here used of prediction by means of a horoscope.

44. *cunning-men:* here fortune-tellers; elsewhere in Jonson magicians and
other charlatans.

happy hour, unless she marry within this sen'night, and when it is, it must be a madman, they say.

LITTLEWIT: Ay, but it must be a gentleman madman.

MISTRESS LITTLEWIT: Yes, so the tother man of Moorfields says.

50 WINWIFE: But does she believe 'em?

LITTLEWIT: Yes, and has been at Bedlam twice since, every day, to inquire if any gentleman be there, or to come there, mad!

WINWIFE: Why, this is a confederacy, a mere piece of practice upon her, by these impostors!

LITTLEWIT: I tell her so; or else say I that they mean some young madcap-gentleman (for the devil can equivocate as well as a shopkeeper) and therefore would I advise you to be a little madder than Master Quarlous, hereafter.

WINWIFE: Where is she? Stirring yet?

60 LITTLEWIT: Stirring! Yes, and studying an old elder, come from Banbury, a suitor that puts in here at meal-tide, to praise the painful Brethren, or pray that the sweet singers may be restored; says a grace as long as his breath lasts him! Sometime the spirit is so strong with him, it gets quite out of him, and then my mother, or Win, are fain to fetch it again with malmsey, or *aqua cœlestis*.

MISTRESS LITTLEWIT: Yes indeed, we have such a tedious life with him for his diet, and his clothes too; he breaks his buttons and cracks seams at every saying he sobs out.

70 LITTLEWIT: He cannot abide my vocation, he says.

MISTRESS LITTLEWIT: No, he told my mother a Proctor was a claw of the Beast, and that she had little less than committed abomination in marrying me so as she has done.

LITTLEWIT: Every line, he says, that a Proctor writes, when it comes to be read in the Bishop's court, is a long black hair, kembed out of the tail of Antichrist.

WINWIFE: When came this proselyte?

LITTLEWIT: Some three days since.

---

46. *sen'night:* week.

62. *sweet singers:* Puritans.

65. *aqua cœlestis:* cordial.

62. *painful:* diligent.

65. *malmsey:* a sweet wine.

72. *Beast:* i.e. the Beast of *Revelation*, 13.

76. *kembed:* combed.　　77. *proselyte:* preacher.

[*Enter* TOM QUARLOUS.]

[QUARLOUS:] O sir, ha' you ta'en soil here? It's well a man may reach you after three hours running, yet! What an unmerciful companion art thou, to quit thy lodging at such ungentlemanly hours! None but a scattered covey of fiddlers, or one of these rag-rakers in dunghills, or some marrow-bone man at most, would have been up when thou wert gone abroad, by all description. I pray thee what ailest thou, thou canst not sleep? Hast thou thorns i' thy eyelids, or thistles i' thy bed?

WINWIFE: I cannot tell. It seems you had neither i' your feet, that took this pain to find me.

QUARLOUS: No, an' I had, all the lyam-hounds o' the City should have drawn after you by the scent rather. Master John Littlewit! God save you, sir. 'Twas a hot night with some of us, last night, John. Shall we pluck a hair o' the same wolf today, Proctor John?

LITTLEWIT: Do you remember, Master Quarlous, what we discoursed on last night?

QUARLOUS: Not I, John. Nothing that I either discourse or do; at those times I forfeit all to forgetfulness.

LITTLEWIT: No? not concerning Win? Look you, there she is, and dressed as I told you she should be. Hark you, sir, had you forgot?

QUARLOUS: By this head, I'll beware how I keep your company, John, when I am drunk, an' you have this dangerous memory! That's certain.

LITTLEWIT: Why sir?

QUARLOUS: Why? We were all a little stained last night, sprinkled with a cup or two, and I agreed with Proctor John here to come and do somewhat with Win (I know not what 'twas) today; and he puts me in mind on't, now; he says he was coming to fetch me. – Before truth, if you have that fearful quality, John, to remember, when you are sober, John, what you promise

1. *ta'en soil*: hunting term for taken refuge or being run to earth.

11. *lyam-hounds*: blood-hounds.

14. *pluck hair o' the same wolf*: drink again today; modern version 'hair of the dog that bit you'.

27. *stained*: tipsy.

drunk, John, I shall take heed of you, John. For this once, I am content to wink at you. Where's your wife? Come hither, Win.

He kisseth her.

MISTRESS LITTLEWIT: Why, John! do you see this, John? Look you! help me, John.

LITTLEWIT: O Win, fie, what do you mean, Win? Be womanly, Win? make an outcry to your mother, Win? Master Quarlous
40 is an honest gentleman, and our worshipful good friend, Win; and he is Master Winwife's friend, too. And Master Winwife comes a suitor to your mother, Win, as I told you before, Win, and may perhaps be our father, Win. They'll do you no harm, Win; they are both our worshipful good friends. Master Quarlous! You must know Master Quarlous, Win; you must not quarrel with Master Quarlous, Win.

QUARLOUS: No, we'll kiss again, and fall in.

LITTLEWIT: Yes, do, good Win.

MISTRESS LITTLEWIT: I' faith you are a fool, John.

50 LITTLEWIT: A fool-John she calls me, do you mark that, gentlemen? Pretty littlewit of velvet! A fool-John!

QUARLOUS: She may call you an apple-John, if you use this.

WINWIFE: Pray thee forbear, for my respect somewhat.

QUARLOUS: Hoy-day! How respective you are become o' the sudden! I fear this family will turn you reformed too; pray you come about again. Because she is in possibility to be your daughter-in-law, and may ask your blessing hereafter, when she courts it to Tottenham to eat cream – well, I will forbear, sir; but i' faith, would thou wouldst leave thy exercise of widow-
60 hunting once, this drawing after an old reverend smock by the splay-foot! There cannot be an ancient tripe or trillibub i' the town, but thou art straight nosing it; and 'tis a fine occupation

47. *fall in:* become reconciled.

52. *apple-John:* an apple eaten when shrivelled after two years keeping; pun on *apple-squire* – pimp.

54. *respective:* respectable, conscious of manners.

56. *come about:* come round to my opinion.

60. *drawing after:* hunting by the scent.

61. *tripe or trillibub:* entrails; used as a mocking term for someone fat.

thou'lt confine thyself to, when thou hast got one – scrubbing a
piece of buff, as if thou hadst the perpetuity of Pannyer Alley to
stink in; or perhaps, worse, currying a carcass that thou hast
bound thyself to alive. I'll be sworn, some of them, that thou
art or hast been a suitor to, are so old as no chaste or married
pleasure can ever become 'em. The honest instrument of pro-
creation has, forty years since, left to belong to 'em. Thou must
visit 'em as thou wouldst do a tomb, with a torch, or three   70
handfuls of link, flaming hot, and so thou mayst hap to make
'em feel thee, and after, come to inherit according to thy inches.
A sweet course for a man to waste the brand of life for, to be
still raking himself a fortune in an old woman's embers; we
shall ha' thee, after thou hast been but a month married to one
of 'em, look like the quartan ague and the black jaundice met
in a face, and walk as if thou hadst borrowed legs of a spinner,
and voice of a cricket. I would endure to hear fifteen sermons a
week 'fore her, and such coarse and loud ones as some of 'em
must be; I would e'en desire of Fate I might dwell in a drum,   80
and take in my sustenance with an old broken tobacco-pipe and
a straw. Dost thou ever think to bring thine ears or stomach to
the patience of a dry grace as long as thy tablecloth, and droned
out by thy son here, that might be thy father, till all the meat o'
thy board has forgot it was that day i' the kitchen? Or to brook
the noise made in a question of predestination, by the good
labourers and painful eaters assembled together, put to 'em by
the matron, your spouse, who moderates with a cup of wine,
ever and anon, and a sentence out of Knox between? Or the
perpetual spitting, before and after a sober drawn exhortation   90
of six hours, whose better part was the hum-ha-hum? Or to
hear prayers groaned out over thy iron-chests, as if they were

64. *buff*: leather, skin.
76. *quartan ague*: a fever in which a paroxysm occurs every fourth day;
malaria.
77. *spinner*: spider.
79. *'fore*: in preference to; Professor Horsman's emendation of 'for' in
Folio.
88. *moderates*: prerides, arbitrates.
89. *sentence*: pronouncement, wise saying.

charms to break 'em? And all this, for the hope of two apostle-spoons, to suffer! And a cup to eat a caudle in! For that will be thy legacy. She'll ha' conveyed her state, safe enough from thee, an' she be a right widow.

WINWIFE: Alas, I am quite off that scent now.

QUARLOUS: How so?

WINWIFE: Put off by a brother of Banbury, one that, they say, is come here and governs all, already.

QUARLOUS: What do you call him? I knew divers of those Ban-burians when I was in Oxford.

WINWIFE: Master Littlewit can tell us.

LITTLEWIT: Sir! Good Win, go in, and if Master Barthol'mew Cokes's man come for the licence (the little old fellow), let him speak with me.

[*Exit* MISTRESS LITTLEWIT.]

What say you, gentlemen?

WINWIFE: What call you the reverend elder you told me of, your Banbury man?

LITTLEWIT: Rabbi Busy, sir. He is more than an elder, he is a prophet, sir.

QUARLOUS: O, I know him! A baker, is he not?

LITTLEWIT: He was a baker, sir, but he does dream now, and see visions; he has given over his trade.

QUARLOUS: I remember that, too – out of a scruple he took, that (in spiced conscience) those cakes he made were served to bridals, may-poles, morrises, and such profane feasts and meetings. His Christian name is Zeal-of-the-Land.

LITTLEWIT: Yes, sir, Zeal-of-the-Land Busy.

WINWIFE: How, what a name's there!

LITTLEWIT: O, they have all such names, sir. He was witness for Win here (they will not be called godfathers), and named her

---

93. *apostle-spoon:* silver spoon – often gift at baptism – with an apostle portrayed on the handle.

94. *caudle:* a warm and nourishing drink for invalids.

95. *conveyed her estate:* made her estate over to someone else.

116. *spiced:* over scrupulous.

116. *bridals:* wedding feasts.

117. *morrises:* morris-dances.

Win-the-Fight. You thought her name had been Winifred, did you not?

WINWIFE: I did indeed.

LITTLEWIT: He would ha' thought himself a stark reprobate, if it had.

QUARLOUS: Ay, for there was a blue-starch-woman o' the name, at the same time. A notable hypocritical vermin it is; I know him. One that stands upon his face more than his faith, at all 130 times; ever in seditious motion, and reproving for vain-glory; of a most lunatic conscience and spleen, and affects the violence of singularity in all he does. (He has undone a grocer here, in Newgate-market, that broke with him, trusted him with currants, as arrant a zeal as he, that's by the way.) By his profession he will ever be i' the state of innocence, though, and childhood; derides all antiquity; defies any other learning than inspiration; and what discretion soever years should afford him, it is all prevented in his original ignorance. Ha' not to do with him; for he is a fellow of a most arrogant and invincible dullness, I assure 140 you. Who is this?

[*Re-enter* MISTRESS LITTLEWIT *with* HUMPHREY WASP.]   I, iv
[WASP:] By your leave, gentlemen, with all my heart to you, and God you good morrow. Master Littlewit, my business is to you. Is this licence ready?

LITTLEWIT: Here, I ha' it for you in my hand, Master Humphrey.

WASP: That's well. Nay, never open or read it to me; it's labour in vain, you know. I am no clerk, I scorn to be saved by my book, i' faith I'll hang first. Fold it up o' your word and gi' it me. What must you ha' for't?

LITTLEWIT: We'll talk of that anon, Master Humphrey.

WASP: Now, or not at all, good Master Proctor; I am for no 10 anons, I assure you.

128. *blue-starch-woman:* laundress (suggesting to the Puritans luxury and display; see Ananias on 'that idol, starch', *The Alchemist*, III, ii, 823.)
135. *profession:* declared religious faith.
138. *prevented:* forestalled.   2. *God you:* God give you.
6. *clerk:* cleric.   6. *saved by my book:* Note.

LITTLEWIT: Sweet Win, bid Solomon send me the little black box within, in my study.

WASP: Ay, quickly, good mistress, I pray you; for I have both eggs o' the spit, and iron i' the fire. Say what you must have, good Master Littlewit.

[*Exit* MISTRESS LITTLEWIT.]

LITTLEWIT: Why, you know the price, Master Numps.

WASP: I know? I know nothing, I. What tell you me of knowing? Now I am in haste, sir, I do not know, and I will not know,
20 and I scorn to know, and yet (now I think on't) I will and do know as well as another; you must have a mark for your thing here, and eightpence for the box. I could ha' saved twopence i' that, an' I had bought it myself, but here's fourteen shillings for you. Good Lord, how long your little wife stays! Pray God, Solomon, your clerk, be not looking i' the wrong box, Master Proctor.

LITTLEWIT: Good i' faith! No. I warrant you, Solomon is wiser than so, sir.

WASP: Fie, fie, fie, by your leave, Master Littlewit, this is scurvy,
30 idle, foolish, and abominable; with all my heart, I do not like it.

WINWIFE: Do you hear? Jack Littlewit, what business does thy pretty head think this fellow may have, that he keeps such a coil with?

QUARLOUS: More than buying of gingerbread i' the Cloister, here (for that we allow him), or a gilt pouch i' the Fair?

LITTLEWIT: Master Quarlous, do not mistake him. He is his master's both-hands, I assure you.

QUARLOUS: What? to pull on his boots, a mornings, or his stockings, does he?

40 LITTLEWIT: Sir, if you have a mind to mock him, mock him softly, and look t'other way; for if he apprehend you flout him once, he will fly at you presently. A terrible testy old fellow, and his name is Wasp too.

QUARLOUS: Pretty insect! make much on him.

16. *Numps:* familiar contraction of Humphrey.
21. *mark:* thirteen shillings and fourpence.
32. *keeps such a coil:* makes such a fuss.
37. *both-hands:* guardian, nurse.

WASP: A plague o' this box, and the pox too, and on him that made it, and her that went for't, and all that should ha' sought it, sent it, or brought it! Do you see, sir?

LITTLEWIT: Nay, good Master Wasp.

WASP: Good Master Hornet, turd i' your teeth, hold you your tongue! Do not I know you? Your father was a 'pothecary, and 50 sold glisters, more than he gave, I wusse. And turd i' your little wife's teeth too – here she comes – 'twill make her spit, as fine as she is, for all her velvet-custard on her head, sir.

[*Re-enter* MISTRESS LITTLEWIT *with the box.*]

LITTLEWIT: O! be civil, Master Numps.

WASP: Why, say I have a humour not to be civil; how then? Who shall compel me? You?

LITTLEWIT: Here is the box now.

WASP: Why a pox o' your box, once again. Let your little wife stale in it, an' she will. Sir, I would have you to understand, and these gentlemen too, if they please – 60

WINWIFE: With all our hearts, sir.

WASP: That I have a charge, gentlemen.

LITTLEWIT: They do apprehend, sir.

WASP: Pardon me, sir, neither they nor you can apprehend me yet. (You are an ass.) I have a young master, he is now upon his making and marring; the whole care of his well-doing is now mine. His foolish schoolmasters have done nothing but run up and down the country with him to beg puddings and cakebread of his tenants, and almost spoiled him; he has learned nothing but to sing catches and repeat 'Rattle bladder rattle' 70 and 'O Madge'. I dare not let him walk alone for fear of learning of vile tunes, which he will sing at supper and in the sermontimes! If he meet but a carman i' the street, and I find him not

49. *turd i' your teeth:* an insulting exclamation; turd = shit.

51. *glisters:* clysters, enema-tubes.

51. *I wusse:* certainly; I know for sure.

53. *velvet-custard:* custard = an open meat (or fruit) pie; here, a pie-shaped hat.

59. *stale:* urinate (of animals).

68. *puddings:* sausages (usage still current in Scotland – e.g. 'black puddings').   73. *carman:* carter.

73. *I find him not talk:* I do not distract him with conversation.

talk to keep him off on him, he will whistle him and all his
tunes over at night in his sleep! He has a head full of bees! I am
fain now, for this little time I am absent, to leave him in charge
with a gentlewoman. 'Tis true, she is a Justice of Peace's wife,
and a gentlewoman o' the hood, and his natural sister; but what
may happen under a woman's government, there's the doubt.
80 Gentlemen, you do not know him. He is another manner of
piece than you think for – but nineteen year old, and yet he is
taller than either of you, by the head, God bless him.

QUARLOUS: Well, methinks this is a fine fellow!

WINWIFE: He has made his master a finer by this description, I
should think.

QUARLOUS: 'Faith, much about one; it's cross and pile whether,
for a new farthing.

WASP: I'll tell you, gentlemen –

LITTLEWIT: Will't please you drink, Master Wasp?

90 WASP: Why, I ha' not talked so long to be dry, sir. You see no
dust or cobwebs come out o' my mouth, do you? You'd ha' me
gone, would you?

LITTLEWIT: No, but you were in haste e'en now, Master Numps.

WASP: What an' I were? So I am still, and yet I will stay, too.
Meddle you with your match, your Win, there; she has as little
wit as her husband, it seems. I have others to talk to.

LITTLEWIT: She's my match indeed, and as little wit as I, good!

WASP: We ha' been but a day and a half in town, gentlemen, 'tis
true; and yesterday i' the afternoon we walked London to show
100 the City to the gentlewoman he shall marry, Mistress Grace;
but afore I will endure such another half day with him I'll be
drawn with a good gib-cat through the great pond at home, as
his Uncle Hodge was! Why, we could not meet that heathen
thing all day, but stayed him. He would name you all the signs
over, as he went, aloud; and where he spied a parrot or a
monkey, there he was pitched with all the little long-coats about

75. *bees:* crazy notions; cf. 'bees in his bonnet'.
78. *hood:* the sign of Overdo's office as a Justice.
86. *cross and pile:* a toss-up.
102. *gib-cat:* tom-cat.
106. *little long-coats:* children in petticoats.

him! I thought he would ha' run mad o' the black boy in
Bucklersbury that takes the scurvy, roguy tobacco there.

LITTLEWIT: You say true, Master Numps; there's such a one
indeed.   110

WASP: It's no matter whether there be or no. What's that to you?

QUARLOUS: He will not allow of John's reading at any hand.

[*Enter* BARTHOLOMEW COKES, MISTRESS OVERDO, *and*   I, V
GRACE WELLBORN.]

COKES: O Numps! are you here, Numps? Look where I am,
Numps! And Mistress Grace, too! Nay, do not look angerly,
Numps: my sister is here, and all; I do not come without her.

WASP: What the mischief, do you come with her? Or she with
you?

COKES: We came all to seek you, Numps.

WASP: To seek me? Why, did you all think I was lost? Or run
away with your fourteen shillings worth of small ware here? Or
that I had changed it i' the Fair for hobby-horses? 'Sprecious – to
seek me!   10

MISTRESS OVERDO: Nay, good Master Numps, do you show
discretion, though he be exorbitant, as Master Overdo says, an't
be but for conservation of the peace.

WASP: Marry gip, Goody She-Justice, Mistress French-hood!
Turd i' your teeth; and turd i' your French-hood's teeth, too, to
do you service, do you see? Must you quote your Adam to me?
You think you are Madam Regent still, Mistress Overdo, when
I am in place? No such matter, I assure you; your reign is out
when I am in, dame.

MISTRESS OVERDO: I am content to be in abeyance, sir, and be   20

112. *reading:* interpretation.
  9. *'Sprecious:* by God's precious blood.
  12. *exorbitant:* abnormal, troublesome.
  14. *Marry gip:* the oath 'by Mary of Egypt', confused with 'gee up!' to
a horse.
  15. *French-hood:* a fashionable head-dress.
  17. *Regent:* deputy for a governor. See I, iv, 79.

governed by you; so should he too, if he did well; but 'twill be expected you should also govern your passions.

WASP: Will't so forsooth? Good Lord! How sharp you are with being at Bedlam yesterday? Whetstone has set an edge upon you, has he?

MISTRESS OVERDO: Nay, if you know not what belongs to your dignity, I do, yet, to mine.

WASP: Very well, then.

COKES: Is this the licence, Numps? For love's sake, let me see't. I never saw a licence.

WASP: Did you not so? Why, you shall not see't, then.

COKES: An' you love me, good Numps.

WASP: Sir, I love you, and yet I do not love you, i' these fooleries; set your heart at rest; there's nothing in't but hard words; and what would you see't for?

COKES: I would see the length and the breadth on't, that's all; and I will see't now, so I will.

WASP: You sha' not see it here.

COKES: Then I'll see't at home, and I'll look upo' the case here.

WASP: Why, do so. [*He shows him the box.*] A man must give way to him a little in trifles, gentlemen. These are errors, diseases of youth, which he will mend when he comes to judgement and knowledge of matters. I pray you conceive so, and I thank you. And I pray you pardon him, and I thank you again.

QUARLOUS: Well, this dry nurse, I say still, is a delicate man.

WINWIFE: And I am for the cosset, his charge! Did you ever see a fellow's face more accuse him for an ass?

QUARLOUS: Accuse him? It confesses him one without accusing. What pity 'tis yonder wench should marry such a cokes!

WINWIFE: 'Tis true.

QUARLOUS: She seems to be discreet, and as sober as she is handsome.

WINWIFE: Ay, and if you mark her, what a restrained scorn she casts upon all his behaviour and speeches!

COKES: Well, Numps, I am now for another piece of business more, the Fair, Numps, and then –

WASP: Bless me! deliver me, help, hold me! the Fair!

46. *cosset:* pet lamb, spoilt child.

COKES: Nay, never fidge up and down, Numps, and vex itself. I am resolute Barthol'mew, in this; I'll make no suit on't to you; 'twas all the end of my journey, indeed, to show Mistress Grace 60 my Fair. I call't my Fair because of Barthol'mew: you know my name is Barthol'mew, and Barthol'mew Fair.

LITTLEWIT: That was mine afore, gentlemen – this morning. I had that i' faith, upon his licence; believe me, there he comes after me.

QUARLOUS: Come, John, this ambitious wit of yours, I am afraid, will do you no good i' the end.

LITTLEWIT: No? Why sir?

QUARLOUS: You grow so insolent with it, and overdoing, John, that if you look not to it, and tie it up, it will bring you to some 70 obscure place in time, and there 'twill leave you.

WINWIFE: Do not trust it too much, John; be more sparing, and use it but now and then. A wit is a dangerous thing in this age; do not over-buy it.

LITTLEWIT: Think you so, gentlemen? I'll take heed on't hereafter.

MISTRESS LITTLEWIT: Yes, do, John.

COKES: A pretty little soul, this same Mistress Littlewit! Would I might marry her.

GRACE [aside]: So would I, or anybody else, so I might 'scape you. 80

COKES: Numps, I will see it, Numps, 'tis decreed. Never be melancholy for the matter.

WASP: Why, see it, sir, do see it! Who hinders you? Why do you not go see it? 'Slid, see it.

COKES: The Fair, Numps, the Fair!

WASP: Would the Fair and all the drums and rattles in't were i' your belly for me! They are already i' your brain; he that had the means to travel your head, now, should meet finer sights than any are i' the Fair, and make a finer voyage on't, to see it all hung with cockle-shells, pebbles, fine wheat-straws, and here 90 and there a chicken's feather and a cobweb.

QUARLOUS: Good faith, he looks, methinks, an' you mark him,

58. *fidge:* fidget, move restlessly.
74. *over-buy:* pay too much for; here, buy too much of.
84. *'Slid:* by God's eyelid.

like one that were made to catch flies, with his Sir Cranion legs.

WINWIFE: And his Numps to flap 'em away.

WASP: God be w'you, sir. There's your bee in a box, and much good do't you.

[*Gives* COKES *the box and starts to go out.*]

COKES: Why, your friend, and Barthol'mew, an' you be so contumacious.

QUARLOUS: What mean you, Numps?

100 WASP: I'll not be guilty, I, gentlemen.

MISTRESS OVERDO: You will not let him go, brother, and lose him?

COKES: Who can hold that will away? I had rather lose him than the Fair, I wusse.

WASP: You do not know the inconvenience, gentlemen, you persuade to, nor what trouble I have with him in these humours. If he go to the Fair, he will buy of everything to a baby there; and household-stuff for that too. If a leg or an arm on him did not grow on, he would lose it i' the press. Pray heaven I bring

110 him off with one stone! And then he is such a ravener after fruit! You will not believe what a coil I had t'other day to compound a business between a Cather'ne-pear-woman and him about snatching! 'Tis intolerable, gentlemen.

WINWIFE: O! but you must not leave him now to these hazards, Numps.

WASP: Nay, he knows too well I will not leave him, and that makes him presume. - Well, sir, will you go now? If you have such an itch i' your feet to foot it to the Fair, why do you stop? Am I your tarriers? Go, will you go, sir? Why do you not go?

120 COKES: O Numps! have I brought you about? Come, Mistress Grace, and sister, I am resolute Bat, i'faith, still.

GRACE: Truly, I have no such fancy to the Fair, nor ambition to see it; there's none goes thither of any quality or fashion.

COKES: O Lord. sir! You shall pardon me, Mistress Grace, we are

---

93. *Sir Cranion:* crane-fly or daddy-long-legs.
98. *contumacious:* quarrelsome, insubordinate.
110. *stone.* testicle.
112. *Cather'ne-pear:* small, early pear; see IV, ii.
119. *tarriers:* hinderers.

enow of ourselves to make it a fashion; and for qualities, let
Numps alone, he'll find qualities.

[*Exeunt* COKES, WASP, GRACE, *and* MISTRESS OVERDO.]

QUARLOUS: What a rogue in apprehension is this, to understand
her language no better!

WINWIFE: Ay, and offer to marry to her! Well, I will leave the
chase of my widow for today, and directly to the Fair. These 130
flies cannot, this hot season, but engender us excellent creeping
sport.

QUARLOUS: A man that has but a spoonful of brain would think
so. Farewell, John.

[*Exeunt* QUARLOUS *and* WINWIFE.]

LITTLEWIT: Win, you see 'tis in fashion to go to the Fair, Win.
We must to the Fair too, you and I, Win. I have an affair i' the
Fair, Win, a puppet-play of mine own making - say nothing -
that I writ for the motion-man, which you must see, Win.

MISTRESS LITTLEWIT: I would I might, John, but my mother
will never consent to such a 'profane motion', she will call it. 140

LITTLEWIT: Tut, we'll have a device, a dainty one. (Now, Wit,
help at a pinch, good Wit come, come, good Wit, an't be thy
will.) I have it, Win, I have it i' faith, and 'tis a fine one. Win,
long to eat of a pig, sweet Win, i' the Fair; do you see? I' the
heart o' the Fair, not at Pie-corner. Your mother will do anything, Win, to satisfy your longing, you know, pray thee long,
presently, and be sick o' the sudden, good Win. I'll go in and
tell her. Cut thy lace i' the meantime, and play the hypocrite,
sweet Win.

MISTRESS LITTLEWIT: No, I'll not make me unready for it. 150
I can be hypocrite enough, though I were never so strait-
laced.

LITTLEWIT: You say true. You have been bred i' the family, and

125. *quality:* social rank; Cokes then uses 'qualities' to mean moral
characteristics.
127. *apprehension:* understanding.
138. *motion-man:* puppet-master.
148. *cut thy lace:* i.e. of her bodice or stays.
150. *make me unready:* undress.
151. *strait-laced:* both with stays or bodice tightly laced and careful in
morality.

brought up to't. Our mother is a most elect hypocrite, and has maintained us all this seven year with it, like gentlefolks.

MISTRESS LITTLEWIT: Ay, let her alone, John; she is not a wise wilful widow for nothing, nor a sanctified sister for a song. And let me alone too; I ha' somewhat o' the mother in me, you shall see. Fetch her, fetch her.

[*Exit* LITTLEWIT.]

160 Ah! ah!

[*She pretends to faint.*]

I, vi   [*Re-enter* LITTLEWIT *with* DAME PURECRAFT.]

[DAME PURECRAFT:] Now the blaze of the beauteous discipline fright away this evil from our house! How now, Win-the-Fight, child, how do you? Sweet child, speak to me.

LITTLEWIT: Yes, forsooth.

DAME PURECRAFT: Look up, sweet Win-the-Fight, and suffer not the enemy to enter you at this door; remember that your education has been with the purest. What polluted one was it that named first the unclean beast, pig, to you, child?

MISTRESS LITTLEWIT: Uh, uh!

10 LITTLEWIT: Not I, o' my sincerity, mother. She longed above three hours ere she would let me know it. Who was it, Win?

MISTRESS LITTLEWIT: A profane black thing with a beard, John.

DAME PURECRAFT: O! resist it, Win-the-Fight, it is the Tempter, the wicked Tempter; you may know it by the fleshly motion of pig. Be strong against it, and its foul temptations, in these assaults, whereby it broacheth flesh and blood, as it were, on the weaker side; and pray against its carnal provocations, good child, sweet child, pray.

20 LITTLEWIT: Good mother, I pray you that she may eat some pig, and her belly-full, too; and do not you cast away your own child,

154. *elect:* predestined to heaven.

158. *mother:* Jacobean pun on literal and metaphorical meanings – pregnancy and hysteria.

  8. *unclean beast:* Puritans took the Old Testament literally.

 15. *motion:* urging, prompting.

and perhaps one of mine, with your tale of the Tempter. How
do you, Win? Are you not sick?

MISTRESS LITTLEWIT: Yes, a great deal, John. Uh, uh!

DAME PURECRAFT: What shall we do? Call our zealous brother
Busy hither, for his faithful fortification in this charge of the
adversary; child, my dear child, you shall eat pig, be comforted,
my sweet child.

[*Exit* LITTLEWIT.]

MISTRESS LITTLEWIT: Ay, but i' the Fair, mother.

DAME PURECRAFT: I mean i' the Fair, if it can be anyway made   30
or found lawful. Where is our brother Busy? Will he not come?
– Look up, child.

[*Re-enter* LITTLEWIT.]

LITTLEWIT: Presently, mother, as soon as he has cleansed his
beard. I found him fast by the teeth i' the cold turkey-pie i' the
cupboard, with a great white loaf on his left hand, and a glass of
malmsey on his right.

DAME PURECRAFT: Slander not the Brethren, wicked one.

LITTLEWIT: Here he is now, purified, mother.

[*Enter* ZEAL-OF-THE-LAND BUSY.]

DAME PURECRAFT: O Brother Busy! your help here to edify
and raise us up in a scruple. My daughter Win-the-Fight is   40
visited with a natural disease of woman, called 'A longing to eat
pig'.

LITTLEWIT: Ay sir, a Barthol'mew-pig, and in the Fair.

DAME PURECRAFT: And I would be satisfied from you, religi-
ously-wise, whether a widow of the sanctified assembly, or a
widow's daughter, may commit the act without offence to the
weaker sisters.

BUSY: Verily, for the disease of longing, it is a disease, a carnal
disease, or appetite, incident to woman; and as it is carnal, and
incident, it is natural, very natural. Now pig, it is a meat, and a   50
meat that is nourishing, and may be longed for, and so conse-
quently eaten; it may be eaten; very exceeding well eaten. But
in the Fair, and as a Barthol'mew-pig, it cannot be eaten, for the
very calling it a Barthol'mew-pig, and to eat it so, is a spice
of idolatry, and you make the Fair no better than one of the

54. *spice:* species, kind.

high places. This, I take it, is the state of the question. A high place.

LITTLEWIT: Ay, but in state of necessity, place should give place, Master Busy. (I have a conceit left, yet.)

60 DAME PURECRAFT: Good Brother Zeal-of-the-Land, think to make it as lawful as you can.

LITTLEWIT: Yes, sir, and as soon as you can; for it must be, sir; you see the danger my little wife is in, sir.

DAME PURECRAFT: Truly, I do love my child dearly, and I would not have her miscarry, or hazard her first fruits, if it might be otherwise.

BUSY: Surely it may be otherwise, but it is subject to construction – subject, and hath a face of offence with the weak, a great face, a foul face, but that face may have a veil put over it, and be 70 shadowed, as it were. It may be eaten, and in the Fair, I take it, in a booth, the tents of the wicked. The place is not much, not very much; we may be religious in midst of the profane, so it be eaten with a reformed mouth, with sobriety, and humbleness; not gorged in with gluttony or greediness; there's the fear: for, should she go there, as taking pride in the place, or delight in the unclean dressing, to feed the vanity of the eye or the lust of the palate, it were not well, it were not fit, it were abominable, and not good.

LITTLEWIT: Nay, I knew that afore, and told her on't; but 80 courage, Win, we'll be humble enough; we'll seek out the homeliest booth i' the Fair, that's certain. Rather than fail we'll eat it o' the ground.

DAME PURECRAFT: Ay, and I'll go with you myself, Win-the-Fight, and my brother Zeal-of-the-Land shall go with us, too, for our better consolation.

MISTRESS LITTLEWIT: Uh! uh!

LITTLEWIT: Ay, and Solomon, too, Win; the more the merrier. Win – [*Aside to* MISTRESS LITTLEWIT] We'll leave Rabbi Busy in a booth. – Solomon, my cloak!

[*Enter* SOLOMON *with the cloak.*]

56. *high places:* biblical association with the worship of idols, as in *Leviticus*, xxvi, 30 (Horsman).
68. *face:* outward appearance.

356

SOLOMON: Here, sir. 90

BUSY: In the way of comfort to the weak, I will go and eat. I will eat exceedingly and prophesy; there may be a good use made of it, too, now I think on't: by the public eating of swine's flesh, to profess our hate and loathing of Judaism, whereof the Brethren stand taxed. I will therefore eat, yea, I will eat exceedingly.

LITTLEWIT: Good, i' faith, I will eat heartily, too, because I will be no Jew; I could never away with that stiff-necked generation. And truly, I hope my little one will be like me, that cries for pig so, i' the mother's belly. 100

BUSY: Very likely, exceeding likely, very exceeding likely.

[*Exeunt.*]

98. *away with:* agree with.

ACT TWO

[*The Fair.*]

[*Enter* LANTERN LEATHERHEAD, JOAN TRASH, *and the people of the Fair; they begin to erect their booths and stalls.*]
[*Enter* JUSTICE OVERDO, *alone, disguised as a madman.*]
[OVERDO (*aside*):] Well, in Justice' name, and the King's, and for the Commonwealth! defy all the world, Adam Overdo, for a disguise, and all story; for thou hast fitted thyself, I swear. Fain would I meet the Lynceus now, that eagle's eye, that piercing Epidaurian serpent (as my Quintus Horace calls him), that could discover a Justice of Peace (and lately of the quorum) under this covering. They may have seen many a fool in the habit of a Justice; but never till now a Justice in the habit of a fool. Thus must we do, though, that wake for the public good; and thus
10   hath the wise magistrate done in all ages. There is a doing of right out of wrong, if the way be found. Never shall I enough commend a worthy worshipful man, sometime a capital member of this City, for his high wisdom in this point, who would take you, now the habit of a porter, now of a carman, now of the dog-killer, in this month of August; and in the winter of a seller of tinder-boxes. And what would he do in all these shapes? Marry, go you into every ale-house, and down into every cellar; measure the length of puddings, take the gauge of black pots and cans, ay, and custards, with a stick; and
20   their circumference, with a thread; weigh the loaves of bread on his middle-finger; then would he send for 'em, home; give the puddings to the poor, the bread to the hungry, the custards to his children; break the pots and burn the cans himself; he

2. *Commonwealth:* the commonweal, the general good.
3. *fitted:* equipped, disguised.
6. *quorum:* those Justices of the Peace whose presence was necessary to constitute a bench.
15. *dog-killer:* man appointed to kill stray dogs as suspect carriers of the plague, especially in hot summers.

would not trust his corrupt officers; he would do't himself.
Would all men in authority would follow this worthy precedent! For, alas, as we are public persons, what do we know?
Nay, what can we know? We hear with other men's ears; we
see with other men's eyes. A foolish constable or a sleepy
watchman is all our information; he slanders a gentleman by
the virtue of his place, as he calls it, and we, by the vice of ours, 30
must believe him. As, a while gone, they made me, yea me, to
mistake an honest zealous pursuivant for a seminary, and a
proper young Bachelor of Music for a bawd. This we are
subject to, that live in high place; all our intelligence is idle, and
most of our intelligencers knaves; and, by your leave, ourselves
thought little better, if not arrant fools, for believing 'em. I,
Adam Overdo, am resolved therefore to spare spy-money hereafter, and make mine own discoveries. Many are the yearly
enormities of this Fair, in whose courts of Pie-powders I have
had the honour during the three days sometimes to sit as judge. 40
But this is the special day for detection of those foresaid enormities. Here is my black book for the purpose; this the cloud
that hides me; under this covert I shall see and not be seen. On,
Junius Brutus! And as I began so I'll end: in Justice' name, and
the King's; and for the Commonwealth!

[LEATHERHEAD:] The Fair's pestilence-dead, methinks; people II, ii
come not abroad today, whatever the matter is. Do you hear,
Sister Trash, Lady o' the Basket? Sit farther with your ginger-
bread-progeny there, and hinder not the prospect of my shop,
or I'll ha' it proclaimed i' the Fair what stuff they are made on.
TRASH: Why, what stuff are they made on, Brother Leatherhead?
Nothing but what's wholesome, I assure you.

32. *pursuivant:* official with powers to execute warrants for arrest.
32. *seminary:* recusant priest trained in Europe in a Catholic seminary.
34. *intelligence:* information.
35. *intelligencers:* informers.
39. *Pie-powders:* Note.
  1. *pestilence–dead:* as deserted as if the plague had closed it (as happened
in 1603).

LEATHERHEAD: Yes, stale bread, rotten eggs, musty ginger, and dead honey, you know.

10 OVERDO [*aside*]: Ay! have I met with enormity so soon?

LEATHERHEAD: I shall mar your market, old Joan.

TRASH: Mar my market, thou too-proud pedlar? Do thy worst; I defy thee, I, and thy stable of hobby-horses. I pay for my ground as well as thou dost; an' thou wrong'st me, for all thou art parcel-poet and an inginer, I'll find a friend shall right me and make a ballad of thee and thy cattel all over. Are you puffed up with the pride of your wares? Your arsedine?

LEATHERHEAD: Go to, old Joan, I'll talk with you anon; and take you down too afore Justice Overdo; he is the man must charm

20 you. I'll ha' you i' the Pie-powders.

TRASH: Charm me? I'll meet thee face to face afore his worship when thou dar'st; and though I be a little crooked o' my body, I'll be found as upright in my dealing as any woman in Smithfield, I. Charm me?

OVERDO [*aside*]: I am glad to hear my name is their terror, yet; this is doing of justice.

[*Enter* PASSENGERS.]

LEATHERHEAD: What do you lack? What is't you buy? What do you lack? Rattles, drums, halberts, horses, babies o' the best? Fiddles o' th' finest?

Enter COSTER-MONGER [*and* NIGHTINGALE.]

30 COSTER-MONGER: Buy any pears, pears, fine, very fine pears!

TRASH: Buy any gingerbread, gilt gingerbread!

NIGHTINGALE: Hey, now the Fair's a-filling!
    O, for a tune to startle
    The birds o' the booths here billing
    Yearly with old Saint Bartle!

15. *parcel-poet:* past poet.
15. *inginer:* inventor, deviser of shows.
16. *cattel:* property.
17. *arsedine:* imitation gold-leaf used to decorate toys.
18. *take down:* humiliate.
19. *charm:* subdue.
31. *gilt:* 'Gold leaf was used to decorate ginger-bread (hence Trash's jibe at Leatherhead's "arsedine")' – Professor Horsman.

The drunkards they are wading,
The punks and chapmen trading;
Who'd see the Fair without his lading?

Buy any ballads; new ballads?

[*Exeunt* PASSENGERS *and* COSTER-MONGER. *Enter* URSULA *from her booth.*]

URSULA: Fie upon't! Who would wear out their youth and prime 40 thus in roasting of pigs, that had any cooler vocation? Hell's a kind of cold cellar to't, a very fine vault, o' my conscience! What Mooncalf!

MOONCALF [*within*]: Here, Mistress.

NIGHTINGALE: How, now, Urs'la? In a heat, in a heat?

URSULA [*to* MOONCALF]: My chair, you false faucet you; and my morning's draught, quickly, a bottle of ale to quench me, rascal. – I am all fire and fat, Nightingale; I shall e'en melt away to the first woman, a rib again, I am afraid. I do water the ground in knots as I go, like a great garden-pot; you may follow me by the 50 S's I make.

NIGHTINGALE: Alas, good Urs; was 'Zekiel here this morning?

URSULA: 'Zekiel? what 'Zekiel?

NIGHTINGALE: 'Zekiel Edgworth, the civil cutpurse; you know him well enough – he that talks bawdy to you still. I call him my secretary.

URSULA: He promised to be here this morning, I remember.

NIGHTINGALE: When he comes, bid him stay. I'll be back again presently.

URSULA: Best take your morning's dew in your belly, Nightin- 60 gale.

MOONCALF *brings in the chair.*

Come, sir, set it here. Did not I bid you should get this chair let out o' the sides for me, that my hips might play? You'll never think of anything till your dame be rump-galled. 'Tis well, changeling; because it can take in your grasshopper's thighs, you

36. *wading:* staggering.
46. *faucet:* tap for drawing liquor out of a barrel.
56. *secretary:* a confidant.
65. *changeling:* stupid or ugly child left by fairies in exchange for an attractive one.

care for no more. Now you look as you had been i' the corner o' the booth, fleaing your breech with a candle's end, and set fire o' the Fair. Fill, stot, fill.

OVERDO [*aside*]: This pig-woman do I know, and I will put her in for my second enormity. She hath been before me, punk, pinnace, and bawd, any time these two and twenty years, upon record i' the Pie-powders.

URSULA: Fill again, you unlucky vermin.

MOONCALF: Pray you be not angry, mistress; I'll ha' it widened anon.

URSULA: No, no, I shall e'en dwindle away to't, ere the Fair be done, you think, now you ha' heated me! A poor vexed thing I am. I feel myself dropping already, as fast as I can; two stone o' suet a day is my proportion. I can but hold life and soul together with this (here's to you, Nightingale) and a whiff of tobacco, at most. Where's my pipe now? Not filled? Thou arrant incubee!

NIGHTINGALE: Nay, Urs'la, thou'lt gall between the tongue and the teeth with fretting, now.

URSULA: How can I hope that ever he'll discharge his place of trust – tapster, a man of reckoning under me – that remembers nothing I say to him?

[*Exit* NIGHTINGALE.]

But look to't, sirrah, you were best; threepence a pipeful I will ha' made of all my whole half-pound of tobacco, and a quarter of a pound of colts-foot mixed with it too, to eke it out. I that have dealt so long in the fire will not be to seek in smoke, now. Then, six and twenty shillings a barrel I will advance o' my beer, and fifty shillings a hundred o' my bottle-ale; I ha' told you the ways how to raise it. Froth your cans well i' the filling, at length, rogue, and jog your bottles o' the buttock, sirrah, then skink out the first glass, ever, and drink with all companies, though you be sure to be drunk; you'll misreckon the

---

69. *stot:* a stupid, clumsy person (Horsman's reading of *stote*).

71. *pinnace:* go-between or whore.

81. *incubee:* incubus – possibly here the offspring of a human being and an evil spirit.

89. *colts-foot:* a herb used to adulterate tobacco.

90. *be to seek:* be at a loss.   91. *advance:* raise.   95. *skink:* pour.

better, and be less ashamed on't. But your true trick, rascal, must be ever busy, and mis-take away the bottles and cans in haste before they be half drunk off, and never hear anybody call (if they should chance to mark you) till you ha' brought fresh, *100* and be able to forswear 'em. Give me a drink of ale.

OVERDO [*aside*]: This is the very womb and bed of enormity, gross as herself! This must all down for enormity, all, every whit on't.

One knocks.

URSULA: Look who's there, sirrah! Five shillings a pig is my price, at least; if it be a sow-pig, sixpence more; if she be a great-bellied wife, and long for't, sixpence more for that.

OVERDO [*aside*]: O tempora! O mores! I would not ha' lost my discovery of this one grievance for my place and worship o' the bench. How is the poor subject abused here! Well, I will fall in *110* with her, and with her Mooncalf, and win out wonders of enormity. [*To* URSULA] By thy leave, goodly woman, and the fatness of the Fair, oily as the King's constable's lamp, and shining as his shoeing-horn! Hath thy ale virtue, or thy beer strength? that the tongue of man may be tickled? and his palate pleased in the morning? Let thy pretty nephew here go search and see.

URSULA: What new roarer is this?

MOONCALF: O Lord! do you not know him, mistress? 'Tis mad Arthur of Bradley, that makes the orations. Brave master, old *120* Arthur of Bradley, how do you? Welcome to the Fair! When shall we hear you again, to handle your matters? With your back again' a booth, ha? I ha' been one o' your little disciples i' my days!

OVERDO: Let me drink, boy, with my love, thy aunt, here, that I may be eloquent; but of thy best, lest it be bitter in my mouth, and my words fall foul on the Fair.

URSULA: Why dost thou not fetch him drink? And offer him to sit?

MOONCALF: Is't ale or beer, Master Arthur? *130*

OVERDO: Thy best, pretty stripling, thy best; the same thy dove drinketh and thou drawest on holy days.

125. *aunt*: gossip or old woman; here possibly euphemism for bawd.

URSULA: Bring him a sixpenny bottle of ale; they say a fool's handsel is lucky.

OVERDO: Bring both, child. Ale for Arthur and beer for Bradley. Ale for thy aunt, boy.

[*Exit* MOONCALF.]

[*Aside.*] My disguise takes to the very wish and reach of it. I shall, by the benefit of this, discover enough and more, and yet get off with the reputation of what I would be: a certain

140   middling thing between a fool and a madman.

II, iii   [*Enter* JORDAN KNOCKEM.]

[KNOCKEM:] What! my little lean Urs'la! my she-bear! art thou alive yet, with thy litter of pigs, to grunt out another Barthol'- mew Fair, ha?

URSULA: Yes, and to amble afoot, when the Fair is done, to hear you groan out of a cart, up the heavy hill.

KNOCKEM: Of Holborn, Urs'la, meanst thou so? For what? For what, pretty Urs?

URSULA: For cutting halfpenny purses, or stealing little penny dogs out o' the Fair.

10   KNOCKEM: O! good words, good words, Urs.

OVERDO [*aside*]: Another special enormity! A cutpurse of the sword, the boot, and the feather! Those are his marks.

[*Re-enter* MOONCALF, *with the ale.*]

URSULA: You are one of those horse-leeches that gave out I was dead in Turnbull Street of a surfeit of bottle-ale and tripes?

KNOCKEM: No, 'twas better meat, Urs: cow's udders, cow's udders!

URSULA: Well, I shall be meet with your mumbling mouth one day.

---

134. *handsel:* first takings of the day – thought to be lucky.

     Jordan: derisive nickname; literally, chamber-pot.

   1. *she-bear: ursa* is Latin for bear.

   5. *heavy hill:* i.e. Holborn Hill, part of the route from Newgate to the gallows at Tyburn.

   13. *horse-leeches:* literally farriers or bloodsuckers; figuratively preda- tory persons.

KNOCKEM: What? Thou'lt poison me with a newt in a bottle of
ale, wilt thou? Or a spider in a tobacco-pipe, Urs? Come, there's 20
no malice in these fat folks. I never fear thee, an' I can 'scape thy
lean Mooncalf here. Let's drink it out, good Urs, and no
vapours!

[*Exit* URSULA.]

OVERDO: Dost thou hear, boy? (There's for thy ale, and the remnant for thee.) Speak in thy faith of a faucet, now; is this goodly
person before us here, this vapours, a knight of the knife?

MOONCALF: What mean you by that, Master Arthur?

OVERDO: I mean a child of the horn-thumb, a babe of booty, boy,
a cutpurse.

MOONCALF: O Lord, sir! far from it. This is Master Dan 30
Knockem – Jordan, the ranger of Turnbull. He is a horse-
courser, sir.

OVERDO: Thy dainty dame, though, called him cutpurse.

MOONCALF: Like enough, sir. She'll do forty such things in an
hour (an' you listen to her) for her recreation, if the toy take
her i' the greasy kerchief. It makes her fat, you see. She battens
with it.

OVERDO [*aside*]: Here might I ha' been deceived, now, and ha'
put a fool's blot upon myself, if I had not played an after-game
o' discretion. 40

URSULA *comes in again, dropping.*

KNOCKEM: Alas, poor Urs, this's an ill season for thee.

URSULA: Hang yourself, hackney-man.

KNOCKEM: How, how, Urs? vapours? motion breed vapours?

URSULA: Vapours? Never tusk nor twirl your dibble, good
Jordan. I know what you'll take to a very drop. Though you be

23. *vapours:* Note.

28. *horn-thumb:* the thimble worn by a cutpurse to protect his thumb
from the knife's edge.

35. *toy:* whim.

39. *after-game:* a second game played to give the loser a chance of re-
versing the result of the first.

43. *motion:* physical exertion.

44. *tusk:* meaning uncertain; 'show the teeth' (Partridge), 'form into a
tuft' (Horsman).

44. *dibble;* a spade-beard.

captain o' the roarers, and fight well at the case of piss-pots, you shall not fright me with your lion-chap, sir, nor your tusks. You angry? You are hungry. Come, a pig's head will stop your mouth and stay your stomach at all times.

50 KNOCKEM: Thou art such another mad merry Urs still! Troth, I do make conscience of vexing thee now i' the dog-days, this hot weather, for fear of found'ring thee i' the body, and melting down a pillar of the Fair. Pray thee take thy chair again, and keep state; and let's have a fresh bottle of ale and a pipe of tobacco; and no vapours. I'll ha' this belly o' thine taken up and thy grass scoured, wench. Look! here's Ezekiel Edgworth, a fine boy of his inches as any is i' the Fair! Has still money in his purse, and will pay all with a kind heart; and good vapours.

II, iv　　　[*Enter*] *to them* [EZEKIEL] EDGWORTH, NIGHTINGALE, CORN-CUTTER, TINDERBOX-MAN, *and* PASSENGERS.

[EDGWORTH:] That I will, indeed, willingly, Master Knockem. [*To* MOONCALF] Fetch some ale and tobacco.

[*Exit* MOONCALF.]

LEATHERHEAD: What do you lack, gentlemen? Maid, see a fine hobby-horse for your young master; cost you but a token a week his provender.

CORN-CUTTER: Ha' you any corns i' your feet and toes?

TINDERBOX-MAN: Buy a mousetrap, a mousetrap, or a tormentor for a flea!

TRASH: Buy some gingerbread!

NIGHTINGALE:

10　　Ballads, ballads! fine new ballads:
　　Hear for your love and buy for your money!
　　A delicate ballad o' 'The Ferret and the Coney'.

52. *found'ring*, etc: an eruptive disease caused by overeating or overwork; in horses it is caused by allowing them to drink when overheated.

54. *keep state*: act as befits your dignity; act royally.

55. *taken up*: reduced.

7. *mousetrap*: the Tinderbox-man is synonymous with the Mousetrapman in 'The Persons of the Play'.

7. *tormentor*: trap.

12. *Ferret, Coney*: underworld jargon for confidence-trickster and dupe.

'A Preservative again the Punks' Evil.'
Another of 'Goose-green Starch and the Devil'.
'A dozen of Divine Points' and 'The Godly Garters'.
'The Fairing of Good Counsel', of an ell and three quarters.
What is't you buy?
'The Windmill blown down by the witch's fart!'
Or 'Saint George, that O! did break the dragon's heart!'
[*Re-enter* MOONCALF.]

EDGWORTH: Master Nightingale, come hither, leave your mart a   20
little.

[*Exeunt* PASSENGERS, CORN-CUTTER, *and* TINDERBOX-
MAN.]

NIGHTINGALE: O my secretary! What says my secretary?

OVERDO: Child o' the bottles, what's he? what's he?

MOONCALF: A civil young gentleman, Master Arthur, that keeps
company with the roarers and disburses all, still. He has ever
money in his purse. He pays for them, and they roar for him –
one does good offices for another. They call him the secretary,
but he serves nobody. A great friend of the ballad-man's – they
are never asunder.

OVERDO: What pity 'tis so civil a young man should haunt this   30
debauched company! Here's the bane of the youth of our time
apparent. A proper penman, I see't in his countenance; he has a
good clerk's look with him, and I warrant him a quick hand.

MOONCALF: A very quick hand, sir.

[*Exit.*]

EDGWORTH [*to* NIGHTINGALE]: All the purses and purchase I give
you today by conveyance, bring hither to   *This*
Urs'la's presently. Here we will meet at night in   *they*
her lodge, and share. Look you choose good   *whisper,*
places for your standing i' the Fair when you   *that*
sing, Nightingale.   OVERDO   40

URSULA: Ay, near the fullest passages; and shift 'em   *hears*
often.   *it*

EDGWORTH: And i' your singing you must use   *not.*

---

14. *Goose-green:* yellowish-green, symbolizing pride.
20. *mart:* marketing.   35. *purchase:* booty.
36. *conveyance:* theft.

your hawk's eye nimbly, and fly the purse to a mark still –
where 'tis worn and o' which side – that you may gi' me the
sign with your beak, or hang your head that way i' the tune.

URSULA: Enough, talk no more on't. Your friendship, masters,
is not now to begin. Drink your draught of indenture, your sup
of covenant, and away. The Fair fills apace, company begins to
50 come in, and I ha' ne'er a pig ready yet.

KNOCKEM: Well said! Fill the cups and light the tobacco. Let's
give fire i' th' works and noble vapours.

EDGWORTH: And shall we ha' smocks, Urs'la and good whimsies,
ha?

URSULA: Come, you are i' your bawdy vein! The best the Fair
will afford, 'Zekiel, if Bawd Whit keep his word.

[Re-enter MOONCALF.]

How do the pigs, Mooncalf?

MOONCALF: Very passionate, mistress; one on 'em has wept out
an eye. Master Arthur o' Bradley is melancholy, here; nobody
60 talks to him. Will you any tobacco, Master Arthur?

OVERDO: No, boy, let my meditations alone.

MOONCALF: He's studying for an oration, now.

OVERDO [aside]: If I can, with this day's travail, and all my policy,
but rescue this youth here out of the hands of the lewd man and
the strange woman, I will sit down at night and say with my
friend Ovid, *Iamque opus exegi, quod nec Iovis ira, nec ignis,* etc.

KNOCKEM: Here 'Zekiel; here's a health to Urs'la, and a kind
vapour. Thou hast money i' thy purse still; and store! How dost
thou come by it? Pray thee vapour thy friends some in a
70 courteous vapour.

[Exit URSULA.]

EDGWORTH: Half I have, Master Dan Knockem, is always at
your service.

43. *fly . . . to a mark:* hawking term used when a falcon indicates to the
falconer the spot where its prey disappeared from view.

53. *smocks, whimsies:* wenches.

58. *passionate:* sorrowful.

58. *wept out an eye:* a sign that a pig is nearly roasted.

63. *policy:* craftiness.

65. *strange woman:* biblical phrase for harlot.

68. *store:* plenty.

OVERDO [*aside*]: Ha, sweet nature! What goshawk would prey upon such a lamb?

KNOCKEM: Let's see what 'tis, 'Zekiel! Count it, come, fill him to pledge me.

[*Enter* WINWIFE *and* QUARLOUS.]   II, V

WINWIFE: We are here before 'em, methinks.

QUARLOUS: All the better; we shall see 'em come in now.

LEATHERHEAD: What do you lack, gentlemen, what is't you lack? A fine horse? A lion? A bull? A bear? A dog, or a cat? An excellent fine Barthol'mew-bird? Or an instrument? What is't you lack?

QUARLOUS: 'Slid! here's Orpheus among the beasts, with his fiddle and all!

TRASH: Will you buy any comfortable bread, gentlemen?

QUARLOUS: And Ceres selling her daughter's picture in ginger-   10
work!

WINWIFE: That these people should be so ignorant to think us chapmen for 'em! Do we look as if we would buy gingerbread? Or hobby-horses?

QUARLOUS: Why, they know no better ware than they have, nor better customers than come. And our very being here makes us fit to be demanded, as well as others. Would Cokes would come! There were a true customer for 'em.

KNOCKEM [*to* EDGWORTH]: How much is't? Thirty shillings? Who's yonder? Ned Winwife? and Tom Quarlous, I think!   20
Yes. (Gi' me it all, gi' me it all.) Master Winwife! Master Quarlous! Will you take a pipe of tobacco with us? (Do not discredit me now, 'Zekiel.)

WINWIFE: Do not see him! He is the roaring horse-courser. Pray thee let's avoid him; turn down this way.

QUARLOUS: 'Slud, I'll see him, and roar with him too, an' he roared as loud as Neptune; pray thee go with me.

9. *comfortable bread*: sustaining, or possibly spiced (i.e. ginger-), bread.
13. *chapmen*: customers.
24. *roaring*: riotous.
26. *'slud*: by God's blood.

WINWIFE: You may draw me to as likely an inconvenience, when you please, as this.

30 QUARLOUS: Go to then, come along. We ha' nothing to do, man, but to see sights now.

KNOCKEM: Welcome, Master Quarlous and Master Winwife! Will you take any froth and smoke with us?

QUARLOUS: Yes, sir, but you'll pardon us if we knew not of so much familiarity between us afore.

KNOCKEM: As what, sir?

QUARLOUS: To be so lightly invited to smoke and froth.

KNOCKEM: A good vapour! Will you sit down, sir? This is old Urs'la's mansion. How like you her bower? Here you may ha'
40 your punk and your pig in state, sir, both piping hot.

QUARLOUS: I had rather ha' my punk cold, sir.

OVERDO [aside]: There's for me; punk! and pig!

URSULA: What, Mooncalf? You rogue.
    She calls [from] within.

MOONCALF: By and by; the bottle is almost off, mistress. Here, Master Arthur.

URSULA [within]: I'll part you and your play-fellow there i' the guarded coat, an' you sunder not the sooner.

KNOCKEM: Master Winwife, you are proud, methinks; you do not talk nor drink; are you proud?

50 WINWIFE: Not of the company I am in, sir, nor the place, I assure you.

KNOCKEM: You do not except at the company, do you? Are you in vapours, sir?

MOONCALF: Nay, good Master Dan Knockem, respect my mistress' bower, as you call it; for the honour of our booth, none o' your vapours here.
    She comes out with a firebrand.

URSULA: Why, you thin lean polecat you, an' they have a mind to be i' their vapours, must you hinder 'em? What did you know, vermin, if they would ha' lost a cloak, or such a trifle?
60 Must you be drawing the air of pacification here, while I am tormented, within, i' the fire, you weasel?

47. *guarded*: trimmed with braid.
52. *except at*: take exception to.

MOONCALF: Good mistress, 'twas in the behalf of your booth's credit that I spoke.

URSULA: Why? Would my booth ha' broke if they had fall'n out in't, sir? Or would their heat ha' fired it? In, you rogue, and wipe the pigs, and mend the fire, that they fall not, or I'll both baste and roast you till your eyes drop out like 'em. (Leave the bottle behind you, and be curst awhile.)

[*Exit* MOONCALF.]

QUARLOUS: Body o' the Fair! what's this? Mother o' the bawds?

KNOCKEM: No, she's mother o' the pigs, sir, mother o' the pigs! 70

WINWIFE: Mother o' the Furies, I think, by her firebrand.

QUARLOUS: Nay, she is too fat to be a Fury, sure some walking sow of tallow!

WINWIFE: An inspired vessel of kitchen-stuff!

She drinks this while.

QUARLOUS: She'll make excellent gear for the coach-makers here in Smithfield to anoint wheels and axle-trees with.

URSULA: Ay, ay, gamesters, mock a plain plump soft wench o' the suburbs, do, because she's juicy and wholesome. You must ha' your thin pinched ware, pent up i' the compass of a dog-collar (or 'twill not do), that looks like a long laced conger, set 80 upright, and a green feather, like fennel, i' the jowl on't.

KNOCKEM: Well said, Urs, my good Urs; to 'em, Urs!

QUARLOUS: Is she your quagmire Dan Knockem? Is this your bog?

NIGHTINGALE: We shall have a quarrel presently.

KNOCKEM: How? Bog? Quagmire? Foul vapours! Hum'h!

QUARLOUS: Yes, he that would venture for't, I assure him, might sink into her and be drowned a week ere any friend he had could find where he were.

WINWIFE: And then he would be a fortnight weighing up again. 90

64. *broke:* gone bankrupt.

74. *inspired:* inflated; infused with divine or supernatural power.

75. *gear:* stuff.

78. *suburbs:* areas outside the City boundaries much-frequented by prostitutes.

80. *laced:* streaked, striped.

80. *conger:* eel.   81. *jowl:* fish-head.

90. *weighing up:* raising up (as of a sunken ship).

QUARLOUS: 'Twere like falling into a whole shire of butter. They had need be a team of Dutchmen, should draw him out.

KNOCKEM: Answer 'em, Urs. Where's thy Barthol'mew-wit, now, Urs? thy Barthol'mew-wit?

URSULA: Hang 'em, rotten, roguy cheaters, I hope to see 'em plagued one day (poxed they are already, I am sure) with lean playhouse poultry, that has the bony rump sticking out like the ace of spades or the point of a partizan, that every rib of 'em is like the tooth of a saw; and will so grate 'em with their hips and shoulders, as (take 'em altogether) they were as good lie with a hurdle.

QUARLOUS: Out upon her, how she drips! She's able to give a man the sweating sickness with looking on her.

URSULA: Marry look off, with a patch o' your face and a dozen i' your breech, though they be o' scarlet, sir. I ha' seen as fine out-sides as either o' yours bring lousy linings to the brokers ere now, twice a week!

QUARLOUS: Do you think there may be a fine new cucking-stool i' the Fair to be purchased? One large enough, I mean. I know there is a pond of capacity for her.

URSULA: For your mother, you rascal! Out, you rogue, you hedge-bird, you pimp, you pannier-man's bastard, you!

QUARLOUS: Ha, ha, ha!

URSULA: Do you sneer, you dog's-head, you trendle-tail! You look as you were begotten atop of a cart in harvest-time, when the whelp was hot and eager. Go, snuff after your brother's bitch, Mistress Commodity. That's the livery you wear; 'twill be out at the elbows shortly. It's time you went to't, for the tother remnant.

KNOCKEM: Peace, Urs, peace, Urs. [*Aside*] They'll kill the poor whale and make oil of her. – Pray thee go in.

96. *poxed:* infected with syphilis.
97. *playhouse poultry:* prostitutes who sought clients in the audience.
98. *partizan:* spear.   104. *patch:* i.e. a sign of the pox.
108. *cucking-stool:* one used for ducking scolds and shrewish women.
112. *hedge-bird:* footpad, bandit.
112. *pannier-man:* hawker.
114. *trendle-tail:* cur, mongrel.
117. *Commodity:* self-interest, gain; here 'swindler'.

URSULA: I'll see 'em poxed first, and piled, and double-piled.

WINWIFE: Let's away; her language grows greasier than her pigs.

URSULA: Does't so, snotty nose? Good Lord! are you snivelling? You were engendered on a she-beggar in a barn when the bald thrasher, your sire, was scarce warm.

WINWIFE: Pray thee, let's go.

QUARLOUS: No, faith; I'll stay the end of her, now; I know she cannot last long; I find by her similes she wanes apace.

URSULA: Does she so? I'll set you gone. Gi' me my pig-pan hither 130 a little. I'll scald you hence, an' you will not go.

[Exit.]

KNOCKEM: Gentlemen, these are very strange vapours! And very idle vapours, I assure you!

QUARLOUS: You are a very serious ass, we assure you.

KNOCKEM: Hum'h! Ass? And serious? Nay, then pardon me my vapour. I have a foolish vapour, gentlemen: any man that does vapour me the ass, Master Quarlous –

QUARLOUS: What then, Master Jordan?

KNOCKEM: I do vapour him the lie.

QUARLOUS: Faith, and to any man that vapours me the lie, I do 140 vapour that.

[Strikes him.]

KNOCKEM: Nay, then, vapours upon vapours.

EDGWORTH, NIGHTINGALE: 'Ware the pan, the pan, the pan; she comes with the pan, gentlemen!

URSULA *comes in with the scalding-pan. They fight. She falls with it.*

God bless the woman.

URSULA: Oh!

[*Exeunt* QUARLOUS *and* WINWIFE.]

TRASH [*running in*]: What's the matter?

OVERDO: Goodly woman!

MOONCALF: Mistress!

URSULA: Curse of hell, that ever I saw these fiends! Oh! I ha' 150 scalded my leg, my leg, my leg, my leg! I ha' lost a limb in the

122. *piled:* diseased; bald as a result of the pox; *double-piled* refers to the pile or nap in velvet, etc.
130. *set you gone:* get you gone.

service! Run for some cream and salad oil, quickly! [*To* MOON-CALF] Are you under-peering, you baboon? Rip off my hose, an' you be men, men, men!

MOONCALF: Run you for some cream, good Mother Joan. I'll look to your basket.

[*Exit* JOAN TRASH.]

LEATHERHEAD: Best sit up i' your chair, Urs'la. Help, gentlemen. [*They lift her up.*]

KNOCKEM: Be of good cheer, Urs; thou hast hindered me the currying of a couple of stallions here, that abused the good race-
160   bawd o' Smithfield; 'twas time for 'em to go.

NIGHTINGALE: I'faith, when the pan came; they had made you run else. [*Aside to* EDGWORTH] This had been a fine time for purchase, if you had ventured.

EDGWORTH: Not a whit; these fellows were too fine to carry money.

KNOCKEM: Nightingale, get some help to carry her leg out o' the air; take off her shoes; body o' me, she has the mallanders, the scratches, the crown scab, and the quitter bone i' the tother leg.

URSULA: Oh! the pox, why do you put me in mind o' my leg
170   thus, to make it prick and shoot? Would you ha' me i' the Hospital afore my time?

KNOCKEM: Patience, Urs. Take a good heart; 'tis but a blister as big as a windgall. I'll take it away with the white of an egg, a little honey, and hog's grease; ha' thy pasterns well rolled, and thou shalt pace again by tomorrow. I'll tend thy booth and look to thy affairs the while; thou shalt sit i' thy chair and give directions, and shine Ursa major.

[*Exeunt* KNOCKEM, MOONCALF, *and* LEATHERHEAD, *carrying* URSULA *in her chair into her booth.*]

II, vi   [OVERDO:] These are the fruits of bottle-ale and tobacco! the foam of the one and the fumes of the other! Stay, young man, and

159. *currying:* dressing down (a horse); beating.
167. *mallanders, quitter-bone,* etc.: scabs and diseases in the legs and feet of horses.   173. *windgall:* tumour on the leg of a horse.
174. *pastern:* lower part of a horse's leg.

despise not the wisdom of these few hairs that are grown grey
in care of thee.

[*Enter* COKES, WASP, MISTRESS OVERDO, *and* GRACE.]

EDGWORTH: Nightingale, stay a little. Indeed I'll hear some o'
this!

COKES: Come, Numps, come, where are you? Welcome into the
Fair, Mistress Grace.

EDGWORTH [*to* NIGHTINGALE]: 'Slight, he will call company,
you shall see, and put us into doings presently.   10

OVERDO: Thirst not after that frothy liquor, ale; for who knows,
when he openeth the stopple, what may be in the bottle? Hath
not a snail, a spider, yea, a newt been found there? Thirst not
after it, youth; thirst not after it.

COKES: This is a brave fellow, Numps; let's hear him.

WASP: 'Sblood, how brave is he? In a guarded coat? You were
best truck with him; e'en strip and truck presently; it will become you. Why will you hear him? Because he is an ass, and
may be akin to the Cokeses?

COKES: O, good Numps!   20

OVERDO: Neither do thou lust after that tawny weed, tobacco.

COKES: Brave words!

OVERDO: Whose complexion is like the Indian's that vents it!

COKES: Are they not brave words, sister?

OVERDO: And who can tell if, before the gathering and making
up thereof, the alligarta hath not pissed thereon?

WASP: 'Heart, let 'em be brave words, as brave as they will! An'
they were all the brave words in a country, how then? Will you
away yet? Ha' you enough on him? Mistress Grace, come you
away, I pray you, be not you accessory. If you do lose your   30
licence, or somewhat else, sir, with list'ning to his fables, say
Numps is a witch, with all my heart, do, say so.

COKES: Avoid, i' your satin doublet, Numps.

OVERDO: The creeping venom of which subtle serpent, as some
late writers affirm, neither the cutting of the perilous plant, nor

17. *truck:* deal.
26. *alligarta:* i.e. alligator.
33. *Avoid:* Be off! as in 'Avoid, Satan!'
34. *some late writers:* Note.

the drying of it, nor the lighting or burning, can any way persway or assuage.

COKES: Good, i' faith! is't not, sister?

OVERDO: Hence it is that the lungs of the tobacconist are rotted,
the liver spotted, the brain smoked like the backside of the pig-
woman's booth, here, and the whole body within, black as her
pan you saw e'en now without.

COKES: A fine similitude, that, sir! Did you see the pan?

EDGWORTH: Yes, sir.

OVERDO: Nay, the hole in the nose here, of some tobacco-takers,
or the third nostril (if I may so call it), which makes that they
can vent the tobacco out like the ace of clubs, or rather the
flower-de-lys, is caused from the tobacco, the mere tobacco!
when the poor innocent pox, having nothing to do there, is
miserably, and most unconscionably slandered.

COKES: Who would ha' missed this, sister?

MISTRESS OVERDO: Not anybody but Numps.

COKES: He does not understand.

EDGWORTH [aside]: Nor you feel.

He picketh his purse.

COKES: What would you have, sister, of a fellow that knows
nothing but a basket-hilt and an old fox in't? The best music i'
the Fair will not move a log.

EDGWORTH [giving the purse to NIGHTINGALE]: In to Urs'la,
Nightingale, and carry her comfort; see it told. This fellow was
sent to us by fortune for our first fairing.

[Exit NIGHTINGALE.]

OVERDO: But what speak I of the diseases of the body, children
of the Fair?

COKES: That's to us, sister. Brave i' faith!

OVERDO: Hark, O you sons and daughters of Smithfield! and hear
what malady it doth the mind: it causeth swearing, it causeth
swaggering, it causeth snuffling, and snarling, and now and then
a hurt.

MISTRESS OVERDO: He hath something of Master Overdo, methinks, brother.

36. *persway:* mitigate, lessen.
39. *tobacconist:* smoker.   56. *fox:* sword.

COKES: So methought, sister, very much of my brother Overdo; *70* and 'tis when he speaks.

OVERDO: Look into any angle o' the town – the Straits, or the Bermudas – where the quarrelling lesson is read, and how do they entertain the time but with bottle-ale and tobacco? The lecturer is o' one side, and his pupils o' the other; but the seconds are still bottle-ale and tobacco, for which the lecturer reads and the novices pay. Thirty pound a week in bottle-ale! forty in tobacco! and ten more in ale again. Then for a suit to drink in, so much, and (that being slavered) so much for another suit, and then a third suit, and a fourth suit! And still the bottle-ale *80* slavereth, and the tobacco stinketh!

WASP: Heart of a madman! are you rooted here? Will you never away? What can any man find out in this bawling fellow to grow here for? He is a full handful higher sin' he heard him. Will you fix here? And set up a booth, sir?

OVERDO: I will conclude briefly –

WASP: Hold your peace, you roaring rascal! I'll run my head i' your chaps else. – You were best build a booth and entertain him; make your will, an' you say the word, and him your heir! Heart, I never knew one taken with a mouth of a peck, afore. *90* By this light, I'll carry you away o' my back, an' you will not come.

He gets him up on pick-pack.

COKES: Stay, Numps, stay, set me down! I ha' lost my purse, Numps, O my purse! One o' my fine purses is gone!

MISTRESS OVERDO: Is't indeed, brother?

COKES: Ay, as I am an honest man, would I were an arrant rogue, else! A plague of all roguy, damned cutpurses for me.

WASP: Bless 'em with all my heart, with all my heart, do you see! Now, as I am no infidel, that I know of, I am glad on't. Ay I am; here's my witness! do you see, sir? I did not tell you of his *100* fables, I? No, no, I am a dull malt-horse, I, I know nothing. Are you not justly served i' your conscience now? Speak i' your

72. *Straits*, etc.: Note.
75. *seconds*: things which assist.
90. *peck*: two gallons.
101. *malt-horse*: dray-horse.

conscience. Much good do you with all my heart, and his good heart that has it, with all my heart again.

EDGWORTH [*aside*]: This fellow is very charitable; would he had a purse, too! But I must not be too bold all at a time.

COKES: Nay, Numps, it is not my best purse.

WASP: Not your best! Death! why should it be your worst? Why should it be any, indeed, at all? Answer me to that. Gi' 110 me a reason from you, why it should be any?

COKES: Nor my gold, Numps; I ha' that yet; look here else, sister. [*Shows his other purse.*]

WASP: Why so, there's all the feeling he has!

MISTRESS OVERDO: I pray you, have a better care of that, brother.

COKES: Nay, so I will, I warrant you; let him catch this, that catch can. I would fain see him get this, look you here.

WASP: So, so, so, so, so, so, so, so! Very good.

COKES: I would ha' him come again, and but offer at it. Sister, will you take notice of a good jest? I will put it just where th' 120 other was, and if we ha' good luck, you shall see a delicate fine trap to catch the cutpurse nibbling.

EDGWORTH [*aside*]: Faith, and he'll try ere you be out o' the Fair.

COKES: Come, Mistress Grace, prithee be not melancholy for my mischance; sorrow wi' not keep it, sweetheart.

GRACE: I do not think on't, sir.

COKES: 'Twas but a little scurvy white money, hang it; it may hang the cutpurse one day. I ha' gold left to gi' thee a fairing, yet, as hard as the world goes. Nothing angers me but that no- 130 body here looked like a cutpurse, unless 'twere Numps.

WASP: How? I? I look like a cutpurse? Death! your sister's a cut-purse! and your mother and father and all your kin were cut-purses! And here is a rogue is the bawd o' the cutpurses, whom I will beat to begin with.

They speak all together, and WASP *beats the* JUSTICE.

COKES: Numps, Numps!	OVERDO: Hold thy hand, child
MISTRESS OVERDO: Good	of wrath and heir of anger.
Master Humphrey.	Make it not Childermass day

127. *white money:* silver.

WASP: You are the Patrico, are you? the patriarch of the cutpurses? You share, sir, they say; let them share this with you. Are you i' your hot fit of preaching again? I'll cool you. in thy fury, or the feast of the French Barthol'mew, parent of the Massacre. Murder, murder, murder!

[*Exeunt.*]

ACT THREE

[*The Fair.*]

[LEATHERHEAD, JOAN TRASH, *and others sit at their booths
and stalls.*]
[*Enter* WHIT, HAGGIS, *and* BRISTLE.]

[WHIT:] Nay, 'tish all gone, now! Dish 'tish, phen tou vilt not be
phitin call, Master Offisher! Phat ish a man te better to lishen
out noishes for tee an' tou art in an oder 'orld – being very
shuffishient noishes and gallantsh too, one o' their brabblesh
would have fed ush all dish fortnight; but tou art so bushy about
beggersh still, tou hast no leshure to intend shentlemen, an't be.

HAGGIS: Why, I told you, Davy Bristle.

BRISTLE: Come, come, you told me a pudding, Toby Haggis; a
matter of nothing; I am sure it came to nothing! You said,
10 'Let's go to Urs'la's,' indeed; but then you met the man with
the monsters, and I could not get you from him. An old fool,
not leave seeing yet?

HAGGIS: Why, who would ha' thought anybody would ha'
quarrelled so early? Or that the ale o' the Fair would ha' been
up so soon?

WHIT: Phy, phat o' clock tost tou tink it ish, man?

HAGGIS: I cannot tell.

WHIT: Tou art a vishe vatchman, i' te mean-teeme.

HAGGIS: Why, should the watch go by the clock, or the clock by
20 the watch, I pray?

BRISTLE: One should go by another, if they did well.

WHIT: Tou art right now! Phen didst tou ever know or hear of
a shuffishient vatchman but he did tell the clock, phat bushiness
soever he had?

BRISTLE: Nay, that's most true, a sufficient watchman knows
what o'clock it is.

4. *brabblesh:* brabbles, i.e. brawls. Whit's accent throughout is 'stage-
Irish'.
11. *monsters:* Note.

WHIT: Shleeping or vaking! ash well as te clock himshelf, or te
jack dat shtrikes him!

BRISTLE: Let's inquire of Master Leatherhead, or Joan Trash here.
Master Leatherhead, do you hear, Master Leatherhead?   30

WHIT: If it be a Ledderhead, tish a very tick Ledderhead, tat sho
mush noish vill not piersh him.

LEATHERHEAD: I have a little business now, good friends; do not
trouble me.

WHIT: Phat? Because o' ty wrought neet-cap and ty phelvet
sherkin, man? Phy? I have sheen tee in ty ledder sherkin ere
now, mashter o' de hobby-horses, as bushy and as stately as tou
sheem'st to be.

TRASH: Why, what an' you have, Captain Whit? He has his
choice of jerkins, you may see by that, and his caps too, I assure   40
you, when he pleases to be either sick or employed.

LEATHERHEAD: God a mercy, Joan, answer for me.

WHIT: Away, be not sheen i' my company; here be shentlemen,
and men of vorship.

[*Exeunt* HAGGIS *and* BRISTLE.]

[*Enter* QUARLOUS *and* WINWIFE.]   III, ii

QUARLOUS: We had wonderful ill luck to miss this prologue o'
the purse, but the best is we shall have five acts of him ere night.
He'll be spectacle enough! I'll answer for't.

WHIT: O Creesh! Duke Quarlous, how dosht tou? Tou dosht not
know me, I fear? I am te vishesht man, but Justish Overdo, in
all Barthol'mew Fair, now. Gi' me twelvepence from tee, I vill
help tee to a vife vorth forty marks for't, an't be.

QUARLOUS: Away, rogue, pimp, away.

WHIT: And she shall show tee as fine cut 'ork for't in her shmock
too as tou cansht vish i' faith. Vilt tou have her, vorshipful   10
Vinvife? I vill help tee to her, here, be an't be, in te pig-quarter,
gi' me ty twel'pence from tee.

WINWIFE: Why, there's twel'pence; pray thee, wilt thou be gone?

WHIT: Tou art a vorthy man, and a vorshipful man still.

28. *jack:* figure which strikes the bell.
9. *cut 'ork* (= cut-work): lace.

QUARLOUS: Get you gone, rascal.

WHIT: I do mean it, man, Prinsh Quarlous, if tou hasht need on me, tou shalt find me here at Urs'la's. I vill see phat ale and punk ish i' te pigshty for tee, bless ty good vorship.

[*Exit.*]

QUARLOUS: Look! who comes here! John Littlewit!

20 WINWIFE: And his wife, and my widow, her mother – the whole family.

[*Enter, at a distance,* BUSY, DAME PURECRAFT, LITTLEWIT, *and* MISTRESS LITTLEWIT.]

QUARLOUS: 'Slight, you must gi' em all fairings, now!

WINWIFE: Not I, I'll not see 'em.

QUARLOUS: They are going a-feasting. What school-master's that is with 'em?

WINWIFE: That's my rival, I believe, the baker!

BUSY: So, walk on in the middle way, fore-right; turn neither to the right hand nor to the left. Let not your eyes be drawn aside with vanity, nor your ear with noises.

30 QUARLOUS: O, I know him by that start!

LEATHERHEAD: What do you lack? What do you buy, pretty mistress? a fine hobby-horse, to make your son a tilter? a drum to make a soldier? a fiddle to make him a reveller? What is't you lack? Little dogs for your daughters? or babies, male or female?

BUSY: Look not toward them, hearken not! The place is Smith-field, or the field of smiths, the grove of hobby-horses and trinkets. The wares are the wares of devils; and the whole Fair is the shop of Satan! They are hooks and baits, very baits, that
40 are hung out on every side to catch you, and to hold you as it were, by the gills and by the nostrils, as the fisher doth; there-fore, you must not look, nor turn toward them. The heathen man could stop his ears with wax against the harlot o' the sea; do you the like, with your fingers, against the bells of the Beast.

WINWIFE: What flashes comes from him!

QUARLOUS: O, he has those of his oven! A notable hot baker

27. *fore-right:* straight ahead.
32. *tilter:* jouster, fighter.
42. *heathen man:* Note.

'twas, when he plied the peel. He is leading his flock into the Fair, now.

WINWIFE: Rather driving 'em to the pens; for he will let 'em look upon nothing.   50

[*Enter* KNOCKEM *and* WHIT, *from* URSULA'S *booth.*]

KNOCKEM: Gentlewomen, the weather's hot! LITTLEWIT *is* Whither walk you? Have a care o' your fine *gazing at the* velvet caps; the Fair is dusty. Take a sweet *sign, which is* delicate booth with boughs, here, i' the way, *the Pig's Head* and cool yourselves i' the shade, you and *with a large* your friends. The best pig and bottle-ale i' *writing under it.* the Fair, sir. Old Urs'la is cook, there you may read: the pig's head speaks it. Poor soul, she has had a stringhalt, the mary-hinchco; but she's prettily amended.

WHIT: A delicate show-pig, little mistress, with shweet sauce, 60 and crackling like de bay leaf i' de fire, la! Tou shalt ha' de clean side o' de table-clot and dy glass vashed with phatersh of Dame Annessh Cleare.

LITTLEWIT: This's fine, verily: 'Here be the best pigs, and she does roast 'em as well as ever she did,' the pig's head says.

KNOCKEM: Excellent, excellent, mistress, with fire o' juniper and rosemary branches! The oracle of the pig's head, that, sir.

DAME PURECRAFT: Son, were you not warned of the vanity of the eye? Have you forgot the wholesome admonition so soon?

LITTLEWIT: Good mother, how shall we find a pig if we do not 70 look about for't? Will it run off o' the spit into our mouths, think you? as in Lubberland? and cry, 'We, we'?

BUSY: No, but your mother, religiously wise, conceiveth it may offer itself by other means to the sense, as by way of steam, which I think it doth here in this place. Huh, huh – yes, it doth.

BUSY *scents after it like a hound.*

And it were a sin of obstinacy, great obstinacy, high and horrible

47. *peel:* baker's shovel.
54. *delicate:* pleasant.
58. *stringhalt, the maryhinchco:* synonyms for a twitching ailment in a horse's legs.
66. *juniper:* burnt to sweeten and purify the air.
72. *Lubberland:* Note.

obstinacy, to decline or resist the good titillation of the famelic sense, which is the smell. Therefore be bold – huh, huh, huh – follow the scent. Enter the tents of the unclean for once, and

80 satisfy your wife's frailty. Let your frail wife be satisfied; your zealous mother and my suffering self will also be satisfied.

LITTLEWIT: Come, Win, as good winny here as go farther and see nothing.

BUSY: We 'scape so much of the other vanities by our early ent'-ring.

DAME PURECRAFT: It is an edifying consideration.

MISTRESS LITTLEWIT: This is scurvy, that we must come into the Fair and not look on't.

LITTLEWIT: Win, have patience, Win, I'll tell you more anon.

90 KNOCKEM: Mooncalf, entertain within there; the best pig i' the booth, a pork-like pig. These are Banbury-bloods, o' the sincere stud, come a pig-hunting. Whit, wait, Whit, look to your charge.

[*Exeunt* DAME PURECRAFT, MISTRESS LITTLEWIT, LITTLE-WIT, *and* WHIT *into the booth.*]

BUSY: A pig prepare presently; let a pig be prepared to us.

[*Exit. Enter* MOONCALF *and* URSULA.]

MOONCALF: 'Slight, who be these?

URSULA: Is this the good service, Jordan, you'd do me?

KNOCKEM: Why, Urs? Why, Urs? Thou'lt ha' vapours i' thy leg again presently; pray thee go in; 't may turn to the scratches else.

100 URSULA: Hang your vapours, they are stale, and stink like you. Are these the guests o' the game you promised to fill my pit withal, today?

KNOCKEM: Ay, what ail they, Urs?

URSULA: Ail they? They are all sippers, sippers o' the City. They look as they would not drink off two pen'orth of bottle-ale amongst 'em.

MOONCALF: A body may read that i' their small printed ruffs.

KNOCKEM: Away, thou art a fool, Urs, and thy Mooncalf, too, i' your ignorant vapours, now! hence! Good guests, I say, right

78. *famelic sense:* sense of hunger. 82. *winny:* stay.
91. *sincere stud:* genuine breed. 107. *small printed ruffs:* Note.

hypocrites, good gluttons. In, and set a couple o' pigs o' the 110
board, and half a dozen of the biggest bottles afore 'em, and call
Whit. I do not love to hear innocents abused. Fine ambling
hypocrites! and a stone-puritan with a sorrel head and beard –
good mouthed gluttons, two to a pig. Away!

    [*Exit* MOONCALF.]

URSULA: Are you sure they are such?

KNOCKEM: O' the right breed; thou shalt try 'em by the teeth,
Urs. Where's this Whit?

    [*Re-enter* WHIT.]

WHIT: Behold, man, and see, what a worthy man am ee!
    With the fury of my sword, and the shaking of my beard,
    I will make ten thousand men afeard. 120

KNOCKEM: Well said, brave Whit; in, and fear the ale out o' the
bottles into the bellies of the Brethren and the Sisters; drink to
the cause, and pure vapours.

    [*Exeunt* KNOCKEM, WHIT, *and* URSULA.]

QUARLOUS: My roarer is turned tapster, methinks. Now were a
fine time for thee, Winwife, to lay aboard thy widow; thou'lt
never be master of a better season or place; she that will venture
herself into the Fair and a pig-box will admit any assault, be
assured of that.

WINWIFE: I love not enterprises of that suddenness, though.

QUARLOUS: I'll warrant thee, then, no wife out o' the widows' 130
hundred. If I had but as much title to her as to have breathed
once on that strait stomacher of hers, I would now assure myself to carry her yet, ere she went out of Smithfield. Or she
should carry me, which were the fitter sight, I confess. But you
are a modest undertaker, by circumstances and degrees; come,
'tis disease in thee, not judgement; I should offer at all together.
Look, here's the poor fool again that was stung by the wasp,
erewhile.

113. *stone-puritan:* male Puritan (analogy with *stone-horse* = stallion).
113. *sorrel:* chestnut-coloured.
125. *lay aboard:* to place one's ship alongside another prior to attacking it.
131. *hundred:* sub-division of a county.
132. *stomacher:* an ornamental covering of stiff material worn over the
bodice.   135. *undertaker:* one who accepts a challenge.
136. *offer at:* make an attempt at.

III, iii   [*Enter* JUSTICE OVERDO.]

[OVERDO:] I will make no more orations shall draw on these
tragical conclusions. And I begin now to think that, by a spice of
collateral justice, Adam Overdo deserved this beating; for I, the
said Adam, was one cause (a by-cause) why the purse was lost;
and my wife's brother's purse too, which they know not of yet.
But I shall make very good mirth with it at supper (that will be
the sport), and put my little friend Master Humphrey Wasp's
choler quite out of countenance; when, sitting at the upper end
o' my table, as I use, and drinking to my brother Cokes and
Mistress Alice Overdo, as I will, my wife, for their good
affection to old Bradley, I deliver to 'em it was I that was cud-
gelled, and show 'em the marks. To see what bad events may
peep out o' the tail of good purposes! The care I had of that
civil young man I took fancy to this morning (and have not left
it yet) drew me to that exhortation, which drew the company,
indeed, which drew the cutpurse; which drew the money;
which drew my brother Cokes's loss; which drew on Wasp's
anger; which drew on my beating: a pretty gradation! And
they shall ha' it i' their dish, i' faith, at night for fruit; I love to
be merry at my table. I had thought once, at one special blow
he ga' me, to have revealed myself; but then (I thank thee,
fortitude) I remembered that a wise man (and who is ever so
great a part o' the Commonwealth in himself) for no particular
disaster ought to abandon a public good design. The husband-
man ought not, for one unthankful year, to forsake the plough;
the shepherd ought not, for one scabbed sheep, to throw by
his tar-box; the pilot ought not, for one leak i' the poop, to
quit the helm; nor the alderman ought not, for one custard
more at a meal, to give up his cloak; the constable ought not to
break his staff and forswear the watch, for one roaring night;
the piper o' the parish (*ut parvis componere magna solebam*) to put
up his pipes for one rainy Sunday. These are certain knocking
conclusions; out of which I am resolved, come what come can –
come beating, come imprisonment, come infamy, come banish-

3. *collateral*: accompanying, concomitant.
4. *by-cause*: incidental cause.
27. *tar-box*: box which held tar ointment for treating sores in sheep.

ment, nay, come the rack, come the hurdle – welcome all – I will not discover who I am till my due time; and yet still all shall be, as I said ever, in Justice' name, and the King's and for the Commonwealth!

WINWIFE: What does he talk to himself, and act so seriously? Poor fool!   40

[*Exit* JUSTICE OVERDO.]

QUARLOUS: No matter what. Here's fresher argument, intend that.

[*Enter* COKES, MISTRESS OVERDO, *and* GRACE, *followed by*   III, iv
WASP, *loaded with toys.*]

COKES: Come, Mistress Grace, come sister, here's more fine sights yet, i' faith. God's lid, where's Numps?

LEATHERHEAD: What do you lack, gentlemen? What is't you buy? Fine rattles? drums? babies? little dogs? and birds for ladies? What do you lack?

COKES: Good honest Numps, keep afore. I am so afraid thou'lt lose somewhat; my heart was at my mouth when I missed thee.

WASP: You were best buy a whip i' your hand to drive me.

COKES: Nay, do not mistake. Numps, thou art so apt to mistake; I would but watch the goods. Look you now, the treble fiddle   10
was e'en almost like to be lost.

WASP: Pray you take heed you lose not yourself. Your best way were e'en get up and ride for more surety. Buy a token's worth of great pins to fasten yourself to my shoulder.

LEATHERHEAD: What do you lack, gentlemen? Fine purses, pouches, pincases, pipes? What is't you lack? A pair o' smiths to wake you i' the morning? or a fine whistling bird?

COKES: Numps, here be finer things than any we ha' bought, by odds! And more delicate horses, a great deal! Good Numps, stay, and come hither.   20

WASP: Will you scourse with him? You are in Smithfield; you may fit yourself with a fine easy-going street-nag for your saddle again' Michaelmas term, do. Has he ne'er a little odd cart

41. *intend:* attend to.
16. *pair o' smiths:* Note.   21. *scourse:* deal.

for you, to make a caroche on, i' the country, with four pied hobby-horses? Why the measles should you stand here with your train, cheaping of dogs, birds, and babies? You ha' no children to bestow 'em on, ha' you?

COKES: No, but again' I ha' children, Numps, that's all one.

WASP: Do, do, do, do. How many shall you have, think you? An' I were as you, I'd buy for all my tenants, too. They are a kind o' civil savages that will part with their children for rattles, pipes, and knives. You were best buy a hatchet or two and truck with 'em.

COKES: Good Numps, hold that little tongue o' thine, and save it a labour. I am resolute Bat, thou know'st.

WASP: A resolute fool you are, I know, and a very sufficient coxcomb, with all my heart; nay, you have it, sir, an' you be angry, turd i' your teeth, twice (if I said it not once afore); and much good do you.

WINWIFE: Was there ever such a self-affliction? And so impertinent?

QUARLOUS: Alas! his care will go near to crack him; let's in and comfort him.

WASP: Would I had been set i' the ground, all but the head on me, and had my brains bowled at, or threshed out, when first I underwent this plague of a charge!

QUARLOUS: How now, Numps! Almost tired i' your protectorship? Overparted? Overparted?

WASP: Why, I cannot tell, sir; it may be I am; does't grieve you?

QUARLOUS: No, I swear does't not, Numps, to satisfy you.

WASP: Numps? 'Sblood, you are fine and familiar! How long ha' we been acquainted, I pray you?

QUARLOUS: I think it may be remembered, Numps, that? 'Twas since morning sure.

---

24. *caroche:* a splendid carriage.
26. *cheaping of:* bargaining for, haggling over.
28. *again':* against, in anticipation of.
31. *civil:* civilized.
42. *crack:* craze.
48. *overparted:* unequal to a task (theatrical metaphor for having too difficult a role to act).

WASP: Why, I hope I know't well enough, sir; I did not ask to be told.

QUARLOUS: No? Why then?

WASP: It's no matter why; you see with your eyes, now, what I said to you today? You'll believe me another time?

QUARLOUS: Are you removing the Fair, Numps?   60

WASP: A pretty question! and a very civil one! Yes faith, I ha' my lading you see, or shall have anon; you may know whose beast I am by my burden. If the pannier-man's jack were ever better known by his loins of mutton, I'll be flayed, and feed dogs for him, when his time comes.

WINWIFE: How melancholy Mistress Grace is yonder! Pray thee let's go enter ourselves in grace with her.

COKES: Those six horses, friend, I'll have

WASP: How!

COKES: And the three Jew's trumps; and a half dozen o' birds,   70 and that drum (I have one drum already) and your smiths (I like that device o' your smiths very pretty well) and four halberts – and (le'me see) that fine painted great lady, and her three women for state, I'll have.

WASP: No, the shop; buy the whole shop, it will be best, the shop, the shop!

LEATHERHEAD: If his worship please.

WASP: Yes, and keep it during the Fair, bobchin.

COKES: Peace, Numps. – Friend, do not meddle with him, an' you be wise, and would show your head above board. He will   80 sting thorough your wrought nightcap, believe me. A set of these violins I would buy too, for a delicate young noise I have i' the country, that are every one a size less than another, just like your fiddles. I would fain have a fine young masque at my marriage, now I think on't; but I do want such a number of things. And Numps will not help me now, and I dare not speak to him.

---

63. *pannier-man:* a servant at the Inns of Court who carried provisions from the market.

63. *jack:* servant.

70. *Jew's trumps:* Jew's harps.

74. *state:* ceremony.

78. *bobchin:* booby.

82. *noise:* group of musicians.

84. *masque:* company of masquers.

TRASH: Will your worship buy any gingerbread, very good bread, comfortable bread?

90 COKES: Gingerbread! Yes, let's see.

He runs to her shop.

WASP: There's the tother springe!

LEATHERHEAD: Is this well, Goody Joan? to interrupt my market? in the midst? and call away my customers? Can you answer this at the Pie-powders?

TRASH: Why, if his mastership have a mind to buy, I hope my ware lies as open as another's. I may show my ware as well as you yours.

COKES: Hold your peace; I'll content you both: I'll buy up his shop and thy basket.

100 WASP: Will you i' faith?

LEATHERHEAD: Why should you put him from it, friend?

WASP: Cry you mercy! you'd be sold too, would you? What's the price on you? Jerkin and all, as you stand? Ha' you any qualities?

TRASH: Yes, Goodman Angry-man, you shall find he has qualities, if you cheapen him.

WASP: Godso, you ha' the selling of him! What are they? Will they be bought for love or money?

TRASH: No indeed, sir.

110 WASP: For what then? Victuals?

TRASH: He scorns victuals, sir; he has bread and butter at home, thanks be to God! And yet he will do more for a good meal, if the toy take him i' the belly. Marry then they must not set him at lower end; if they do, he'll go away, though he fast. But put him atop o' the table, where his place is, and he'll do you forty fine things. He has not been sent for, and sought out, for nothing, at your great City suppers, to put down Coriat and Cokely, and been laughed at for his labour. He'll play you all the puppets

91. *springe:* trap or snare for birds.

92. *Goody:* goodwife; indicates low social status. See *Goodman* below, line 105.

104. *qualities:* accomplishments.

107. *Godso:* vulgar expletive (from the Italian *cazzo* = penis).

115. *atop o' the table:* i.e. the jester's place.

i' the town over, and the players, every company, and his own
company too; he spares nobody! 120

COKES: I' faith?

TRASH: He was the first, sir, that ever baited the fellow i' the
bear's skin, an't like your worship. No dog ever came near him
since. And for fine motions!

COKES: Is he good at those too? Can he set out a masque, trow?

TRASH: O Lord, master! sought to, far and near, for his inventions; and he engrosses all, he makes all the puppets i' the Fair.

COKES: Dost thou, in troth, old velvet jerkin? Give me thy hand.

TRASH: Nay, sir, you shall see him in his velvet jerkin, and a scarf
too, at night, when you hear him interpret Master Littlewit's 130
motion.

COKES: Speak no more, but shut up shop presently, friend. I'll
buy both it and thee too, to carry down with me, and her
hamper beside. Thy shop shall furnish out the masque, and hers
the banquet. I cannot go less, to set out anything with credit.
What's the price, at a word, o' thy whole shop, case and all as it
stands?

LEATHERHEAD: Sir, it stands me in six and twenty shillings seven-
pence halfpenny, besides three shillings for my ground.

COKES: Well, thirty shillings will do all, then! And what comes 140
yours to?

TRASH: Four shillings and elevenpence, sir, ground and all, an't
like your worship.

COKES: Yes, it does like my worship very well, poor woman;
that's five shillings more. What a masque shall I furnish out for
forty shillings (twenty pound Scotch)! And a banquet of gingerbread! There's a stately thing! Numps! Sister! And my wedding
gloves too! (That I never thought on afore.) All my wedding
gloves gingerbread! O me! what a device will there be to make
'em eat their fingers' ends! And delicate brooches for the 150
bride-men and all! And then I'll ha' this posy to put to 'em:

122. *baited*, etc.: Note.   124. *motions:* puppet-shows.
125. *trow?:* do you suppose?   127. *engrosses:* monopolizes.
135. *banquet:* (here) dessert.   138. *stands me in:* costs.
146. *pound Scotch:* worth 1s. 8d. at the accession of King James in 1603.
151. *posy:* motto or verse.

'For the best grace,' meaning Mistress Grace, my wedding posy.

GRACE: I am beholden to you, sir, and to your Barthol'mew-wit.

WASP: You do not mean this, do you? Is this your first purchase?

COKES: Yes, faith, and I do not think, Numps, but thou'lt say, it was the wisest act that ever I did in my wardship.

WASP: Like enough! I shall say anything, I!

III, V   [*Enter* EDGWORTH *and* NIGHTINGALE, *followed by* JUSTICE OVERDO.]

[OVERDO (*aside*):] I cannot beget a project, with all my political brain, yet; my project is how to fetch off this proper young man from his debauched company. I have followed him all the Fair over, and still I find him with this songster; and I begin shrewdly to suspect their familiarity; and the young man of a terrible taint, poetry! with which idle disease if he be infected, there's no hope of him in a state-course. *Actum est* of him for a commonwealth's-man if he go to't in rhyme once.

EDGWORTH [*to* NIGHTINGALE]: Yonder he is buying o' ginger-
10 bread. Set in quickly, before he part with too much on his money.

NIGHTINGALE [*singing*]: My masters and friends and good people, draw near, etc.

COKES: Ballads! hark, hark! Pray thee, fellow, stay a little! Good Numps, look to the goods. What ballads hast thou? Let me see, let me see myself.

He runs to the ballad-man.

WASP: Why so! He's flown to another lime-bush; there he will flutter as long more, till he ha' ne'er a feather left. Is there a vexation like this, gentlemen? Will you believe me now? Here-after shall I have credit with you?

1. *political:* politic, i.e. prudent, shrewd.

7. *state-course:* Professor Horsman suggests a 'life concerned with public affairs or welfare'.

7. *Actum est of him:* it's all up with him.

8. *commonwealth's man:* good citizen.

15. *lime-bush:* bush sprayed with lime to snare birds.

QUARLOUS: Yes faith, shalt thou, Numps, an' thou art worthy
on't, for thou sweatest for't. I never saw a young pimp-errant *20*
and his squire better matched.

WINWIFE: Faith, the sister comes after 'em well, too.

GRACE: Nay, if you saw the Justice her husband, my guardian,
you were fitted for the mess; he is such a wise one his way –

WINWIFE: I wonder we see him not here.

GRACE: O! he is too serious for this place, and yet better sport
than the other three, I assure you, gentlemen, where'er he is,
though't be o' the bench.

COKES: How dost thou call it? 'A Caveat Against Cutpurses!' A
good jest, i' faith; I would fain see that demon, your cutpurse, *30*
you talk of, that delicate-handed devil; they say he walks hereabout. I would see him walk, now. Look you, sister, here, here,
let him come, sister, and welcome.

He shows his purse boastingly.

Ballad-man, does any cutpurses haunt hereabout? Pray thee
raise me one or two; begin and show me one.

NIGHTINGALE: Sir, this is a spell against 'em, spick and span
new; and 'tis made as 'twere in mine own person, and I sing it
in mine own defence. But 'twill cost a penny alone, if you buy it.

COKES: No matter for the price; thou dost not know me, I see;
I am an odd Barthol'mew. *40*

MISTRESS OVERDO: Has't a fine picture, brother?

COKES: O sister, do you remember the ballads over the nursery-
chimney at home o' my own pasting up? There be brave
pictures! Other manner of pictures than these, friend.

WASP: Yet these will serve to pick the pictures out o' your
pockets, you shall see.

COKES: So I heard 'em say. Pray thee mind him not, fellow; he'll
have an oar in everything.

NIGHTINGALE: It was intended, sir, as if a purse should chance to
be cut in my presence, now, I may be blameless, though; as by *50*
the sequel will more plainly appear.

COKES: We shall find that i' the matter. Pray thee begin.

NIGHTINGALE: To the tune of *Paggington's Pound*, sir.

24. *mess:* group who eat together at a banquet.
44. *pictures:* i.e. pictures of the sovereign – on coins.

COKES: Fa, la la la, la la la, fa la la la la. Nay, I'll put thee in tune, and all! Mine own country dance! Pray thee begin.

NIGHTINGALE: It is a gentle admonition, you must know, sir, both to the purse-cutter and the purse-bearer.

COKES: Not a word more, out o' the tune, an' thou lov'st me. Fa, la la la, la la la, fa la la la. Come, when?

60 NIGHTINGALE [singing]: My masters and friends and good people draw near,
And look to your purses, for that I do say;

COKES: Ha, ha, this chimes! Good counsel at first dash.

NIGHTINGALE: And though little money in them you do bear,
It cost more to get than to lose in a day.   COKES: Good!
    You oft have been told,
    Both the young and the old,
And bidden beware of the cutpurse so bold;   COKES: Well
Then if you take heed not, free me from the   said! He were
70   curse,   to blame that
Who both give you warning for and the   would not,
  cutpurse.   i' faith.
Youth, youth, thou hadst better been starved by thy nurse,
Than live to be hangèd for cutting a purse.

COKES: Good i' faith, how say you, Numps? Is there any harm i' this?

NIGHTINGALE: It hath been upbraided to   COKES: The
  men of my trade   more coxcombs
That oftentimes we are the cause of this   they that did
80   crime.   it, I wusse.
Alack and for pity, why should it be said?
As if they regarded or places or time.
    Examples have been
    Of some that were seen
In Westminster Hall, yea the pleaders be-   COKES: God a
  tween;   mercy for that!
Then why should the judges be free from   Why should
  this curse,   they be more
More than my poor self, for cutting the   free indeed?
90   purse?

63. *chimes:* sounds well, is pleasing.   71. *for and:* and also, moreover.

Youth, youth, thou hadst better been   *He sings the*
   starved by thy nurse,   *burden with him.*
Than live to be hangèd for cutting a purse.

COKES: That again, good ballad-man, that again. O rare! I would fain rub mine elbow now, but I dare not pull out my hand. On, I pray thee; he that made this ballad shall be poet to my masque.

NIGHTINGALE: At Worcester 'tis known well, and even i' the jail,
A knight of good worship did there show his face,
Against the foul sinners, in zeal for to rail,   *100*
And lost (*ipso facto*) his purse in the place.   COKES: Is it
   Nay, once from the seat   possible?
   Of judgement so great
A judge there did lose a fair pouch of velvet.   COKES: I' faith?
O Lord for thy mercy, how wicked or worse
Are those that so venture their necks for a purse!
Youth, youth, etc.

COKES [*sings the burden with him again*]: Youth, youth, etc.
Pray thee stay a little, friend. Yet o' thy conscience, Numps, speak, is there any harm i' this?   *110*

WASP: To tell you true, 'tis too good for you, 'less you had grace to follow it.

OVERDO [*aside*]: It doth discover enormity, I'll mark it more; I ha' not liked a paltry piece of poetry so well, a good while.

COKES: Youth, youth, etc.
Where's this youth, now? A man must call upon him, for his own good, and yet he will not appear. Look here, here's for him; handy-dandy, which hand will he have?
   He shows his purse.
On, I pray thee, with the rest; I do hear of him, but I cannot see him, this Master Youth, the cutpurse.   *120*

NIGHTINGALE: At plays and at sermons, and at the sessions,
'Tis daily their practice such booty to make:
Yea, under the gallows, at executions,
They stick not the stare-abouts' purses to take.

95. *rub mine elbow:* show pleasure.
118. *handy-dandy:* a game in which children guess which hand holds a concealed object.

Nay, one without grace,
At a better place,
At court, and in Christmas, before the
King's face.
Alack then for pity, must I bear the curse
130 That only belongs to the cunning cutpurse?

COKES: That was a fine fellow! I would have him, now.

COKES: But where's their cunning now, when they should use it? They are all chained now, I warrant you.

Youth, youth, etc.

The rat-catcher's charms are all fools and asses to this! A pox on 'em, that they will not come! that a man should have such a desire to a thing and want it!

QUARLOUS: 'Fore God, I'd give half the Fair, an' 'twere mine, for a cutpurse for him, to save his longing.

COKES: Look you, sister, here, here, where is't now? which
140 pocket is't in, for a wager?

He shows his purse again.

WASP: I beseech you leave your wagers and let him end his matter, an't may be.

COKES: O, are you edified, Numps?

OVERDO [*aside*]: Indeed he does interrupt him too much; there Numps spoke to purpose.

COKES: Sister, I am an ass, I cannot keep my purse.

[*He shows it*] *again.*

On on, I pray thee, friend.

EDGWORTH *gets up to him and tickles him in the ear with a straw twice to draw his hand out of his pocket.*

NIGHTINGALE: But O, you vile nation of cutpurses all,
150 Relent and repent, and amend and be sound,
And know that you ought not, by honest men's fall,
Advance your own fortunes, to die above ground;
    And though you go gay
    In silks as you may,

WINWIFE [*aside*]: Will you see sport? Look, there's a fellow gathers up to him, mark.

QUARLOUS [*aside*]: Good, i' faith! O, he has lighted on

134. *rat-catcher's charms:* Note.

It is not the highway to heaven (as they say).

Repent then, repent you, for better, for worse:

And kiss not the gallows for cutting a purse.

Youth, youth, thou hadst better been starved by thy nurse,

Than live to be hangèd for cutting a purse.

the wrong pocket.

WINWIFE: He 160 has it, 'fore God he is a brave fellow; pity he should be detected.

ALL: An excellent ballad! an excellent ballad!

EDGWORTH: Friend, let me ha' the first, let me ha' the first, I pray you.

COKES: Pardon me, sir. First come, first served; and I'll buy the 170 whole bundle too.

[EDGWORTH *gives the purse to* NIGHTINGALE.]

WINWIFE [*aside*]: That conveyance was better than all, did you see't?

He has given the purse to the ballad-singer.

QUARLOUS: Has he?

EDGWORTH: Sir, I cry you mercy; I'll not hinder the poor man's profit; pray you, mistake me not.

COKES: Sir, I take you for an honest gentleman, if that be mistaking; I met you today afore. Ha! humh! O God! my purse is gone, my purse, my purse, etc.! 180

WASP: Come, do not make a stir and cry yourself an ass thorough the Fair afore your time.

COKES: Why, hast thou it, Numps? Good Numps, how came you by it? I mar'l!

WASP: I pray you seek some other gamester to play the fool with. You may lose it time enough, for all your Fair-wit.

COKES: By this good hand, glove and all, I ha' lost it already, if thou hast it not; feel else, and Mistress Grace's handkercher, too, out o' the tother pocket.

WASP: Why, 'tis well; very well, exceeding pretty, and well. 190

EDGWORTH: Are you sure you ha' lost it, sir?

COKES: O God! yes; as I am an honest man, I had it but e'en now, at 'Youth, youth'.

184. *mar'l*: marvel.   188. *handkercher*: handkerchief.

NIGHTINGALE: I hope you suspect not me, sir.

EDGWORTH: Thee? That were a jest indeed! Dost thou think the gentleman is foolish? Where hadst thou hands, I pray thee? [*To* NIGHTINGALE] Away, ass, away.

[*Exit* NIGHTINGALE.]

OVERDO [*aside*]: I shall be beaten again if I be spied.

EDGWORTH: Sir, I suspect an odd fellow, yonder, is stealing away.

200 MISTRESS OVERDO: Brother, it is the preaching fellow! You shall suspect him. He was at your tother purse, you know! Nay, stay, sir, and view the work you ha' done; an' you be beneficed at the gallows and preach there, thank your own handiwork.

COKES: Sir, you shall take no pride in your preferment; you shall be silenced quickly.

[*They seize* JUSTICE OVERDO.]

OVERDO: What do you mean, sweet buds of gentility?

COKES: To ha' my pennyworths out on you, bud. No less than two purses a day serve you? I thought you a simple fellow, when my man Numps beat you i' the morning, and pitied you –

210 MISTRESS OVERDO: So did I, I'll be sworn, brother; but now I see he is a lewd and pernicious enormity (as Master Overdo calls him).

OVERDO [*aside*]: Mine own words turned upon me like swords.

COKES: Cannot a man's purse be at quiet for you i' the master's pocket, but you must entice it forth and debauch it?

WASP: Sir, sir, keep your debauch and your fine Barthol'mew-terms to yourself, and make as much on 'em as you please. But gi' me this from you i' the meantime; I beseech you, see if I can look to this.

[WASP *tries to get the box with the licence.*]

220 COKES: Why, Numps?

WASP: Why? Because you are an ass, sir; there's a reason the shortest way, an' you will needs ha' it. Now you ha' got the trick of losing, you'd lose your breech, an't were loose. I know you sir; come, deliver.

WASP *takes the licence from him.*

194. *suspect:* take note of.   202. *beneficed:* given a cleric's living.
215. *entice, debauch:* almost synonyms in Jacobean times – hence Wasp calls them 'fine terms' because the distinction is slight.

You'll go and crack the vermin you breed now, will you? 'Tis very fine, will you ha' the truth on't? They are such retchless flies as you are, that blow cutpurses abroad in every corner; your foolish having of money makes 'em. An' there were no wiser than I, sir, the trade should lie open for you, sir; it should i' faith, sir. I would teach your wit to come to your head, sir, as 230 well as your land to come into your hand, I assure you, sir.

WINWIFE: Alack, good Numps.

WASP: Nay, gentlemen, never pity me; I am not worth it. Lord send me at home once, to Harrow o' the Hill again; if I travel any more, call me Coriat, with all my heart.

[*Exeunt* WASP, COKES, *and* MISTRESS OVERDO; JUSTICE OVERDO *is carried out.*]

QUARLOUS: Stay, sir, I must have a word with you in private. Do you hear?

EDGWORTH: With me, sir? What's your pleasure, good sir?

QUARLOUS: Do not deny it, you are a cutpurse, sir; this gentle-man here, and I, saw you, nor do we mean to detect you 240 (though we can sufficiently inform ourselves toward the danger of concealing you), but you must do us a piece of service.

EDGWORTH: Good gentlemen, do not undo me; I am a civil young man, and but a beginner, indeed.

QUARLOUS: Sir, your beginning shall bring on your ending, for us. We are no catchpoles nor constables. That you are to under-take is this; you saw the old fellow with the black box here?

EDGWORTH: The little old governor, sir?

QUARLOUS: That same. I see you have flown him to a mark already. I would ha' you get away that box from him, and 250 bring it us.

EDGWORTH: Would you ha' the box and all, sir? or only that that is in't? I'll get you that, and leave him the box to play with still (which will be the harder o' the two), because I would gain your worships' good opinion of me.

WINWIFE: He says well; 'tis the greater mastery, and 'twill make the more sport when 'tis missed.

226. *retchless:* heedless.
246. *catchpoles:* officers of the sheriff.
248. *governor:* tutor.

EDGWORTH: Ay, and 'twill be the longer a-missing, to draw on the sport.

260 QUARLOUS: But look you do it now, sirrah, and keep your word, or –

EDGWORTH: Sir, if ever I break my word with a gentleman, may I never read word at my need. Where shall I find you?

QUARLOUS: Somewhere i' the Fair, hereabouts. Dispatch it quickly. I would fain see the careful fool deluded! Of all beasts I love the serious ass – he that takes pains to be one, and plays the fool with the greatest diligence that can be.

GRACE: Then you would not choose, sir, but love my guardian, Justice Overdo, who is answerable to that description in every 270 hair of him.

QUARLOUS: So I have heard. But how came you, Mistress Well-born, to be his ward, or have relation to him, at first?

GRACE: Faith, through a common calamity; he bought me, sir; and now he will marry me to his wife's brother, this wise gentleman that you see, or else I must pay value o' my land.

QUARLOUS: 'Slid, is there no device of disparagement, or so? Talk with some crafty fellow, some picklock o' the law! Would I had studied a year longer i' the Inns of Court, an't had been but i' your case.

280 WINWIFE [aside]: Ay, Master Quarlous, are you proffering?

GRACE: You'd bring but little aid, sir.

WINWIFE [aside]: I'll look to you i' faith, gamester. – An unfortunate foolish tribe you are fall'n into, lady; I wonder you can endure 'em.

GRACE: Sir, they that cannot work their fetters off must wear 'em.

WINWIFE: You see what care they have on you, to leave you thus.

GRACE: Faith, the same they have of themselves, sir. I cannot greatly complain if this were all the plea I had against 'em.

WINWIFE: 'Tis true! but will you please to withdraw with us a 290 little, and make them think they have lost you? I hope our manners ha' been such hitherto, and our language, as will give you no cause to doubt yourself in our company.

263. *read word*: see I, iv, 6.
273. *bought me*: made me his ward. Note.
276. *disparagement*: Note.   292. *doubt yourself*: to fear.

GRACE: Sir, I will give myself no cause; I am so secure of mine own manners as I suspect not yours.

QUARLOUS: Look where John Littlewit comes.

WINWIFE: Away, I'll not be seen by him.

QUARLOUS: No, you were not best, he'd tell his mother, the widow.

WINWIFE: Heart, what do you mean?

QUARLOUS: Cry you mercy, is the wind there? Must not the *300* widow be named?

[*Exeunt* GRACE, WINWIFE, *and* QUARLOUS.]

[*Enter* LITTLEWIT *and* MISTRESS LITTLEWIT.]   III, vi

[LITTLEWIT:] Do you hear, Win, Win?

MISTRESS LITTLEWIT: What say you, John?

LITTLEWIT: While they are paying the reckoning, Win, I'll tell you a thing, Win: we shall never see any sights i' the Fair, Win, except you long still, Win. Good Win, sweet Win, long to see some hobby-horses and some drums and rattles and dogs and fine devices, Win. The bull with the five legs, Win, and the great hog. Now you ha' begun with pig, you may long for anything, Win, and so for my motion, Win.

MISTRESS LITTLEWIT: But we sha' not eat o' the bull and the *10* hog, John; how shall I long then?

LITTLEWIT: O yes, Win! you may long to see as well as to taste, Win. How did the 'pothecary's wife, Win, that longed to see the anatomy, Win? Or the lady, Win, that desired to spit i' the great lawyer's mouth after an eloquent pleading? I assure you they longed, Win; good Win, go in, and long.

[*Exeunt* LITTLEWIT *and* MISTRESS LITTLEWIT.]

TRASH: I think we are rid of our new customer, Brother Leatherhead; we shall hear no more of him.

They plot to be gone.

LEATHERHEAD: All the better; let's pack up all and be gone before he find us.   *20*

TRASH: Stay a little, yonder comes a company; it may be we may take some more money.

14. *anatomy:* skeleton.

[*Enter* KNOCKEM *and* BUSY.]

KNOCKEM: Sir, I will take your counsel, and cut my hair, and leave vapours. I see that tobacco, and bottle-ale, and pig, and Whit, and very Urs'la herself, is all vanity.

BUSY: Only pig was not comprehended in my admonition; the rest were. For long hair, it is an ensign of pride, a banner, and the world is full of those banners, very full of banners. And bottle-ale is a drink of Satan's, a diet-drink of Satan's, devised
30   to puff us up and make us swell in this latter age of vanity, as the smoke of tobacco to keep us in mist and error; but the fleshly woman, which you call Urs'la, is above all to be avoided, having the marks upon her of the three enemies of man: the World, as being in the Fair; the Devil, as being in the fire; and the Flesh, as being herself.

[*Enter* DAME PURECRAFT.]

DAME PURECRAFT: Brother Zeal-of-the-Land! what shall we do? My daughter, Win-the-Fight, is fall'n into her fit of longing again.

BUSY: For more pig? There is no more, is there?

40 DAME PURECRAFT: To see some sights i' the Fair.

BUSY: Sister, let her fly the impurity of the place swiftly, lest she partake of the pitch thereof. Thou art the seat of the Beast, O Smithfield, and I will leave thee. Idolatry peepeth out on every side of thee.

KNOCKEM [*aside*]: An excellent right hypocrite! Now his belly is full, he falls a-railing and kicking, the jade. A very good vapour! I'll in and joy Urs'la with telling how her pig works; two and a half he eat to his share. And he has drunk a pailful. He eats with his eyes as well as his teeth.

[*Exit.*]

50 LEATHERHEAD: What do you lack, gentlemen? What is't you buy? Rattles, drums, babies –

BUSY: Peace with thy apocryphal wares, thou profane publican –

---

29. *diet-drink:* medicine.

52. *apocryphal:* spurious, sham – the Puritans did not accept the Apocrypha.

52. *publican:* excommunicated person.

thy bells, thy dragons, and thy Toby's dogs. Thy hobby-horse is an idol, a very idol, a fierce and rank idol; and thou the Nebuchadnezzar, the proud Nebuchadnezzar of the Fair, that sett'st it up for children to fall down to and worship.

LEATHERHEAD: Cry you mercy, sir, will you buy a fiddle to fill up your noise?

[Re-enter LITTLEWIT and MISTRESS LITTLEWIT.]

LITTLEWIT: Look, Win; do look o' God's name, and save your longing. Here be fine sights.   60

DAME PURECRAFT: Ay, child, so you hate 'em, as our brother Zeal does, you may look on 'em.

LEATHERHEAD: Or what do you say to a drum, sir?

BUSY: It is the broken belly of the Beast, and thy bellows there are his lungs, and these pipes are his throat, those feathers are of his tail, and thy rattles the gnashing of his teeth.

TRASH: And what's my gingerbread, I pray you?

BUSY: The provender that pricks him up. Hence with thy basket of popery, thy nest of images, and whole legend of ginger-work.   70

LEATHERHEAD: Sir, if you be not quiet the quicklier, I'll ha' you clapped fairly by the heels for disturbing the Fair.

BUSY: The sin of the Fair provokes me; I cannot be silent.

DAME PURECRAFT: Good Brother Zeal!

LEATHERHEAD: Sir, I'll make you silent, believe it.

LITTLEWIT [aside to LEATHERHEAD]: I'd give a shilling you could, i' faith, friend.

LEATHERHEAD: Sir, give me your shilling; I'll give you my shop if I do not, and I'll leave it in pawn with you i' the meantime.

LITTLEWIT: A match i' faith, but do it quickly, then.   80

[Exit LEATHERHEAD.]

BUSY: Hinder me not, woman.

He speaks to the widow.

I was moved in spirit to be here this day in this Fair, this wicked

---

53. *Toby's dogs:* the dogs in the Punch-and-Judy show; probably the dog which accompanies Tobias in the *Book of Tobit* in the Apocrypha.

68. *pricks him up:* stimulates.

69. *images:* gingerbread cakes shaped like St Bartholomew.

69. *legend:* a collection of saints' lives.

and foul Fair – and fitter may it be called a Foul than a Fair – to protest against the abuses of it, the foul abuses of it, in regard of the afflicted Saints, that are troubled, very much troubled, exceedingly troubled, with the opening of the merchandise of Babylon again, and the peeping of popery upon the stalls, here, here, in the high places. See you not Goldylocks, the purple strumpet, there, in her yellow gown and green sleeves? the pro-
90   fane pipes, the tinkling timbrels? A shop of relics!

LITTLEWIT: Pray you forbear, I am put in trust with 'em.

BUSY: And this idolatrous grove of images, this flasket of idols! which I will pull down –

Overthrows the gingerbread.

TRASH: O my ware, my ware, God bless it!

BUSY: – in my zeal, and glory to be thus exercised.

    LEATHERHEAD *enters with* OFFICERS.

LEATHERHEAD: Here he is. Pray you lay hold on his zeal; we cannot sell a whistle, for him, in tune. Stop his noise first!

BUSY: Thou canst not; 'tis a sanctified noise. I will make a loud and most strong noise, till I have daunted the profane enemy.
100   And for this cause –

LEATHERHEAD: Sir, here's no man afraid of you or your cause. You shall swear it i' the stocks, sir.

BUSY: I will thrust myself into the stocks, upon the pikes of the land.

LEATHERHEAD: Carry him away.

DAME PURECRAFT: What do you mean, wicked men?

BUSY: Let them alone; fear I them not.

    [*Exeunt* OFFICERS *with* BUSY, *followed by* DAME PURE-
    CRAFT.]

LITTLEWIT: Was not this shilling well ventured, Win, for our liberty? Now we may go play, and see over the Fair, where we
110   list, ourselves. My mother is gone after him, and let her e'en go and lose us.

MISTRESS LITTLEWIT: Yes, John, but I know not what to do.

LITTLEWIT: For what, Win?

    92. *flasket:* a long shallow basket.

    103. *thrust myself . . . upon the pikes:* rush into martyrdom or danger; *pikes* = bayonets.

MISTRESS LITTLEWIT: For a thing I am ashamed to tell you, i'
faith, and 'tis too far to go home.

LITTLEWIT: I pray thee be not ashamed, Win. Come, i' faith thou
shall not be ashamed. Is it anything about the hobby-horse-
man? An't be, speak freely.

MISTRESS LITTLEWIT: Hang him, base bobchin, I scorn him.
No, I have very great what sha' call 'um, John.   *120*

LITTLEWIT: O! is that all, Win? We'll go back to Captain Jordan;
to the pig-woman's, Win. He'll help us, or she with a dripping
pan, or an old kettle, or something. The poor greasy soul loves
you, Win, and after we'll visit the Fair all over, Win, and see
my puppet-play, Win; you know it's a fine matter, Win.

[*Exeunt* LITTLEWIT *and* MISTRESS LITTLEWIT.]

LEATHERHEAD: Let's away; I counselled you to pack up afore,
Joan.

TRASH: A pox of his Bedlam purity. He has spoiled half my ware;
but the best is, we lose nothing if we miss our first merchant.

LEATHERHEAD: It shall be hard for him to find or know us when   *130*
we are translated, Joan.

[*Exeunt.*]

129. *merchant:* customer.
131. *translated:* transformed, disguised.

ACT FOUR

IV, i   *[The Fair.]*

[Booths and stalls, as before, and a pair of stocks.]
[Enter BRISTLE *and* HAGGIS, *with* JUSTICE OVERDO, *followed by* COKES *and* TROUBLE-ALL.]

[TROUBLE-ALL:] My Masters, I do make no doubt but you are officers.

BRISTLE: What then, sir?

TROUBLE-ALL: And the King's loving and obedient subjects.

BRISTLE: Obedient, friend? Take heed what you speak, I advise you; Oliver Bristle advises you. His loving subjects, we grant you; but not his obedient, at this time, by your leave. We know ourselves a little better than so. We are to command, sir, and such as you are to be obedient. Here's one of his obedient sub-
10   jects going to the stocks, and we'll make you such another, if you talk.

TROUBLE-ALL: You are all wise enough i' your places, I know.

BRISTLE: If you know it, sir, why do you bring it in question?

TROUBLE-ALL: I question nothing, pardon me. I do only hope you have warrant for what you do, and so, quit you, and so, multiply you.

He goes away again.

HAGGIS: What's he? Bring him up to the stocks there. Why bring you him not up?

[TROUBLE-ALL] comes again.

TROUBLE-ALL: If you have Justice Overdo's warrant, 'tis well;
20   you are safe. This is the warrant of warrants. I'll not give this button for any man's warrant else.

BRISTLE: Like enough, sir; but let me tell you, an' you play away your buttons thus, you will want 'em ere night, for any store I see about you. You might keep 'em, and save pins, I wusse.

6. *Oliver:* earlier Davy.
15. *quit you:* God requite (i.e. reward) you.
16. *multiply you:* God increase your family.   23. *store:* supply.

[TROUBLE-ALL] *goes away.*

OVERDO [*aside*]: What should he be, that doth so esteem and advance my warrant? He seems a sober and discreet person! It is a comfort to a good conscience to be followed with a good fame in his sufferings. The world will have a pretty taste by this, how I can bear adversity; and it will beget a kind of reverence toward me hereafter, even from mine enemies, when they shall   *30* see I carry my calamity nobly, and that it doth neither break me nor bend me.

HAGGIS: Come, sir, here's a place for you to preach in. Will you put in your leg?

They put him in the stocks.

OVERDO: That I will, cheerfully.

BRISTLE: O' my conscience, a seminary! He kisses the stocks.

COKES: Well, my masters, I'll leave him with you; now I see him bestowed, I'll go look for my goods and Numps.

HAGGIS: You may, sir, I warrant you; where's the tother bawler? Fetch him too, you shall find 'em both fast enough.   *40*

[*Exit* COKES.]

OVERDO [*aside*]: In the midst of this tumult I will yet be the author of mine own rest, and, not minding their fury, sit in the stocks in that calm as shall be able to trouble a triumph.

[TROUBLE-ALL] *comes again.*

TROUBLE-ALL: Do you assure me upon your words? May I undertake for you, if I be asked the question, that you have this warrant?

HAGGIS: What's this fellow, for God's sake?

TROUBLE-ALL: Do but show me Adam Overdo, and I am satisfied.

Goes out.

BRISTLE: He is a fellow that is distracted, they say – one Trouble-   *50* all. He was an officer in the court of Pie-powders here last year, and put out on his place by Justice Overdo.

OVERDO: Ha!

BRISTLE: Upon which he took an idle conceit, and's run mad upon't. So that ever since, he will do nothing but by Justice Overdo's warrant; he will not eat a crust, nor drink a little, nor make him in his apparel ready. His wife, sir reverence, cannot get him make his water or shift his shirt without his warrant.

60 OVERDO [aside]: If this be true, this is my greatest disaster! How am I bound to satisfy this poor man, that is of so good a nature to me, out of his wits, where there is no room left for dissembling!

[TROUBLE-ALL] comes in.

TROUBLE-ALL: If you cannot show me Adam Overdo, I am in doubt of you. I am afraid you cannot answer it.

Goes again.

HAGGIS: Before me, neighbour Bristle, (and now I think on't better) Justice Overdo is a very peremptory person.

BRISTLE: O! are you advised of that? And a severe Justicer, by your leave.

70 OVERDO [aside]: Do I hear ill o' that side, too?

BRISTLE: He will sit as upright o' the bench, an' you mark him, as a candle i' the socket, and give light to the whole court in every business.

HAGGIS: But he will burn blue and swell like a boil (God bless us!) an' he be angry.

BRISTLE: Ay, and he will be angry too, when he list, that's more; and when he is angry, be it right or wrong, he has the law on's side ever. I mark that too.

OVERDO [aside]: I will be more tender hereafter. I see compassion
80 may become a Justice, though it be a weakness, I confess, and nearer a vice than a virtue.

HAGGIS: Well, take him out o' the stocks again. We'll go a sure way to work; we'll ha' the ace of hearts of our side, if we can.

They take the JUSTICE out.

[Enter POACHER and OFFICERS with BUSY, followed by DAME PURECRAFT.]

POACHER: Come, bring him away to his fellow, there. Master Busy, we shall rule your legs, I hope, though we cannot rule your tongue.

BUSY: No, minister of darkness, no, thou canst not rule my

65. *answer*: justify, answer for.   68. *advised*: aware.

76. *list*: please (Folio reads 'his list'. Herford–Simpson read 'when him list'.)

tongue; my tongue it is mine own, and with it I will both knock
and mock down your Barthol'mew-abominations, till you be
made a hissing to the neighbour parishes round about.   *90*

HAGGIS: Let him alone; we have devised better upon't.

DAME PURECRAFT: And shall he not into the stocks then?

BRISTLE: No, mistress, we'll have 'em both to Justice Overdo,
and let him do over 'em as is fitting. Then I and my gossip
Haggis and my beadle Poacher are discharged.

DAME PURECRAFT: O, I thank you, blessed, honest men!

BRISTLE: Nay, never thank us, but thank this madman that comes
here. He put it in our heads.

   [TROUBLE-ALL] *comes again.*

DAME PURECRAFT: Is he mad? Now heaven increase his madness, and bless it, and thank it; sir, your poor handmaid thanks   *100*
you.

TROUBLE-ALL: Have you a warrant? An' you have a warrant,
show it.

DAME PURECRAFT: Yes, I have a warrant out of the Word, to
give thanks for removing any scorn intended to the Brethren.

   [*Exeunt all but* TROUBLE-ALL.]

TROUBLE-ALL: It is Justice Overdo's warrant that I look for. If
you have not that, keep your word, I'll keep mine. Quit ye, and
multiply ye.

   [*Enter* EDGWORTH *and* NIGHTINGALE.]   IV, ii

EDGWORTH: Come away, Nightingale, I pray thee.

TROUBLE-ALL: Whither go you? Where's your warrant?

EDGWORTH: Warrant, for what, sir?

TROUBLE-ALL: For what you go about; you know how fit it is;
an' you have no warrant, bless you, I'll pray for you, that's all I
can do.

   Goes out.

EDGWORTH: What means he?

NIGHTINGALE: A madman that haunts the Fair; do you not
know him? It's marvel he has not more followers after his ragged
heels.   *10*

95. *discharged:* freed from responsibility.   104. *the Word:* the Bible.

EDGWORTH: Beshrew him, he startled me. I thought he had known of our plot. Guilt's a terrible thing! Ha' you prepared the coster-monger?

NIGHTINGALE: Yes, and agreed for his basket of pears. He is at the corner here, ready.

[*Enter* COSTER-MONGER.]

And your prize, he comes down, sailing that way, all alone, without his protector; he is rid of him, it seems.

EDGWORTH: Ay, I know; I should ha' followed his protector-ship for a feat I am to do upon him; but this offered itself so i'
20 the way, I could not let it 'scape. Here he comes; whistle. Be this sport called 'Dorring the Dottrel'.

[*Enter* COKES.]

Nightingale whistles.

NIGHTINGALE: Wh, wh, wh, wh, etc.

COKES: By this light, I cannot find my gingerbread-wife nor my hobby-horse-man in all the Fair, now, to ha' my money again. And I do not know the way out on't, to go home for more. Do you hear, friend, you that whistle? what tune is that you whistle?

NIGHTINGALE: A new tune I am practising, sir.

COKES: Dost thou know where I dwell, I pray thee? Nay, on with
30 thy tune, I ha' no such haste for an answer. I'll practise with thee.

COSTER-MONGER: Buy any pears, very fine pears, pears fine!

NIGHTINGALE *sets his foot afore him, and he falls with his basket.*

COKES: Godso! a muss, a muss, a muss, a muss!

[*He helps to pick up the pears.*]

COSTER-MONGER: Good gentleman, my ware, my ware! I am a poor man. Good sir, my ware.

NIGHTINGALE [*to* COKES]: Let me hold your sword, sir, it troubles you.

COKES: Do, and my cloak, an' thou wilt; and my hat too.

COKES *falls a-scrambling whilst they run away with his things.*

EDGWORTH: A delicate great boy! Methinks he out-scrambles 'em all. I cannot persuade myself but he goes to grammar-
40 school yet, and plays the truant today.

21. *Dorring the Dottrel:* tricking the simpleton.
32. *muss:* scramble.

NIGHTINGALE: Would he had another purse to cut, 'Zekiel.

EDGWORTH: Purse? a man might cut out his kidneys, I think, and he never feel 'em, he is so earnest at the sport.

NIGHTINGALE: His soul is half-way out on's body at the game.

EDGWORTH: Away, Nightingale; that way!

[*Exit* NIGHTINGALE *with* COKES'S *sword, cloak, and hat.*]

COKES: I think I am furnished for Cather'ne pears for one under-meal. Gi' me my cloak.

COSTER-MONGER: Good gentleman, give me my ware.

COKES: Where's the fellow I ga' my cloak to? My cloak? and my hat? Ha! God's lid, is he gone? Thieves, thieves! Help me to 50 cry, gentlemen.

He runs out.

EDGWORTH: Away, coster-monger, come to us to Urs'la's.

[*Exit* COSTER-MONGER.]

Talk of him to have a soul? 'Heart, if he have any more than a thing given him instead of salt, only to keep him from stinking, I'll be hanged afore my time, presently. Where should it be, trow? In his blood? He has not so much toward it in his whole body as will maintain a good flea. And if he take this course, he will not ha' so much land left as to rear a calf within this twelvemonth. Was there ever green plover so pulled! That his little overseer had been here now, and been but tall enough, 60 to see him steal pears in exchange for his beaver-hat and his cloak thus! I must go find him out next, for his black box and his patent (it seems) he has of his place; which I think the gentleman would have a reversion of, that spoke to me for it so earnestly.

[*Exit.*]

He [COKES] *comes again.*

COKES: Would I might lose my doublet, and hose too, as I am an honest man, and never stir, if I think there be anything but thieving and coz'ning i' this whole Fair. Barthol'mew Fair, quoth he; an' ever any Barthol'mew had that luck in't that I

46. *under-meal:* afternoon meal.
59. *pulled:* plucked, tricked.
63. *patent:* a document conferring an office or job.
64. *reversion:* future possession, right of inheriting.

70 have had, I'll be martyred for him, and in Smithfield, too. I ha'
paid for my pears, a rot on 'em, I'll keep 'em no longer.

Throws away his pears.

You were choke-pears to me; I had better ha' gone to mum-
chance for you, I wusse. Methinks the Fair should not have used
me thus, an' 'twere but for my name's sake; I would not ha'
used a dog o' the name so. O, Numps will triumph now!

TROUBLE-ALL *comes again.*

Friend, do you know who I am? Or where I lie? I do not myself, I'll be sworn. Do but carry me home, and I'll please thee; I
ha' money enough there. I ha' lost myself, and my cloak and
my hat; and my fine sword, and my sister, and Numps, and
80 Mistress Grace (a gentlewoman that I should ha' married), and
a cut-work handkercher she ga' me, and two purses, today. And
my bargain o' hobby-horses and gingerbread, which grieves
me worst of all.

TROUBLE-ALL: By whose warrant, sir, have you done all this?

COKES: Warrant? thou art a wise fellow, indeed – as if a man need
a warrant to lose anything with.

TROUBLE-ALL: Yes, Justice Overdo's warrant, a man may get
and lose with, I'll stand to't.

COKES: Justice Overdo? Dost thou know him? I lie there, he is
90 my brother-in-law; he married my sister. Pray thee show me
the way, dost thou know the house?

TROUBLE-ALL: Sir, show me your warrant; I know nothing
without a warrant, pardon me.

COKES: Why, I warrant thee, come along. Thou shalt see I have
wrought pillows there, and cambric sheets, and sweet bags too.
Pray thee guide me to the house.

TROUBLE-ALL: Sir, I'll tell you: go you thither yourself, first,
alone; tell your worshipful brother your mind; and but bring
me three lines of his hand, or his clerk's, with Adam Overdo
100 underneath. Here I'll stay you; I'll obey you, and I'll guide you
presently.

72. *choke-pears:* coarse cider-pears.
72. *mum-chance:* game played with dice, or cards.
77. *carry:* lead.   89. *lie:* lodge.
95. *sweet bags:* lavender bags.   96. *wrought:* embroidered.

COKES [*aside*]: 'Slid, this is an ass; I ha' found him. Pox upon me, what do I talking to such a dull fool? – Farewell. You are a very coxcomb, do you hear?

TROUBLE-ALL: I think I am; if Justice Overdo sign to it, I am, and so we are all; he'll quit us all, multiply us all.

[*Exeunt.*]

[*Enter* GRACE *with* QUARLOUS *and* WINWIFE.] *They enter* IV, iii *with their swords drawn.*

[GRACE:] Gentlemen, this is no way that you take. You do but breed one another trouble and offence, and give me no contentment at all. I am no she that affects to be quarrelled for, or have my name or fortune made the question of men's swords.

QUARLOUS: 'Slood, we love you.

GRACE: If you both love me, as you pretend, your own reason will tell you but one can enjoy me; and to that point there leads a directer line than by my infamy, which must follow if you fight. 'Tis true, I have professed it to you ingenuously, that rather than to be yoked with this bridegroom is appointed me, 10 I would take up any husband, almost upon any trust. Though subtlety would say to me, I know, he is a fool, and has an estate, and I might govern him and enjoy a friend beside. But these are not my aims. I must have a husband I must love, or I cannot live with him. I shall ill make one of these politic wives!

WINWIFE: Why, if you can like either of us, lady, say which is he, and the other shall swear instantly to desist.

QUARLOUS: Content; I accord to that willingly.

GRACE: Sure you think me a woman of an extreme levity, gentlemen, or a strange fancy, that (meeting you by chance in such a 20 place as this, both at one instant, and not yet of two hours' acquaintance, neither of you deserving afore the other of me) I should so forsake my modesty (though I might affect one more particularly) as to say, 'This is he,' and name him.

QUARLOUS: Why, wherefore should you not? What should hinder you?

GRACE: If you would not give it to my modesty, allow it yet to

102. *found:* detected.   3. *affects:* likes.

413

my wit; give me so much of woman and cunning as not to
betray myself impertinently. How can I judge of you so far as
to a choice without knowing you more? You are both equal
and alike to me yet; and so indifferently affected by me as each
of you might be the man if the other were away. For you are
reasonable creatures; you have understanding and discourse.
And if fate send me an understanding husband, I have no fear
at all but mine own manners shall make him a good one.

QUARLOUS: Would I were put forth to making for you, then!

GRACE: It may be you are; you know not what's toward you.
Will you consent to a motion of mine, gentlemen?

WINWIFE: Whatever it be, we'll presume reasonableness, coming
from you.

QUARLOUS: And fitness too.

GRACE: I saw one of you buy a pair of tables, e'en now.

WINWIFE: Yes, here they be, and maiden ones too, unwritten in.

GRACE: The fitter for what they may be employed in. You shall
write, either of you, here, a word or a name – what you like
best – but of two or three syllables at most; and the next person
that comes this way (because destiny has a high hand in business
of this nature) I'll demand which of the two words he or she
doth approve; and according to that sentence fix my resolution
and affection without change.

QUARLOUS: Agreed. My word is conceived already.

WINWIFE: And mine shall not be long creating after.

GRACE: But you shall promise, gentlemen, not to be curious to
know which of you it is, taken; but give me leave to conceal
that till you have brought me either home, or where I may
safely tender myself.

WINWIFE: Why, that's but equal.

QUARLOUS: We are pleased.

GRACE: Because I will bind both your endeavours to work together, friendly and jointly, each to the other's fortune, and

33. *discourse:* rationality.   36. *to making:* to be trained.
37. *toward:* in store for.   38. *motion:* suggestion.
42. *tables:* writing tablets.
56. *tender:* take care of.
57. *equal:* fair.

have myself fitted with some means to make him that is forsaken a part of amends.

QUARLOUS: These conditions are very courteous. Well, my word
is out of the *Arcadia*, then: 'Argalus'.

WINWIFE: And mine out of the play, 'Palemon'.

TROUBLE-ALL *comes again.*

TROUBLE-ALL: Have you any warrant for this, gentlemen?

QUARLOUS, WINWIFE: Ha!

TROUBLE-ALL: There must be a warrant had, believe it.

WINWIFE: For what?

TROUBLE-ALL: For whatsoever it is, anything indeed, no matter   70
what.

QUARLOUS: 'Slight, here's a fine ragged prophet, dropped down
i' the nick!

TROUBLE-ALL: Heaven quit you, gentlemen.

QUARLOUS: Nay, stay a little. Good lady, put him to the question.

GRACE: You are content, then?

WINWIFE, QUARLOUS: Yes, yes.

GRACE: Sir, here are two names written –

TROUBLE-ALL: Is Justice Overdo one?

GRACE: How, sir? I pray you read 'em to yourself – it is for a   80
wager between these gentlemen – and with a stroke or any
difference, mark which you approve best.

TROUBLE-ALL: They may be both worshipful names for ought I
know, mistress, but Adam Overdo had been worth three of 'em,
I assure you, in this place; that's in plain English.

GRACE: This man amazes me! I pray you, like one of 'em, sir.

TROUBLE-ALL: I do like him there, that has the best warrant.
Mistress, to save your longing (and multiply him), it may be
this. [*Marks the book.*] But I am ay still for Justice Overdo,
that's my conscience. And quit you.   90
[*Exit.*]

WINWIFE: Is't done, lady?

GRACE: Ay, and strangely as ever I saw! What fellow is this, trow?

QUARLOUS: No matter what, a fortune-teller we ha' made him.
Which is't, which is't?

GRACE: Nay, did you not promise not to inquire?

82. *difference:* distinguishing marks.

[*Enter* EDGWORTH.]

QUARLOUS: 'Slid, I forgot that, pray you pardon me. Look, here's our Mercury come. The licence arrives i' the finest time, too! 'Tis but scraping out Cokes's name, and 'tis done.

WINWIFE: How now, lime-twig? Hast thou touched?

100 EDGWORTH: Not yet, sir; except you would go with me and see't, it's not worth speaking on. The act is nothing without a witness. Yonder he is, your man with the box, fall'n into the finest company, and so transported with vapours; they ha' got in a northern clothier and one Puppy, a western man, that's come to wrestle before my Lord Mayor anon, and Captain Whit, and one Val Cutting, that helps Captain Jordan to roar, a circling boy; with whom your Numps is so taken that you may strip him of his clothes, if you will. I'll undertake to geld him for you, if you had but a surgeon ready to sear him. And

110 Mistress Justice, there, is the goodest woman! She does so love 'em all over, in terms of justice and the style of authority, with her hood upright – that I beseech you come away, gentlemen, and see't.

QUARLOUS: 'Slight, I would not lose it for the Fair; what'll you do, Ned?

WINWIFE: Why, stay here about for you; Mistress Wellborn must not be seen.

QUARLOUS: Do so, and find out a priest i' the meantime; I'll bring the licence. [*To* EDGWORTH] Lead, which way is't?

[*Exeunt* WINWIFE *and* GRACE.]

120 EDGWORTH: Here, sir, you are o' the backside o' the booth already; you may hear the noise.

IV, iv [KNOCKEM, NORTHERN, PUPPY, CUTTING, WHIT, WASP, *and* MISTRESS OVERDO *discovered drinking in Ursula's booth.*]

[KNOCKEM:] Whit, bid Val Cutting continue the vapours for a lift, Whit, for a lift.

99. *lime-twig:* see III, v; (here): a thief.
105. *wrestle:* Note.
107. *circling boy:* a thief's bully or decoy; see IV, iv.
2. *lift:* theft, trick.

NORTHERN: I'll ne mare, I'll ne mare, the eale's too meeghty.

KNOCKEM: How now! my Galloway Nag, the staggers? Ha! Whit, gi' him a slit i' the forehead. Cheer up, man; a needle and thread to stitch his ears. I'd cure him now, an' I had it, with a little butter and garlic, long-pepper, and grains. Where's my horn? I'll gi' him a mash, presently, shall take away this dizziness.

PUPPY: Why, where are you, zurs? Do you vlinch and leave us i' the zuds, now? 10

NORTHERN: I'll ne mare, I is e'en as vull as a paiper's bag, by my troth, I.

PUPPY: Do my northern cloth zhrink i' the wetting, ha?

KNOCKEM: Why, well said, old flea-bitten, thou'lt never tire, I see.

   They fall to their vapours, again.

CUTTING: No, sir, but he may tire, if it please him.

WHIT: Who told dee sho? that he vuld never teer, man?

CUTTING: No matter who told him so, so long as he knows.

KNOCKEM: Nay, I know nothing, sir, pardon me there. 20

EDGWORTH [*to* QUARLOUS]: They are at it still, sir; this they call vapours.

WHIT: He shall not pardon dee, Captain, dou shalt not be pardoned. Pre'de shweetheart, do not pardon him.

CUTTING: 'Slight, I'll pardon him, an' I list, whosoever says nay to't.

QUARLOUS: Where's Numps? I miss him.

WASP: Why, I say nay to't.

QUARLOUS: O there he is!

KNOCKEM: To what do you say nay, sir? 30

   Here they continue their game of vapours, which is nonsense: every man to oppose the last man that spoke, whether it concerned him or no.

WASP: To anything, whatsoever it is, so long as I do not like it.

WHIT: Pardon me, little man, dou musht like it a little.

CUTTING: No, he must not like it at all, sir; there you are i' the wrong.

   4. *Galloway Nag:* a small, hardy Scots horse.
   4. *the staggers:* a dizziness in horses.   11. *i' the zuds:* in difficulty.

WHIT: I tink I be; he musht not like it, indeed.

CUTTING: Nay, then he both must and will like it, sir, for all you.

KNOCKEM: If he have reason, he may like it, sir.

WHIT: By no meansh, Captain, upon reason; he may like nothing upon reason.

40 WASP: I have no reason, nor I will hear of no reason, nor I will look for no reason, and he is an ass that either knows any or looks for't from me.

CUTTING: Yes, in some sense you may have reason, sir.

WASP: Ay, in some sense, I care not if I grant you.

WHIT: Pardon me, thou ougsht to grant him nothing, in no shensh, if dou do love dyshelf, angry man.

WASP: Why then, I do grant him nothing; and I have no sense.

CUTTING: 'Tis true, thou hast no sense indeed.

WASP: 'Slid, but I have sense, now I think on't better, and I will
50 grant him anything, do you see?

KNOCKEM: He is i' the right, and does utter a sufficient vapour.

CUTTING: Nay, it is no sufficient vapour, neither; I deny that.

KNOCKEM: Then it is a sweet vapour.

CUTTING: It may be a sweet vapour.

WASP: Nay, it is no sweet vapour, neither, sir; it stinks, and I'll stand to't.

WHIT: Yes, I tink it doesh shtink, Captain. All vapour doesh shtink.

WASP: Nay, then it does not stink, sir, and it shall not stink.

60 CUTTING: By your leave, it may, sir.

WASP: Ay, by my leave, it may stink; I know that.

WHIT: Pardon me, thou knowesht nothing; it cannot by thy leave, angry man.

WASP: How can it not?

KNOCKEM: Nay, never question him, for he is i' the right.

WHIT: Yesh, I am i' de right, I confesh it; so ish de little man too.

WASP: I'll have nothing confessed that concerns me. I am not i' the right, nor never was i' the right, nor never will be i' the right, while I am in my right mind.

70 CUTTING: Mind? Why, here's no man minds you, sir, nor anything else.

They drink again.

PUPPY: Vriend, will you mind this that we do?

QUARLOUS [to EDGWORTH]: Call you this vapours? This is such belching of quarrel as I never heard. Will you mind your business, sir?

EDGWORTH: You shall see, sir.

NORTHERN: I'll ne mair, my waimb warks too mickle with this aureaddy.

EDGWORTH: Will you take that, Master Wasp, that nobody should mind you? 80

WASP: Why? What ha' you to do? Is't any matter to you?

EDGWORTH: No, but methinks you should not be unminded, though.

WASP: Nor I wu' not be, now I think on't; do you hear, new acquaintance, does no man mind me, say you?

CUTTING: Yes, sir, every man here minds you, but how?

WASP: Nay, I care as little how as you do; that was not my question.

WHIT: No, noting was ty question; tou art a learned man, and I am a valiant man; i' faith la, tou shalt speak for me, and I vill 90 fight for tee.

KNOCKEM: Fight for him, Whit? A gross vapour; he can fight for himself.

WASP: It may be I can, but it may be I wu' not, how then?

CUTTING: Why, then you may choose.

WASP: Why, and I'll choose whether I'll choose or no.

KNOCKEM: I think you may, and 'tis true; and I allow it for a resolute vapour.

WASP: Nay, then, I do think you do not think and it is no resolute vapour. 100

CUTTING: Yes, in some sort he may allow you.

KNOCKEM: In no sort, sir, pardon me, I can allow him nothing. You mistake the vapour.

WASP: He mistakes nothing, sir, in no sort.

WHIT: Yes, I pre dee now, let him mistake.

WASP: A turd i' your teeth, never pre dee me, for I will have nothing mistaken.

KNOCKEM: Turd, ha, turd? A noisome vapour; strike, Whit.

77. *waimb*: stomach.

419

They fall by the ears.

[EDGWORTH *steals the licence out of the box. Exit.*]

MISTRESS OVERDO: Why gentlemen, why gentlemen, I charge
110   you upon my authority, conserve the peace. In the King's name,
and my husband's, put up your weapons; I shall be driven to
commit you myself, else.

QUARLOUS: Ha, ha, ha.

WASP: Why do you laugh, sir?

QUARLOUS: Sir, you'll allow me my Christian liberty. I may
laugh, I hope.

CUTTING: In some sort you may, and in some sort you may not,
sir.

KNOCKEM: Nay, in some sort, sir, he may neither laugh nor hope
120   in this company.

WASP: Yes, then he may both laugh and hope in any sort, an't
please him.

QUARLOUS: Faith, and I will then, for it doth please me exceedingly.

WASP: No exceeding neither, sir.

KNOCKEM: No, that vapour is too lofty.

QUARLOUS: Gentlemen, I do not play well at your game of
vapours; I am not very good at it, but –

CUTTING: Do you hear, sir? I would speak with you in circle!
He draws a circle on the ground.

130 QUARLOUS: In circle, sir? What would you with me in circle?

CUTTING: Can you lend me a piece, a jacobus, in circle?

QUARLOUS: 'Slid, your circle will prove more costly than your
vapours, then. Sir, no, I lend you none.

CUTTING: Your beard's not well turned up, sir.

QUARLOUS: How, rascal? Are you playing with my beard? I'll
break circle with you.
They draw all, and fight.

PUPPY, NORTHERN: Gentlemen, gentlemen!

KNOCKEM [*aside*]: Gather up, Whit, gather up, Whit. Good
vapours!

112. *commit:* send to prison.   117. *in some sort:* to some extent.
125. *exceeding:* being presumptuous.
131. *jacobus:* gold sovereign issued at King James's accession.

[*Exit.*]

[WHIT *takes the cloaks and hides them.*]

MISTRESS OVERDO: What mean you? are you rebels, gentle- 140
men? Shall I send out a sergeant-at-arms or a writ o' rebellion
against you? I'll commit you, upon my womanhood, for a riot,
upon my justice-hood, if you persist.

[*Exeunt* QUARLOUS *and* CUTTING.]

WASP: Upon your justice-hood? Marry, shit o' your hood; you'll
commit? Spoke like a true Justice of Peace's wife, indeed, and a
fine female lawyer! Turd i' your teeth for a fee, now.

MISTRESS OVERDO: Why, Numps, in Master Overdo's name, I
charge you.

WASP: Good Mistress Underdo, hold your tongue.

MISTRESS OVERDO: Alas! poor Numps. 150

WASP: Alas! And why alas from you, I beseech you? Or why
poor Numps, Goody Rich? Am I come to be pitied by your
tuft taffeta now? Why mistress, I knew Adam, the clerk, your
husband, when he was Adam scrivener, and writ for twopence
a sheet, as high as he bears his head now, or you your hood,
dame.

The watch comes in.

What are you, sir?

BRISTLE: We be men, and no infidels. What is the matter here,
and the noises? Can you tell?

WASP: Heart, what ha' you to do? Cannot a man quarrel in quiet- 160
ness, but he must be put out on't by you? What are you?

BRISTLE: Why, we be His Majesty's Watch, sir.

WASP: Watch? 'Sblood, you are a sweet watch, indeed. A body
would think, an' you watched well a-nights, you should be contented to sleep at this time a-day. Get you to your fleas and
your flock-beds, you rogues, your kennels, and lie down close.

BRISTLE: Down? Yes, we will down, I warrant you – down with
him in His Majesty's name, down, down with him, and carry
him away to the pigeon-holes!

142. *commit:* see line 112, above; here pun on other sense, 'fornicate'.
153. *tuft taffeta:* tufted or fancily woven taffeta.
166. *flock-beds:* beds filled with wool or cotton, not feathers.
169. *pigeon-holes:* the stocks.

[BRISTLE *and* POACHER *seize* WASP.]

170 MISTRESS OVERDO: I thank you, honest friends, in the behalf o' the Crown and the peace, and in Master Overdo's name, for suppressing enormities.

WHIT: Stay, Bristle, here ish a noder brash o' drunkards, but very quiet, special drunkards, will pay dee five shillings very well. Take 'em to dee, in de graish o' God. One of 'em does change cloth for ale in the Fair here, te toder ish a strong man, a mighty man, my Lord Mayor's man, and a wrestler. He has wreshled so long with the bottle, here, that the man with the beard hash almost streek up hish heelsh.

180 BRISTLE: 'Slid, the Clerk o' the Market has been to cry him all the Fair over, here, for my Lord's service.

WHIT: Tere he ish, pre de taik him hensh and make ty best on him.

[*Exit the* WATCH *with* WASP, NORTHERN, *and* PUPPY.]

How now, woman o' shilk, vat ailsh ty shweet faish? Art tou melancholy?

MISTRESS OVERDO: A little distempered with these enormities. Shall I entreat a courtesy of you, Captain?

WHIT: Entreat a hundred, velvet voman, I vill do it; shpeak out.

MISTRESS OVERDO: I cannot with modesty speak it out, but –
[*Whispers.*]

WHIT: I vill do it, and more, and more, for dee. What, Urs'la,

190 an't be bitch, an't be bawd, an't be!
[*Enter* URSULA.]

URSULA: How now, rascal? What roar you for, old pimp?

WHIT [*to* URSULA]: Here, put up de cloaks, Ursh; de purchase; pre dee now, shweet Ursh, help dis good brave voman to a jordan, an't be.

URSULA: 'Slid, call your Captain Jordan to her, can you not?

WHIT: Nay, pre dee leave dy consheits, and bring the velvet woman to de –

URSULA: I bring her! Hang her! Heart, must I find a common pot for every punk i' your purlieus?

200 WHIT: O good voordsh, Ursh; it ish a guest o' velvet, i' fait la.

178. *man with the beard:* jug with a face on it; toby-jug.
180. *Clerk o' the Market:* official in charge of the Fair.
199. *purlieus:* suburbs, disreputable areas.

URSULA. Let her sell her hood and buy a sponge, with a pox to
her. My vessel is employed, sir. I have but one, and 'tis the
bottom of an old bottle. An honest proctor and his wife are at
it, within; if she'll stay her time, so.
[*Exit* URSULA.]

WHIT: As soon ash tou cansht, shweet Ursh. Of a valiant man I
tink I am the patientsh man i' the world, or in all Smithfield.
[*Re-enter* KNOCKEM.]

KNOCKEM: How now, Whit? Close vapours, stealing your leaps?
Covering in corners, ha?

WHIT: No, fait, Captain, dough tou beesht a vishe man, dy vit is
a mile hence, now. I vas procuring a shmall courtesy for a   210
woman of fashion here.

MISTRESS OVERDO: Yes, Captain, though I am Justice of Peace's
wife, I do love men of war and the sons of the sword, when they
come before my husband.

KNOCKEM: Say'st thou so, filly? Thou shalt have a leap presently;
I'll horse thee myself, else.
[*Re-enter* URSULA, *followed by* LITTLEWIT *and* MISTRESS
LITTLEWIT.]

URSULA: Come, will you bring her in now? and let her take her
turn?

WHIT: Gramercy, good Ursh, I tank dee.

MISTRESS OVERDO: Master Overdo shall thank her.   220
[*Exit.*]

[LITTLEWIT:] Good Gammer Urs, Win and I are exceedingly   IV, V
beholden to you, and to Captain Jordan and Captain Whit.
Win, I'll be bold to leave you i' this good company, Win, for
half an hour or so, Win, while I go and see how my matter goes
forward, and if the puppets be perfect; and then I'll come and
fetch you, Win.

MISTRESS LITTLEWIT: Will you leave me alone with two men,
John?

LITTLEWIT: Ay, they are honest gentlemen, Win, Captain

207. *leaps:* sexual acts.
208. *covering:* copulating.

423

10 Jordan and Captain Whit; they'll use you very civilly, Win; God b' w' you, Win.

[*Exit.*]

URSULA [*to* KNOCKEM *and* WHIT]: What, 's her husband gone?

KNOCKEM: On his false gallop, Urs, away.

URSULA: An' you be right Barthol'mew-birds, now show yourselves so: we are undone for want of fowl i' the Fair, here. Here will be 'Zekiel Edgworth and three or four gallants with him at night, and I ha' neither plover nor quail for 'em. Persuade this between you two to become a bird o' the game, while I work the velvet woman within, as you call her.

20 KNOCKEM: I conceive thee, Urs! go thy ways.

[*Exit* URSULA.]

Dost thou hear, Whit? is't not pity my delicate dark chestnut here – with the fine lean head, large forehead, round eyes, even mouth, sharp ears, long neck, thin crest, close withers, plain back, deep sides, short fillets, and full flanks; with a round belly, a plump buttock, large thighs, knit knees, straight legs, short pasterns, smooth hoofs, and short heels – should lead a dull honest woman's life, that might live the life of a lady?

WHIT: Yes, by my fait and trot it is, Captain. De honesht woman's life is a scurvy dull life, indeed la.

30 MISTRESS LITTLEWIT: How, sir? Is an honest woman's life a scurvy life?

WHIT: Yes, fait, shweetheart, believe him, de leef of a bondwoman! But if dou vilt harken to me, I vill make tee a freewoman and a lady. Dou shalt live like a lady, as te Captain saish.

KNOCKEM: Ay, and be honest too, sometimes; have her wires and her tires, her green gowns and velvet petticoats.

WHIT: Ay, and ride to Ware and Rumford i' dy coach, shee de players, be in love vit 'em; sup vit gallantsh, be drunk, and cost de noting.

---

12. *What's:* for what reason is.

17. *plover, quail:* whores.

18. *bird o' the game:* as above.

35. *wires:* stiffeners in ruffs.   36. *tires.* attire, dresses.

36. *green gowns:* play of words suggesting seduction on the grass; thus green was a colour associated with prostitutes.

KNOCKEM: Brave vapours! 40

WHIT: And lie by twenty on 'em, if dou pleast, shweetheart.

MISTRESS LITTLEWIT: What, and be honest still? That were fine sport.

WHIT: Tish common, shweetheart; tou may'st do it, by my hand. It shall be justified to ty husband's faish, now; tou shalt be as honesht as the skin between his hornsh, la!

KNOCKEM: Yes, and wear a dressing, top and top-gallant, to compare with e'er a husband on 'em all, for a fore-top. It is the vapour of spirit in the wife to cuckold, nowadays, as it is the vapour of fashion in the husband not to suspect. Your prying 50 cat-eyed-citizen is an abominable vapour.

MISTRESS LITTLEWIT: Lord, what a fool have I been!

WHIT: Mend, then, and do everyting like a lady hereafter; never know ty husband from another man.

KNOCKEM: Nor any one man from another, but i' the dark.

WHIT: Ay, and then it ish no dishgrash to know any man.

[*Re-enter* URSULA.]

URSULA: Help, help here!

KNOCKEM: How now? What vapour's there?

URSULA: O, you are a sweet ranger! and look well to your walks! Yonder is your punk of Turnbull, Ramping Alice, has fall'n 60 upon the poor gentlewoman within, and pulled her hood over her ears, and her hair through it.

ALICE *enters, beating the Justice's wife.*

MISTRESS OVERDO: Help, help, i' the King's name!

PUNK ALICE: A mischief on you, they are such as you are that undo us, and take our trade from us, with your tuft taffeta haunches.

KNOCKEM: How now, Alice!

PUNK ALICE: The poor common whores can ha' no traffic for the privy rich ones; your caps and hoods of velvet call away our customers and lick the fat from us. 70

URSULA: Peace, you foul ramping jade, you –

PUNK ALICE: Od's foot, you bawd in grease, are you talking?

47. *top and top-gallant:* in full sail.
48. *fore-top:* top of a mast.
72. *in grease:* fattened for the killing.

KNOCKEM: Why, Alice, I say.

PUNK ALICE: Thou sow of Smithfield, thou!

URSULA: Thou tripe of Turnbull!

KNOCKEM: Cat-a-mountain vapours! ha!

URSULA: You know where you were tawed lately, both lashed and slashed you were in Bridewell.

PUNK ALICE: Ay, by the same token, you rid that week, and
80   broke out the bottom o' the cart, night-tub.

KNOCKEM: Why, lion face! ha! do you know who I am? Shall I tear ruff, slit waistcoat, make rags of petticoat? Ha! go to, vanish, for fear of vapours. Whit, a kick, Whit, in the parting vapour.

[*They kick out* PUNK ALICE.]

Come, brave woman, take a good heart, thou shalt be a lady, too.

WHIT: Yes, fait, dey shall all both be ladies and write Madam. I vill do't myself for dem. Do is the vord, and D is the middle letter of Madam. DD, put 'em together and make deeds, with-
90   out which all words are alike, la.

KNOCKEM: 'Tis true. Urs'la, take 'em in, open thy wardrobe, and fit 'em to their calling. Green gowns, crimson petticoats, green women! My Lord Mayor's green women! guests o' the game, true bred. I'll provide you a coach to take the air in.

MISTRESS LITTLEWIT: But do you think you can get one?

KNOCKEM: O, they are as common as wheelbarrows where there are great dunghills. Every pettifogger's wife has 'em; for first he buys a coach, that he may marry, and then he marries that he may be made cuckold in't. For if their wives ride not to their
100   cuckolding, they do 'em no credit. Hide and be hidden; ride and be ridden, says the vapour of experience.

[*Exeunt* URSULA, MISTRESS LITTLEWIT, *and* MISTRESS OVERDO.]

76. *Cat-a-mountain*: panther or leopard.
77. *tawed*: softened by beating (tanners' term); here, beaten.
79. *rid*: i.e. in the cart, as a public punishment for being a whore.
80. *night-tub*: synonym for jordan, chamber-pot.
82. *waistcoat*: a woman's undergarment: as an outer garment usually a sign of a whore or '*waistcoateer*'.

[*Enter* TROUBLE-ALL.]

TROUBLE-ALL: By what warrant does it say so?

KNOCKEM: Ha! mad child o' the Pie-powders, art thou there? Fill us a fresh can, Urs; we may drink together.

TROUBLE-ALL: I may not drink without a warrant, Captain.

KNOCKEM: 'Slood, thou'll not stale without a warrant, shortly. Whit, give me pen, ink, and paper. I'll draw him a warrant presently.

TROUBLE-ALL: It must be Justice Overdo's.

KNOCKEM: I know, man. Fetch the drink, Whit.

[KNOCKEM *writes on a paper.*]

WHIT: I pre dee now, be very brief, Captain; for de new ladies 10 stay for dee.

[KNOCKEM *gives* TROUBLE-ALL *the paper.*]

KNOCKEM: O, as brief as can be; here 'tis already. 'Adam Overdo.'

TROUBLE-ALL: Why, now I'll pledge you, Captain.

KNOCKEM: Drink it off. I'll come to thee, anon, again.

[*Exit* KNOCKEM *into Ursula's booth. Exit* TROUBLE-ALL. *Enter* QUARLOUS, EDGWORTH.]

QUARLOUS: Well, sir, you are now discharged;   QUARLOUS beware of being spied, hereafter.   *to the cutpurse.*

EDGWORTH: Sir, will it please you enter in here at Urs'la's and take part of a silken gown, a velvet petticoat, or a wrought smock? I am promised such, and I can spare any gentleman a 20 moiety.

QUARLOUS: Keep it for your companions in beastliness; I am none of 'em, sir. If I had not already forgiven you a greater trespass, or thought you yet worth my beating, I would instruct your manners, to whom you made your offers. But go your ways, talk not to me, the hangman is only fit to discourse with you; the hand of beadle is too merciful a punishment for your trade of life.

[*Exit* EDGWORTH.]

I am sorry I employed this fellow; for he thinks me such: *Facinus quos inquinat, aequat.* But it was for sport. And would I 30

7. *presently:* at once.   19. *take part of:* partake of, share.
21. *moiety:* a half.

make it serious, the getting of this licence is nothing to me, without other circumstances concur. I do think how impertinently I labour, if the word be not mine that the ragged fellow marked; and what advantage I have given Ned Winwife in this time now, of working her, though it be mine. He'll go near to form to her what a debauched rascal I am, and fright her out of all good conceit of me. I should do so by him, I am sure, if I had the opportunity. But my hope is in her temper, yet; and it must needs be next to despair, that is grounded on any part of
40 a woman's discretion. I would give, by my troth, now, all I could spare (to my clothes and my sword) to meet my tattered soothsayer again, who was my judge i' the question, to know certainly whose word he has damned or saved. For till then I live but under a reprieve. I must seek him. Who be these?

[*Enter* BRISTLE *and* POACHER *with* WASP.]

WASP: Sir, you are a Welsh cuckold, and a prating runt, and no constable.

BRISTLE: You say very well. Come put in his leg in the middle roundel, and let him hole there.

[*They put him in the stocks.*]

WASP: You stink of leeks, metheglin, and cheese, you rogue.

50 BRISTLE: Why, what is that to you, if you sit sweetly in the stocks in the meantime? If you have a mind to stink too, your breeches sit close enough to your bum. Sit you merry, sir.

QUARLOUS: How now, Numps?

WASP: It is no matter how; pray you look off.

QUARLOUS: Nay, I'll not offend you, Numps. I thought you had sat there to be seen.

WASP: And to be sold, did you not? Pray you mind your business, an' you have any.

QUARLOUS: Cry you mercy, Numps. Does your leg lie high
60 enough?

[*Enter* HAGGIS *and others of the Watch with* JUSTICE OVERDO, *still disguised, and* BUSY.]

---

32. *impertinently:* to no purpose. 36. *form:* formulate, describe.
37. *conceit:* opinion, estimate.
45. *runt:* ignorant lout.
49. *metheglin:* Welsh mead.

BRISTLE: How now, neighbour Haggis, what says Justice Over-do's worship to the other offenders?

HAGGIS: Why, he says just nothing; what should he say? Or where should he say? He is not to be found, man. He ha' not been seen i' the Fair, here, all this live-long day, never since seven o'clock i' the morning. His clerks know not what to think on't. There is no court of Pie-powders yet. Here they be returned.

BRISTLE: What shall be done with 'em, then, in your discretion?

HAGGIS: I think we were best put 'em in the stocks, in discretion 70 (there they will be safe in discretion) for the valour of an hour or such a thing, till his worship come.

BRISTLE: It is but a hole matter if we do, neighbour Haggis. [To WASP] Come, sir, here is company for you. Heave up the stocks.

WASP [aside]: I shall put a trick upon your Welsh diligence, perhaps.

As they [re-]open the stocks, WASP puts his shoe on his hand and slips it in for his leg.

BRISTLE [To BUSY]: Put in your leg, sir.

They bring BUSY, and put him in.

QUARLOUS: What, Rabbi Busy! Is he come?

BUSY: I do obey thee; the lion may roar, but he cannot bite. I am glad to be thus separated from the heathen of the land, and put 80 apart in the stocks for the holy cause.

WASP: What are you, sir?

BUSY: One that rejoiceth in his affliction and sitteth here to prophesy the destruction of fairs and May-games, wakes and Whitsun-ales, and doth sigh and groan, for the reformation of these abuses.

[They put JUSTICE OVERDO in the stocks.]

WASP [to OVERDO]: And do you sigh and groan, too, or rejoice in your affliction?

OVERDO: I do not feel it, I do not think of it, it is a thing without

69. *discretion:* successively used here in different senses – (1) judgement, opinion; (2) prudence; (3) separation.
71. *valour:* amount.
80. *separated:* reference to Separatists, or Nonconformists.
89. *without:* outside of.

90   me. Adam, thou art above these batt'ries, these contumelies. *In te manca ruit fortuna*, as thy friend Horace says; thou art one, *Quem neque pauperies, neque mors, neque vincula terrent*. And therefore, as another friend of thine says (I think it be thy friend Persius), *Non te quaesiveris extra*.

QUARLOUS: What's here? A stoic i' the stocks? The fool is turned philosopher.

BUSY: Friend, I will leave to communicate my spirit with you if I hear any more of those superstitious relics, those lists of Latin, the very rags of Rome and patches of Popery.

100 WASP: Nay, an' you begin to quarrel, gentlemen, I'll leave you. I ha' paid for quarrelling too lately. Look you, a device, but shifting in a hand for a foot. God b' w' you.

   He gets out.

BUSY: Wilt thou then leave thy brethren in tribulation?

WASP: For this once, sir.

   [*Exit.*]

BUSY: Thou art a halting neutral – Stay him there, stop him! – that will not endure the heat of persecution.

BRISTLE: How, now, what's the matter?

BUSY: He is fled, he is fled, and dares not sit it out.

BRISTLE: What, has he made an escape? Which way? Follow,
110   neighbour Haggis!

   [*Exeunt* BRISTLE *and* HAGGIS. *Enter* DAME PURECRAFT.]

DAME PURECRAFT: O me! In the stocks! Have the wicked prevailed?

BUSY: Peace, religious sister; it is my calling, comfort yourself, an extraordinary calling, and done for my better standing, my surer standing hereafter.

   The madman enters.

TROUBLE-ALL: By whose warrant, by whose warrant, this?

QUARLOUS: O, here's my man dropped in, I looked for.

OVERDO: Ha!

DAME PURECRAFT: O good sir, they have set the faithful here to
120   be wondered at; and provided holes for the holy of the land.

         90. *contumelies:* insults.
         98. *lists:* strips (of cloth).
         105. *a halting neutral:* someone not of the elect.

TROUBLE-ALL: Had they warrant for it? Showed they Justice
Overdo's hand? If they had no warrant, they shall answer it.

[*Re-enter* BRISTLE *and* HAGGIS.]

BRISTLE: Sure you did not lock the stocks sufficiently, neighbour
Toby!

HAGGIS: No? See if you can lock 'em better.

BRISTLE [*tries the lock*]: They are very sufficiently locked, and
truly, yet something is in the matter.

TROUBLE-ALL: True, your warrant is the matter that is in
question; by what warrant?

BRISTLE: Madman, hold your peace; I will put you in his room 130
else, in the very same hole, do you see?

QUARLOUS: How? Is he a madman?

TROUBLE-ALL: Show me Justice Overdo's warrant, I obey you.

HAGGIS: You are a mad fool; hold your tongue.

TROUBLE-ALL: In Justice Overdo's name I drink to you, and
here's my warrant.

Shows his can.

[*Exeunt* BRISTLE *and* HAGGIS.]

OVERDO [*aside*]: Alas, poor wretch! How it earns my heart for
him!

QUARLOUS [*aside*]: If he be mad, it is in vain to question him. I'll
try, though. [*To him*] Friend, there was a gentlewoman showed 140
you two names, some hour since, Argalus and Palemon, to
mark in a book. Which of 'em was it you marked?

TROUBLE-ALL: I mark no name but Adam Overdo; that is the
name of names; he only is the sufficient magistrate; and that
name I reverence; show it me.

QUARLOUS [*aside*]: This fellow's mad indeed. I am further off now
than afore.

OVERDO [*aside*]: I shall not breathe in peace till I have made him
some amends.

QUARLOUS [*aside*]: Well, I will make another use of him, is come 150
in my head: I have a nest of beards in my trunk, one something
like his.

[*Exit.*]

137. *earns:* grieves. Some editors read 'yearns', following Whalley
(1736).

The watchmen come back again.

BRISTLE: This mad fool has made me that I know not whether I have locked the stocks or no; I think I locked 'em.

[*He tries the lock.*]

TROUBLE-ALL: Take Adam Overdo in your mind and fear nothing.

BRISTLE: 'Slid, madness itself, hold thy peace, and take that.

[*Strikes him.*]

TROUBLE-ALL: Strikes thou without a warrant? Take thou that.

The madman fights with 'em, and they leave open the stocks.

BUSY: We are delivered by miracle; fellow in fetters, let us not
160 refuse the means; this madness was of the spirit. The malice of the enemy hath mocked itself.

[*Exeunt* BUSY *and* JUSTICE OVERDO.]

DAME PURECRAFT: Mad, do they call him! The world is mad in error, but he is mad in truth. I love him o' the sudden (the cunning-man said all true), and shall love him more and more. How well it becomes a man to be mad in truth! O, that I might be his yoke-fellow and be mad with him! What a many should we draw to madness in truth with us!

[*Exit.*]

The watch, missing them, are affrighted.

BRISTLE: How now? All 'scaped? Where's the woman? It is witchcraft! Her velvet hat is a witch, o' my conscience, or my key, t'one! The madman was a devil and I am an ass; so bless
170 me, my place, and mine office.

[*Exeunt.*]

169. *t'one:* the one or the other.

ACT FIVE

[*The Fair.*]

[*Enter* LEATHERHEAD *with* FILCHER *and* SHARKWELL, *door-keepers. They begin to erect the puppet-theatre.*]

[LEATHERHEAD:] Well, luck and Saint Barthol'mew! Out with the sign of our invention, in the name of wit, and do you beat the drum the while. All the fowl i' the Fair, I mean all the dirt in Smithfield (that's one of Master Littlewit's carwitchets now), will be thrown at our banner today if the matter does not please the people. O the motions that I, Lantern Leatherhead, have given light to i' my time, since my Master Pod died! *Jerusalem* was a stately thing, and so was *Nineveh*, and *The City of Norwich*, and *Sodom and Gomorrah*, with the rising o' the prentices and pulling down the bawdy-houses there, upon Shrove 10 Tuesday; but *The Gunpowder Plot*, there was a get-penny! I have presented that to an eighteen- or twenty-pence audience nine times in an afternoon. Your home-born projects prove ever the best, they are so easy and familiar. They put too much learning i' their things nowadays, and that I fear will be the spoil o' this. Littlewit? I say Micklewit! if not too mickle! – Look to your gathering there, Goodman Filcher.

FILCHER: I warrant you, sir.

LEATHERHEAD: An' there come any gentlefolks, take twopence a piece, Sharkwell. 20

SHARKWELL: I warrant you, sir, three pence an' we can.

The JUSTICE *comes in like a porter.*　　　　　v, ii

[OVERDO:] This later disguise, I have borrowed of a porter, shall carry me out to all my great and good ends; which, however

---

2. *sign:* the 'banner' mentioned in line 5. Note.
2. *invention:* here puppet-play.　　4. *carwitchets:* quibbles, puns.
11. *get-penny:* box-office draw.
13. *home-born projects:* subjects of local and national origin.
16. *mickle:* great.

interrupted, were never destroyed in me. Neither is the hour of my severity yet come, to reveal myself, wherein, cloud-like, I will break out in rain and hail, lightning and thunder, upon the head of enormity. Two main works I have to prosecute: first, one is to invent some satisfaction for the poor kind wretch who is out of his wits for my sake; and yonder I see him coming. I will walk aside and project for it.

[*Enter* WINWIFE *and* GRACE.]

10 WINWIFE: I wonder where Tom Quarlous is, that he returns not; it may be he is struck in here to seek us.

GRACE: See, here's our madman again.

[*Enter* QUARLOUS *and* DAME PURECRAFT.] QUARLOUS *in the habit of the madman is mistaken by* MISTRESS PURECRAFT.

QUARLOUS [*aside*]: I have made myself as like him as his gown and cap will give me leave.

DAME PURECRAFT: Sir, I love you, and would be glad to be mad with you in truth.

WINWIFE: How! my widow in love with a madman?

DAME PURECRAFT: Verily, I can be as mad in spirit as you.

QUARLOUS: By whose warrant? Leave your canting. [*To* GRACE]
20 Gentlewoman, have I found you? (Save ye, quit ye, and multiply ye.) Where's your book? 'Twas a sufficient name I marked, let me see't, be not afraid to show't me.

He desires to see the book of MISTRESS GRACE.

GRACE: What would you with it, sir?

QUARLOUS: Mark it again and again, at your service.

GRACE: Here it is, sir; this was it you marked.

QUARLOUS: 'Palemon'? Fare you well, fare you well.

WINWIFE: How, Palemon!

GRACE: Yes, faith, he has discovered it to you now, and therefore 'twere vain to disguise it longer: I am yours. sir, by the benefit
30 of your fortune.

WINWIFE: And you have him, Mistress, believe it, that shall never give you cause to repent her benefit, but make you rather to think that, in this choice, she had both her eyes.

GRACE: I desire to put it to no danger of protestation.

9. *project:* plan.
19. *canting:* pious Puritan jargon.

434

[*Exeunt* WINWIFE *and* GRACE.]

QUARLOUS [*aside*]: Palemon the word and Winwife the man?

DAME PURECRAFT: Good sir, vouchsafe a yoke-fellow in your madness; shun not one of the sanctified sisters, that would draw with you in truth.

QUARLOUS: Away! You are a herd of hypocritical proud ignorants, rather wild than mad, fitter for woods and the society 40 of beasts than houses and the congregation of men. You are the second part of the society of canters, outlaws to order and discipline, and the only privileged church-robbers of Christendom. Let me alone. – [*Aside*] Palemon the word and Winwife the man?

DAME PURECRAFT [*aside*]: I must uncover myself unto him or I shall never enjoy him, for all the cunning-men's promises. – Good sir, hear me: I am worth six thousand pound; my love to you is become my rack; I'll tell you all, and the truth, since you hate the hypocrisy of the party-coloured Brotherhood. These 50 seven years I have been a wilful holy widow only to draw feasts and gifts from my entangled suitors. I am also by office an assisting sister of the Deacons and a devourer, instead of a distributor, of the alms. I am a special maker of marriages for our decayed Brethren with our rich widows, for a third part of their wealth, when they are married, for the relief of the poor elect; as also our poor handsome young virgins with our wealthy bachelors or widowers, to make them steal from their husbands when I have confirmed them in the faith and got all put into their custodies. And if I ha' not my bargain, they may 60 sooner turn a scolding drab into a silent minister than make me leave pronouncing reprobation and damnation unto them. Our elder, Zeal-of-the-Land, would have had me, but I know him to be the capital knave of the land, making himself rich by being made feoffee in trust to deceased Brethren, and coz'ning their heirs by swearing the absolute gift of their inheritance. And thus, having eased my conscience and uttered my heart with

42. *canters*: Puritans.
50. *party-coloured Brotherhood*: Note.
61. *silent minister*: Note.
65. *feoffee in trust*: a trustee of freehold estate in land.

the tongue of my love, enjoy all my deceits together, I beseech you. I should not have revealed this to you, but that in time I
70 think you are mad; and I hope you'll think me so too, sir?

QUARLOUS: Stand aside, I'll answer you presently.

He considers with himself of it.

Why should not I marry this six thousand pound, now I think on't? And a good trade too, that she has beside, ha? The tother wench Winwife is sure of; there's no expectation for me there! Here I may make myself some saver yet, if she continue mad – there's the question. It is money that I want. Why should I not marry the money, when 'tis offered me? I have a licence and all; it is but razing out one name and putting in another. There's no playing with a man's fortune. I am resolved! I were truly
80 mad an' I would not! [*To* DAME PURECRAFT] Well, come your ways, follow me an' you will be mad, I'll show you a warrant!

He takes her along with him.

DAME PURECRAFT: Most zealously; it is that I zealously desire.

The JUSTICE *calls him.*

OVERDO: Sir, let me speak with you.

QUARLOUS: By whose warrant?

OVERDO: The warrant that you tender and respect so: Justice Overdo's! I am the man, friend Trouble-all, though thus disguised (as the careful magistrate ought) for the good of the republic, in the Fair, and the weeding out of enormity. Do you
90 want a house or meat or drink or clothes? Speak whatsoever it is, it shall be supplied you. What want you?

QUARLOUS: Nothing but your warrant.

OVERDO: My warrant? For what?

QUARLOUS: To be gone, sir.

OVERDO: Nay, I pray thee stay. I am serious, and have not many words nor much time to exchange with thee. Think what may do thee good.

QUARLOUS: Your hand and seal will do me a great deal of good; nothing else in the whole Fair, that I know.

100 OVERDO: If it were to any end, thou should'st have it willingly.

69. *in time:* probably at a suitable time.
75. *make myself some saver:* compensate for my loss (gambling jargon).

QUARLOUS: Why, it will satisfy me; that's end enough to look on. An' you will not gi' it me, let me go.

OVERDO: Alas! thou shalt ha' it presently. I'll but step into the scrivener's hereby and bring it. Do not go away.

The JUSTICE goes out.

QUARLOUS [*aside*]: Why, this madman's shape will prove a very fortunate one, I think! Can a ragged robe produce these effects? If this be the wise Justice, and he bring me his hand, I shall go near to make some use on't.

[JUSTICE OVERDO *returns.*]

He is come already!

OVERDO: Look thee! here is my hand and seal, Adam Overdo; if 110 there be anything to be written above in the paper, that thou want'st now or at any time hereafter, think on't; it is my deed, I deliver it so; can your friend write?

QUARLOUS: Her hand for a witness, and all is well.

OVERDO: With all my heart.

He urgeth MISTRESS PURECRAFT.

QUARLOUS [*aside*]: Why should not I ha' the conscience to make this a bond of a thousand pound, now? or what I would else?

OVERDO: Look you, there it is; and I deliver it as my deed again.

QUARLOUS: Let us now proceed in madness.

He takes her in with him.

OVERDO: Well, my conscience is much eased; I ha' done my part, 120 though it doth him no good, yet Adam hath offered satisfaction! The sting is removed from hence. Poor man, he is much altered with his affliction; it has brought him low! Now, for my other work, reducing the young man I have followed so long in love from the brink of his bane to the centre of safety. Here, or in some such like vain place, I shall be sure to find him. I will wait the good time.

[*Enter* COKES, *followed by the boys of the Fair.*]   v, iii

[COKES:] How now? What's here to do? Friend, art thou the master of the monuments?

116. *conscience:* good sense, judgement.   124. *reducing:* bringing back.
2. *master of the monuments:* person in charge here.

SHARKWELL: 'Tis a motion, an't please your worship.

OVERDO [aside]: My fantastical brother-in-law, Master Barthol'-mew Cokes!

COKES: A motion? What's that?

He reads the bill.

'The ancient modern history of *Hero and Leander*, otherwise called *The Touchstone of True Love*, with as true a trial of friend-ship between Damon and Pythias, two faithful friends o' the Bankside.' Pretty i' faith; what's the meaning on't? Is't an inter-lude, or what is't?

FILCHER: Yes, sir; please you come near, we'll take your money within.

The boys o' the Fair follow him.

COKES: Back with these children; they do so follow me up and down.

[*Enter* LITTLEWIT.]

LITTLEWIT: By your leave, friend.

FILCHER: You must pay, sir, an' you go in.

LITTLEWIT: Who, I? I perceive thou know'st not me. Call the master o' the motion.

SHARKWELL: What, do you not know the author, fellow Filcher? You must take no money of him; he must come in *gratis*. Master Littlewit is a voluntary; he is the author.

LITTLEWIT: Peace, speak not too loud; I would not have any notice taken that I am the author till we see how it passes.

COKES: Master Littlewit, how dost thou?

LITTLEWIT: Master Cokes! you are exceeding well met. What, in your doublet and hose, without a cloak or a hat?

COKES: I would I might never stir, as I am an honest man, and by that fire; I have lost all i' the Fair, and all my acquaintance too. Didst thou meet anybody that I know, Master Littlewit? my man Numps, or my sister Overdo, or Mistress Grace? Pray thee, Master Littlewit, lend me some money to see the interlude here. I'll pay thee again, as I am a gentleman. If thou'lt but carry me home, I have money enough there.

4. *fantastical:* hair-brained.
10. *interlude:* short comic or farcical entertainment.
22. *voluntary:* Note.   29. *fire:* evidently the fire in Ursula's booth.

LITTLEWIT: O, sir, you shall command it. What, will a crown serve you?

COKES: I think it will. What do we pay for coming in, fellows?

FILCHER: Twopence, sir.

COKES: Twopence? there's twelvepence, friend. Nay, I am a gallant, as simple as I look now, if you see me with my man *40* about me and my artillery again.

LITTLEWIT: Your man was i' the stocks e'en now, sir.

COKES: Who, Numps?

LITTLEWIT: Yes, faith.

COKES: For what, i' faith? I am glad o' that. Remember to tell me on't anon; I have enough now! What manner of matter is this, Master Littlewit? What kind of actors ha' you? Are they good actors?

LITTLEWIT: Pretty youths, sir, all children, both old and young; here's the master of 'em – *50*

[*Enter* LEATHERHEAD.]

LEATHERHEAD: Call me not Leatherhead, but Lantern.

LEATHERHEAD *whispers to* LITTLEWIT.

LITTLEWIT: Master Lantern, that gives light to the business.

COKES: In good time, sir, I would fain see 'em; I would be glad drink with the young company. Which is the tiring-house?

LEATHERHEAD: Troth sir, our tiring-house is somewhat little; we are but beginners, yet, pray pardon us; you cannot go upright in't.

COKES: No? Not now my hat is off? What would you have done with me if you had had me, feather and all, as I was once today? *60* Ha' you none of your pretty impudent boys, now, to bring stools, fill tobacco, fetch ale, and beg money, as they have at other houses? Let me see some o' your actors.

LITTLEWIT: Show him 'em, show him 'em. Master Lantern, this is a gentleman that is a favourer of the quality.

[LEATHERHEAD *goes to the puppet-theatre.*]

OVERDO [*aside*]: Ay, the favouring of this licentious quality is the consumption of many a young gentleman, a pernicious enormity.

55. *tiring-house:* dressing-room.　　63. *at other houses:* Note.
65. *the quality:* the acting profession.　　67. *consumption:* financial ruin.

439

He [LEATHERHEAD] *brings them out in a basket.*

COKES: What, do they live in baskets?

70 LEATHERHEAD: They do lie in a basket, sir; they are o' the small players.

COKES: These be players minors, indeed. Do you call these players?

LEATHERHEAD: They are actors, sir, and as good as any, none dispraised, for dumb shows; indeed I am the mouth of 'em all!

COKES: Thy mouth will hold 'em all. I think one Taylor would go near to beat all this company, with a hand bound behind him.

LITTLEWIT: Ay, and eat 'em all, too, an' they were in cake-bread.

COKES: I thank you for that, Master Littlewit, a good jest! Which is your Burbage now?

80 LEATHERHEAD: What mean you by that, sir?

COKES: Your best actor, your Field?

LITTLEWIT: Good, i' faith! You are even with me, sir.

LEATHERHEAD: This is he that acts young Leander, sir. He is extremely beloved of the womenkind, they do so affect his action, the green gamesters that come here; and this is lovely Hero; this with the beard, Damon; and this, pretty Pythias. This is the ghost of King Dionysius in the habit of a scrivener, as you shall see anon, at large.

COKES: Well, they are a civil company. I like 'em for that; they
90 offer not to fleer, nor jeer, nor break jests, as the great players do. And then there goes not so much charge to the feasting of 'em or making 'em drunk, as to the other, by reason of their littleness. Do they use to play perfect? Are they never flustered?

LEATHERHEAD: No, sir, I thank my industry and policy for it; they are as well-governed a company, though I say it – And here is young Leander, is as proper an actor of his inches; and shakes his head like an ostler.

72. *players minors:* boy-actors.
76. *eat 'em all:* Note.
87. *habit of a scrivener:* a gown with fur trimmings.
88. *at large:* in full.
93. *perfect:* i.e. word-perfect.
98. *ostler:* or possibly Ostler, alluding to an actor of that name.

COKES: But do you play it according to the printed book? I have read that. 100

LEATHERHEAD: By no means, sir.

COKES: No? How then?

LEATHERHEAD: A better way, sir; that is too learned and poetical for our audience. What do they know what Hellespont is, 'Guilty of true love's blood'? Or what Abydos is? Or 'the other Sestos hight'?

COKES: Th' art i' the right. I do not know myself.

LEATHERHEAD: No, I have entreated Master Littlewit to take a little pains to reduce it to a more familiar strain for our people.

COKES: How, I pray thee, good Master Littlewit? 110

LITTLEWIT: It pleases him to make a matter of it, sir. But there is no such matter I assure you. I have only made it a little easy and modern for the times, sir, that's all; as, for the Hellespont, I imagine our Thames here; and then Leander I make a dyer's son, about Puddle Wharf; and Hero a wench o' the Bankside, who going over one morning to Old Fish Street, Leander spies her land at Trig Stairs, and falls in love with her. Now do I introduce Cupid, having metamorphosed himself into a drawer, and he strikes Hero in love with a pint of sherry; and other pretty passages there are o' the friendship, that will delight you, 120 sir, and please you of judgement.

COKES: I'll be sworn they shall. I am in love with the actors already, and I'll be allied to them presently. (They respect gentlemen, these fellows.) Hero shall be my fairing; but which of my fairings? Le'me see – i' faith, my fiddle! and Leander my fiddlestick; then Damon my drum, and Pythias my pipe, and the ghost of Dionysius my hobby-horse. All fitted.

[*Enter* WINWIFE *and* GRACE.]   v, iv

[WINWIFE:] Look, yonder's your Cokes gotten in among his playfellows. I thought we could not miss him at such a spectacle.

GRACE: Let him alone. He is so busy, he will never spy us.

COKES *is handling the puppets.*

99. *printed book*: Note.   113. *modern*: commonplace.
18. *drawer*: tapster.

LEATHERHEAD: Nay, good sir.

COKES: I warrant thee, I will not hurt her, fellow; what, dost think me uncivil? I pray thee be not jealous; I am toward a wife.

LITTLEWIT: Well, good Master Lantern, make ready to begin, that I may fetch my wife, and look you be perfect; you undo me else i' my reputation.

10 LEATHERHEAD: I warrant you, sir. Do not you breed too great an expectation of it among your friends. That's the only hurter of these things.

LITTLEWIT; No, no, no.

[Exit.]

COKES: I'll stay here and see; pray thee let me see.

WINWIFE: How diligent and troublesome he is!

GRACE: The place becomes him, methinks.

OVERDO [aside]: My ward, Mistress Grace, in the company of a stranger? I doubt I shall be compelled to discover myself before my time!

[Enter KNOCKEM, EDGWORTH, and WHIT with MISTRESS OVERDO and MISTRESS LITTLEWIT, masked.]

20 FILCHER: Twopence apiece, gentlemen, an excellent motion!   *The door-keepers speak.*

KNOCKEM: Shall we have fine fireworks and good vapours?

SHARKWELL: Yes, Captain, and waterworks too.

WHIT: I pree dee, take a care o' dy shmall lady, there, Edgworth; I will look to dish tall lady myself.

LEATHERHEAD: Welcome, gentlemen; welcome, gentlemen.

WHIT: Predee, mashter o' de monshtersh, help a very sick lady here to a chair to shit in.

30 LEATHERHEAD: Presently, sir.

They bring MISTRESS OVERDO *a chair.*

WHIT: Good fait now, Urs'la's ale and *aqua vitae* ish to blame for't; shit down, shweetheart, shit down and shleep a little.

EDGWORTH [to MISTRESS LITTLEWIT]: Madam, you are very welcome hither.

KNOCKEM: Yes, and you shall see very good vapours.

6. *toward:* in prospect of, about to have.
15. *troublesome:* painstaking.

OVERDO [*aside*]: Here is my care come! I like to   *By*
see him in so good company; and yet I   EDGWORTH.
wonder that persons of such fashion should resort hither!

   The CUTPURSE *courts* MISTRESS LITTLEWIT.

EDGWORTH: This is a very private house, madam.

LEATHERHEAD: Will it please your ladyship sit, madam?   *40*

MISTRESS LITTLEWIT: Yes, good-man. They do so all-to-be-madam me, I think they think me a very lady!

EDGWORTH: What else, madam?

MISTRESS LITTLEWIT: Must I put off my mask to him?

EDGWORTH: O, by no means.

MISTRESS LITTLEWIT: How should my husband know me, then?

KNOCKEM: Husband? an idle vapour. He must not know you, nor you him; there's the true vapour.

OVERDO [*aside*]: Yea, I will observe more of this. [*To* WHIT] Is   *50*
this a lady, friend?

WHIT: Aye, and dat is anoder lady, shweetheart; if dou hasht a mind to 'em, give me twelvepence from tee, and dou shalt have eider-oder on 'em!

OVERDO [*aside*]: Ay? This will prove my chiefest enormity. I will follow this.

EDGWORTH: Is not this a finer life, lady, than to be clogged with a husband?

MISTRESS LITTLEWIT: Yes, a great deal. When will they begin, trow, in the name o' the motion?   *60*

EDGWORTH: By and by, madam; they stay but for company.

KNOCKEM: Do you hear, puppet-master, these are tedious vapours; when begin you?

LEATHERHEAD: We stay but for Master Littlewit, the author, who is gone for his wife; and we begin presently.

MISTRESS LITTLEWIT: That's I, that's I.

EDGWORTH: That was you, lady; but now you are no such poor thing.

36. *By:* standing by, indicating.
39. *private house:* Note.
41. *all-to-be-madam:* always call me madam.
54. *eider-oder:* any.

KNOCKEM: Hang the author's wife, a running vapour! Here be
70   ladies will stay for ne'er a Delia o' em all.

WHIT: But hear me now, here ish one o' de ladish ashleep; stay
  till she but vake, man.

  [Enter WASP.]

WASP: How now, friends? What's here to do?   *The door-*

FILCHER: Twopence apiece, sir, the best motion in   *keepers*
  the Fair!   *again.*

WASP: I believe you lie. If you do, I'll have my money again and
  beat you.

WINWIFE: Numps is come!

WASP: Did you see a master of mine come in here, a tall young
80   squire of Harrow o' the Hill, Master Barthol'mew Cokes?

FILCHER: I think there be such a one within.

WASP: Look he be, you were best; but it is very likely. I wonder
  I found him not at all the rest. I ha' been at the eagle, and the
  black wolf, and the bull with the five legs and two pizzles (he
  was a calf at Uxbridge Fair, two years agone), and at the dogs
  that dance the morris, and the hare o' the tabor, and missed him
  at all these! Sure this must needs be some fine sight that holds
  him so, if it have him.

COKES: Come, come, are you ready now?

90 LEATHERHEAD: Presently, sir.

WASP: Hoyday, he's at work in his doublet and hose. Do you
  hear, sir? are you employed, that you are bare-headed and so
  busy?

COKES: Hold your peace, Numps; you ha' been i' the stocks, I
  hear.

WASP: Does he know that? Nay, then the date of my authority
  is out; I must think no longer to reign, my government is at an
  end. He that will correct another must want fault in himself.

WINWIFE: Sententious Numps! I never heard so much from him
100   before.

LEATHERHEAD: Sure, Master Littlewit will not come. Please you
  take your place, sir, we'll begin.

COKES: I pray thee do; mine ears long to be at it, and my eyes

86. *hare o' the tabor:* performing hare which played the drum.

too. O Numps, i' the stocks, Numps? Where's your sword, Numps?

WASP: I pray you intend your game, sir; let me alone.

COKES: Well then, we are quit for all. Come, sit down, Numps; I'll interpret to thee. Did you see Mistress Grace? It's no matter, neither, now I think on't, tell me anon.

WINWIFE: A great deal of love and care he expresses.   110

GRACE: Alas! would you have him to express more than he has? That were tyranny.

[*The curtains of the puppet-theatre are drawn.*]

COKES: Peace, ho; now, now.

LEATHERHEAD: *Gentles, that no longer your expectations may wander,*
Behold our chief actor, amorous Leander,
With a great deal of cloth lapped about him like a scarf,
For he yet serves his father, a dyer at Puddle Wharf,
Which place we'll make bold with, to call it our Abydos,
As the Bankside is our Sestos, and let it not be denied us.
Now, as he is beating, to make the dye take the fuller,   120
Who chances to come by but fair Hero in a sculler?
And seeing Leander's naked leg and goodly calf,
Cast at him, from the boat, a sheep's eye and a half.
Now she is landed, and the sculler come back;
By and by you shall see what Leander doth lack.

PUPPET LEANDER: *Cole, Cole, old Cole.*

LEATHERHEAD: *That is the sculler's name*
without control.

PUPPET LEANDER: *Cole, Cole, I say, Cole.*

LEATHERHEAD: *We do hear you.*

PUPPET LEANDER: *Old Cole.*

LEATHERHEAD: *Old Cole? Is the dyer turned collier? How do you*
sell?

PUPPET LEANDER: *A pox o' your manners, kiss my hole here and*
smell.

106. *intend:* attend to.

115. *amorous Leander*, etc.: Note.

126. *Cole:* name for a pander.

128. *collier:* an abusive term; colliers (sellers of charcoal) were reputed to cheat their customers.

130 LEATHERHEAD: *Kiss your hole and smell? There's manners indeed.*

PUPPET LEANDER: *Why, Cole, I say, Cole.*

LEATHERHEAD: *It's the sculler you need!*

PUPPET LEANDER: *Ay, and be hanged.*

LEATHERHEAD: *Be hanged! Look you yonder,*
Old Cole, you must go hang with Master Leander.

PUPPET COLE: *Where is he?*

PUPPET LEANDER: *Here, Cole. What fairest of fairs*
Was that fare that thou landedst but now a' Trig Stairs?

COKES: What was that, fellow? Pray thee tell me; I scarce understand 'em.

LEATHERHEAD: Leander does ask, sir: *What fairest of fairs*
Was the fare that he landed but now at Trig Stairs?

140 PUPPET COLE: *It is lovely Hero.*

PUPPET LEANDER: *Nero?*

PUPPET COLE: *No, Hero.*

LEATHERHEAD: *It is Hero*
Of the Bankside, he saith, to tell you truth without erring,
Is come over into Fish Street to eat some fresh herring.
Leander says no more, but as fast as he can,
Gets on all his best clothes, and will after to the Swan.

COKES: Most admirable good, is't not?

LEATHERHEAD: *Stay, sculler.*

PUPPET COLE: *What say you?*

LEATHERHEAD: *You must stay for*
Leander,
150 *And carry him to the wench.*

PUPPET COLE: *You rogue, I am no pander.*

COKES: He says he is no pander. 'Tis a fine language; I understand it now.

LEATHERHEAD: *Are you no pander, Goodman Cole? Here's no man*
says you are.
You'll grow a hot Cole, it seems; pray you stay for your fare.

PUPPET COLE: *Will he come away?*

LEATHERHEAD: *What do you say?*

PUPPET COLE: *I'd ha' him come*
away.

147. *the Swan*: the inn of that name rather than the theatre

LEATHERHEAD: *Would you ha' Leander come away? Why pray, sir,*
stay.

You are angry, Goodman Cole; I believe the fair maid
Came over w' you o' trust. Tell us, sculler, you are paid?

PUPPET COLE: *Yes, Goodman Hogrubber o' Pickt-hatch.*

LEATHERHEAD: *How, Hogrubber o' Pickt-hatch?*

PUPPET COLE: *Ay, Hogrubber o'* 160
Pickt-hatch.

Take you that. The PUPPET

LEATHERHEAD: *O, my head!* strikes him

PUPPET COLE: *Harm watch, harm* over the pate.
catch.

COKES: Harm watch, harm catch, he says. Very good i' faith; the
sculler had like to ha' knocked you, sirrah.

LEATHERHEAD: Yes, but that his fare called him away.

PUPPET LEANDER: *Row apace, row apace, row, row, row, row, row.*

LEATHERHEAD: *You are knavishly 'vaden, sculler, take heed where*
you go.

PUPPET COLE: *Knave i' your face, Goodman Rogue.*

PUPPET LEANDER: *Row, row, row,*
row, row, row.

COKES: He said knave i' your face, friend.

LEATHERHEAD: Aye, sir, I heard him. But there's no talking to
these watermen; they will ha' the last word. 170

COKES: God's my life! I am not allied to the sculler yet; he shall
be Dauphin my boy. But my fiddle-stick does fiddle in and out
too much; I pray you speak to him on't; tell him, I would have
him tarry in my sight more.

LEATHERHEAD: I pray you be content; you'll have enough on
him, sir.

Now gentles, I take it, here is none of you so stupid,
But that you have heard of a little god of love, called Cupid;
Who out of kindness to Leander, hearing he but saw her
This present day and hour, doth turn himself to a drawer. 180
And because he would have their first meeting to be merry,
He strikes Hero in love to him with a pint of sherry.

159. *Hogrubber:* swineherd.
172. *fiddle-stick:* Leander (see v, iii).

Which he tells her from amorous Leander is sent PUPPET
her, LEANDER
Who after him into the room of Hero doth goes into
venter. Mistress Hero's

PUPPET JONAS: *A pint of sack, score a pint of* room.
sack i' the Coney.

COKES: Sack? You said but e'en now it should be sherry.

PUPPET JONAS: *Why so it is: sherry, sherry, sherry.*

COKES: Sherry, sherry, sherry. By my troth he makes me merry.
I must have a name for Cupid too. Let me see, thou mightst
190   help me now, an' thou wouldst, Numps, at a dead lift, but thou art
dreaming o' the stocks still! Do not think on't, I have forgot it.
'Tis but a nine days' wonder, man; let it not trouble thee.

WASP: I would the stocks were about your neck, sir; condition 1
hung by the heels in them till the wonder were off from you,
with all my heart.

COKES: Well said, resolute Numps. But hark you, friend, where
is the friendship, all this while, between my drum, Damon, and
my pipe, Pythias?

LEATHERHEAD: You shall see by and by, sir.

200 COKES: You think my hobby-horse is forgotten, too. No, I'll see
'em all enact before I go; I shall not know which to love best,
else.

KNOCKEM: This gallant has interrupting vapours, troublesome
vapours, Whit; puff with him.

WHIT: No, I pre dee, Captain, let him alone. He is a child i' faith,
la.

LEATHERHEAD: *Now, gentles, to the friends, who in number are two,*
And lodged in that ale-house in which fair Hero does do:
Damon (for some kindness done him the last week)
210 *Is come fair Hero in Fish Street this morning to seek.*
Pythias does smell the knavery of the meeting,
And now you shall see their true friendly greeting.

185. *sack . . . sherry:* Note.
185. *the Coney:* name of a room in the tavern.
190 *at a dead lift:* at a last extremity.
193. *condition:* on condition that.
200. *hobby-horse,* etc.: Note.   204. *puff:* quarrel, bully.

PUPPET PYTHIAS: *You whoremasterly slave, you.*

COKES: Whoremasterly slave you? Very friendly and familiar, that!

PUPPET DAMON: *Whoremaster i' thy face,*
Thou hast lien with her thyself, I'll prove 't i' this place.

COKES: Damon says Pythias has lien with her himself; he'll prove't in this place.

LEATHERHEAD: *They are whoremasters both, sir, that's a plain case.* 220

PUPPET PYTHIAS: *You lie like a rogue.*

LEATHERHEAD: *Do I lie like a rogue?*

PUPPET PYTHIAS: *A pimp and a scab.*

LEATHERHEAD: *A pimp and a scab?*
I say between you, you have both but one drab.

PUPPET DAMON: *You lie again.*

LEATHERHEAD: *Do I lie again?*

PUPPET DAMON: *Like a rogue again.*

LEATHERHEAD: *Like a rogue again?*

PUPPET PYTHIAS: *And you are a pimp again.*

COKES: And you are a pimp again, he says.

PUPPET DAMON: *And a scab again.* 230

COKES: And a scab again, he says.

LEATHERHEAD: *And I say again you are both whoremasters again,*
And you have both but one drab again. They fight.

PUPPETS DAMON and PYTHIAS: *Dost thou, dost thou, dost thou?*

LEATHERHEAD: *What, both at once?*

PUPPET PYTHIAS: *Down with him, Damon.*

PUPPET DAMON: *Pink his guts, Pythias.*

LEATHERHEAD: *What, so malicious?*
Will ye murder me, masters both, i' mine own house?

COKES: Ho! well acted, my drum, well acted, my pipe, well acted 240
still.

WASP: Well acted, with all my heart.

LEATHERHEAD: *Hold, hold your hands.*

COKES: Ay, both your hands, for my sake! for you ha' both done well.

PUPPET DAMON: *Gramercy, pure Pythias.*

222. *scab*: scoundrel.
237. *pink*: stab.

449

PUPPET PYTHIAS: *Gramercy, dear Damon.*

COKES: Gramercy to you both, my pipe and my drum.

PUPPETS DAMON *and* PYTHIAS: *Come now we'll together to break-*
fast to Hero.

250 LEATHERHEAD: *'Tis well, you can now go to breakfast to Hero,*
You have given me my breakfast, with a hone and honero.

COKES: How is't, friend, ha' they hurt thee?

LEATHERHEAD: O no!
Between you and I, sir, we do but make show.
Thus, gentles, you perceive, without any denial,
'Twixt Damon and Pythias here, friendship's true trial.
Though hourly they quarrel thus and roar each with other,
They fight you no more than does brother with brother.
But friendly together, at the next man they meet,
They let fly their anger, as here you might see't.

260 COKES: Well, we have seen't, and thou hast felt it, whatsoever
thou sayest. What's next? What's next?

LEATHERHEAD: *This while young Leander with fair Hero is drinking,*
And Hero grown drunk, to any man's thinking!
Yet was it not three pints of sherry could flaw her,
Till Cupid, distinguished like Jonas the drawer,
From under his apron, where his lechery lurks,
Put love in her sack. Now mark how it works.

PUPPET HERO: *O Leander, Leander, my dear, my dear Leander,*
I'll forever be thy goose, so thou'lt be my gander.

270 COKES: Excellently well said, fiddle! She'll ever be his goose, so
he'll be her gander: was't not so?

LEATHERHEAD: Yes, sir, but mark his answer, now.

PUPPET LEANDER: *And sweetest of geese, before I go to bed,*
I'll swim o'er the Thames, my goose, thee to tread.

COKES: Brave! he will swim o'er the Thames and tread his goose
tonight, he says.

LEATHERHEAD: Ay, peace, sir, they'll be angry if they hear you
eavesdropping, now they are setting their match.

251. *hone and honero:* from the Scots *ochone, ochonarie:* alas! (evidently a
    ballad-refrain).
275. *tread:* copulate with.
278. *setting their match:* fixing a time to meet.

PUPPET LEANDER: *But lest the Thames should be dark, my goose, my*
    dear friend,
Let thy window be provided of a candle's end.   280

PUPPET HERO: *Fear not, my gander, I protest I should handle*
My matters very ill, if I had not a whole candle.

PUPPET LEANDER: *Well then, look to 't, and kiss me to boot.*

LEATHERHEAD: *Now here come the friends again,*   DAMON and
    Pythias and Damon,   PYTHIAS enter
And under their cloaks they have of bacon a gammon.

PUPPET PYTHIAS: *Drawer, fill some wine here.*

LEATHERHEAD: *How, some wine there?*
There's company already, sir, pray forbear!

PUPPET DAMON: *'Tis Hero.*

LEATHERHEAD: *Yes, but she will not be taken,*
After sack and fresh herring, with your Dunmow-bacon.

PUPPET PYTHIAS: *You lie, it's Westfabian.*

LEATHERHEAD: *Westphalian, you should*
    say.   290

DAMON: *If you hold not your peace, you are a*   LEANDER and
    coxcomb, I would say.   HERO are kissing.

PUPPET PYTHIAS: *What's here? What's here? Kiss, kiss upon kiss.*

LEATHERHEAD: *Ay, wherefore should they not? What harm is in*
    this?
'Tis Mistress Hero.

PUPPET DAMON: *Mistress Hero's a whore.*

LEATHERHEAD: *Is she a whore? Keep you quiet, or Sir Knave out of*
    door.

PUPPET DAMON: *Knave out of door?*   Here the PUP-

PUPPET HERO: *Yes, knave*   PETS quarrel
    out of door.   and fall together

PUPPET DAMON: *Whore out of door.*   by the ears.

PUPPET HERO: *I say knave out of door.*

PUPPET DAMON: *I say whore out of door.*

PUPPET PYTHIAS: *Yea, so say I too.*

PUPPET HERO: *Kiss the whore o' the arse.*

LEATHERHEAD: *Now you ha' something to*
    do:

289. *Dunmow-bacon*: Note.   290. *Westfalian*: celebrated kind of ham.

300   *You must kiss her o' the arse, she says.*

PUPPETS DAMON *and* PYTHIAS: *So we will, so we will.*
   [*They kick her.*]

PUPPET HERO: *O my haunches, o my haunches, hold, hold!*

LEATHERHEAD: *Stand'st thou still?*
   Leander, where art thou? Stand'st thou still like a sot,
   And not offer'st to break both their heads with a pot?
   See who's at thine elbow there! Puppet Jonas and Cupid.

PUPPET JONAS: *Upon 'em, Leander, be not so stupid.*
   They fight.

PUPPET LEANDER: *You goat-bearded slave!*

PUPPET DAMON: *You whoremaster knave!*

PUPPET LEANDER: *Thou art a whoremaster.*

PUPPET JONAS: *Whoremasters all.*

LEATHERHEAD: *See, Cupid with a word has ta'en up the brawl.*

KNOCKEM: These be fine vapours!

310 COKES: By this good day they fight bravely, do they not, Numps?

WASP: Yes, they lacked but you to be their second, all this while.

LEATHERHEAD: *This tragical encounter, falling out thus to busy us,*
   It raises up the ghost of their friend Dionysius,
   Not like a monarch, but the master of a school,
   In a scrivener's furred gown, which shows he is no fool.
   For therein he hath wit enough to keep himself warm.
   'O Damon,' he cries, 'and Pythias, what harm
   Hath poor Dionysius done you in his grave,
   That after his death you should fall out thus, and rave,
320   *And call amorous Leander whoremaster knave?'*

PUPPET DIONYSIUS: *I cannot, I will not, I promise you, endure it.*

V, V   [*Enter* BUSY.]

BUSY: Down with Dagon, down with Dagon! 'Tis I will no
   longer endure your profanations.

LEATHERHEAD: What mean you, sir?

BUSY: I will remove Dagon there, I say, that idol, that heathenish
   idol, that remains, as I may say, a beam, a very beam, not a
   beam of the sun, nor a beam of the moon, nor a beam of a

balance, neither a house-beam nor a weaver's beam, but a beam in the eye, in the eye of the Brethren; a very great beam, an exceeding great beam; such as are your stage-players, rhymers, and morris-dancers, who have walked hand in hand in con- *10* tempt of the Brethren and the Cause, and been borne out by instruments of no mean countenance.

LEATHERHEAD: Sir, I present nothing but what is licensed by authority.

BUSY: Thou art all license, even licentiousness itself, Shimei!

LEATHERHEAD: I have the Master of the Revels' hand for it, sir.

BUSY: The master of rebels' hand thou hast – Satan's! Hold thy peace; thy scurrility shut up thy mouth. Thy profession is damnable, and in pleading for it thou dost plead for Baal. I have long opened my mouth wide and gaped, I have gaped as the *20* oyster for the tide, after thy destruction; but cannot compass it by suit or dispute; so that I look for a bickering ere long, and then a battle.

KNOCKEM: Good Banbury-vapours.

COKES: Friend, you'd have an ill match on't if you bicker with him here; though he be no man o' the fist, he has friends that will go to cuffs for him. Numps, will not you take our side?

EDGWORTH: Sir, it shall not need; in my mind, he offers him a fairer course, to end it by disputation! Hast thou nothing to say for thyself, in defence of thy quality? *30*

LEATHERHEAD: Faith, sir, I am not well studied in these controversies between the hypocrites and us. But here's one of my motion, Puppet Dionysius, shall undertake him, and I'll venture the cause on't.

COKES: Who? My hobby-horse? Will he dispute with him?

LEATHERHEAD: Yes, sir, and make a hobby-ass of him, I hope.

COKES: That's excellent! Indeed he looks like the best scholar of 'em all. Come, sir, you must be as good as your word, now.

BUSY: I will not fear to make my spirit and gifts known! Assist me, zeal; fill me, fill me, that is, make me full! *40*

WINWIFE: What a desperate, profane wretch is this! Is there any

12. *instruments:* agents.
12. *countenance:* repute.
29. *disputation:* formal debate.

453

ignorance or impudence like his? To call his zeal to fill him
against a puppet?

GRACE: I know no fitter match than a puppet to commit with an
hypocrite!

BUSY: First, I say unto thee, idol, thou hast no calling.

PUPPET DIONYSIUS: You lie; I am called Dionysius.

LEATHERHEAD: The motion says you lie, he is called Dionysius i'
the matter, and to that calling he answers.

50 BUSY: I mean no vocation, idol, no present lawful calling.

PUPPET DIONYSIUS: Is yours a lawful calling?

LEATHERHEAD: The motion asketh if yours be a lawful calling.

BUSY: Yes, mine is of the spirit.

PUPPET DIONYSIUS: Then idol is a lawful calling.

LEATHERHEAD: He says, then idol is a lawful calling! For you
called him idol, and your calling is of the spirit.

COKES: Well disputed, hobby-horse!

BUSY: Take not part with the wicked, young gallant. He neigheth
and hinnyeth; all is but hinnying sophistry. I call him idol again.

60 Yet, I say, his calling, his profession is profane, it is profane, idol.

PUPPET DIONYSIUS: It is not profane!

LEATHERHEAD: It is not profane, he says.

BUSY: It is profane.

PUPPET DIONYSIUS: It is not profane.

BUSY: It is profane.

PUPPET DIONYSIUS: It is not profane.

LEATHERHEAD: Well said, confute him with 'not', still. You
cannot bear him down with your base noise, sir.

BUSY: Nor he me with his treble creaking, though he creak like

70 the chariot wheels of Satan. I am zealous for the Cause –

LEATHERHEAD: As a dog for a bone.

BUSY: And I say it is profane, as being the page of pride and the
waiting-woman of vanity.

PUPPET DIONYSIUS: Yea? What say you to your tire-women
then?

LEATHERHEAD: Good.

44. *commit with:* fight with.   46. *calling:* vocation.
55. *hinnyeth:* whinnies.   69. *creaking:* shrill way of speaking.
74. *tire-women:* dress-makers.

PUFPET DIONYSIUS: Or feather-makers i' the Friars, that are o'
your faction of faith? Are not they with their perukes and their
puffs, their fans and their huffs, as much pages of pride and
waiters upon vanity? What say you? What say you? What say   *80*
you?

BUSY: I will not answer for them.

PUPPET DIONYSIUS: Because you cannot, because you cannot. Is
a bugle-maker a lawful calling? or the confect-maker's? such
you have there; or your French fashioner? You'd have all the
sin within yourselves, would you not? would you not?

BUSY: No, Dagon.

PUPPET DIONYSIUS: What then, Dagonet? Is a puppet worse
than these?

BUSY: Yes, and my main argument against you is that you are an   *90*
abomination; for the male among you putteth on the apparel
of the female, and the female of the male.

PUPPET DIONYSIUS: You lie, you lie, you lie abominably.

COKES: Good, by my troth, he has given him the lie thrice.

PUPPET DIONYSIUS: It is your old stale argument against the
players, but it will not hold against the puppets; for we have
neither male nor female amongst us. And that thou may'st see,
if thou wilt, like a malicious purblind zeal as thou art!

THE PUPPET *takes up his garment.*

EDGWORTH: By my faith, there he has answered you, friend, by   *100*
plain demonstration.

PUPPET DIONYSIUS: Nay, I'll prove, against e'er a rabbin of 'em
all, that my standing is as lawful as his; that I speak by inspiration as well as he; that I have as little to do with learning as he;
and do scorn her helps as much as he.

BUSY: I am confuted; the Cause hath failed me.

PUPPET DIONYSIUS: Then be converted, be converted.

LEATHERHEAD: Be converted, I pray you, and let the play go on!

77. *feather-makers:* dealers in feathers.   78. *perukes:* wigs.
79. *puffs:* bunches of ribbons, feathers, or hair.
79. *huffs:* padded shoulders, etc.
84. *bugle-maker:* maker of glass beads.
84. *confect-maker:* maker of sweets or confectionery.
85. *fashioner:* tailor.   90. *main argument:* Note.
103. *standing:* employment, vocation.

BUSY: Let it go on. For I am changed, and will become a beholder
110   with you!

COKES: That's brave i' faith. Thou hast carried it away, hobby-
horse; on with the play!

THE JUSTICE *discovers himself.*

OVERDO: Stay, now do I forbid, I, Adam Overdo! Sit still, I
charge you.

COKES: What, my brother-i'-law!

GRACE: My wise guardian!

EDGWORTH: Justice Overdo!

OVERDO: It is time to take enormity by the forehead, and brand
it; for I have discovered enough.

v, vi   [*Enter*] *to them* QUARLOUS (*like the madman*) [*and* DAME]
PURECRAFT (*a while after*).

[QUARLOUS:] Nay, come, mistress bride. You must do as I do,
now. You must be mad with me in truth. I have here Justice
Overdo for it.

OVERDO [*to* QUARLOUS]: Peace, good Trouble-all; come hither,
and you shall trouble none. I will take the charge of you and
your friend, too.

To THE CUTPURSE *and* MISTRESS LITTLEWIT.

You also, young man, shall be my care; stand there.

EDGWORTH: Now, mercy upon me.

KNOCKEM: Would we were away, Whit; these   *The rest are*
10   are dangerous vapours; best fall off with our   *stealing away.*
birds, for fear o' the cage.

OVERDO: Stay, is not my name your terror?

WHIT: Yesh, faith, man, and it ish for tat we would be gone, man.

[*Enter* LITTLEWIT.]

LITTLEWIT: O gentlemen, did you not see a wife of mine? I ha'
lost my little wife, as I shall be trusted, my little pretty Win. I
left her at the great woman's house in trust yonder, the pig-
woman's, with Captain Jordan and Captain Whit, very good

111. *carried it away:* won.
    discovers himself: reveals himself, drops his disguise.
11. *cage:* gaol.

men, and I cannot hear of her. Poor fool, I fear she's stepped
aside. Mother, did you not see Win?

OVERDO: If this grave matron be your mother, sir, stand by her, 20
et digito compesce labellum; I may perhaps spring a wife for you
anon. Brother Barthol'mew, I am sadly sorry to see you so
lightly given, and such a disciple of enormity, with your grave
governor Humphrey; but stand you both there, in the middle-
place; I will reprehend you in your course. Mistress Grace, let
me rescue you out of the hands of the stranger.

WINWIFE: Pardon me, sir, I am a kinsman of hers.

OVERDO: Are you so? Of what name, sir?

WINWIFE: Winwife, sir.

OVERDO: Master Winwife? I hope you have won no wife of her, 30
sir. If you have, I will examine the possibility of it at fit leisure.
Now to my enormities: look upon me, O London! and see me,
O Smithfield! the example of justice and mirror of magistrates,
the true top of formality and scourge of enormity! Hearken
unto my labours and but observe my discoveries, and compare
Hercules with me, if thou dar'st, of old; or Columbus, Magellan,
or our countryman Drake of later times. Stand forth you weeds
of enormity, and spread. (*To* BUSY) First, Rabbi Busy, thou
superlunatical hypocrite. (*To* LANTERN) Next, thou other
extremity, thou profane professor of puppetry, little better than 40
poetry. (*To* THE HORSE-COURSER *and* CUTPURSE) Then thou
strong debaucher and seducer of youth; witness this easy and
honest young man. (*Then* CAPTAIN WHIT *and* MISTRESS
LITTLEWIT) Now thou esquire of dames, madams, and twelve-
penny ladies. Now my green madam herself, of the price. Let
me unmask your ladyship.

[*He removes* MISTRESS LITTLEWIT's *mask.*]

LITTLEWIT: O my wife, my wife, my wife!

OVERDO: Is she your wife? *Redde te Harpocratem!*

Enter TROUBLE-ALL [*with a dripping-pan, followed by* URSULA
and NIGHTINGALE].

TROUBLE-ALL: By your leave, stand by, my masters; be uncovered. 50

18. *stepped aside:* gone astray.
49. *be uncovered:* remove your hats.

URSULA: O stay him, stay him! Help to cry, Nightingale; my pan, my pan!

OVERDO: What's the matter?

NIGHTINGALE: He has stol'n Gammer Urs'la's pan.

TROUBLE-ALL: Yes, and I fear no man but Justice Overdo.

OVERDO: Urs'la? Where is she? O the sow of enormity, this! (*To* URSULA *and* NIGHTINGALE) Welcome, stand you there; you songster, there.

URSULA: An' please your worship, I am in no fault. A gentleman stripped him in my booth, and borrowed his gown and his hat; and he ran away with my goods, here, for it.

OVERDO (*To* QUARLOUS): Then this is the true madman, and you are the enormity!

QUARLOUS: You are i' the right, I am mad but from the gown outward.

OVERDO: Stand you there.

QUARLOUS: Where you please, sir.

MISTRESS OVERDO [*wakes up and*] *is sick, and her husband is silenced.*

MISTRESS OVERDO: O lend me a basin, I am sick, I am sick. Where's Master Overdo? Bridget, call hither my Adam.

OVERDO: How?

WHIT: Dy very own wife, i' fait, worshipful Adam.

MISTRESS OVERDO: Will not my Adam come at me? Shall I see him no more then?

QUARLOUS: Sir, why do you not go on with the enormity? Are you oppressed with it? I'll help you, sir, i' your ear: your 'innocent young man', you have ta'en such care of all this day, is a cutpurse, that hath got all your brother Cokes's things, and helped you to your beating and the stocks. If you have a mind to hang him now and show him your magistrate's wit, you may; but I should think it were better recovering the goods, and to save your estimation in him. I thank you, sir, for the gift of your ward, Mistress Grace. Look you, here is your hand and seal, by the way. Master Winwife, give you joy, you are Palemon; you are possessed of the gentlewoman, but she must

69. *Bridget:* a Jonsonian slip for 'Grace'.
81. *estimation:* repute.

pay me value, here's warrant for it. And honest madman, there's
thy gown and cap again; I thank thee for my wife. (*To* THE
WIDOW.) Nay, I can be mad, sweetheart, when I please, still;
never fear me. And careful Numps, where's he? I thank him for
my licence.

WASP: How! 90

QUARLOUS: 'Tis true, Numps.

WASP: I'll be hanged then.

QUARLOUS: Look i' your box, Numps.

>   WASP *misseth the licence.*

[*To* OVERDO] Nay, sir, stand not you fixed here, like a stake in
Finsbury to be shot at, or the whipping post i' the Fair, but get
your wife out o' the air; it will make her worse else. And
remember you are but Adam, flesh and blood! You have your
frailty; forget your other name of Overdo and invite us all to
supper. There you and I will compare our discoveries, and
drown the memory of all enormity in your bigg'st bowl at 100
home.

COKES: How now, Numps, ha' you lost it? I warrant 'twas when
thou wert i' the stocks. Why dost not speak?

WASP: I will never speak while I live, again, for aught I know.

OVERDO: Nay, Humphrey, if I be patient, you must be so, too;
this pleasant conceited gentleman hath wrought upon my
judgement, and prevailed. I pray you take care of your sick
friend, Mistress Alice, and my good friends all –

QUARLOUS: And no enormities.

OVERDO: I invite you home with me to my house, to supper. I 110
will have none fear to go along, for my intents are *ad correctionem,
non ad destructionem; ad aedificandum, non ad diruendum.* So lead
on.

COKES: Yes, and bring the actors along, we'll ha' the rest o' the
play at home.

>   [*Exeunt.*]

94. *stake:* archery-post.

THE END

THE EPILOGUE

Your Majesty hath seen the play, and you
  Can best allow it from your ear and view.
You know the scope of writers, and what store
  Of leave is given them, if they take not more,
And turn it into licence. You can tell
  If we have used that leave you gave us well;
Or whether we to rage or licence break,
  Or be profane, or make profane men speak.
This is your power to judge, great sir, and not
  The envy of a few. Which if we have got,
We value less what their dislike can bring,
  If it so happy be, t' have pleased the King.

ADDITIONAL NOTES

VOLPONE

THE EPISTLE

The epistle dedicatory is addressed to the Universities of Oxford and Cambridge, appropriately (and tactfully) hailed as 'most *equal* Sisters'. The epistle is important in that it states Jonson's high aims in writing comedies. The stand-point is similar to Sir Philip Sidney's (see the Introduction, pp. 12–13). The address and date are in the quarto.

57. *Sejanus:* The production of *Sejanus* had involved Jonson in charges of Popish sympathies.

89. *Sibi,* etc.: Horace, *Satires*, II, i, 23. There is a free translation by Jonson of the line in *Poetaster*, III, v:

> In satires, each man (though untouched) complains
> As he were hurt; and hates such biting strains.

114. *turning back to my promise:* not fulfilling my undertaking to bring back to the theatre the practice of the ancients. In the matter of the catastrophe, Jonson is here saying, *Volpone* is too harsh.

142. *Cinnamus the barber:* a barber-surgeon is indicated here.

THE PERSONS OF THE PLAY

The principal characters' names are derived from animals. *Volpone* is Italian for fox ('an old fox, an old reynard, an old crafty, sly, subtle companion, sneaking lurking wily deceiver' was John Florio's gloss on the word in *A World of Words* in 1598); *Mosca* is Italian for fly ('flesh-fly' in the play), *Voltore* for vulture, *Corbaccio* for raven, and *Corvino* for crow (i.e. carrion crow). The name *Sir Politic Would-be* expresses the character's aspirations, but the familiar form *Sir Pol* makes him a parrot; and J. J. Enck suggests that *Peregrine*, 'the single sound person in the play', is the peregrine falcon, the pilgrim hawk. Lady Would-be is once referred to in the play as a kite, and once as a she-wolf. Mosca also talks of a physician Signior Lupo, the wolf.

PROLOGUE

17. *coadjutor; novice; journeyman; tutor:* four different kinds of collaborator in the Elizabethan Theatre: a joint-author, sharing responsibility for a play with someone else – for example, Beau-

mont and Fletcher; an apprentice, learning the craft; a hack-writer or adaptor of old plays; a supervisor of apprentice-work. Jonson had been novice, journeyman, and coadjutor in his time, but here puts forward his claim to be considered a serious dramatic artist.

21. *quaking custards:* may be an allusion to the huge custard set out at the Lord Mayor's feasts for the fool to jump into, and, in conjunction with the reference to eggs above, may indicate the sort of slap-stick which Jonson has avoided. A. B. Kernan believes that this is a literary allusion and that it describes such plays as Marston's *Histriomastix*.

23. *Nor hales he in a gull old ends reciting:* the author does not haul in a dupe reciting bits of poetry from old plays.

24. *Make Bedlam a faction:* turn lunatics into enthusiasts for the play, Bedlam being a madhouse.

31. *The laws of time, place, persons:* the 'unities'. See the Introduction, p. 14, and the notes on location and time-scheme, p. 38, p. 176, and p. 321.

ACT ONE

I,

5. *the celestial Ram:* the sun enters Aries, the Ram, on 21 March, the spring equinox, when the 'teeming earth' needs sunshine.

10. *son of Sol:* gold is referred to as the offspring of Sol, the sun, in alchemical writings.

19. *Venus:* Latin poets frequently referred to Venus as 'golden'.

33. *I use no trade . . .:* Volpone here lists the various new capitalist and mercantile practices which he himself scorns, including speculative ventures.

I, ii 1. The interlude, which is supposed to have been written by Mosca, is in the loose four-stressed verse of the old morality-plays, and is recited by the dwarf and the hermaphrodite. It is a cynical account of the transmigration of souls. The suggestion that the soul of Pythagoras, itself having transmigrated from various mythical and Homeric figures (lines 8–16), could now inhabit the body of the freak, Androgyno, contributes to the general debasing effect of the human into the animal which is a major theme in *Volpone*. The classical references and thematic relevance of all this are impossible to convey in the modern theatre, and readers who are interested in the background and the significance of this scene to Jonson's work as a whole are directed to Harry Levin's article 'Jonson's Metempsychosis', *Philological Quarterly*, XXII. Mosca's source is Lucian, a Greek satirist of the 2nd century, whose *Dream of the Cobbler and the Cock* is referred to in line 24.

6. *Pythagoras*: Greek philosopher of the sixth century B.C. who believed in transmigration of souls after death from one body to another. In lines 8–16 Nano reels off the names of those whose bodies Pythagoras's soul had previously inhabited.

26. '*By quater!*': Pythagoras and his followers believed that number was the basis of harmony in the universe, and they invented a numerical and geometrical symbolism. The quater is the triangle with four as its base:

.
. .
. . .
. . . .

27. *golden thigh*: Pythagoras was reputed to have had a thigh of gold.

33. *forbid meats*: Pythagoreans were not allowed to eat fish or beans (see line 40).

35. *dogmatical silence*: Pythagoreans were expected to maintain a five years' silence.

46. *nativity-pie*: Puritans avoided the Catholic implications of Christmas by saying 'the Nativity' or 'Christ-*tide*.' See *The Alchemist*, III, ii, 43 (p. 246).

10. *bought at St Mark*: bought at one of the celebrated goldsmiths' I, iii shops in the square of St Mark.

21. *Your love hath taste in this*: I can sense from this plate how great your love is.

53. *speak to every cause, and things mere contraries*: act as advocate in any case, and support opposite positions.

58. *take provoking gold on either hand, and put it up*: 'to provoke' is to ask a court to take up one's case: Voltore accepts fees from both parties in a case, and pockets it himself.

46. *from his brain*: Mosca here describes correctly (according to I, iv Jacobean medical views) the final symptoms of apoplexy – fluid flowing from the brain and visible in the eyes.

73. *aurum palpabile, if not potabile*: a play on words by Corbaccio who in Latin calls his 'bag of bright chequins' touchable but not drinkable gold – *aurum potabile* being a medicine containing gold particles.

128. *My brother*: i.e. Bonario, Corbaccio's son. The allusion is to Jacob cheating Esau of Isaac's blessing.

125–6. . . . *have all their charge, when he goes out, when he comes in*, I, v *examined*: every time Corvino enters or leaves his house, he interrogates the ten guards who have to watch Celia and to spy on each other.

129. *Maintain mine own shape still:* keep up the pretence of being a dying man.

ACT TWO

[SCENE ONE]

10. *with Ulysses:* like Ulysses – the great Homeric traveller and observer whom Sir Politic here lightly dismisses.

17. *my lord Ambassador:* i.e. the English Ambassador to Venice (Sir Henry Wotton).

30. *the spider and the bee:* insects who are natural enemies (proverbial).

34. *lion's whelping in the Tower:* King James I owned a lioness which twice gave birth to cubs in the Tower of London: in 1604 and 1605. Sir Politic sees this as another omen.

36. *the fires at Berwick:* in 1604 apparitions were reported fighting on the Scottish border.

37. *the new star:* in 1604 also Kepler discovered a new star in the constellation Serpentarius.

38. *meteors:* any disruption in the Elizabethan heavens suggested imminent corresponding social or political disorder.

40. *porpoises:* a porpoise, and (soon after) a whale were seen in England in January 1606; Jonson's audience would appreciate these references, but the dramatic point is Sir Politic's persistent superstitious interest in them.

49. *the Stode fleet:* Stode – a port at the mouth of the Elbe, where the ships of the English Merchant Adventurers were based.

50. *the Archdukes:* the joint title given to the Infanta Isabella and her husband Albert when they were granted the Spanish Netherlands by her father, Philip II of Spain.

51. *Spinola's Whale:* Ambrosio Spinola commanded the Spanish Army in the Netherlands from 1604. Sir Politic thinks the whale must be one of his secret weapons; rumours show he was not alone in this.

55. *Mas' Stone:* Master Stone, a clown, famous for his quips, who was flogged for making fun of the Lord Admiral.

90. *Mamuluchi:* the Mamelukes, a military class, who seized power in Egypt c. 1250, and ruled till 1517; they held power until 1811.

101. *though I live out, free from the active torrent:* though I am not involved in public affairs.

113. *vulgar grammar:* grammar-book or guide to speaking a language

such as *The Italian Schoolmaster, containing Rules for the perfect pro-nouncing of the Italian Tongue* (1597). Grammar-books then, as often now, used commonplaces and proverbial sayings as exercises for translation. These are the common 'rules' (1: iii, above) which Sir Politic has laboriously memorized.

4. *Mountebanks:* from the Italian *monta in banco*, where *banco* means ... II, ii a platform or bench. A Mountebank was a travelling quack who, by persuasive sales-talk and fairground patter, got the bystanders to buy his medicines, as Sir Politic correctly explains to Peregrine.

22. *Scoto of Mantua:* a professional actor, leading member of an Italian troupe, and known in London chiefly as a juggler and sleight-of-hand performer in Elizabethan times. In England his name was proverbially linked with skill and deceit.

46. *Cardinal Bembo's - cook:* One presumes that cook is here an euphemism for mistress. Cardinal Bembo was a great Italian humanist.

92. *malignant humours:* throughout his speech Volpone's medical reference is to the theory of humours, the physiological theory derived from Hippocrates and current throughout the Middle Ages and the Renaissance. The four elements in the universe were earth, air, fire, and water. Everything was made out of these, including Man in whom the elements took the form of four fluid 'humours' - blood (hot and moist), phlegm (cold and moist), choler or yellow bile (hot and dry), and melancholy or black bile (cold and dry). The balance within any individual of these four humours produced what we would call a well-adjusted personality, but imbalance meant that one humour predominated to produce a particular temperament: hence the adjectives sanguine, phlegmatic, choleric, and melancholic. Jonson's early comedies, *Every Man in His Humour* and *Every Man out of His Humour* used these physiological traits as psychological ones: see the General Introduction p. 10.

114. *Broughton's books:* the works of Hugh Broughton (1549-1617), a Puritan divine and scholar, whose learned works are also satirized by Jonson in *The Alchemist*, II, iii, 238, (p. 230).

123. *Raymund Lully:* a medieval Catalan scholar (1235-1315) believed (erroneously) to have been an alchemist and (equally erroneously) to have discovered the elixir. See note on *The Alchemist*, II, v, 8.

124. *Danish Gonswart:* even Herford and the Simpsons could not identify this figure satisfactorily.

125. *Paracelsus:* the pseudonym of Theophrastus Bombastus von Hohenheim (1493–1541), the physician and alchemist, who carried his special drugs in the pommel of his long sword.

133. *the signiory of the Sanita:* the official board in Venice for licensing medical men.

234. *like virginal jacks:* Jonson seems to use jacks wrongly as the keys of a virginal (a spinet or harpsichord), but the technical point is unimportant.

II, iii 3. *Signior Flaminio:* Flaminio Scale was a well-known commedia dell'arte performer.

4. *Franciscina:* the usual name for the stock character of the amorous maid-servant in the improvised commedia dell'arte.

8. *the Pantalone di Besogniosi:* Pantalone was the jealous old Venetian always cuckolded in the commedia dell'arte: the role that Corvino obsessively dreads.

II, iv [SCENE TWO]

9. *my liver melts:* traditionally the liver (now the heart) was the seat of violent or romantic feelings, such as jealousy or love.

33. *I would escape your epilogue:* I would prefer not to end as you did (getting beaten by Corvino); the lines also point, with irony, to Mosca's later scheme to deceive Volpone, and, with greater irony, to the eventual downfall of them both.

II, v [SCENE THREE]

12. *toad-stone:* the precious stone popularly thought to be between the eyes of a toad, and imagined to have special qualities as an antidote against poisons.

24. *save your dowry:* if a wife was unfaithful, her dowry reverted completely to her husband.

24. *I am a Dutchman:* you must think I am a Dutchman, i.e. complacent and not like an Italian.

55. *a conjurer that had heedless left his circle's safety ere his devil was laid:* a magician who wished to conjure up a devil used to draw a magic circle within which he remained protected until the devil was 'laid' – i.e. sent back to Hell.

70. *make thee an anatomy:* 'anatomize you' – i.e. 'analyze your moral qualities in detail'; Corvino seems to extend the metaphor to mean 'dissect you like an anatomical exhibit'.

II, vi 59. *God's so:* here probably God's soul, but see note on v, iv, 73.

III, i

[SCENE ONE]

22. *lick away a moth:* this extends the suggestion of dog-like fawning on the patron.

[SCENE TWO]   III, iv

47. *the golden mediocrity:* Lady Would-be's malapropism for 'the golden mean' of moderation, a principle to which none of the legacy-hunters adhere.

79-81. *Petrarch,* etc.: Lady Would-be correctly names the major Italian poets, including Giovanni Guarini (whose *Pastor Fido* or *Faithful Shepherd* she is carrying with her), but Pietro Aretino, who wrote scurrilous and obscene satires, and Cieco di Hadria – 'the Blind Man of Hadria' – do not belong in this great company.

60. *prints:* the same pornographic illustrations to poems by Aretino   III, vii that Lady Would-be called 'a little obscene' – III, iv, 97.

153. *the blue Proteus:* the god who looked after Neptune's sea-flocks and who could change into any 'Protean shape' he wished; 'blue' suggests the sea, and is the Latin 'caeruleus'.

153. *the hornèd flood:* the river Achelous which fought with Hercules in his three assumed shapes – bull; serpent; half-man, half-ox.

161. *the entertainment for the great Valois:* a masque in Venice in honour of the future Henry III of France (historical date: 1574).

162. *young Antinous:* the favourite of the Emperor Hadrian and famous for his youthful good looks. Volpone equates his own youth and beauty with sex-appeal.

165. *Come, my Celia . . .:* the educated members of the audience would recognize that the opening lines are adapted from Catullus's '*Vivamus, mea Lesbia . . .*' Though the song is beautiful, it is commending sensuality; Volpone's insidious argument is that time is passing, that youth will not last, and that illicit love is illicit only when it is discovered. Compare the tempting speeches of Comus to the Lady in Milton's masque.

192. *Than that the brave Egyptian queen caroused:* Pliny records that Cleopatra once, as an extravagant gesture, drank priceless pearls dissolved in vinegar. Volpone suggests that Celia does the same with a whole rope of pearls.

193. *a carbuncle may put out both the eyes of our St Mark:* perhaps a gem exceeding both those set in the statue of St Mark – or, possibly, a gem which would dazzle even our patron saint of Venice

195. *Lollia Paulina:* mistress of the Emperor Claudius, (eventually murdered by Agrippina); see Tacitus, *Annals*, Book 12, Chapter 1 ff. and Suetonius' *Claudius*, Chapter 25; the point is that Volpone sees her (as he sees everyone) as someone to be 'bought' – a prostitute.

215. *panthers' breath:* this reference is not just exotic; panthers were thought to attract their prey by sweet and alluring breath.

221. *Ovid's tales:* the *Metamorphoses*, which deal with transformations – Zeus, disguised as a bull, carried off Europa; Erycine is another name for Venus.

262. *Nestor's hernia:* Nestor, ancient and wise Greek in *The Iliad*. His hernia (an invention of Juvenal's) here suggests sexual incapacity.

III, viii 15. *since we have lived like Grecians:* since we have led dissolute, self-indulgent lives. London, or Troynovant, was, according to tradition, founded by a Trojan, and the English sided with Troy in retelling the stories of antiquity.

17. *I do feel the brand:* branding on the forehead was a common punishment for certain crimes.

19. *Mine ears are boring:* I feel (in imagination) my ears being slit (or even cut off).

III, ix 36. *stated in a double hope:* set in a doubly advantageous position (with Corbaccio murdered, Bonario disinherited, Volpone would get their money and bequeath all to Voltore).

IV, i ACT FOUR

[SCENE ONE]

26. *Nick Machiavell and Monsieur Bodin:* Niccolo Machiavelli (1469–1527) who wrote *The Prince*, a realistic analysis of political power; Jean Bodin (1530–96), whose work advocated religious toleration, on the realistic grounds that religious unity could never be achieved within a state.

28. *silver fork:* forks were a novelty in England.

40. *Contarini:* Cardinal Contarini (1483–1542), author of a book about Venice.

74. *the Great Council . . . the Forty . . . the Ten:* the Venetian governing bodies in order of importance.

79. *such as they are put in their mouths what they should say, sometimes, as well as greater:* sometimes *commendatori* and the like are just as influential in telling administrators what to say as great men are.

35. *The Courtier: Il Cortegiano* by Baldassar Castiglione (published IV, ii 1528) was the great manual on civilized conduct; Lady Would-be's own behaviour falls short of her reading.

42. *is not warranted from being a solecism:* may well be an impropriety.

48. *Your Sporus:* Sporus was a youth much favoured by Nero, who dressed him as a woman, and eventually married him. The link is transvestism, Lady Would-be insisting that Peregrine is the 'cunning courtesan' dressed up as a youth.

51. *Whitefriars nation:* Whitefriars was a 'liberty' without the jurisdiction of the City of London, and a noted haunt of prostitutes, criminals, etc.

[SCENE TWO]   IV, iv

22. *the French Hercules:* Gallic or Celtic god of eloquence.

89. *Bountiful bones!* This sarcastic aside refers to the miserliness of IV, vi Corbaccio's tip to Mosca.

ACT FIVE   V, i

[SCENE ONE]

17. *This heat is life; 'tis blood by this time!* Volpone is referring to the warming effect of the liquor as it enters his veins.

93. *rope and dagger:* madmen, especially those in a frenzy of despair, V, ii carried these (possibly as a means to suicide) in Elizabethan literature and the drama. See *Faerie Queene*, I, ix, and *The Spanish Tragedy*, IV, iv, when Hieronimo goes mad.

102. *Cestus:* marginal note by Jonson elucidating 'the strange poetical girdle' – the *cestus*, or girdle, of Venus.

104. *Acrisius:* the father of Danaë, who imprisoned her in a tower, where Jove visited her as a shower of gold.

[SCENE TWO]   V, iv

73. *Godso:* nineteenth-century editors took this as a contraction of *God's soul*, but modern scholars reckon it to be a euphemistic form of catso, a vulgar exclamation (from the Italian *cazzo:* penis).

[SCENE FOUR]   V, viii

12–14. *moral emblems:* Volpone suggests that Corvino's name ('Crow') is associated with moral fables such as the one in which the Crow, by too much talking, lets the cheese drop from his beak, while the Fox watches all. The irony here is that Volpone the Fox, *is* watching Corvino's discomfiture.

v, ix 10. *Justinian:* the code of Roman law drawn up by the Emperor Justinian.

v, xii [SCENE SEVEN]

25. *crooked pins*, etc.: Volpone's description of Voltore's feigned fit accords with Jacobean accounts of bewitched persons. See notes in Herford-Simpson *Ben Jonson*, ix, pp. 731-2.

125. *mortifying:* humiliating; but also, in cooking, a word for keeping game till it is high, thus linking with the animal imagery throughout.

THE ALCHEMIST

TO THE READER

This appears only in the quarto text of 1612. Two passages are reprinted in *Timber, or Discoveries*.

THE PERSONS OF THE PLAY

[*Pertinax*] *Surly:* Sir Epicure calls him Pertinax (Latin: obstinate) which seems to reinforce the Elizabethan sense of *surly* as haughty, arrogant, or supercilious, rather than ill-humoured. *Gamester:* gambler, play-boy. For Surly's role, see the introduction, p. 22.

ACT ONE

3-4. *lick figs:* Subtle's vulgar suggestion alludes to Rabelais, Book IV, chapter 45 - or *figs* may be *Ficus morbus*, piles (F. H. Mares).

16. *livery-three-pound-thrum:* shabby, poorly paid drudge; (*livery*, uniform; *thrum*, coarse cloth).

18 *vacations:* i.e. between the terms at the Inns of Court, which roughly corresponded to 'the London season'.

25. *Pic-corner:* near Smithfield; famous for cooks' shops and for pigs prepared there for Bartholomew Fair. See p. 483.

52-3. *chippings, dole-beer:* scraps of bread and beer 'doled out' at great houses to the poor. Subtle is saying Face sold this free beer to wine-merchants instead.

64. *Thou vermin,* etc.: E. H. Duncan has shown that Subtle is here using an extended metaphor from alchemy to describe how he raised Face in the social scale. The image is of the systematic refining and preparation of the elixir or Philosopher's Stone from crude substances. The *dung* refers to the heat (that '*equi clibanum/* The heat of horse-dung' mentioned by Subtle later), for which horse-manure was sometimes used, and which helped to achieve the first stage of the experiment. Subtle claims he has raised *vermin* (i.e. Face), his crude material *ta'en out of dung*, through the appropriate alchemical processes (*sublimation* and *exaltation*) to the point (*projection*) at which Face can turn base metals into gold - i.e. get gold from the 'clients'. See *Publications of the Modern Language Association of America,* LXI (1946), p. 701.

74. *quarrelling dimensions:* the limits within which a quarrel can be

conducted with safety. See II, vi, 65–9 and IV, ii, 16–33. The reference is to 'quarrelling by the book', the rules of which Kastril wishes to learn.

79. *projection:* successful completion of an experiment; *fly out i' the projection* means to fail at the very last moment – when success is in sight.

93. *Paul's:* precincts of St Paul's Cathedral, a meeting-place where bills and notices were posted.

99. *Gamaliel Ratsey:* a highway-man, executed in 1605.

106. *lying too heavy o' the basket:* eating more than his share of the prisoners' rations.

112–13. *statute,* etc.: statute against witchcraft in Henry VIII's thirty-third year, i.e. 1541.

114. *laund'ring gold:* washing off the surface of coins in acid; *barbing:* clipping coins.

165. *sin' the King came in:* i.e. in seven years (James I succeeded to the throne in 1603).

170. *Don Provost:* the hangman who was entitled to the criminals' clothes.

175. *Claridiana:* heroine of a popular prose novel.

I, ii 17–20. *Read:* Dr Simon Read was convicted in 1608 of magic practices on behalf of a young clerk like Dapper, hence the analogy.

24. *court-hand:* the official legal style of handwriting; different for different documents as in line 54 below.

46. *Clim–o'–the–Cloughs,* etc.: heroes of romantic ballads.

56. *Greek Xenophon:* 'Testament' in earlier quarto edition; changed in view of strict Jacobean laws about profanity.

69. *assumpsit:* legal term for an oral promise involving an initial payment.

109. *Holland, Isaac:* probably well-known gamblers.

128. *born with a caul:* the caul is the inner membrane enclosing the foetus before birth, and a portion of it sometimes covers the head of a new-born child. It was a popular fallacy that this was a good omen, especially against death by drowning.

I, iii 5. *free of the Grocers:* a member of the Grocers' Company, or guild, i.e. no longer merely an apprentice.

28–31. *lily-pots,* etc.: tobacconists' shops in Jacobean times were places where customers could sit and smoke as well as merely purchase tobacco – and, the art being a novelty, they could also be instructed in smoking. The *lily-pot* is an ornamental jar; the *maple-block* was the wooden slab on which the tobacco was shredded; the *tongs* were for holding an ember or piece of charcoal to light one's pipe – and *the fire of juniper* was kept alight in the shop for this purpose. Drugger's shop, thus equipped, has pretensions to grandeur as a smoking academy.

36. *of the clothing of his company:* wear the livery of his guild (i.e. the Grocers' Company), as an office-holder.

37. *called to the scarlet:* made a Sheriff, a higher officer, gowned in scarlet.

66. *Mathlai*, etc.: the names of spirits are taken from *Elementa Magica* by Pietro d'Albano.

ACT TWO   II, i

[SCENE ONE]

1. *Come on, sir . . .:* the action is continuous from Act One.
2. *Novo Orbe:* the New World (metaphor for untold riches).
17. *Madam Augusta's:* evidently a brothel.
33. *Lothbury:* a London street where copper-smiths lived.
35. *Devonshire, Cornwall:* the principal English counties where tin and copper were mined.
36. *make them perfect Indies:* turn their copper and tin into gold.
39–40. *Mercury:* quicksilver; *Venus:* copper; *Moon:* silver; *Sun:* gold
48. *elixir:* Mammon uses the word in a double sense: (a) in its alchemical meaning of the substance which would turn all metals into gold, i.e. the Philosopher's Stone, etc., and (b) in its medical sense of a liquid (*elixir vitae*) capable of prolonging life indefinitely. Many people thought the two elixirs to be identical, as Mammon clearly does here, and this gives free range to his imagination. See E. B. Partridge *The Broken Compass*, pp. 132–4.
55. *fifth age:* Mammon is referring to the commonplace of the Seven Ages of Man: see Jaques' speech in *As You Like It*.
62. *Pickt-hatch:* low district of London frequented by whores and pick-pockets.
63–9. *the secret*, etc.: Jonson is satirizing here claims about the Stone's powers put forward in all earnest by the alchemists. The powers attributed to the Stone are taken from Arnold of Villa Nova's *Rosarium Philosophorum*.
71. *the players:* the London actors had to close their playhouses whenever the plague became dangerously virulent, and they would therefore be especially grateful to anyone capable of 'frighting the plague out of the kingdom' and thus guaranteeing their livelihood.

81–3. *Moses, Solomon,* etc.: the belief that Adam understood the mysteries of the Stone is a commonplace in alchemical writings, and occurs in Paracelsus, who also mentions Moses' possession of the elixir. Fifteenth-century manuscripts exist of an alchemical treatise attributed to Solomon.

89–104. *Jason's fleece,* etc.: This passage Professor Duncan styles 'a barrage of mythological–alchemical erudition', and it lists the connexions alchemists traced between mythology and their own science. Duncan points out that 'the legend that the true object of Jason's quest was an alchemical treatise or recipe is at least as old as the tenth century', and he believes that Jonson may have gone to Nicholas Flamel's *Hieroglyphicall Figures* (not translated until 1624) for the alchemists' interpretation of details in the myth as symbols for materials and processes in alchemy. *Publications of the Modern Language Association of America,* LXI, p. 703.

92. *Pythagoras' thigh:* see *Volpone,* I, ii, 27 for reference to 'Pythagoras' golden thigh'.

92. *Pandora's tub:* this (more usually a box or jar) contained all the ills and diseases of mankind which Pandora unwittingly released.

96. *dragon's teeth:* the equation of these with *mercury sublimate* in alchemy, seems to be a Jonsonian invention as is the identification of Jason's helmet as an *alembic* (the top part of a distilling vessel). See Duncan's article.

102. *Demogorgon:* in Boccaccio's *Genealogia Deorum* he is the ancestor of the gods. Alchemically he was interpreted as Chaos, as the *quinta essentia,* and as the *parentum omnium rerum.*

II, ii [SCENE TWO]

Stage direction: i.e. they pass from fore-stage to the main acting area which represents the interior of the house.

44. *Elephantis, Aretine:* both seem to have written poems which were accompanied by pornographic pictures. Elephantis is known only because of references in Suetonius's life of Tiberius and in Martial. For Aretine, see *Volpone* III, iv, 96.

77. *Apicius' diet,* etc.: Jonson took many of the exotic delicacies from Lampridius's *Vita Heliogabali.*

87. *be a knight:* contemporary joke against King James's indiscriminate and mercenary creation of knights.

II, iii 32. *Ulen Spiegel:* Subtle's name for his 'servant' Face: originally the knave-hero of a popular German jest-book.

33. *aludels,* etc.: In this passage Jonson uses accurately a number of alchemical terms, a fact which would be appreciated by only a

small, sophisticated part of his audience. For many Jacobeans, as for most of us, the expressions would sound impressive jargon merely. Compare once more Volpone's spiel, II, ii (pp. 79–85); see note on Alchemy pp. 179–84.

49. *pious uses:* Mammon here expresses a perhaps sincere wish for lasting fame through charitable acts performed with the Stone; but compare the sensual delights and fantasies he proposed to Surly earlier, and his earlier speeches to Dol.

185. *Your Stone*, etc.: Surly, the critic of alchemy, no less than Subtle, the bogus practitioner, uses correctly terms from contemporary alchemical lore.

225. *Bradamante:* heroine in the *Orlando Furioso* of Ariosto.

230. *Paracelsian:* follower of Paracelsus (1493–1541), who studied medicine and mineralogy. His interest in alchemy stemmed from a concern with healing. See *Volpone*, II, ii, 125.

238. *Broughton:* the rabbinical scholar who died in 1612; mentioned also in *Volpone*, II, ii, 114; source of Dol's 'mad' speech.

8. *Lullianist; Ripley:* disciple of Ramón Lull or of Sir George Ripley, **II, v** noted alchemists. Lull (*c.* 1232–1315) was born in Majorca and founded an influential school of philosophy. His disciples wrote systematic alchemical treatises and attributed them to him. Ripley (died 1490) was a Canon of Bridlington, Yorks, studied in Italy, and wrote the *Compound of Alchemy. Filius artis:* son of the art. Subtle is pretending to think that Ananias by 'Brother' meant brother- or fellow-alchemist.

13. *Knipperdoling:* leader of the Anabaptist sect.

2. *Bayards:* blind fools (named from the horse Charlemagne gave **II, vi** to the sons of Aymon).

20. *Dee:* Dr John Dee, astrologer and mathematician, who died in 1608.

ACT THREE

[SCENE TWO]   III, ii

Stage direction: they pass from the fore-stage to the main acting area, as did Mammon and Surly in II, ii. The action is continuous.

43. *Christ-tide:* the Puritans regarded Christ-*mas* as a Popish term. See also *Bartholomew Fair.*

18. *Cinque Port:* The Cinque Ports are five Channel ports, at this **III, iii** period strategically important: Dover, Sandwich, Romney, Hastings, and Hythe. The use here is metaphorical.

24. *John Leydens:* Puritans (John Brockholdt or John of Leyden an Anabaptist was leader).

III, v *Final stage-direction:* Face and Subtle lock Dapper into a privy, probably on-stage. If Act IV is played as continuous, Face must also be changing from his Captain's clothes into his disguise as Lungs. The final moments of the scene (lines 50–81) are full of farcical action.

IV, i

ACT FOUR

[SCENE ONE]

90. *[Edward] Kelly:* an alchemist and associate of Dr Dee. The Emperor Rudolph II of Germany was his patron and dupe. Kelly died in 1595.

93. *Thunderer:* Zeus who struck Æsculapius dead with a thunderbolt.

IV, ii 23. *intentions, canons,* etc.: the technical terms in Subtle's two speeches are from scholastic logic.

IV, iii 30. *d'Alva:* governor of the Netherlands from 1567 to 1573; *Count Egmont,* a Fleming executed at Alva's orders.

IV, iv [SCENE TWO]

48. *Bedlam:* Bethlehem Hospital – visiting the lunatics there was regarded as an amusement; *China-houses:* shops selling articles from the East.

IV, v [SCENE THREE]

Stage-direction 'fit': Mammon thinks Dol is being cured of madness. Her 'mad' speeches incorporate phrases from Hugh Broughton's *Concent of Scriptures.*

IV, vi [SCENE FOUR]

Location: older editors suggest the garden, but the scene can be played indoors. See my preliminary note to the comedy, p. 176.

IV, vii 53. *seventy-seven:* i.e. 1577; no editor has satisfactorily explained this Elizabethan allusion, which may be to the invasion of the Netherlands by d'Alva in 1567, or to the Armada, 1588. The *unclean birds* are from *Revelation,* xviii, 2.

V, i

ACT FIVE

[SCENE ONE]

6. *Pimlico:* a popular London place for entertainment near Hogsden.

V, iv

76. *Ratcliff:* a place in Stepney, frequented by sailors.
77. *Brainford:* Brentford.
115. *Ward:* notorious as a pirate.
141. *Mistress Amo:* a brothel-keeper (*Madam Caesarean* also).
117. *Harry Nicholas:* a well-known religious fanatic.   V, v

BARTHOLOMEW FAIR

TITLE-PAGE

Note the spelling 'Bartholmew', which probably represented the Jacobean pronunciation, Bartle-mew or Bartle-my. See also p. 322.

PROLOGUE

In other words, for the performance at Court on 1 November 1614 – the day after the first public performance.

THE PERSONS OF THE PLAY

Minor characters, such as Solomon, Haggis, Filcher, etc., do not appear in the Folio cast-list.

Banbury: town in Oxfordshire, proverbially noted for Puritans and cakes.

Turnbull: a street in Clerkenwell infamous on account of its brothels.

THE PERSONS IN THE INDUCTION

Not in the Folio cast-list. It is conceivable that the actual stage-keeper and book-holder at the Hope Theatre appeared in these parts, but more likely that they were imitated by acting members of their company, the Lady Elizabeth's Servants.

THE INDUCTION

5. *Arches:* here, an officer of the Court of Arches, the ecclesiastical court of appeal, at Bow Church.

5. *Hospital:* i.e. St Bartholomew in Smithfield.

7. *Master Brome:* Richard Brome, servant, friend, and imitator of Jonson – a successful member of 'the tribe of Ben'.

10. *Smithfield:* the site of the Fair just outside the City of London.

13. *little Davy:* a well-known bully.

14. *Kindheart:* an itinerant tooth-drawer.

31. *Inns o' Court:* houses for the law students belonging to the four societies (Lincoln's Inn, the Inner Temple, the Middle Temple, Gray's Inn) constituting what was, after Oxford and Cambridge, virtually the 'Third University of England'.

33. [*Richard*] *Tarlton:* a leading comedian (died 1588) of the previous reign. See Chambers, *Elizabethan Stage* (1923), vol. ii, pp. 342–5.

36. *cloth-quarter:* the booths or stalls along the north wall of St Bartholomew's Church; one of Tarlton's jests hinged on his being cheated of his clothes there.

36. [*John?*] *Adams:* a fellow-actor of Tarlton's.

59. *Bankside:* the area on the South Bank of the Thames where theatres, bear-baiting arenas, and other centres of entertainment were situated.

80. *six pen'orth:* six-pence-worth: the high cost of admission here seems to indicate, as it were, 'first-night' prices.

85. *the lottery:* i.e. the one started in 1612 to raise money for the plantation of the colonies in Virginia.

96. *Jeronimo: The Spanish Tragedy* by Kyd; *Andronicus: Titus Andronicus* by Shakespeare. By 1614 both were old-fashioned, heavily rhetorical and over-bloody Elizabethan revenge-plays, and Jonson's 'five and twenty or thirty years' deliberately exaggerates their age. He had himself written additional speeches for Kyd's play.

115. *servant-monster:* i.e. Caliban in *The Tempest*, which, with *The Winter's Tale*, is alluded to in the lines following; *antics, jigs,* etc., refer to the masque-like dances characteristic of Shakespeare's Romances or Last Plays, an indecorous *genre* of which Jonson disapproved.

128. *Mirror:* here 'paragon'; but possibly also an allusion to *A Mirror for Magistrates*, the sixteenth century collection of exemplary stories about the fall of rulers. A work by Whetstone of this title advised the magistrate to disguise himself and frequent places of entertainment to discover what happened there as Justice Overdo (to so little effect) does in this comedy. Compare Hal in Shakespeare's *Henry IV* plays and the Duke in *Measure for Measure*. In warning his audience not to identify his characters with actual people, Jonson has been judged by scholars to be especially avoiding any identification of Overdo with Sir Thomas Hayes, Lord Mayor of London in 1614.

ACT ONE

I, i

11. *Paul's:* St Paul's, where the middle aisle was a recognized meeting-place of courtiers and professional men for conversation and the transaction of business.

15. *archdeacon's court:* the Court of Arches; See the Induction, line 5.

21. *Budge Row:* a street where fur was sold. *budge*=lambskin fur.

23. *The Spanish lady:* an allusion to a fashionable English widow who dressed in the Spanish style, with high-heeled shoes, etc. In the production at Edinburgh in 1950 Dorothy Tutin as Mistress Littlewit paraded like a mannequin in this scene to Littlewit's admiring commentary.

31. *Three Cranes, Mitre,* etc.: London taverns, the *Mermaid* being Jonson's particular haunt.

I, ii   6. *Cheapside:* the 'garment district' of London.

6. *Moorfields:* a park reclaimed from marshlands outside the City.

6. *Pimlico:* a tavern in Hoxton noted for cakes and ale.

7. *Exchange:* the New Exchange, built in 1608–9 as a fashionable shopping area for ladies.

51. *Bedlam:* the mad-house, a visit to which was popularly regarded as entertainment.

I, iii   57. *Tottenham:* Tottenham Court, a popular place for buying cakes and cream.

64. *Pannyer Alley:* street associated with leather-making and tripe-selling. Quarlous's speech stresses through vigorous, homely imagery the sexual unattractiveness of the old widows whom Winwife pursues.

72. *inherit according to thy inches:* allusion to a passage in the first satire of Juvenal in which the two lovers of an old woman are rewarded, in G. G. Ramsay's euphemistic translation, 'each in proportion to his *services*'. See *Satires*, I, 40–41.

89. *[John] Knox:* the Scots religious leader.

I, iv   6. *saved by my book:* exempted from punishment for a crime by pleading benefit of clergy. This involved demonstrating the ability to read (as Ben Jonson himself had done after killing Gabriel Spencer; see Introduction p. 10).

34. *Cloister:* the market held during Fair-time in part of a former monastery, Christ Church cloisters.

103. *Uncle Hodge:* the old man who is said to have accepted a wager that a cat could not pull him across a pond. A rope was tied round him and the other end fastened to the cat, but the actual pulling was done by men in hiding who made it appear that the cat was responsible. This was evidently a standard practical joke in Jonson's day.

107. *blackboy:* figure on a tobacconist's sign.

108. *Bucklersbury:* a street inhabited by grocers and apothecaries – the latter being also tobacconists.

24. *Whetstone:* probably a keeper of Bedlam. There is a pun on I, v
whetstone – a stone for sharpening knives.

145. *Pie-corner:* at the sign of the Magpie, an inn at the edge of Smithfield. Face recalls that he first met Subtle there 'taking [his] meal
of steam in, from cooks' stalls' (*The Alchemist*, I, i.), and, since food
was sold outside at the street-corner, the etymology of *Pie*-corner
may have become obscured.

ACT TWO   II, i

Opening stage-directions: for the rest of the play the scene is the Fair.
How the change is effected in any production is the individual
director's business, but Act One should be followed by a bustling
'transformation scene'. See pp. 321–2.

4. *Lynceus:* one of the Argonauts, famous for his keen sight.

5. *Epidaurian serpent:* Horace in his *Satires* mentions the serpents,
which were thought to have keen sight and to be incarnations of
Æsculapius, whose temple was at Epidaurus.

12. *a worthy worshipful man, sometime a capital member of this City:*
i.e. Thomas Hayes, Lord Mayor of the City of London.

39. *Pie-powders:* corruption of *pieds poudrés*, dusty feet; 'a summary
court formerly held at fairs and markets to administer justice
among itinerant dealers and others temporarily present.' – *The
Oxford English Dictionary*. The point is that Overdo, for all his
gravity and self-importance, is a mere Justice of the Peace pre-
siding over the humblest kind of court.

42. *cloud:* Aeneas and his followers were hidden in a cloud as they
entered Carthage – the *Aeneid*, I, 412.

44. *Junius Brutus:* in order to escape execution at the hands of
Tarquinius Superbus he disguised himself as an idiot; also famous
as an inflexible judge – hence Justice Overdo's two-fold self-
identification with this Roman.
    One knocks (stage-direction in Folio): i.e. Justice Overdo knocks II, ii
(presumably at the door of Ursula's booth).

108. *O tempora! O mores!:* 'What times! What manners!' Overdo
is quoting Cicero, *In Catilinam*, I, i, 2.

120. *Arthur of Bradley:* a figure in ballads who assumed the disguise
of a madman, as Justice Overdo has done. His habit of speechify-
ing is described by Ursula.

23. *vapours:* this term is used habitually and often tiresomely by II, iii
Knockem – indeed Eugene Waith in his Yale edition of the

comedy calls his use of the word 'a kind of verbal tic'. 'Vapours' means deliberate quarrelsomeness - as in the formal game of vapours played in Act Four - but in the play it is often synonymous with Jonsonian 'humours', so that the more eccentric, one-idea characters can be said to have their own 'vapours'.

II, iv 66. *Iamque opus*, etc.: 'And now I have finished my task, which neither Jove's wrath, nor fire ...' - *Metamorphoses*, XV, 871-2. The passage continues: 'nor sword, nor the gnawing tooth of time shall ever be able to undo'.

II, v 7. *Orpheus*: the god of music.

10. *Ceres*: mother of Proserpina.

92. *Dutchmen*: it was a popular fallacy that they ate a great deal of butter.

159. *race-bawd*: breeder of bawds; on the analogy of *race-mare* - a brood mare.

177. *Ursa major*: the constellation of the Great Bear; astronomical pun on Ursula's shorter name, Urs, and on her hugeness.

II, vi 34. *some late writers*: see note following.

45. *hole in the nose ... third nostril*: this disfigurement would normally be the result of syphilis; Justice Overdo is railing against the evils of tobacco by claiming that smoking can have the same effects as the pox. His speech is a parody of Jacobean pamphlets against smoking by 'some late writers' (see lines above), of whom King James VI was one.

72. *the Straits, the Bermudas*: disreputable alleys, court-yards, etc.; haunts of thieves and prostitutes.

73. *quarrelling lesson*: discharged soldiers often instructed people in duelling.

136. *Childermass Day*: 28 December - feast of the Massacre of the Holy Innocents.

138. *French Barthol'mew*: the massacre of French Protestants on St Bartholomew's Day, 1572.

III, i   ACT THREE

Opening stage-directions: the bustling life of the Fair continues in the background, while Whit, Haggis, and Bristle enter. Captain Whit, a stage-Irishman, works as a paid informer for the watch - Haggis and Bristle - but he is really a pimp, as becomes clear in the next scene.

11. *monsters*: freaks. Littlewit mentions some of these in III, vi, and Wasp extends the catalogue in V, iv.

42. *heathen man:* Ulysses, who did not succumb to the song of the   III, ii
sirens, but had himself lashed to the mast; it was his crew who
had their ears stopped with wax.

62. *Dame Annessh Cleare:* a spring called after Annis Clare, a rich
London widow.

72. *Lubberland:* a 'Land of Cockayne' or Never-Never Land where,
traditionally, the pigs run about, ready-roasted, and cry 'Come eat
me!'

107. *small printed ruffs:* the Puritans wore their small ruffs 'in print',
i.e. neatly folded. Compare Ananias on 'that ruff of pride' in
The Alchemist, IV, vii, 51.

31. *ut parvis*, etc.: 'as I was accustomed to compare great things with   III, iii
small', misquoted from Virgil, *Eclogues*, I, 23.

16. *pair of smiths:* possibly a bell-like clockwork device which served   III, iv
as a sort of alarm-clock.

23. *Michaelmas term:* the autumn term at the Inns of Court (from
29 September), marking the beginning of 'the London season'.

117. *[Thomas] Coriat, or Coryate:* the Jacobean traveller and entertainer (c, 1577–1617); *Coryat's Crudities* (1611) described his extensive European journey.

117. *Cokeley:* another jester.

122. *the fellow i' the bear's skin:* an actor from the Fortune Theatre
once dressed in a bearskin and was baited by butchers dressed as
dogs. A ballad was made out of this in 1612.

53. *'Paggington's Pound':* an old dance-tune.   III, v

85. *Westminster Hall:* the great hall of the Palace of Westminster
where certain Courts sat.

134. *rat-catcher's charms:* the rhyme which rid Ireland of rats. 'Cokes
thinks of himself as a kind of Pied Piper to the pickpockets' –
Professor Horsman.

273. *bought me:* 'The King had the right to sell the guardship and
marriage of royal wards (minors who were heirs to tenants
holding land from him)' – Professor Horsman.

276. *disparagement:* the legal situation is that Grace must either marry
Cokes or forfeit her land – unless, as Quarlous now suggests, she
can prove that Cokes is her inferior and that marriage to him
would be a 'disparagement'.

55. *Nebuchadnezzar:* a ruler who enforced the worshipping of idols.   III, vi

Opening stage-directions: the scene is substantially as before, save for the stocks. See p. 321.

IV, ii 70. *martyred:* a reference to Bartholomew Leggat who was martyred at Smithfield in 1611.

IV, iii 64. *Argalus:* a lover in Sir Philip Sidney's pastoral romance, the *Arcadia.*

65. *the play: The Two Noble Kinsmen* (1613) by John Fletcher and William Shakespeare from *The Knight's Tale* by Chaucer.

65. *Palemon:* Palemon and Arcite are rival lovers in Chaucer. Argalus and Palemon are typical figures from romance, and it is ironic that Quarlous and Winwife should associate their names with such courtly paragons.

97. *Mercury:* appropriate nickname for Edgworth since the messenger-god was swift of foot and thieving.

105. *wrestle:* a wrestling contest in front of the tent of the Lord Mayor, Aldermen, and sheriffs was one of the events of St Bartholomew's Day.

IV, v 37. *Ware, Rumford:* places of assignation.

78. *Bridewell:* a prison, or house of correction, for bawds, rogues, and whores.

IV, vi 30. *Facinus,* etc.: 'Crime levels those whom it pollutes' – Lucan, *Pharsalia,* v, 290 (J. D. Duff's translation).

90. *In te . . . terrent:* 'in her attacks upon you Fate is powerless' and 'whom neither poverty nor death nor bonds dismay' – snatches from Horace, *Satires,* II, vii.

94. *Non te,* etc.: 'Look to no one outside yourself' – Persius, *Satires,* I.

150. *another use:* this is the first hint we have that Quarlous is going to disguise as Trouble-all as part of a plot to see what was written in Grace Wellborn's book.

Opening stage-directions: Leatherhead and his door-keepers erect their puppet-stage in full view of the audience, possibly dismantling or removing the stocks. They perhaps continue their work while the second scene is acted, rather as the people of the Fair may have erected their booths and stalls during Justice Overdo's soliloquy at the beginning of Act Two. See also pp. 321–2.

2. *sign:* the play-bill, usually with a summary or description of the entertainment, advertising the performance; possibly the 'banner' mentioned a second later and certainly the long-winded 'bill' which Cokes reads in v, iii.

7. *my Master Pod:* the Folio has a marginal note by Jonson: 'Pod was a Master of motions before him.' Leatherhead is claiming to have been apprentice to an actual puppeteer. Some scholars have interpreted Leatherhead and his puppetry as a satirical attack on Inigo Jones and his splendid spectacular stage-effects and *décors.*

7. *Jerusalem,* etc: the five puppet-plays mentioned here on biblical and English historical themes were probably well-known to the original audience at the Hope. No Jacobean puppet-script has survived. The puppet-play later in the act (which is supposed to be the work of Littlewit) is a burlesque of the *genre.*

10. *Shrove Tuesday:* the holiday on which London apprentices traditionally thronged the theatres and behaved riotously.

11. *Gunpowder Plot:* Guy Fawkes's unsuccessful plot to blow up Parliament on 5 November 1605. Puppet-theatres, no less than others, obviously made box-office hits out of recent history.

50. *party-coloured:* literally, but also with the punning sense of party v, ii as faction or division, suggesting that the Puritans were divided among themselves. This speech of Dame Purecraft's is the greatest admission of Puritan deviousness in the play.

61. *silent minister:* one of the Puritans excommunicated for failure to comply with the laws approved by the Hampton Court conference of 1604. See Tribulation Wholesome's speech, *The Alchemist,* iii, i, 38.

Stage-direction 'the bill': the advertisement. See above, v, i. v, iii

22. *voluntary:* a volunteer, i.e. here one who has given his literary services free and is entitled to free admission. This possibly suggests that Littlewit was anxious to preserve his amateur status.

51. *not Leatherhead but Lantern:* Leatherhead's whispered aside to Littlewit is necessitated by his eagerness to conceal his surname from Cokes whom he robbed earlier.

63. *at other houses:* i.e. at the play-houses of the leading acting companies.

70. *the small players,* etc.: Leatherhead – or rather Master Lantern – shows Cokes his basketful of puppets, rather as a leading actor might take a young gallant to the tiring-house (see lines 54–60, above) to meet the other players. George Speaight, the puppet-master and scholar who supervised the play-within-the-play for

George Devine's Old Vic production in 1950, believes that the puppets should be glove-puppets (see his *History of the English Puppet Theatre*, 1955, p. 65) and glove-puppets were used in that production – but Puppet Dionysius who, in the debate with Busy, has to 'take up his garment' is surely a marionette.

75. *one Taylor:* a pun referring first to 'one tailor' (and tailors were supposed to be timid), second to Joseph Taylor, an actor who was probably in the original cast of *Bartholomew Fair* at the Hope Theatre in 1614, and third to the Water-poet, John Taylor, who had won a wit combat (by default) at the Hope Theatre.

76. *eat 'em all:* tailors were proverbially greedy – hence Cokes's 'a goodly jest'.

79. *[Richard] Burbage:* the greatest of Elizabethan actors (1573–1619), creator of many Shakespearean and Jonsonian characters.

81. *[Nathan] Field:* actor, dramatist, friend of Jonson, probably a member of the original cast of the play (1587–1619).

98. *printed book:* Christopher Marlowe's *Hero and Leander* (1598).

v, iv 39. *private house:* Elizabethan play-houses were of two broad categories: large open-air theatres where actors played by daylight in the afternoon – the *public* houses; and small, indoor theatres where performances were given by artificial light, at higher prices and to a more select audience – the *private* houses.

70. *Delia:* the lady in Samuel Daniel's sonnet-sequence (1592).

115. *amorous Leander*, etc.: the puppet-play is a travesty of Marlowe's poem *Hero and Leander* and of Richard Edwardes' old-fashioned play.

160. *Pict-hatch:* haunt of prostitutes near Charterhouse.

172. *Dauphin*, etc.: a ballad, also quoted in *King Lear*, III, iv.

185. *sack . . . sherry:* 'sack' was a loose term for all white wines imported from Spain, including sherry. Cokes's ignorance is shown here.

197. *Damon and Pythias* (acted 1565).

200. *hobby-horse is forgotten:* another snatch from a well-known ballad.

289. *Dunmow bacon:* a flitch of bacon presented to any couple who could prove to a jury of bachelors and maidens of Little Dunmow in Essex that they had spent the past year of their marriage without quarrelling.

313. *Dionysius:* Dionysius the younger, who was reported to have become a school-master after being expelled from Syracuse.

321. *Puppet Dionysius:* the folio reads 'Pup D.' and most editors give 'Pup. Damon'. The emendation is Harry Levin's.

1. *Dagon:* god of the Philistines; used of an idol in general.   v, v

15. *Shimei:* follower of Saul's who cursed King David (*2 Samuel*, xvi).

16. *Master of the Revels:* the official of the Court whose duties included licencing all plays.

19. *Baal:* heathen god.

44. *Grace:* the speech is usually given to Quarlous, but Eugene Waith argues that the printer of the Folio confused the abbreviations *Qua.* and *Gra.* in this instance.

46. *calling:* there is a large body of anti-theatrical pamphlets by Puritans who denied that acting could be recognized as a profession. Zeal-of-the-Land Busy marshals the conventional arguments against the profession and when, in line 90, he comes to his 'main argument' it is that in Elizabethan theatres boys dressed up as women, against biblical injunctions. Similar charges occur in such writers as Philip Stubbs, Stephen Gosson, and William Prynne. As the Jacobean theatre did not employ *actresses*, Busy's line about 'the male among you putteth on the apparel of the female, *and the female of the male*' seems to stem from biblical rhythms.

88. *Dagonet:* King Arthur's jester.

90. *main argument:* see Note on *calling,* above, line 46.

21. *et digito*, etc.: 'and restrain your lips with a finger' – Juvenal, v, vi *Satires,* I, 160.

48. *Redde te Harpocratem!:* 'Make yourself a Harpocrates' – god of silence.

111. *ad correctionem*, etc.: 'for correction not destruction; for building up not tearing down,' from Horace, *Epistles,* I.

READ MORE IN PENGUIN

In every corner of the world, on every subject under the sun, Penguin represents quality and variety – the very best in publishing today.

For complete information about books available from Penguin – including Puffins, Penguin Classics and Arkana – and how to order them, write to us at the appropriate address below. Please note that for copyright reasons the selection of books varies from country to country.

In the United Kingdom: Please write to *Dept. EP, Penguin Books Ltd, Bath Road, Harmondsworth, West Drayton, Middlesex UB7 0DA*

In the United States: Please write to *Consumer Services, Penguin Putnam Inc., 405 Murray Hill Parkway, East Rutherford, New Jersey 07073-2136.* VISA and MasterCard holders call 1-800-631-8571 to order Penguin titles

In Canada: Please write to *Penguin Books Canada Ltd, 10 Alcorn Avenue, Suite 300, Toronto, Ontario M4V 3B2*

In Australia: Please write to *Penguin Books Australia Ltd, 487 Maroondah Highway, Ringwood, Victoria 3134*

In New Zealand: Please write to *Penguin Books (NZ) Ltd, Private Bag 102902, North Shore Mail Centre, Auckland 10*

In India: Please write to *Penguin Books India Pvt Ltd, 11 Community Centre, Panchsheel Park, New Delhi 110017*

In the Netherlands: Please write to *Penguin Books Netherlands bv, Postbus 3507, NL-1001 AH Amsterdam*

In Germany: Please write to *Penguin Books Deutschland GmbH, Metzlerstrasse 26, 60594 Frankfurt am Main*

In Spain: Please write to *Penguin Books S. A., Bravo Murillo 19, 1°B, 28015 Madrid*

In Italy: Please write to *Penguin Italia s.r.l., Via Vittorio Emanuele 45/a, 20094 Corsico, Milano*

In France: Please write to *Penguin France, 12, Rue Prosper Ferradou, 31700 Blagnac*

In Japan: Please write to *Penguin Books Japan Ltd, Iidabashi KM-Bldg, 2-23-9 Koraku, Bunkyo-Ku, Tokyo 112-0004*

In South Africa: Please write to *Penguin Books South Africa (Pty) Ltd, P.O. Box 751093, Gardenview, 2047 Johannesburg*